3/3

image® COMICS PRESENTS

TREKS ON

BY SCOTT R. KURTZ

Contributing artists: Frank Cho, Paul Southworth, Chris Giarrusso.

Collecting issues 25-31 of PvP, Vol. 2
Originally published by Image Comics

D1383838

FOR IMAGE COMICS

Erik Larsen - Publisher
Todd McFarlane - President
Marc Silvestri - CEO
Jim Valentino - Vice-President

Eric Stephenson - Executive Director
Joe Keatinge - PR & Marketing Coordinator
Branwyn Bigglestone - Accounts Manager
Paige Richardson - Administrative Assistant
Traci Hui - Traffic Manager
Allen Hui - Production Manager
Drew Gill - Production Artist
Jonathan Chan - Production Artist
Monica Garcia - Production Artist

www.imagecomics.com

PvP, VOL. 5: PVP . 2008. Published by Image Comics, Inc., Office of publication: 1942 University Avenue, Suite 305, Berkeley, California 94704. Copyright © 2008
Scott R. Kurtz. Originally published in single magazine form as PvP vol. 2 #25-31. All rights reserved. PVP™ (including all prominent characters featured herein), its logo and all character
likenesses are trademarks of Scott R. Kurtz, unless otherwise noted. Image Comics® is a trademark of Image Comics, Inc. All rights reserved. Liberty Meadows appears courtesy Frank Cho.
All characters copyright Frank Cho. No part of this publication may be reproduced or transmitted, in any form or by any means (except for short excerpts for review purposes) without the
express written permission of Image Comics, Inc. All names, characters, events and locales in this publication are entirely fictional. Any resemblance to actual persons (living or dead) events or
places, without satiric intent, is coincidental. PRINTED IN CANADA
ISBN# 978-1-58240-932-0

For Ashley.

CHOOSE YOUR PLAYER

1P PRESS A TO SELECT

COLE RICHARDS
Editor in Chief

SPECIAL MOVE:
Assign Overtime.

The glue that holds PvP together, Cole tries to retain a small semblance of sanity amidst the chaos of his employees. This makes him an obvious target. Confused and disturbed by the latest computer game releases, Cole is happiest playing classic 80's arcade game emulators on his computer.

BRENT SIENNA
Creative Director

SPECIAL MOVE:
Caffeine Rage

Brent has little time to play computer games, however he always finds time to mock those who do. Pretentious and pompous, Brent is the master of the inappropriate comment. Despite his rough exterior, he's managed to show Jade his softer side and the two have become romantically involved.

JADE FONTAINE
Lead Staff Writer

SPECIAL MOVE:
"The Stare"

"Women play games too." That's what Jade Fontaine wants to tell the world. Jade can compete with the best of the boys but prefers the escape of a good online RPG and is hopelessly addicted to chat and email. Despite herself, Jade has fallen for Brent Sienna, the Magazine's Creative Director.

FRANCIS OTTOMAN
Tech Support

SPECIAL MOVE:
Spinning Cobra Clutch

If you have ever wanted to kill someone you've met online, then you know Francis Ray Ottoman. That's not to say that Francis is all bad, he does call in sick every once in a while. Francis knows everything there is to know about gaming, mostly because his life revolves around it.

CHOOSE YOUR PLAYER

PREPARE FOR HUMOR BATTLE!

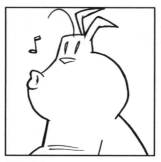

SKULL
The Troll

SPECIAL MOVE:
Stand Dumbfounded

⊡

The heart of PvP Magazine lies deep within the chest of this gentle giant. Skull was living in the janitor's closet when the staff moved in. Being a creature of Myth, Skull's only need is attention; something the staff is more than willing to provide. Skull holds the position of intern, a title he's quite proud of.

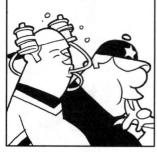

ROBBIE & JASE
Charity Cases.

SPECIAL MOVE:
Convert beer to pee

⊡ ⊡ ⊡ P

Their asses firmly attached to their old couch, these two ex-jocks spend all day playing sports games, drinking beer and eating junk food. Despite his better judgment, Cole can't bring himself to fire Robbie and Jase, who he used to dorm with back in college. The two serve no practical function whatsoever.

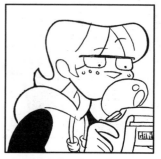

Marcy Wisniewsky
World's top ranked cyber-athlete

SPECIAL MOVE:
Invincibility.

↓ → ⊡

Little is known about this fifteen year old spitfire who goes by the online name DEVILFISH. Not only did she steal Francis' title, but she seems to have stolen his heart. Whether this is simply friendly competition or the start of something more remains to be seen.

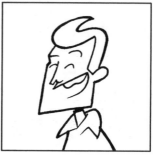

Max Powers
The Jerk

SPECIAL MOVE:
Passive Aggressive attack

↙ ↙ L ⊗

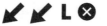

Years ago, something happened between Cole and Max that turned Cole sour. Years later, Max has popped up again to be a thorn in Cole's side. He started a rival video-game review magazine and set up his own offices in the same building, just one floor above the PvP offices.

Art by Paul Southworth

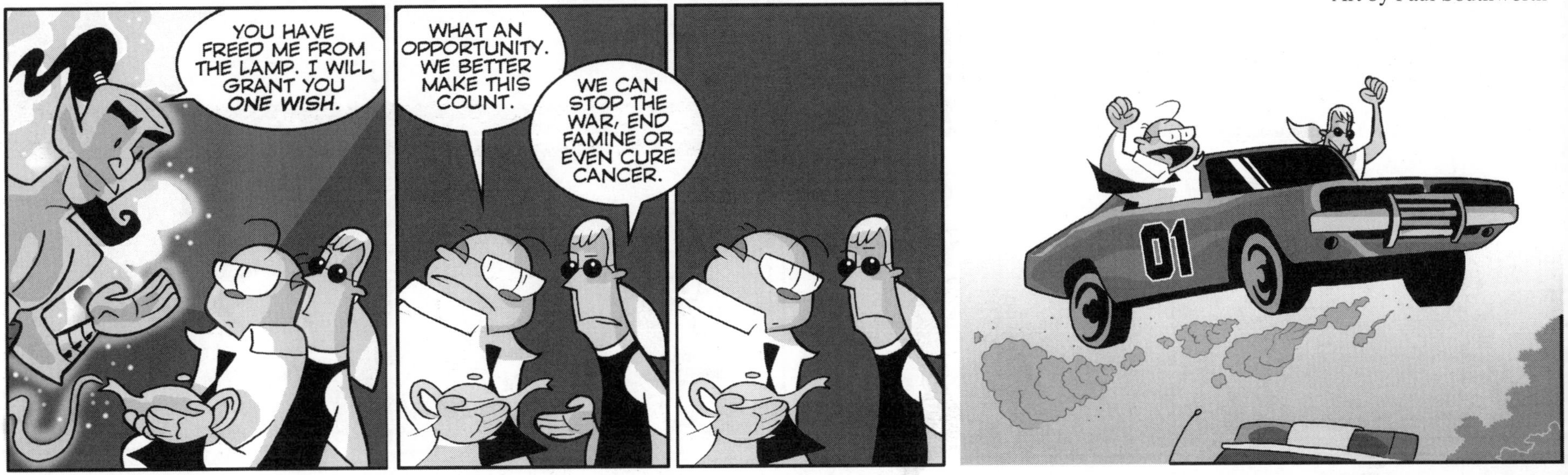

YOU HAVE FREED ME FROM THE LAMP. I WILL GRANT YOU *ONE WISH.*
WHAT AN OPPORTUNITY. WE BETTER MAKE THIS COUNT.
WE CAN STOP THE WAR, END FAMINE OR EVEN CURE CANCER.
01

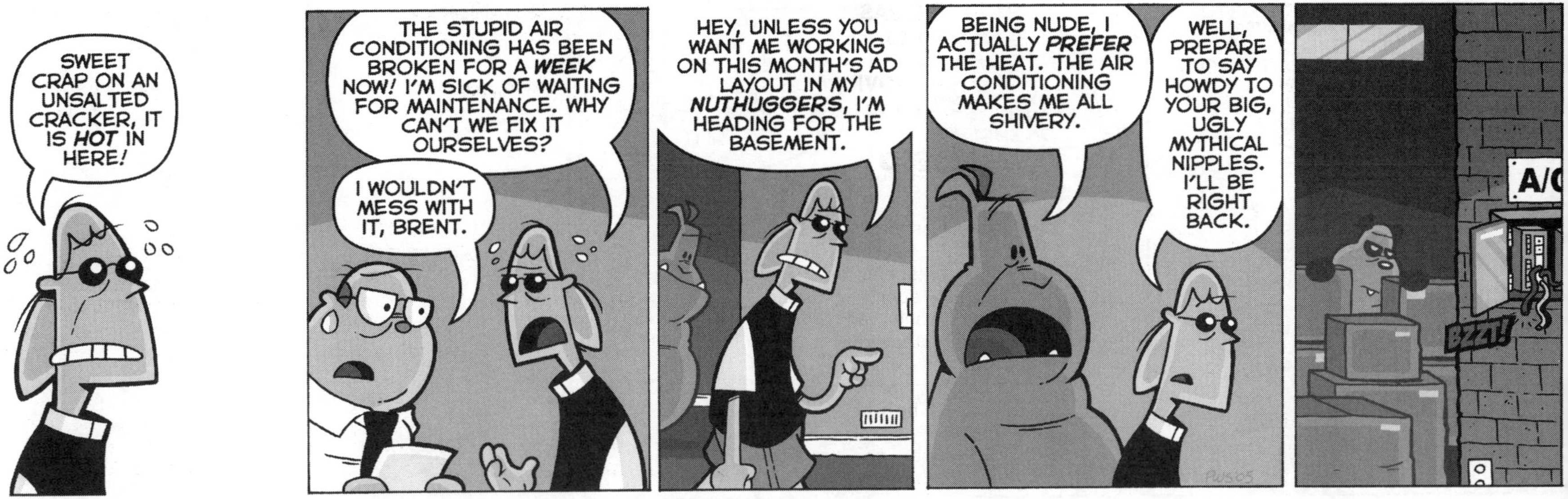

SWEET CRAP ON AN UNSALTED CRACKER, IT IS *HOT* IN HERE!
THE STUPID AIR CONDITIONING HAS BEEN BROKEN FOR A *WEEK* NOW! I'M SICK OF WAITING FOR MAINTENANCE. WHY CAN'T WE FIX IT OURSELVES?
I WOULDN'T MESS WITH IT, BRENT.
HEY, UNLESS YOU WANT ME WORKING ON THIS MONTH'S AD LAYOUT IN MY *NUTHUGGERS*, I'M HEADING FOR THE BASEMENT.
BEING NUDE, I ACTUALLY *PREFER* THE HEAT. THE AIR CONDITIONING MAKES ME ALL SHIVERY.
WELL, PREPARE TO SAY HOWDY TO YOUR BIG, UGLY MYTHICAL NIPPLES. I'LL BE RIGHT BACK.
A/C
BZZT!

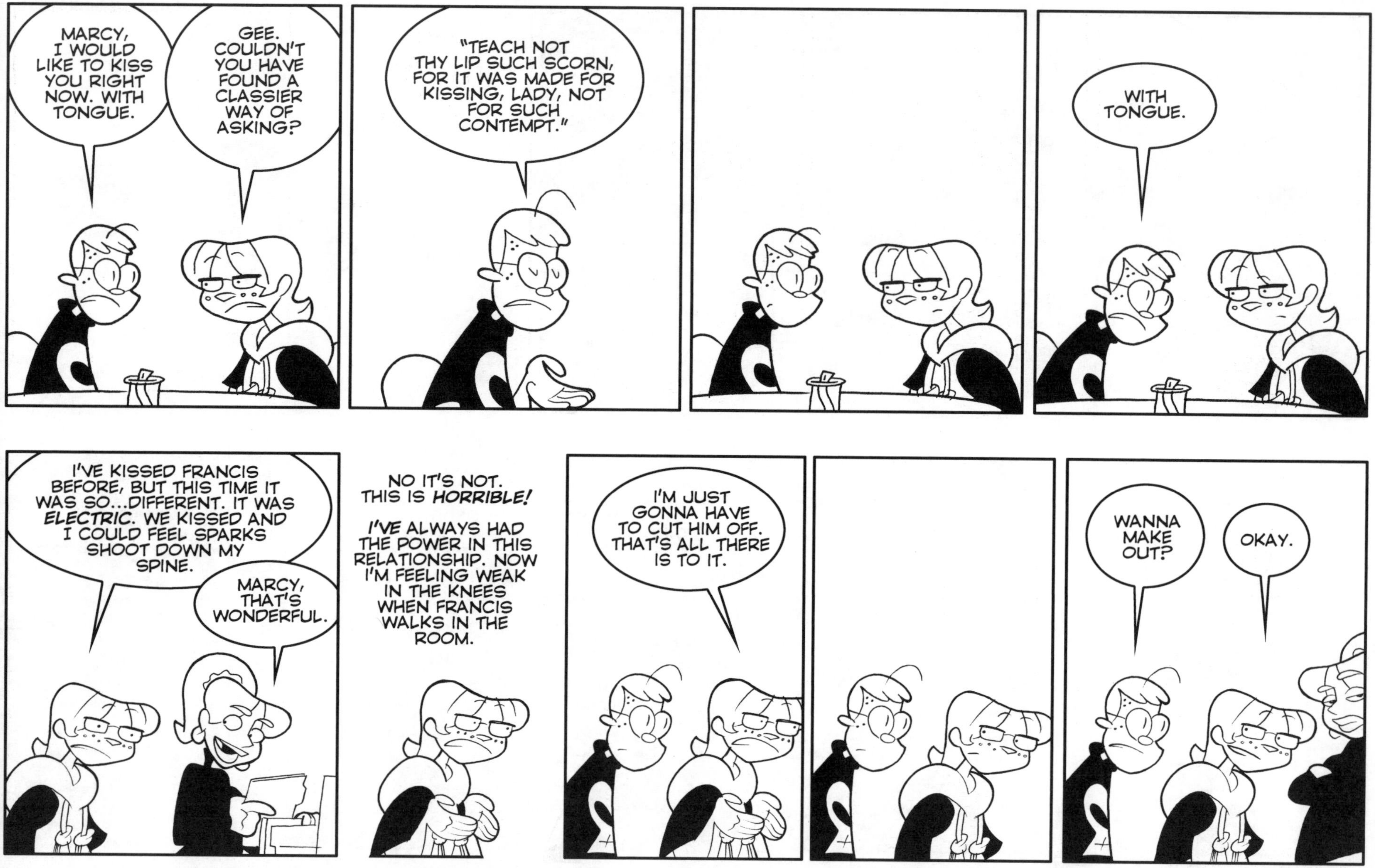
MARCY, I WOULD LIKE TO KISS YOU RIGHT NOW. WITH TONGUE.
GEE. COULDN'T YOU HAVE FOUND A CLASSIER WAY OF ASKING?
"TEACH NOT THY LIP SUCH SCORN, FOR IT WAS MADE FOR KISSING, LADY, NOT FOR SUCH CONTEMPT."
WITH TONGUE.
I'VE KISSED FRANCIS BEFORE, BUT THIS TIME IT WAS SO...DIFFERENT. IT WAS *ELECTRIC*. WE KISSED AND I COULD FEEL SPARKS SHOOT DOWN MY SPINE.
MARCY, THAT'S WONDERFUL.
NO IT'S NOT. THIS IS *HORRIBLE!*
I'VE ALWAYS HAD THE POWER IN THIS RELATIONSHIP. NOW I'M FEELING WEAK IN THE KNEES WHEN FRANCIS WALKS IN THE ROOM.
I'M JUST GONNA HAVE TO CUT HIM OFF. THAT'S ALL THERE IS TO IT.
WANNA MAKE OUT?
OKAY.

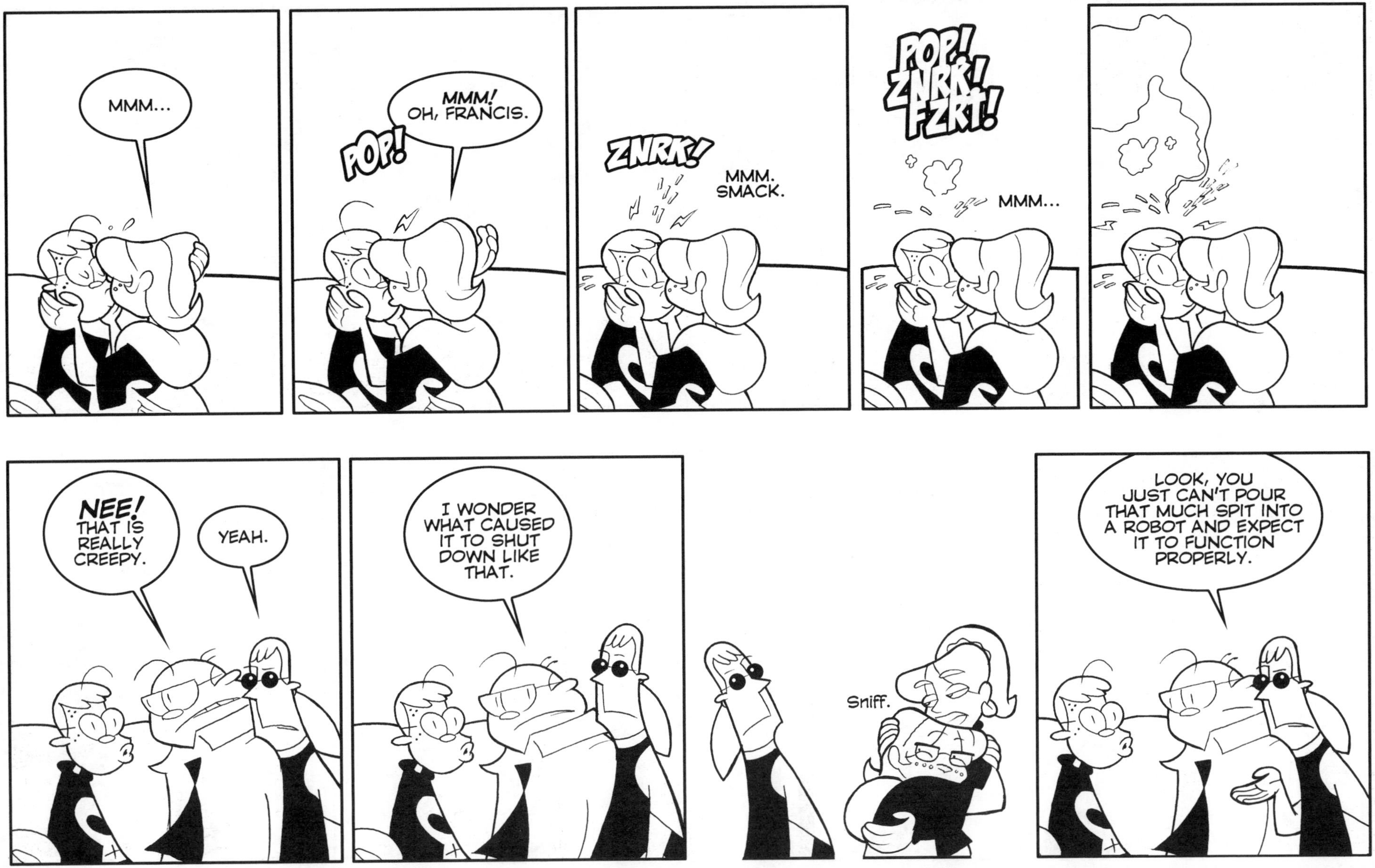
MMM...
POP!
MMM! OH, FRANCIS.
ZNRK!
MMM. SMACK.
POP! ZNRK! FZRT!
MMM...
NEE! THAT IS REALLY CREEPY.
YEAH.
I WONDER WHAT CAUSED IT TO SHUT DOWN LIKE THAT.
Sniff.
LOOK, YOU JUST CAN'T POUR THAT MUCH SPIT INTO A ROBOT AND EXPECT IT TO FUNCTION PROPERLY.

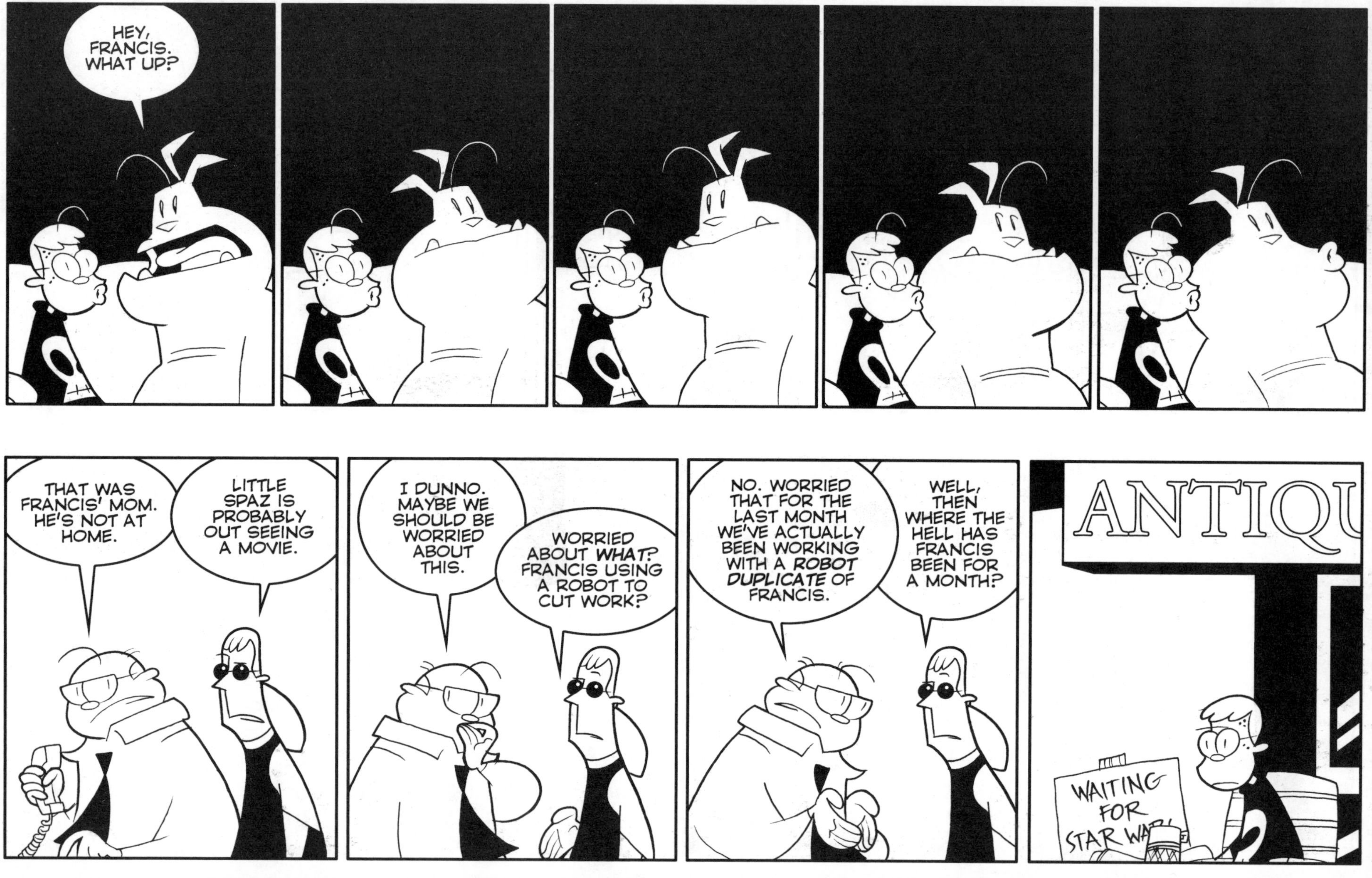

HEY, FRANCIS. WHAT UP?
THAT WAS FRANCIS' MOM. HE'S NOT AT HOME.
LITTLE SPAZ IS PROBABLY OUT SEEING A MOVIE.
I DUNNO. MAYBE WE SHOULD BE WORRIED ABOUT THIS.
WORRIED ABOUT ***WHAT***? FRANCIS USING A ROBOT TO CUT WORK?
NO. WORRIED THAT FOR THE LAST MONTH WE'VE ACTUALLY BEEN WORKING WITH A ***ROBOT DUPLICATE*** OF FRANCIS.
WELL, THEN WHERE THE HELL HAS FRANCIS BEEN FOR A MONTH?
ANTIQU
WAITING FOR STAR WA

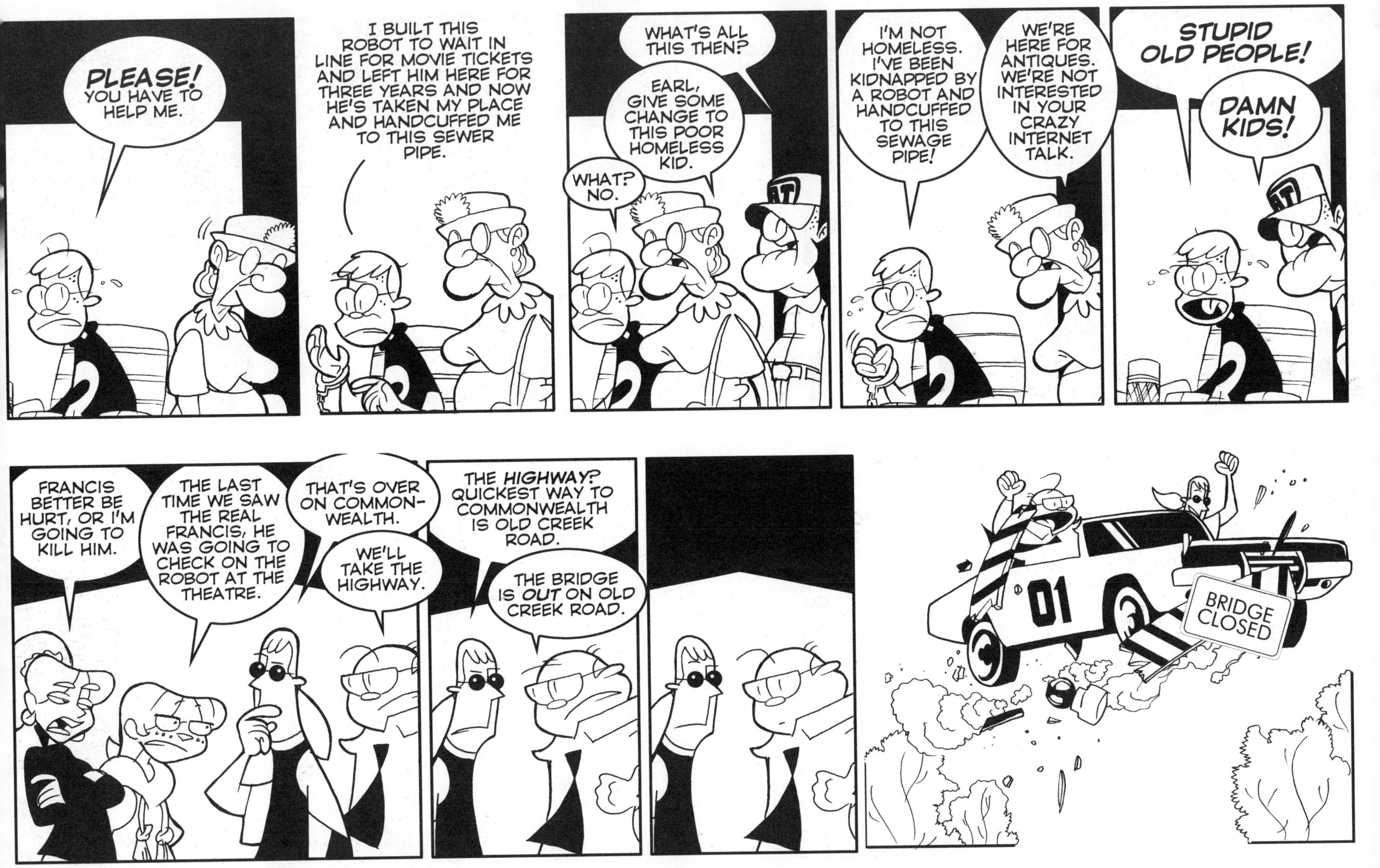
PLEASE! YOU HAVE TO HELP ME.
I BUILT THIS ROBOT TO WAIT IN LINE FOR MOVIE TICKETS AND LEFT HIM HERE FOR THREE YEARS AND NOW HE'S TAKEN MY PLACE AND HANDCUFFED ME TO THIS SEWER PIPE.
WHAT'S ALL THIS THEN?
EARL, GIVE SOME CHANGE TO THIS POOR HOMELESS KID.
WHAT? NO.
I'M NOT HOMELESS. I'VE BEEN KIDNAPPED BY A ROBOT AND HANDCUFFED TO THIS SEWAGE PIPE!
WE'RE HERE FOR ANTIQUES. WE'RE NOT INTERESTED IN YOUR CRAZY INTERNET TALK.
STUPID OLD PEOPLE!
DAMN KIDS!
FRANCIS BETTER BE HURT, OR I'M GOING TO KILL HIM.
THE LAST TIME WE SAW THE REAL FRANCIS, HE WAS GOING TO CHECK ON THE ROBOT AT THE THEATRE.
THAT'S OVER ON COMMON-WEALTH.
WE'LL TAKE THE HIGHWAY.
THE HIGHWAY? QUICKEST WAY TO COMMONWEALTH IS OLD CREEK ROAD.
THE BRIDGE IS OUT ON OLD CREEK ROAD.
01
BRIDGE CLOSED

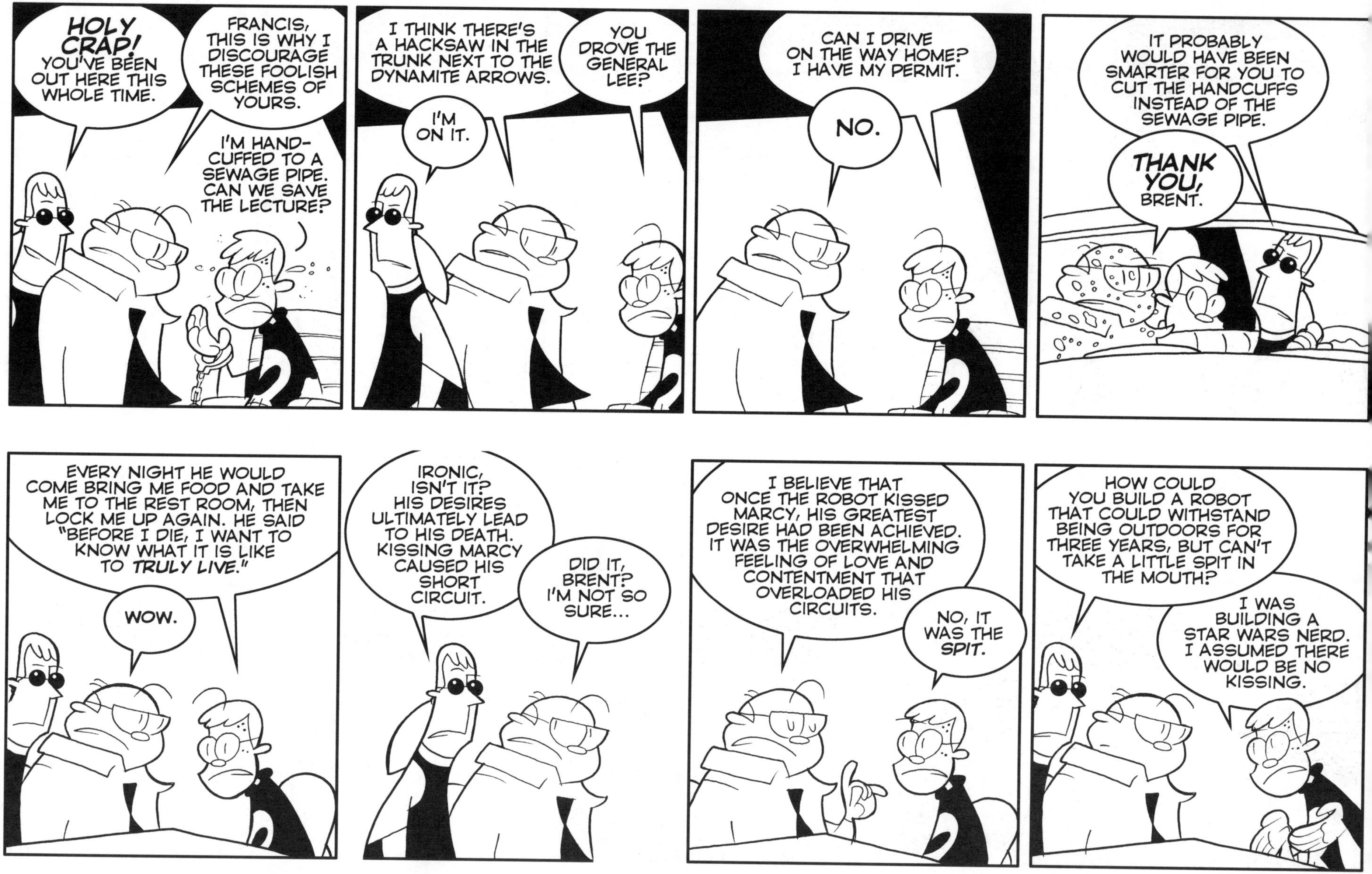
HOLY CRAP! YOU'VE BEEN OUT HERE THIS WHOLE TIME.
FRANCIS, THIS IS WHY I DISCOURAGE THESE FOOLISH SCHEMES OF YOURS.
I'M HAND-CUFFED TO A SEWAGE PIPE. CAN WE SAVE THE LECTURE?
I THINK THERE'S A HACKSAW IN THE TRUNK NEXT TO THE DYNAMITE ARROWS.
I'M ON IT.
YOU DROVE THE GENERAL LEE?
CAN I DRIVE ON THE WAY HOME? I HAVE MY PERMIT.
NO.
IT PROBABLY WOULD HAVE BEEN SMARTER FOR YOU TO CUT THE HANDCUFFS INSTEAD OF THE SEWAGE PIPE.
THANK YOU, BRENT.
EVERY NIGHT HE WOULD COME BRING ME FOOD AND TAKE ME TO THE REST ROOM, THEN LOCK ME UP AGAIN. HE SAID "BEFORE I DIE, I WANT TO KNOW WHAT IT IS LIKE TO TRULY LIVE."
WOW.
IRONIC, ISN'T IT? HIS DESIRES ULTIMATELY LEAD TO HIS DEATH. KISSING MARCY CAUSED HIS SHORT CIRCUIT.
DID IT, BRENT? I'M NOT SO SURE...
I BELIEVE THAT ONCE THE ROBOT KISSED MARCY, HIS GREATEST DESIRE HAD BEEN ACHIEVED. IT WAS THE OVERWHELMING FEELING OF LOVE AND CONTENTMENT THAT OVERLOADED HIS CIRCUITS.
NO, IT WAS THE SPIT.
HOW COULD YOU BUILD A ROBOT THAT COULD WITHSTAND BEING OUTDOORS FOR THREE YEARS, BUT CAN'T TAKE A LITTLE SPIT IN THE MOUTH?
I WAS BUILDING A STAR WARS NERD. I ASSUMED THERE WOULD BE NO KISSING.

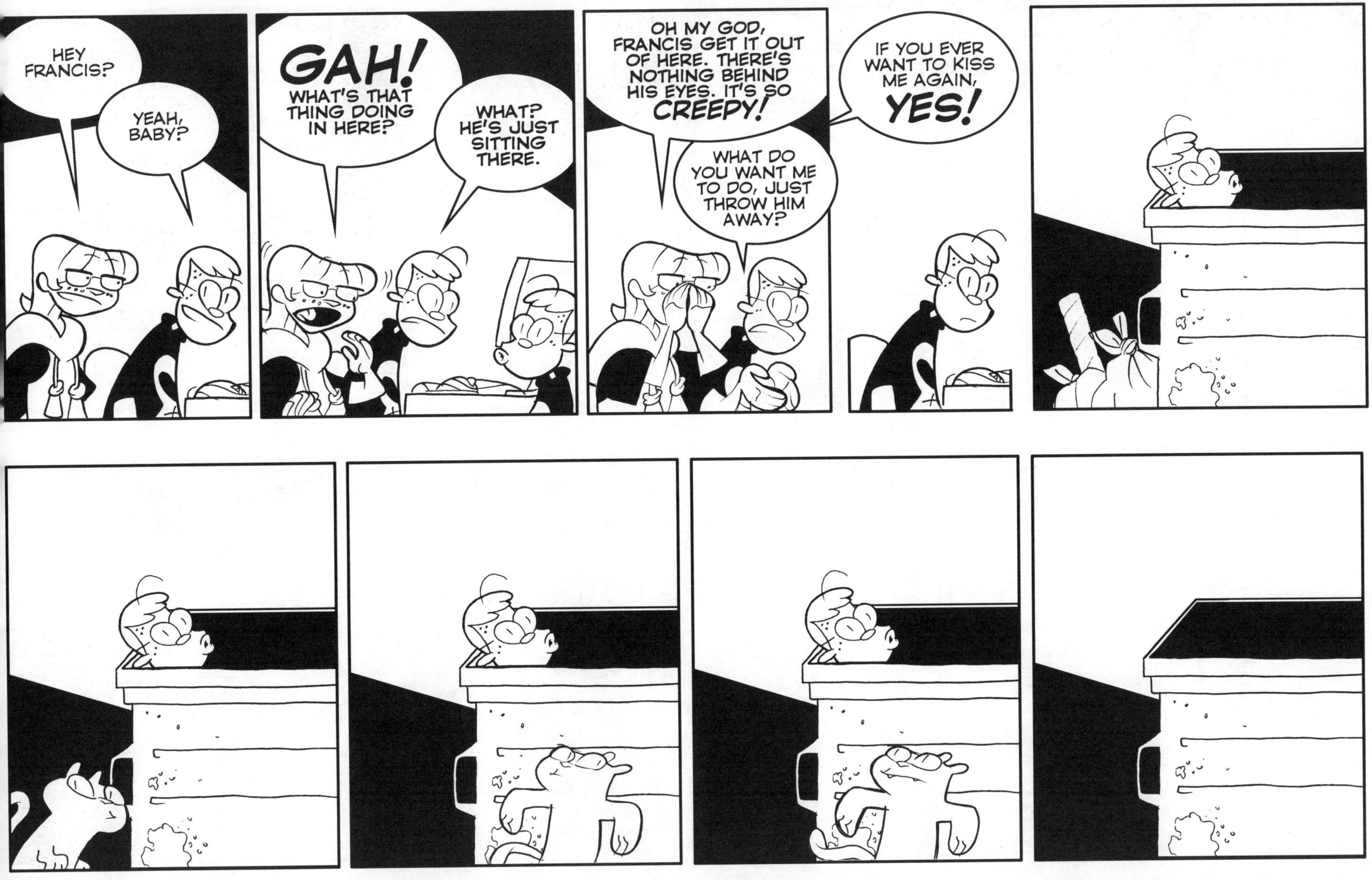
HEY FRANCIS?
YEAH, BABY?
GAH! WHAT'S THAT THING DOING IN HERE?
WHAT? HE'S JUST SITTING THERE.
OH MY GOD, FRANCIS GET IT OUT OF HERE. THERE'S NOTHING BEHIND HIS EYES. IT'S SO CREEPY!
WHAT DO YOU WANT ME TO DO, JUST THROW HIM AWAY?
IF YOU EVER WANT TO KISS ME AGAIN, YES!

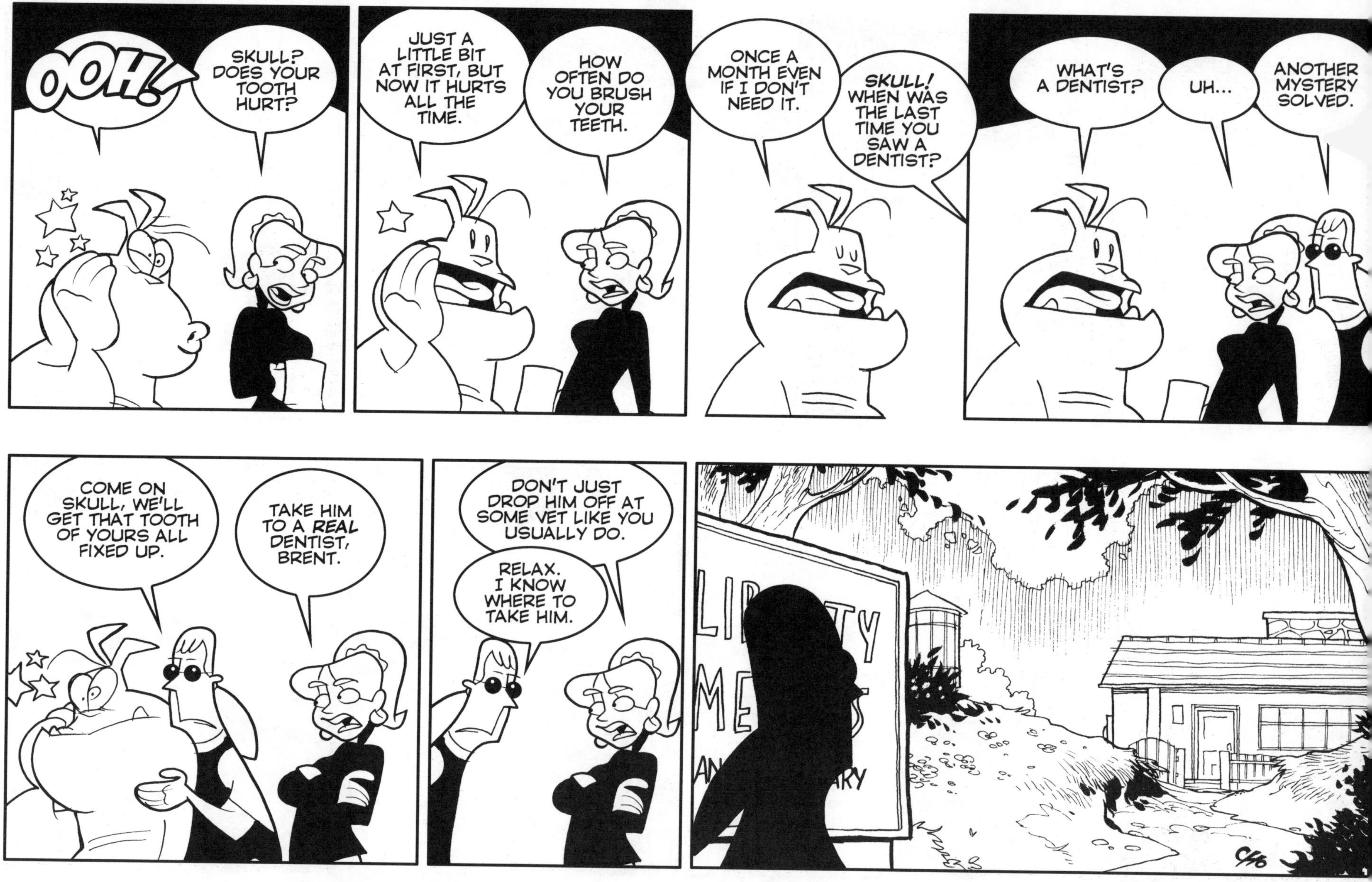
OOH!
SKULL? DOES YOUR TOOTH HURT?
JUST A LITTLE BIT AT FIRST, BUT NOW IT HURTS ALL THE TIME.
HOW OFTEN DO YOU BRUSH YOUR TEETH.
ONCE A MONTH EVEN IF I DON'T NEED IT.
SKULL! WHEN WAS THE LAST TIME YOU SAW A DENTIST?
WHAT'S A DENTIST?
UH...
ANOTHER MYSTERY SOLVED.
COME ON SKULL, WE'LL GET THAT TOOTH OF YOURS ALL FIXED UP.
TAKE HIM TO A REAL DENTIST, BRENT.
DON'T JUST DROP HIM OFF AT SOME VET LIKE YOU USUALLY DO.
RELAX. I KNOW WHERE TO TAKE HIM.

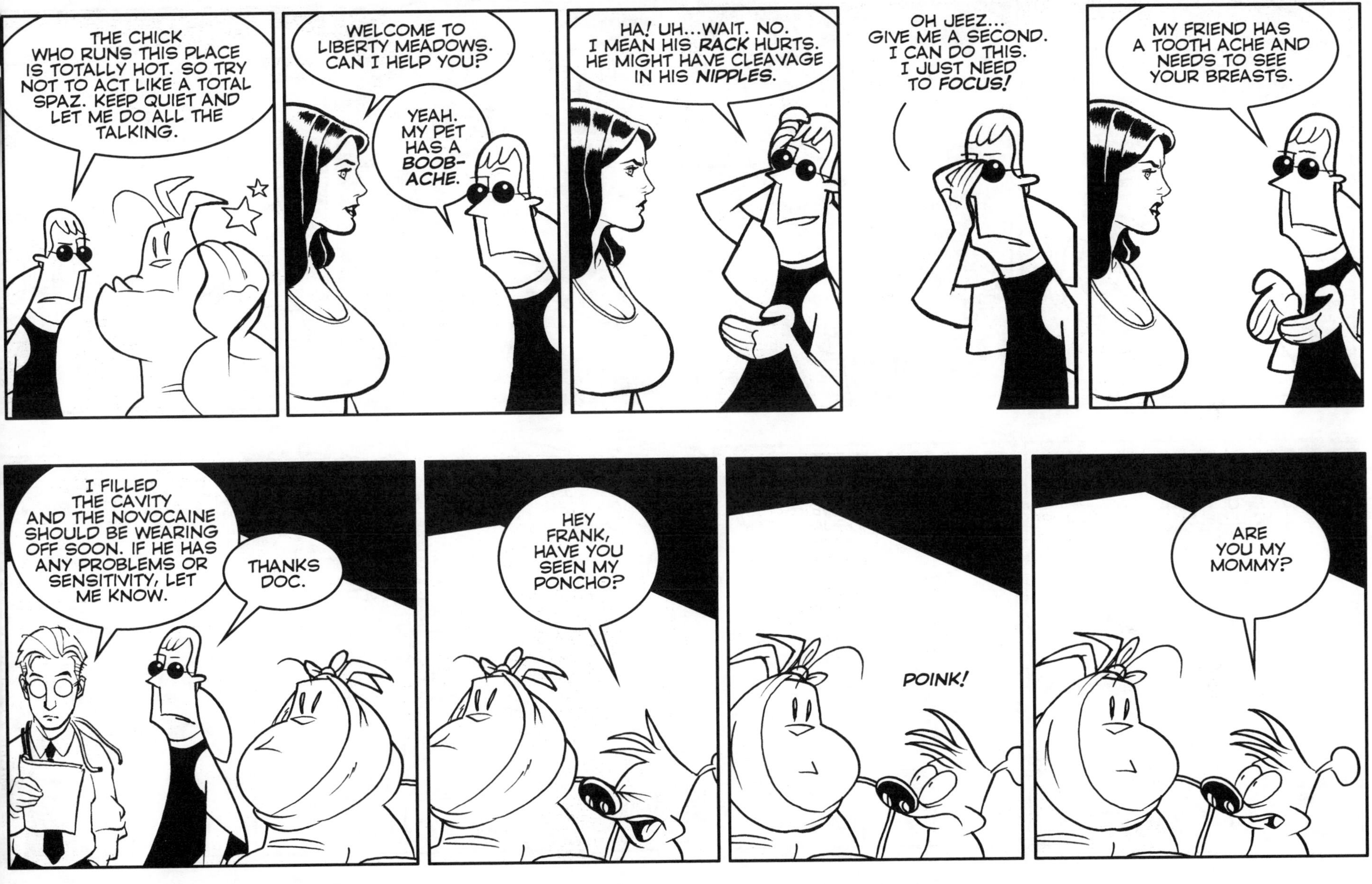
THE CHICK WHO RUNS THIS PLACE IS TOTALLY HOT. SO TRY NOT TO ACT LIKE A TOTAL SPAZ. KEEP QUIET AND LET ME DO ALL THE TALKING.
WELCOME TO LIBERTY MEADOWS. CAN I HELP YOU?
YEAH. MY PET HAS A *BOOB-ACHE*.
HA! UH...WAIT. NO. I MEAN HIS *RACK* HURTS. HE MIGHT HAVE CLEAVAGE IN HIS *NIPPLES*.
OH JEEZ... GIVE ME A SECOND. I CAN DO THIS. I JUST NEED TO *FOCUS!*
MY FRIEND HAS A TOOTH ACHE AND NEEDS TO SEE YOUR BREASTS.
I FILLED THE CAVITY AND THE NOVOCAINE SHOULD BE WEARING OFF SOON. IF HE HAS ANY PROBLEMS OR SENSITIVITY, LET ME KNOW.
THANKS DOC.
HEY FRANK, HAVE YOU SEEN MY PONCHO?
POINK!
ARE YOU MY MOMMY?

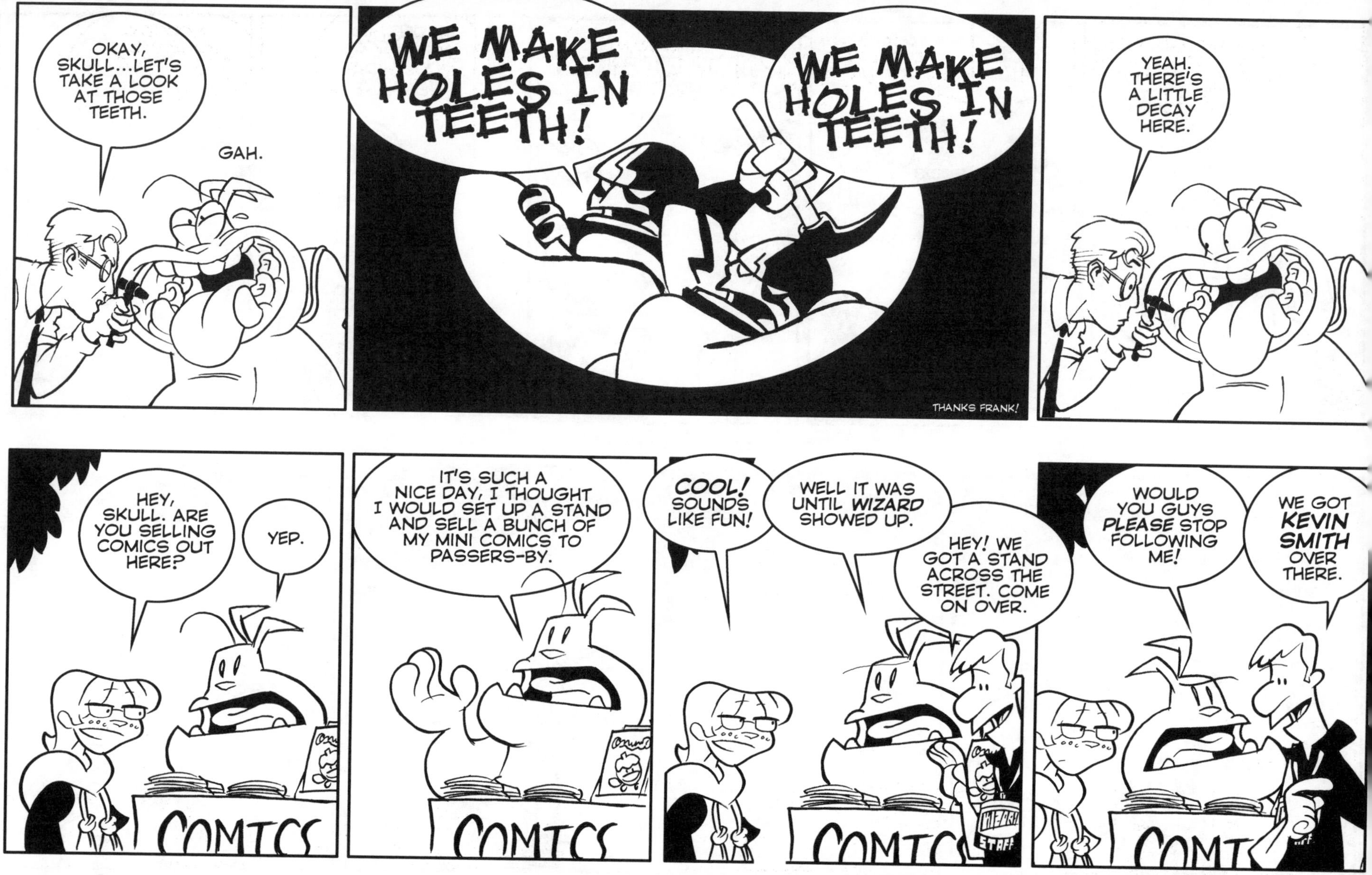
OKAY, SKULL...LET'S TAKE A LOOK AT THOSE TEETH.
GAH.
WE MAKE HOLES IN TEETH!
WE MAKE HOLES IN TEETH!
THANKS FRANK!
YEAH. THERE'S A LITTLE DECAY HERE.
HEY, SKULL. ARE YOU SELLING COMICS OUT HERE?
YEP.
COMICS
IT'S SUCH A NICE DAY, I THOUGHT I WOULD SET UP A STAND AND SELL A BUNCH OF MY MINI COMICS TO PASSERS-BY.
COMICS
COOL! SOUNDS LIKE FUN!
WELL IT WAS UNTIL WIZARD SHOWED UP.
HEY! WE GOT A STAND ACROSS THE STREET. COME ON OVER.
COMICS
STAFF
WOULD YOU GUYS PLEASE STOP FOLLOWING ME!
WE GOT KEVIN SMITH OVER THERE.
COMI

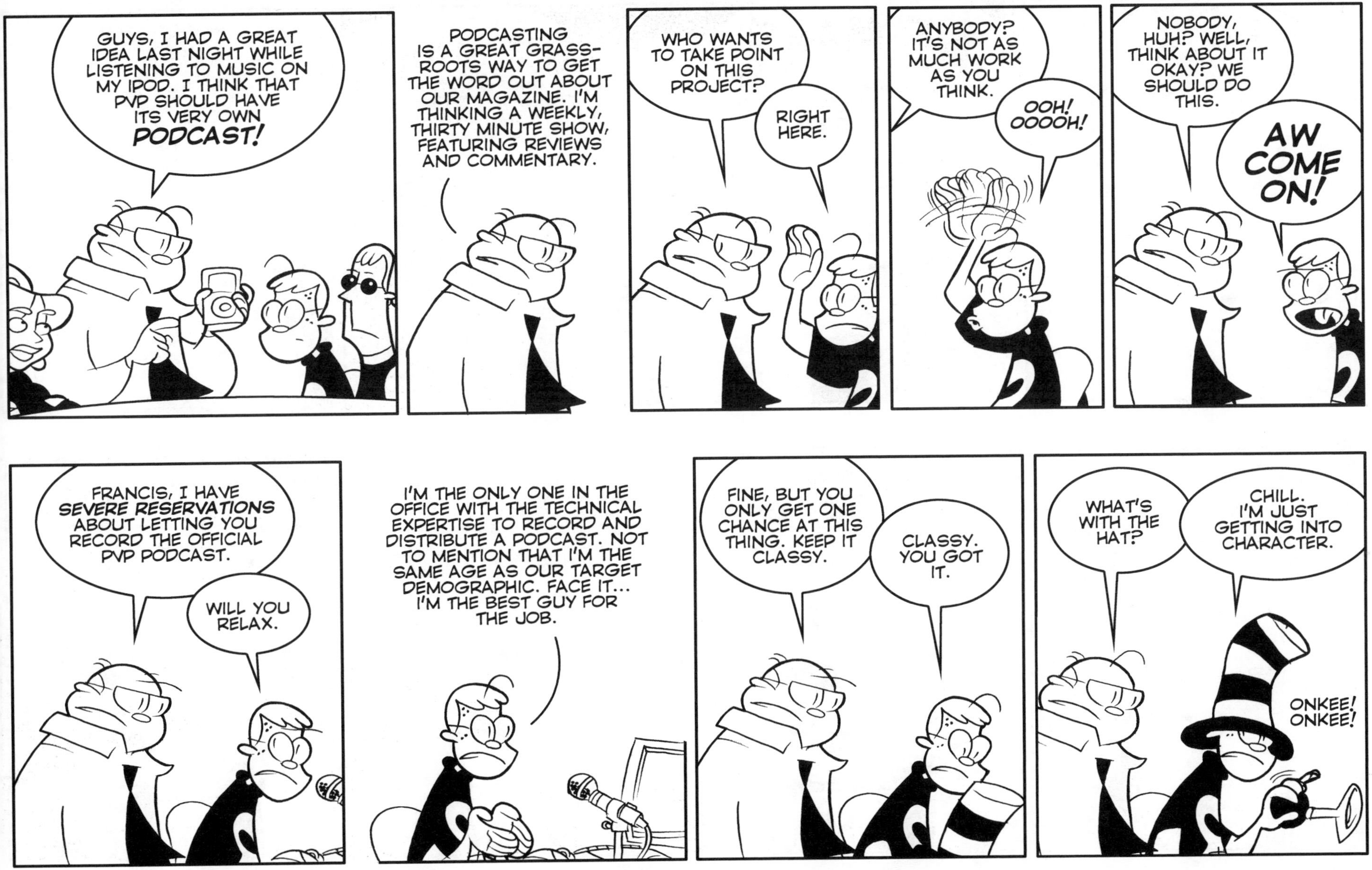
GUYS, I HAD A GREAT IDEA LAST NIGHT WHILE LISTENING TO MUSIC ON MY IPOD. I THINK THAT PVP SHOULD HAVE ITS VERY OWN PODCAST!
PODCASTING IS A GREAT GRASS-ROOTS WAY TO GET THE WORD OUT ABOUT OUR MAGAZINE. I'M THINKING A WEEKLY, THIRTY MINUTE SHOW, FEATURING REVIEWS AND COMMENTARY.
WHO WANTS TO TAKE POINT ON THIS PROJECT?
RIGHT HERE.
ANYBODY? IT'S NOT AS MUCH WORK AS YOU THINK.
OOH! OOOOH!
NOBODY, HUH? WELL, THINK ABOUT IT OKAY? WE SHOULD DO THIS.
AW COME ON!
FRANCIS, I HAVE SEVERE RESERVATIONS ABOUT LETTING YOU RECORD THE OFFICIAL PVP PODCAST.
WILL YOU RELAX.
I'M THE ONLY ONE IN THE OFFICE WITH THE TECHNICAL EXPERTISE TO RECORD AND DISTRIBUTE A PODCAST. NOT TO MENTION THAT I'M THE SAME AGE AS OUR TARGET DEMOGRAPHIC. FACE IT... I'M THE BEST GUY FOR THE JOB.
FINE, BUT YOU ONLY GET ONE CHANCE AT THIS THING. KEEP IT CLASSY.
CLASSY. YOU GOT IT.
WHAT'S WITH THE HAT?
CHILL. I'M JUST GETTING INTO CHARACTER.
ONKEE! ONKEE!

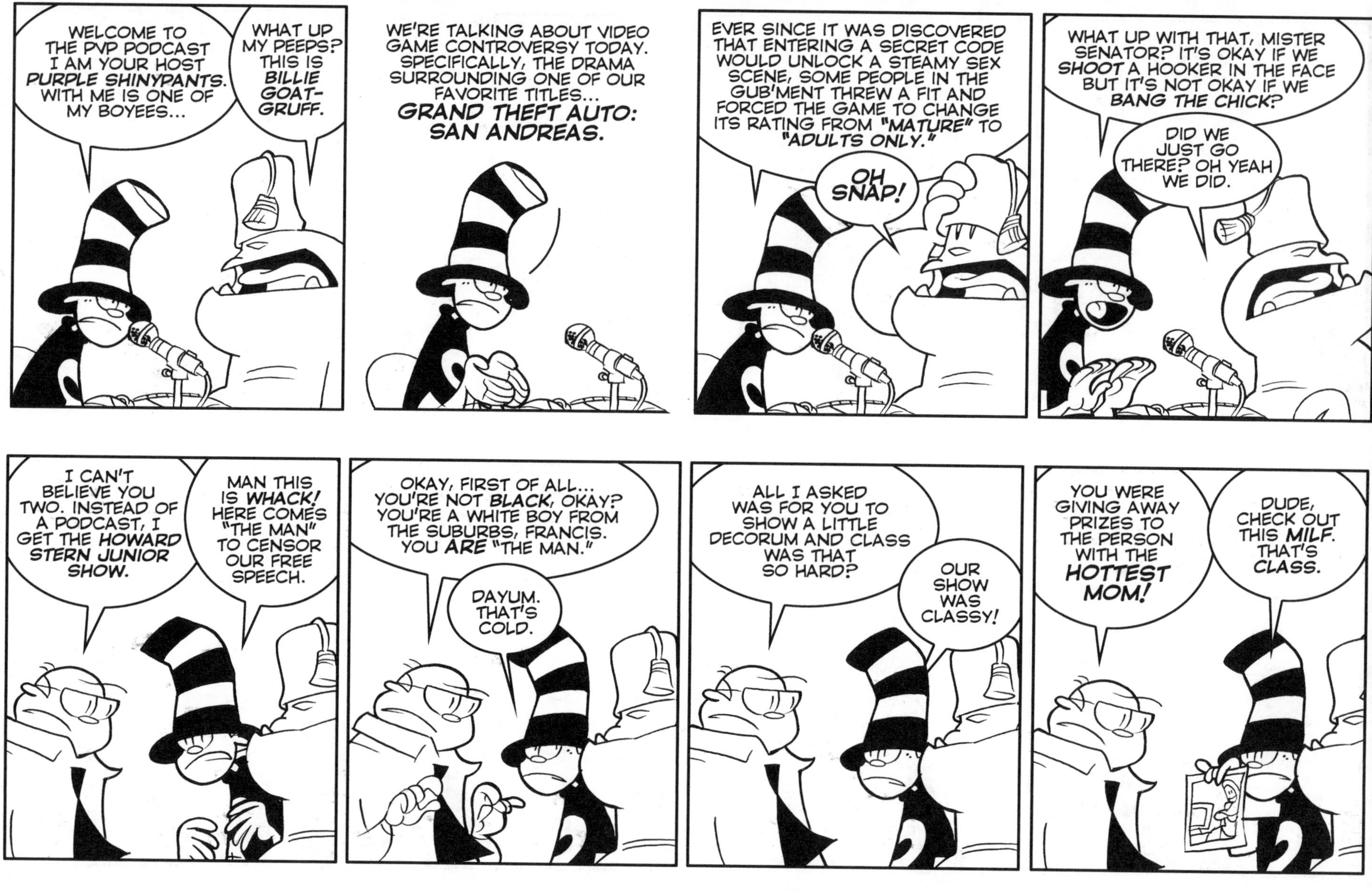
WELCOME TO THE PVP PODCAST I AM YOUR HOST PURPLE SHINYPANTS. WITH ME IS ONE OF MY BOYEES...
WHAT UP MY PEEPS? THIS IS BILLIE GOAT-GRUFF.
WE'RE TALKING ABOUT VIDEO GAME CONTROVERSY TODAY. SPECIFICALLY, THE DRAMA SURROUNDING ONE OF OUR FAVORITE TITLES... GRAND THEFT AUTO: SAN ANDREAS.
EVER SINCE IT WAS DISCOVERED THAT ENTERING A SECRET CODE WOULD UNLOCK A STEAMY SEX SCENE, SOME PEOPLE IN THE GUB'MENT THREW A FIT AND FORCED THE GAME TO CHANGE ITS RATING FROM "MATURE" TO "ADULTS ONLY."
OH SNAP!
WHAT UP WITH THAT, MISTER SENATOR? IT'S OKAY IF WE SHOOT A HOOKER IN THE FACE BUT IT'S NOT OKAY IF WE BANG THE CHICK?
DID WE JUST GO THERE? OH YEAH WE DID.
I CAN'T BELIEVE YOU TWO. INSTEAD OF A PODCAST, I GET THE HOWARD STERN JUNIOR SHOW.
MAN THIS IS WHACK! HERE COMES "THE MAN" TO CENSOR OUR FREE SPEECH.
OKAY, FIRST OF ALL... YOU'RE NOT BLACK, OKAY? YOU'RE A WHITE BOY FROM THE SUBURBS, FRANCIS. YOU ARE "THE MAN."
DAYUM. THAT'S COLD.
ALL I ASKED WAS FOR YOU TO SHOW A LITTLE DECORUM AND CLASS WAS THAT SO HARD?
OUR SHOW WAS CLASSY!
YOU WERE GIVING AWAY PRIZES TO THE PERSON WITH THE HOTTEST MOM!
DUDE, CHECK OUT THIS MILF. THAT'S CLASS.

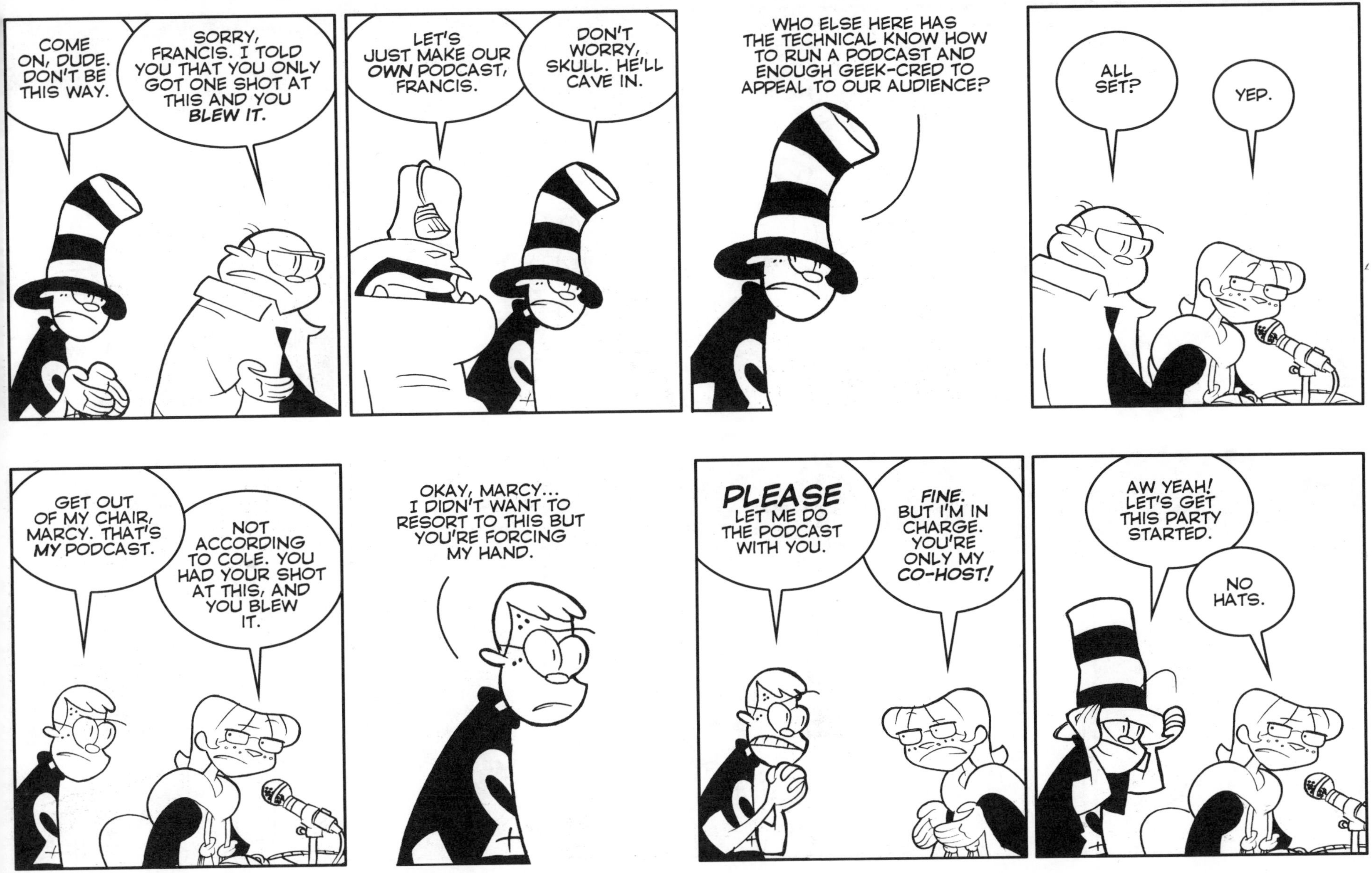
COME ON, DUDE. DON'T BE THIS WAY.
SORRY, FRANCIS. I TOLD YOU THAT YOU ONLY GOT ONE SHOT AT THIS AND YOU *BLEW IT.*
LET'S JUST MAKE OUR *OWN* PODCAST, FRANCIS.
DON'T WORRY, SKULL. HE'LL CAVE IN.
WHO ELSE HERE HAS THE TECHNICAL KNOW HOW TO RUN A PODCAST AND ENOUGH GEEK-CRED TO APPEAL TO OUR AUDIENCE?
ALL SET?
YEP.
GET OUT OF MY CHAIR, MARCY. THAT'S *MY* PODCAST.
NOT ACCORDING TO COLE. YOU HAD YOUR SHOT AT THIS, AND YOU BLEW IT.
OKAY, MARCY... I DIDN'T WANT TO RESORT TO THIS BUT YOU'RE FORCING MY HAND.
PLEASE LET ME DO THE PODCAST WITH YOU.
FINE. BUT I'M IN CHARGE. YOU'RE ONLY MY *CO-HOST!*
AW YEAH! LET'S GET THIS PARTY STARTED.
NO HATS.

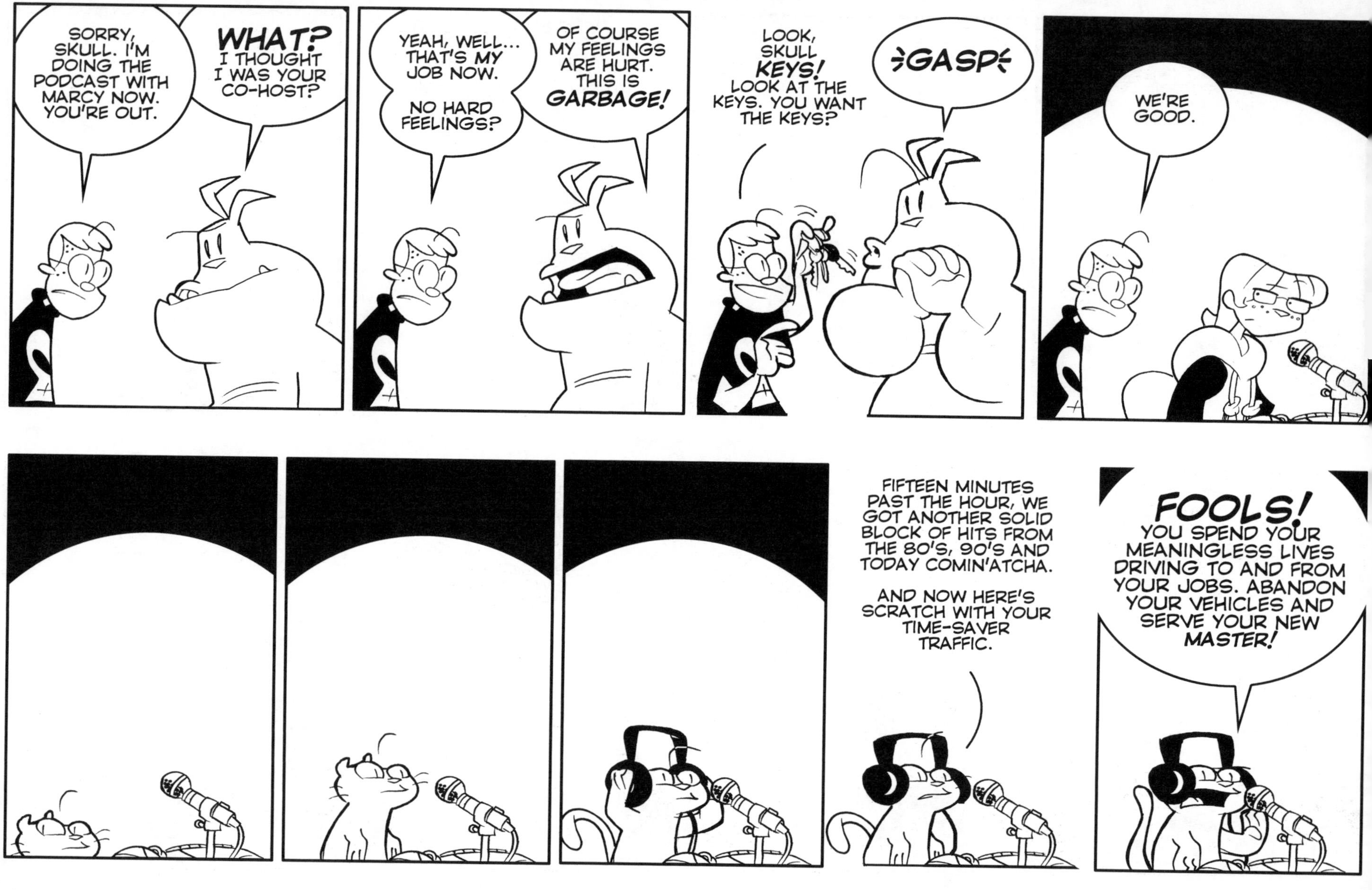
SORRY, SKULL. I'M DOING THE PODCAST WITH MARCY NOW. YOU'RE OUT.
WHAT? I THOUGHT I WAS YOUR CO-HOST?
YEAH, WELL... THAT'S MY JOB NOW.
NO HARD FEELINGS?
OF COURSE MY FEELINGS ARE HURT. THIS IS GARBAGE!
LOOK, SKULL KEYS! LOOK AT THE KEYS. YOU WANT THE KEYS?
GASP
WE'RE GOOD.
FIFTEEN MINUTES PAST THE HOUR, WE GOT ANOTHER SOLID BLOCK OF HITS FROM THE 80'S, 90'S AND TODAY COMIN'ATCHA.
AND NOW HERE'S SCRATCH WITH YOUR TIME-SAVER TRAFFIC.
FOOLS! YOU SPEND YOUR MEANINGLESS LIVES DRIVING TO AND FROM YOUR JOBS. ABANDON YOUR VEHICLES AND SERVE YOUR NEW MASTER!

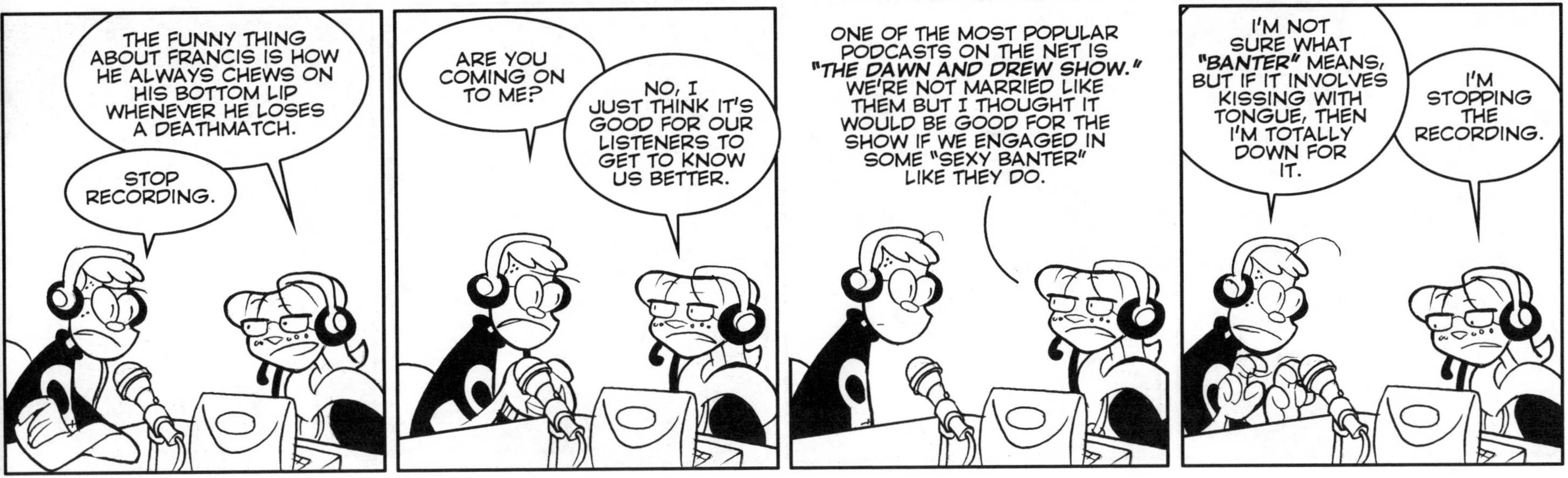
THE FUNNY THING ABOUT FRANCIS IS HOW HE ALWAYS CHEWS ON HIS BOTTOM LIP WHENEVER HE LOSES A DEATHMATCH.
STOP RECORDING.
ARE YOU COMING ON TO ME?
NO, I JUST THINK IT'S GOOD FOR OUR LISTENERS TO GET TO KNOW US BETTER.
ONE OF THE MOST POPULAR PODCASTS ON THE NET IS *"THE DAWN AND DREW SHOW."* WE'RE NOT MARRIED LIKE THEM BUT I THOUGHT IT WOULD BE GOOD FOR THE SHOW IF WE ENGAGED IN SOME "SEXY BANTER" LIKE THEY DO.
I'M NOT SURE WHAT **"BANTER"** MEANS, BUT IF IT INVOLVES KISSING WITH TONGUE, THEN I'M TOTALLY DOWN FOR IT.
I'M STOPPING THE RECORDING.

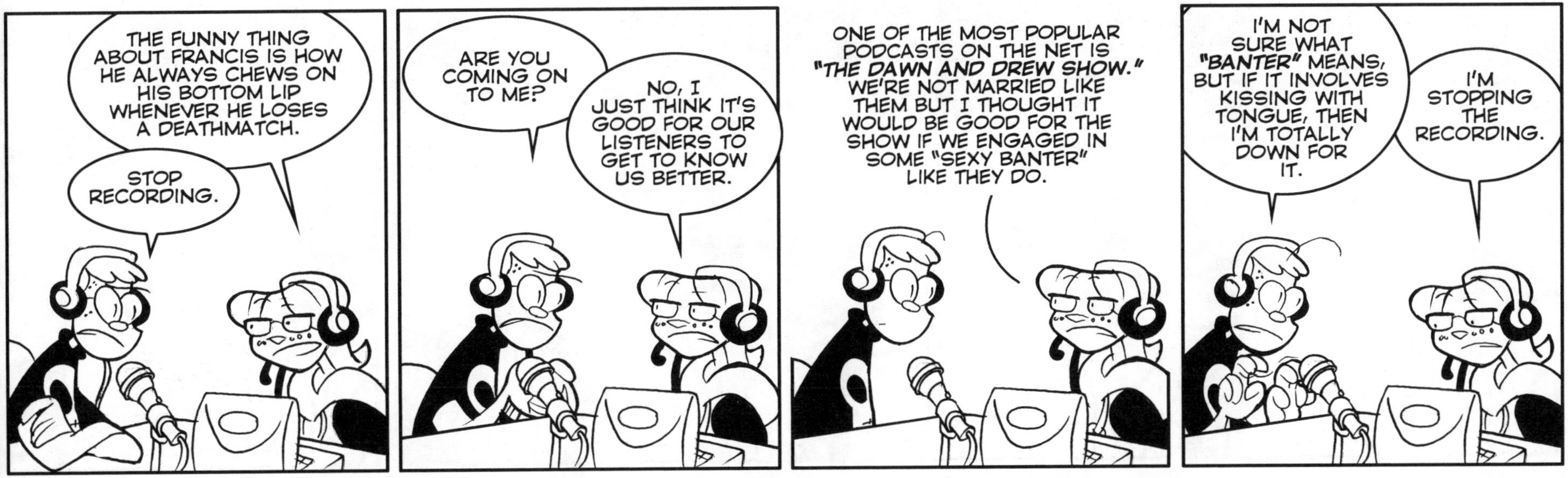
THE FUNNY THING ABOUT FRANCIS IS HOW HE ALWAYS CHEWS ON HIS BOTTOM LIP WHENEVER HE LOSES A DEATHMATCH.
STOP RECORDING.
ARE YOU COMING ON TO ME?
NO, I JUST THINK IT'S GOOD FOR OUR LISTENERS TO GET TO KNOW US BETTER.
ONE OF THE MOST POPULAR PODCASTS ON THE NET IS *"THE DAWN AND DREW SHOW."* WE'RE NOT MARRIED LIKE THEM BUT I THOUGHT IT WOULD BE GOOD FOR THE SHOW IF WE ENGAGED IN SOME "SEXY BANTER" LIKE THEY DO.
I'M NOT SURE WHAT **"BANTER"** MEANS, BUT IF IT INVOLVES KISSING WITH TONGUE, THEN I'M TOTALLY DOWN FOR IT.
I'M STOPPING THE RECORDING.

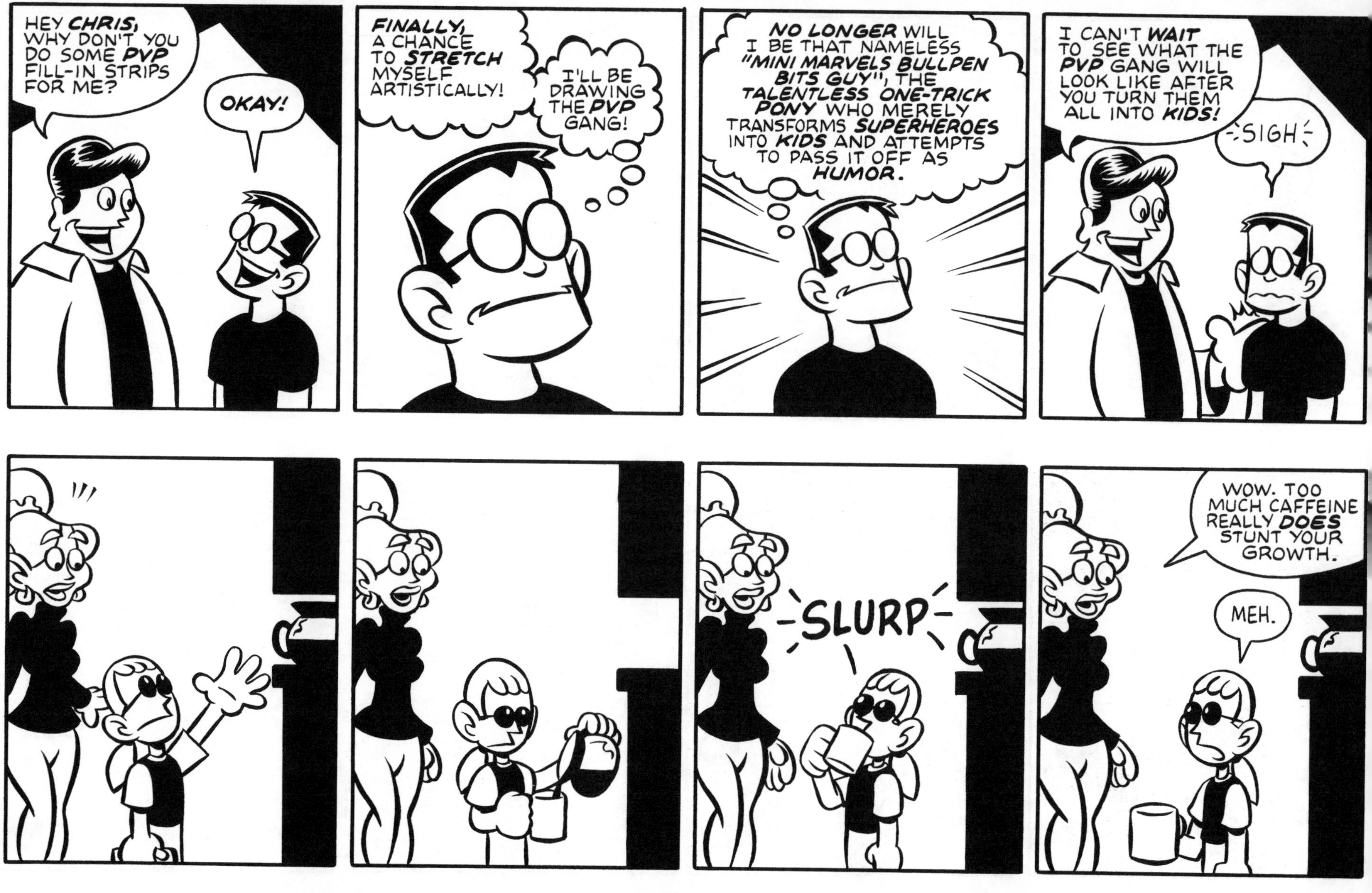
HEY CHRIS, WHY DON'T YOU DO SOME PVP FILL-IN STRIPS FOR ME?
OKAY!
FINALLY, A CHANCE TO STRETCH MYSELF ARTISTICALLY!
I'LL BE DRAWING THE PVP GANG!
NO LONGER WILL I BE THAT NAMELESS "MINI MARVELS BULLPEN BITS GUY", THE TALENTLESS ONE-TRICK PONY WHO MERELY TRANSFORMS SUPERHEROES INTO KIDS AND ATTEMPTS TO PASS IT OFF AS HUMOR.
I CAN'T WAIT TO SEE WHAT THE PVP GANG WILL LOOK LIKE AFTER YOU TURN THEM ALL INTO KIDS!
SIGH
SLURP
WOW. TOO MUCH CAFFEINE REALLY DOES STUNT YOUR GROWTH.
MEH.

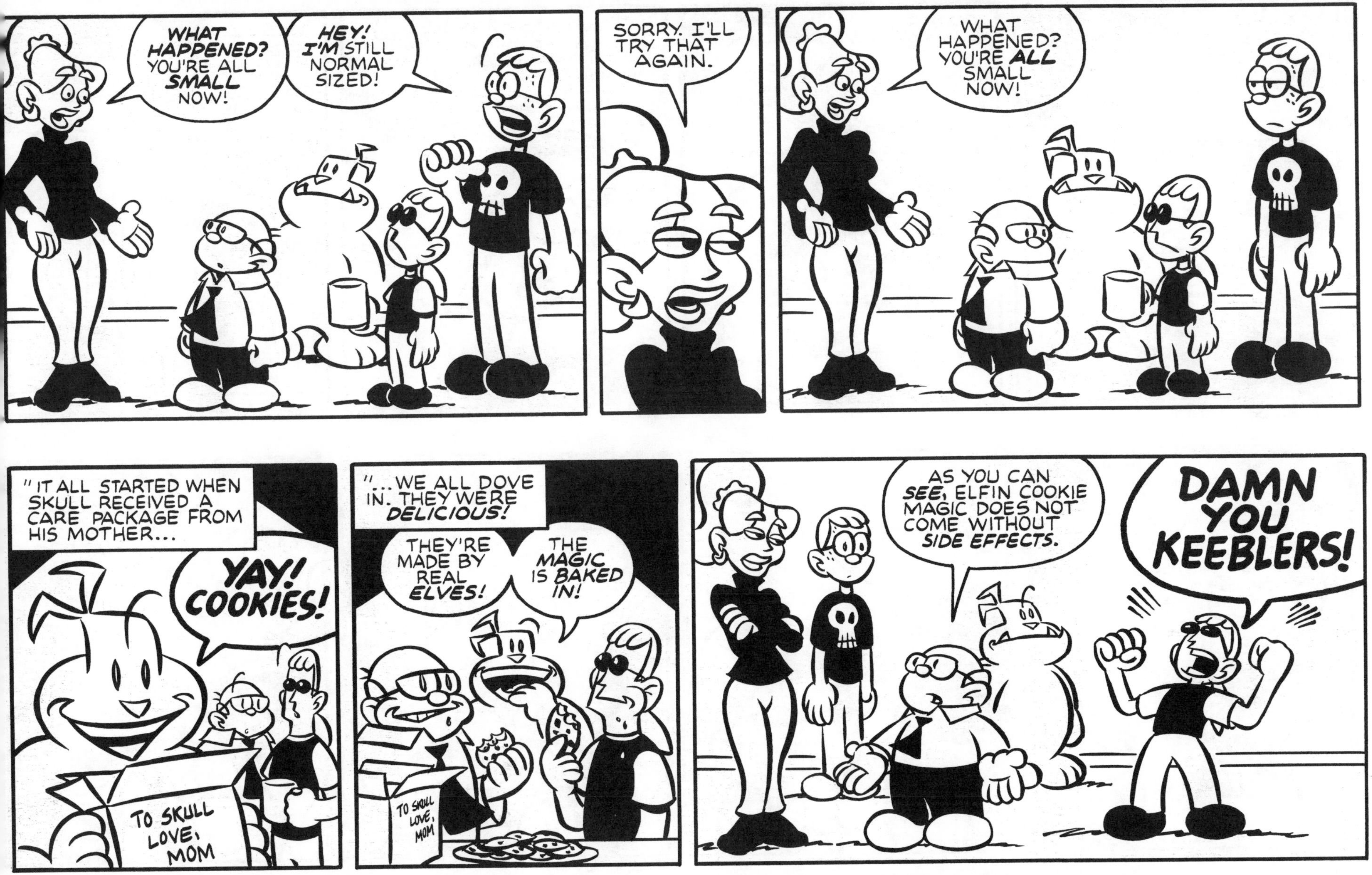

WHAT HAPPENED? YOU'RE ALL SMALL NOW!
HEY! I'M STILL NORMAL SIZED!
SORRY. I'LL TRY THAT AGAIN.
WHAT HAPPENED? YOU'RE ALL SMALL NOW!
"IT ALL STARTED WHEN SKULL RECEIVED A CARE PACKAGE FROM HIS MOTHER...
YAY! COOKIES!
TO SKULL LOVE, MOM
"...WE ALL DOVE IN. THEY WERE DELICIOUS!
THEY'RE MADE BY REAL ELVES!
THE MAGIC IS BAKED IN!
TO SKULL LOVE, MOM
AS YOU CAN SEE, ELFIN COOKIE MAGIC DOES NOT COME WITHOUT SIDE EFFECTS.
DAMN YOU KEEBLERS!

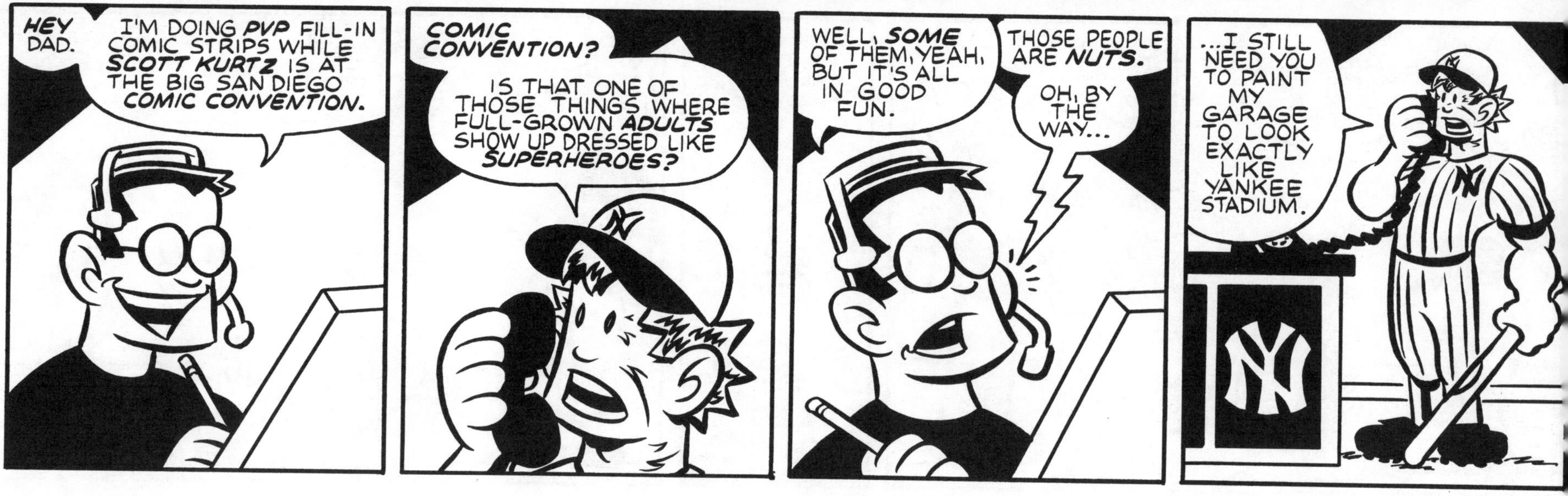
HEY DAD.
I'M DOING PVP FILL-IN COMIC STRIPS WHILE SCOTT KURTZ IS AT THE BIG SAN DIEGO COMIC CONVENTION.
COMIC CONVENTION?
IS THAT ONE OF THOSE THINGS WHERE FULL-GROWN ADULTS SHOW UP DRESSED LIKE SUPERHEROES?
WELL, SOME OF THEM, YEAH, BUT IT'S ALL IN GOOD FUN.
THOSE PEOPLE ARE NUTS.
OH, BY THE WAY...
...I STILL NEED YOU TO PAINT MY GARAGE TO LOOK EXACTLY LIKE YANKEE STADIUM.

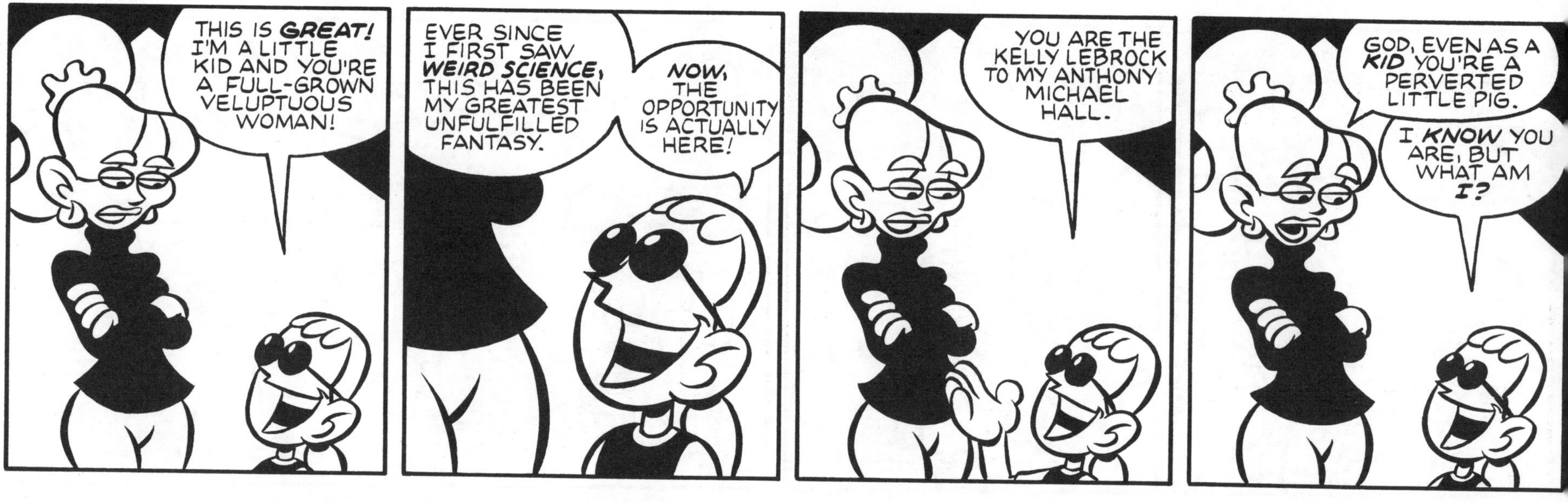
THIS IS GREAT! I'M A LITTLE KID AND YOU'RE A FULL-GROWN VELUPTUOUS WOMAN!
EVER SINCE I FIRST SAW WEIRD SCIENCE, THIS HAS BEEN MY GREATEST UNFULFILLED FANTASY.
NOW, THE OPPORTUNITY IS ACTUALLY HERE!
YOU ARE THE KELLY LEBROCK TO MY ANTHONY MICHAEL HALL.
GOD, EVEN AS A KID YOU'RE A PERVERTED LITTLE PIG.
I KNOW YOU ARE, BUT WHAT AM I?

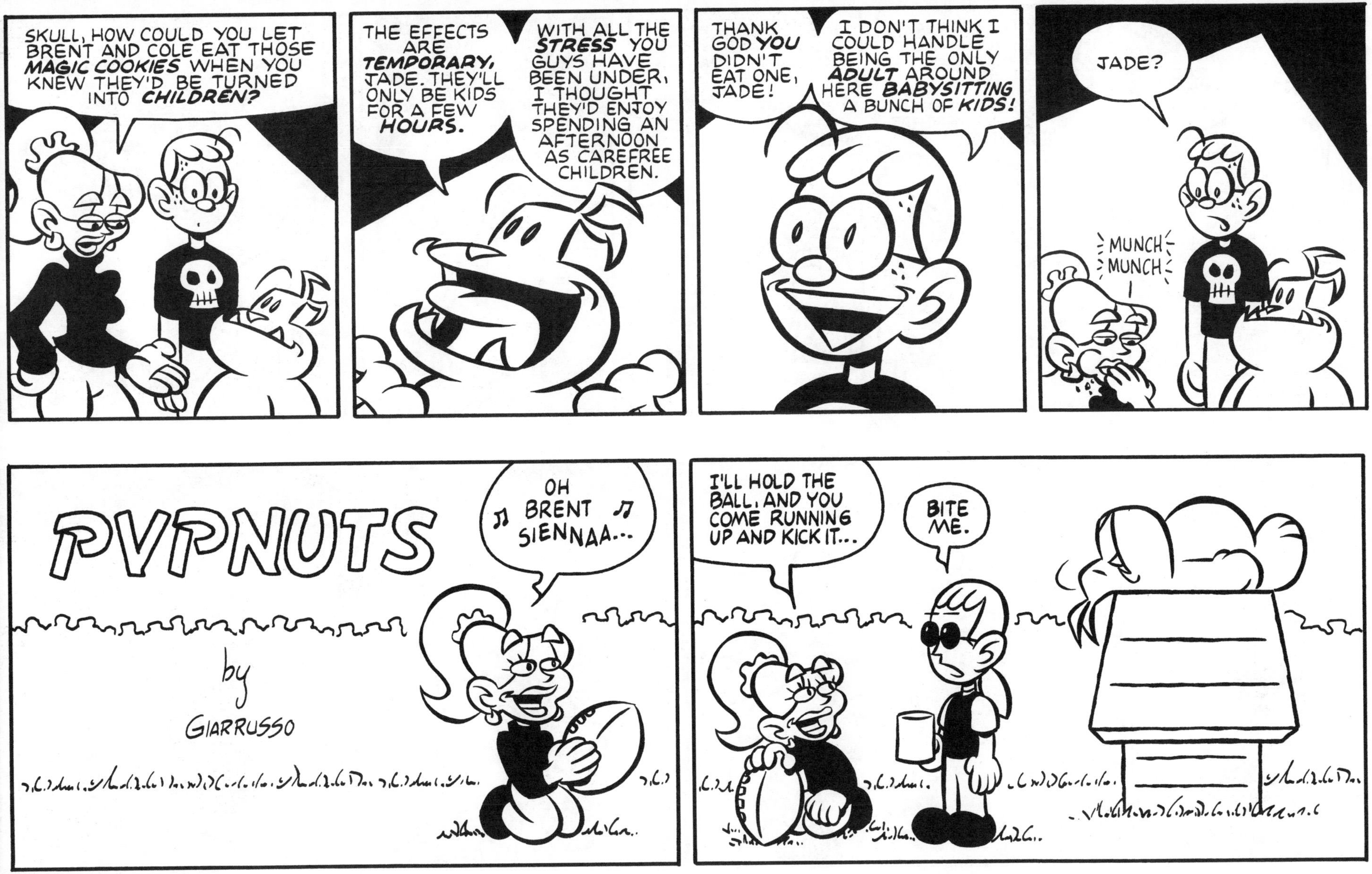
SKULL, HOW COULD YOU LET BRENT AND COLE EAT THOSE MAGIC COOKIES WHEN YOU KNEW THEY'D BE TURNED INTO CHILDREN?
THE EFFECTS ARE TEMPORARY, JADE. THEY'LL ONLY BE KIDS FOR A FEW HOURS.
WITH ALL THE STRESS YOU GUYS HAVE BEEN UNDER, I THOUGHT THEY'D ENJOY SPENDING AN AFTERNOON AS CAREFREE CHILDREN.
THANK GOD YOU DIDN'T EAT ONE, JADE!
I DON'T THINK I COULD HANDLE BEING THE ONLY ADULT AROUND HERE BABYSITTING A BUNCH OF KIDS!
JADE?
MUNCH MUNCH
PVPNUTS
by
GIARRUSSO
OH ♫ BRENT ♫ SIENNAA...
I'LL HOLD THE BALL, AND YOU COME RUNNING UP AND KICK IT...
BITE ME.

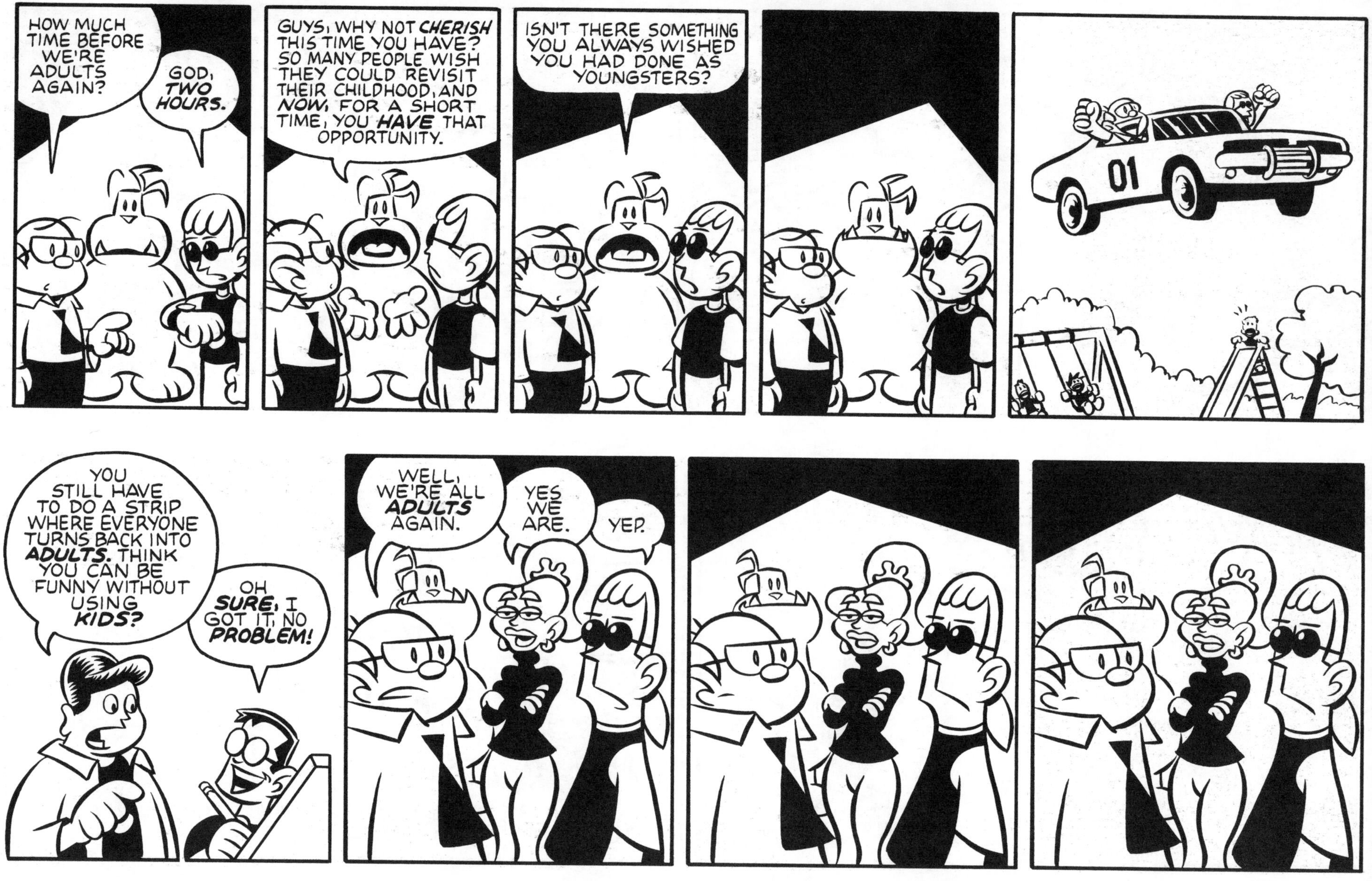
HOW MUCH TIME BEFORE WE'RE ADULTS AGAIN?
GOD, **TWO HOURS.**
GUYS, WHY NOT **CHERISH** THIS TIME YOU HAVE? SO MANY PEOPLE WISH THEY COULD REVISIT THEIR CHILDHOOD, AND **NOW**, FOR A SHORT TIME, YOU **HAVE** THAT OPPORTUNITY.
ISN'T THERE SOMETHING YOU ALWAYS WISHED YOU HAD DONE AS YOUNGSTERS?
01
YOU STILL HAVE TO DO A STRIP WHERE EVERYONE TURNS BACK INTO **ADULTS.** THINK YOU CAN BE FUNNY WITHOUT USING **KIDS?**
OH **SURE**, I GOT IT, NO **PROBLEM!**
WELL, WE'RE ALL **ADULTS** AGAIN.
YES WE ARE.
YEP.

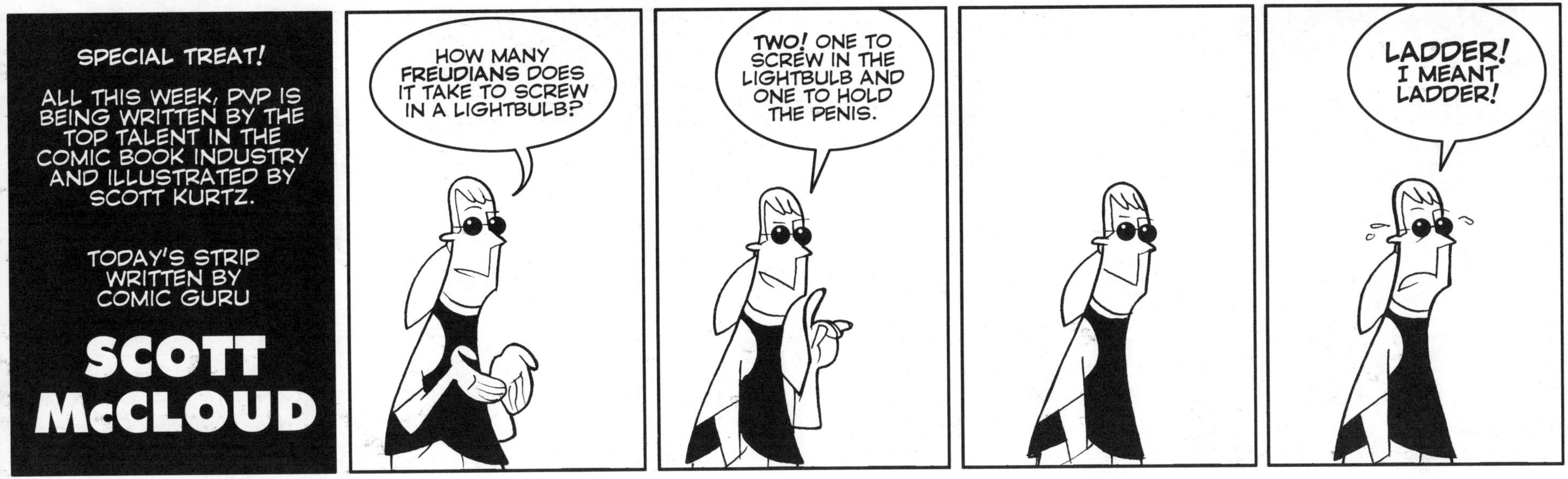
SPECIAL TREAT!
ALL THIS WEEK, PVP IS BEING WRITTEN BY THE TOP TALENT IN THE COMIC BOOK INDUSTRY AND ILLUSTRATED BY SCOTT KURTZ.
TODAY'S STRIP WRITTEN BY COMIC GURU
SCOTT McCLOUD
HOW MANY FREUDIANS DOES IT TAKE TO SCREW IN A LIGHTBULB?
TWO! ONE TO SCREW IN THE LIGHTBULB AND ONE TO HOLD THE PENIS.
LADDER! I MEANT LADDER!

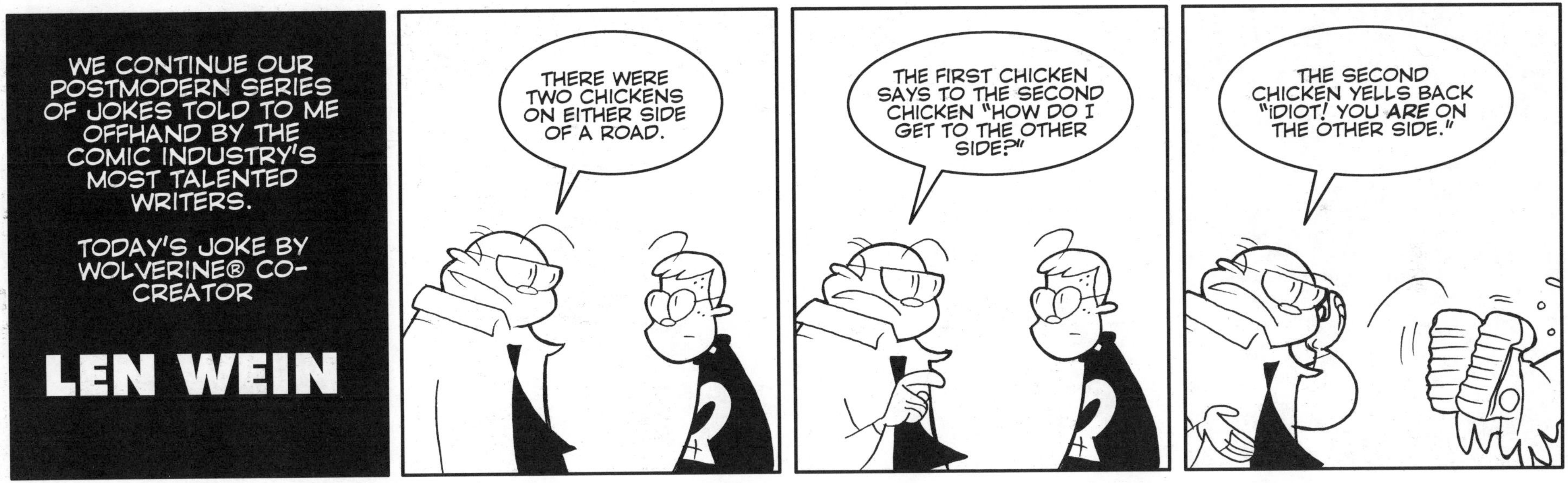
WE CONTINUE OUR POSTMODERN SERIES OF JOKES TOLD TO ME OFFHAND BY THE COMIC INDUSTRY'S MOST TALENTED WRITERS.
TODAY'S JOKE BY WOLVERINE® CO-CREATOR
LEN WEIN
THERE WERE TWO CHICKENS ON EITHER SIDE OF A ROAD.
THE FIRST CHICKEN SAYS TO THE SECOND CHICKEN "HOW DO I GET TO THE OTHER SIDE?"
THE SECOND CHICKEN YELLS BACK "¡IDIOT! YOU ARE ON THE OTHER SIDE."

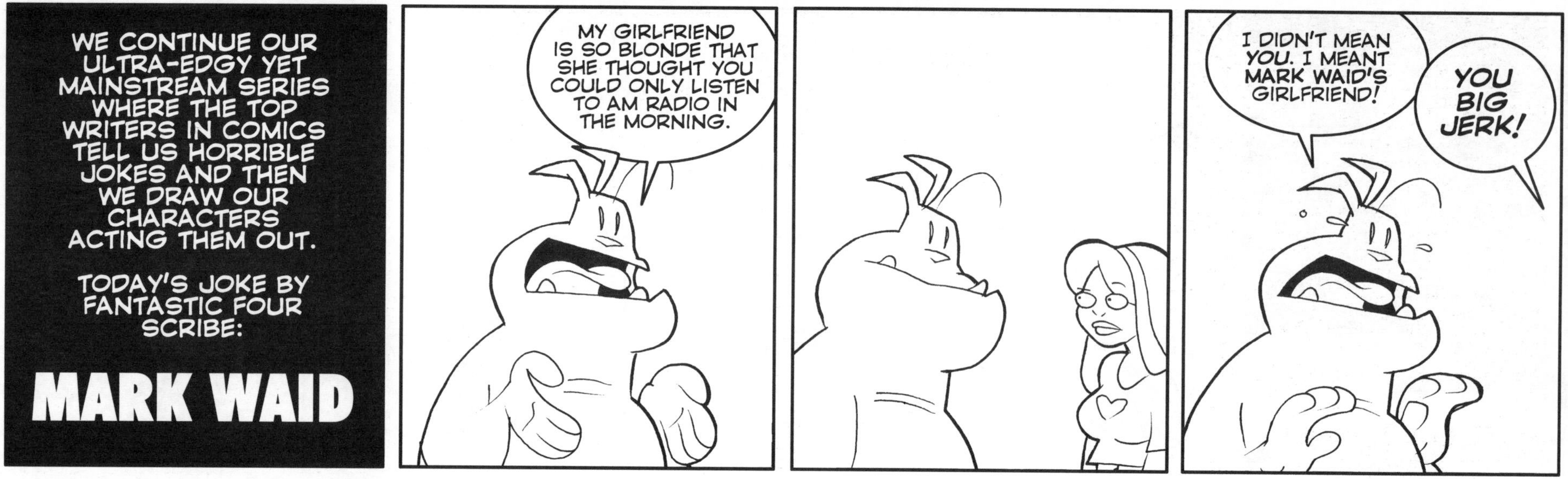
WE CONTINUE OUR ULTRA-EDGY YET MAINSTREAM SERIES WHERE THE TOP WRITERS IN COMICS TELL US HORRIBLE JOKES AND THEN WE DRAW OUR CHARACTERS ACTING THEM OUT.
TODAY'S JOKE BY FANTASTIC FOUR SCRIBE:
MARK WAID
MY GIRLFRIEND IS SO BLONDE THAT SHE THOUGHT YOU COULD ONLY LISTEN TO AM RADIO IN THE MORNING.
I DIDN'T MEAN YOU. I MEANT MARK WAID'S GIRLFRIEND!
YOU BIG JERK!

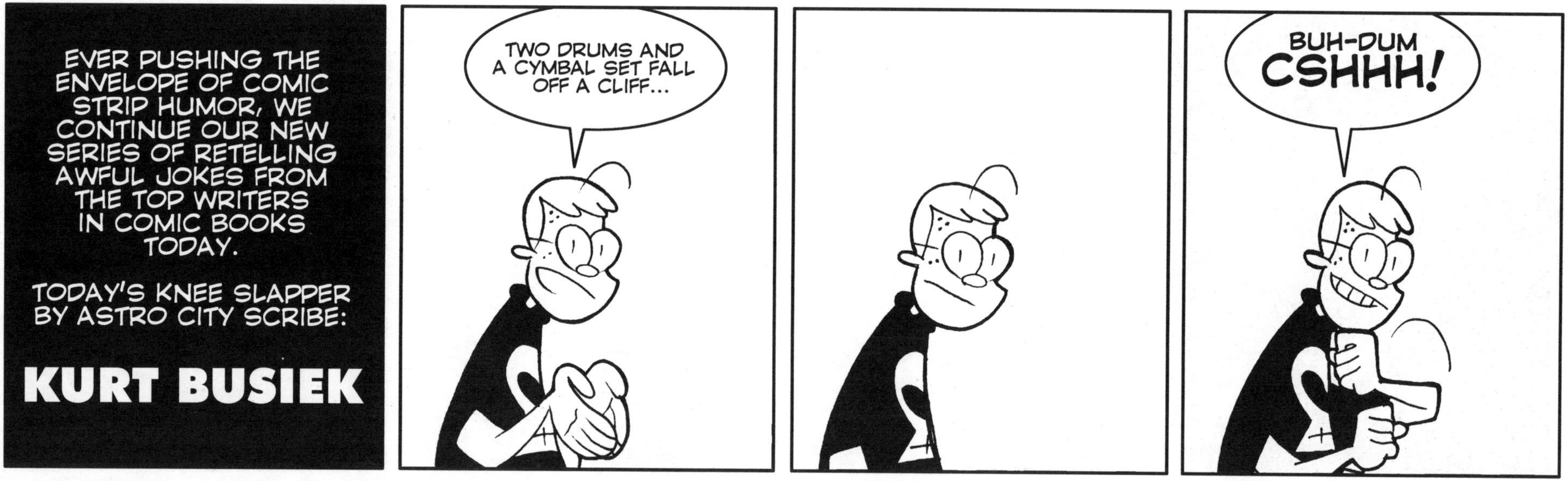
EVER PUSHING THE ENVELOPE OF COMIC STRIP HUMOR, WE CONTINUE OUR NEW SERIES OF RETELLING AWFUL JOKES FROM THE TOP WRITERS IN COMIC BOOKS TODAY.
TODAY'S KNEE SLAPPER BY ASTRO CITY SCRIBE:
KURT BUSIEK
TWO DRUMS AND A CYMBAL SET FALL OFF A CLIFF...
BUH-DUM CSHHH!

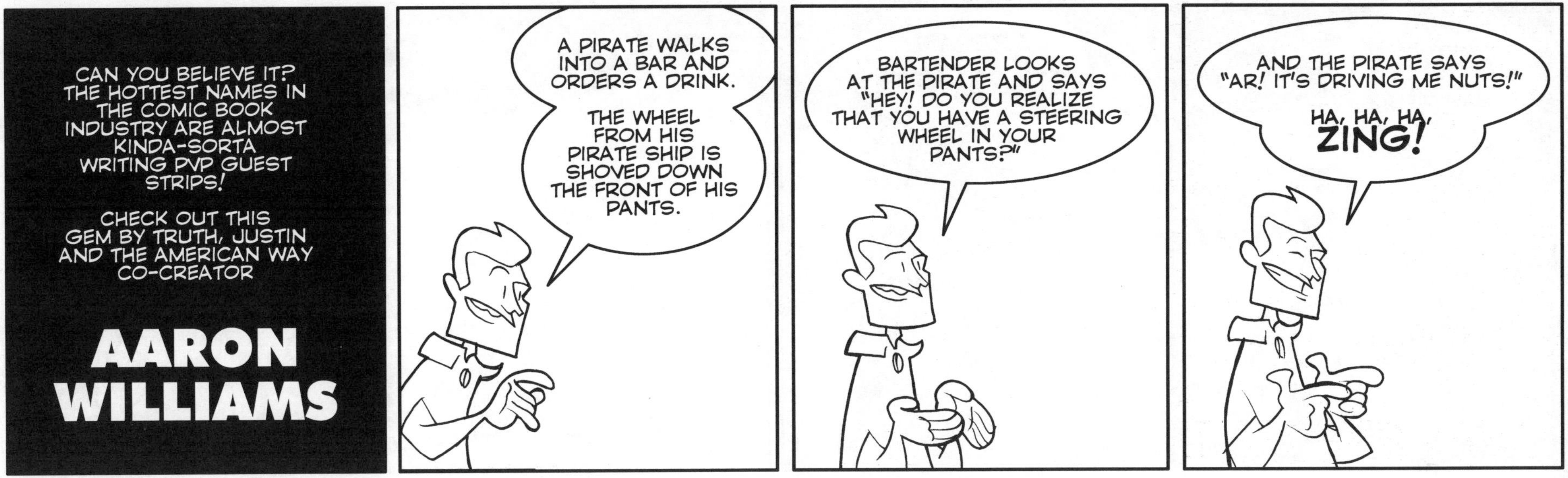
CAN YOU BELIEVE IT? THE HOTTEST NAMES IN THE COMIC BOOK INDUSTRY ARE ALMOST KINDA-SORTA WRITING PVP GUEST STRIPS!
CHECK OUT THIS GEM BY TRUTH, JUSTIN AND THE AMERICAN WAY CO-CREATOR
AARON WILLIAMS
A PIRATE WALKS INTO A BAR AND ORDERS A DRINK.
THE WHEEL FROM HIS PIRATE SHIP IS SHOVED DOWN THE FRONT OF HIS PANTS.
BARTENDER LOOKS AT THE PIRATE AND SAYS "HEY! DO YOU REALIZE THAT YOU HAVE A STEERING WHEEL IN YOUR PANTS?"
AND THE PIRATE SAYS "AR! IT'S DRIVING ME NUTS!"
HA, HA, HA, ZING!

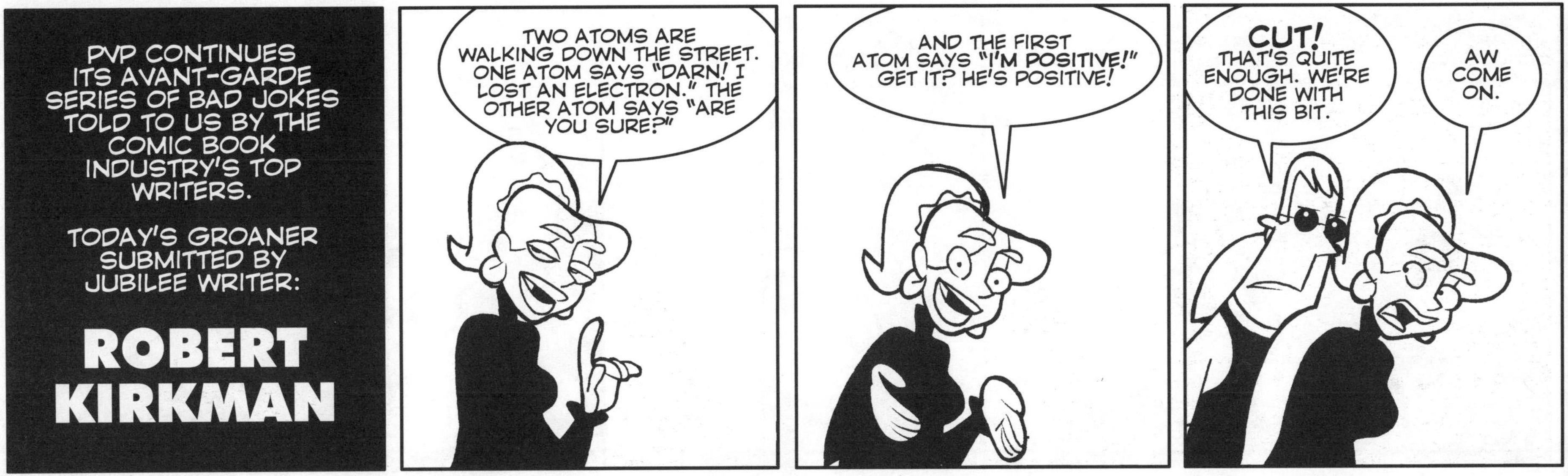
PVP CONTINUES ITS AVANT-GARDE SERIES OF BAD JOKES TOLD TO US BY THE COMIC BOOK INDUSTRY'S TOP WRITERS.
TODAY'S GROANER SUBMITTED BY JUBILEE WRITER:
ROBERT KIRKMAN
TWO ATOMS ARE WALKING DOWN THE STREET. ONE ATOM SAYS "DARN! I LOST AN ELECTRON." THE OTHER ATOM SAYS "ARE YOU SURE?"
AND THE FIRST ATOM SAYS "I'M POSITIVE!" GET IT? HE'S POSITIVE!
CUT! THAT'S QUITE ENOUGH. WE'RE DONE WITH THIS BIT.
AW COME ON.

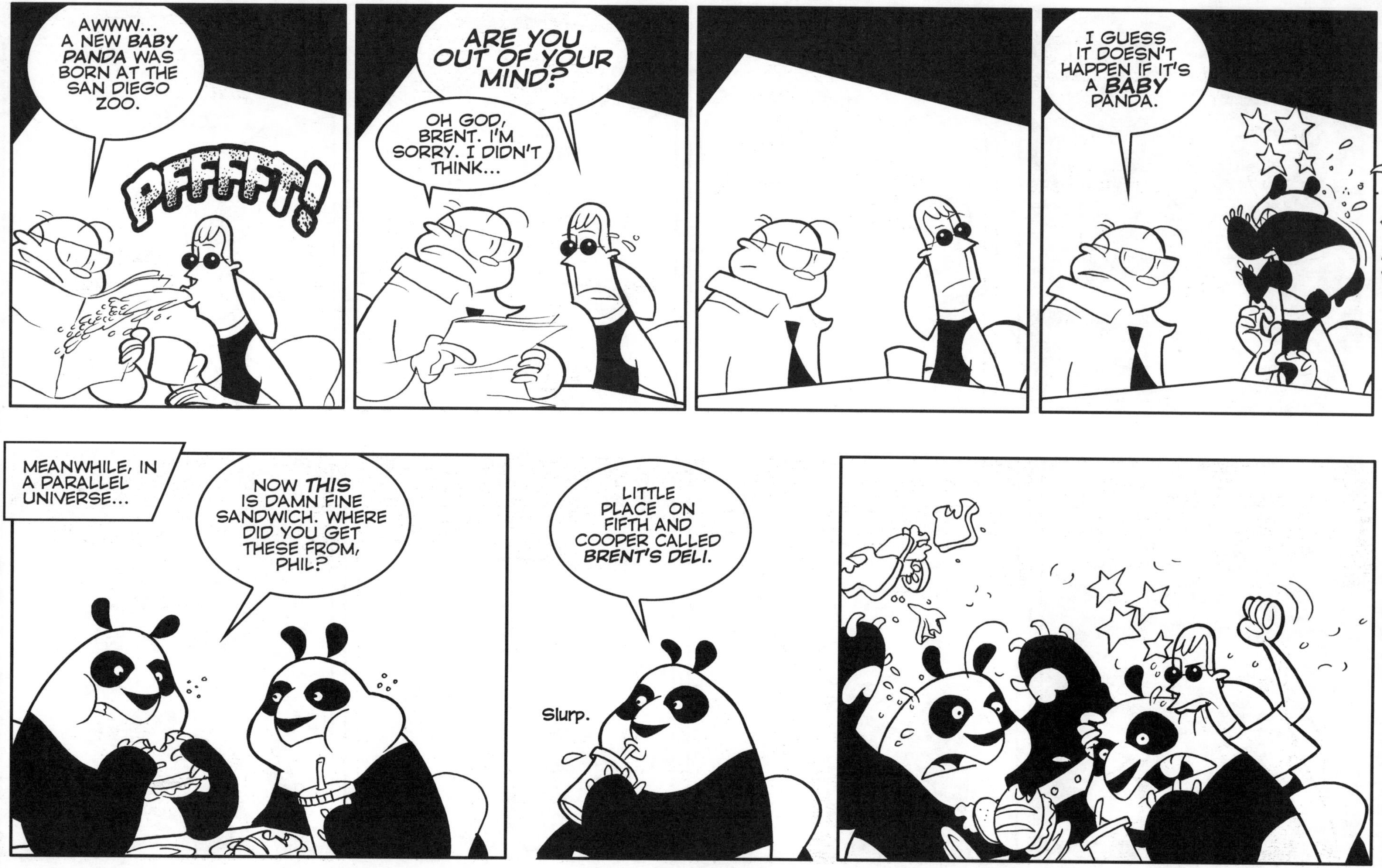
AWWW... A NEW BABY PANDA WAS BORN AT THE SAN DIEGO ZOO.
PFFFFT!
ARE YOU OUT OF YOUR MIND?
OH GOD, BRENT. I'M SORRY. I DIDN'T THINK...
I GUESS IT DOESN'T HAPPEN IF IT'S A BABY PANDA.
MEANWHILE, IN A PARALLEL UNIVERSE...
NOW THIS IS DAMN FINE SANDWICH. WHERE DID YOU GET THESE FROM, PHIL?
LITTLE PLACE ON FIFTH AND COOPER CALLED BRENT'S DELI.
Slurp.

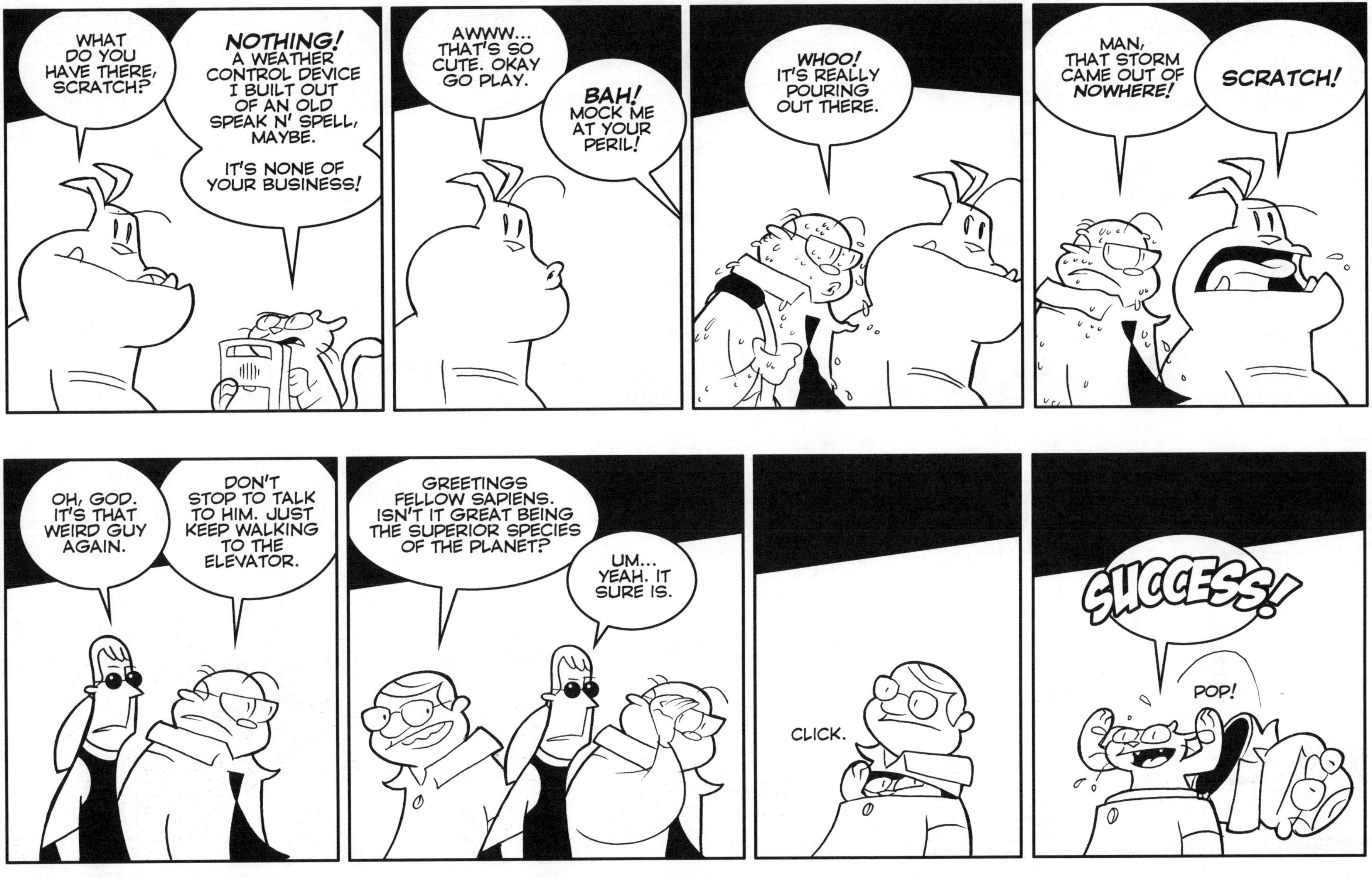
WHAT DO YOU HAVE THERE, SCRATCH?
NOTHING! A WEATHER CONTROL DEVICE I BUILT OUT OF AN OLD SPEAK N' SPELL, MAYBE.
IT'S NONE OF YOUR BUSINESS!
AWWW... THAT'S SO CUTE. OKAY GO PLAY.
BAH! MOCK ME AT YOUR PERIL!
WHOO! IT'S REALLY POURING OUT THERE.
MAN, THAT STORM CAME OUT OF NOWHERE!
SCRATCH!
OH, GOD. IT'S THAT WEIRD GUY AGAIN.
DON'T STOP TO TALK TO HIM. JUST KEEP WALKING TO THE ELEVATOR.
GREETINGS FELLOW SAPIENS. ISN'T IT GREAT BEING THE SUPERIOR SPECIES OF THE PLANET?
UM... YEAH. IT SURE IS.
CLICK.
SUCCESS!
POP!

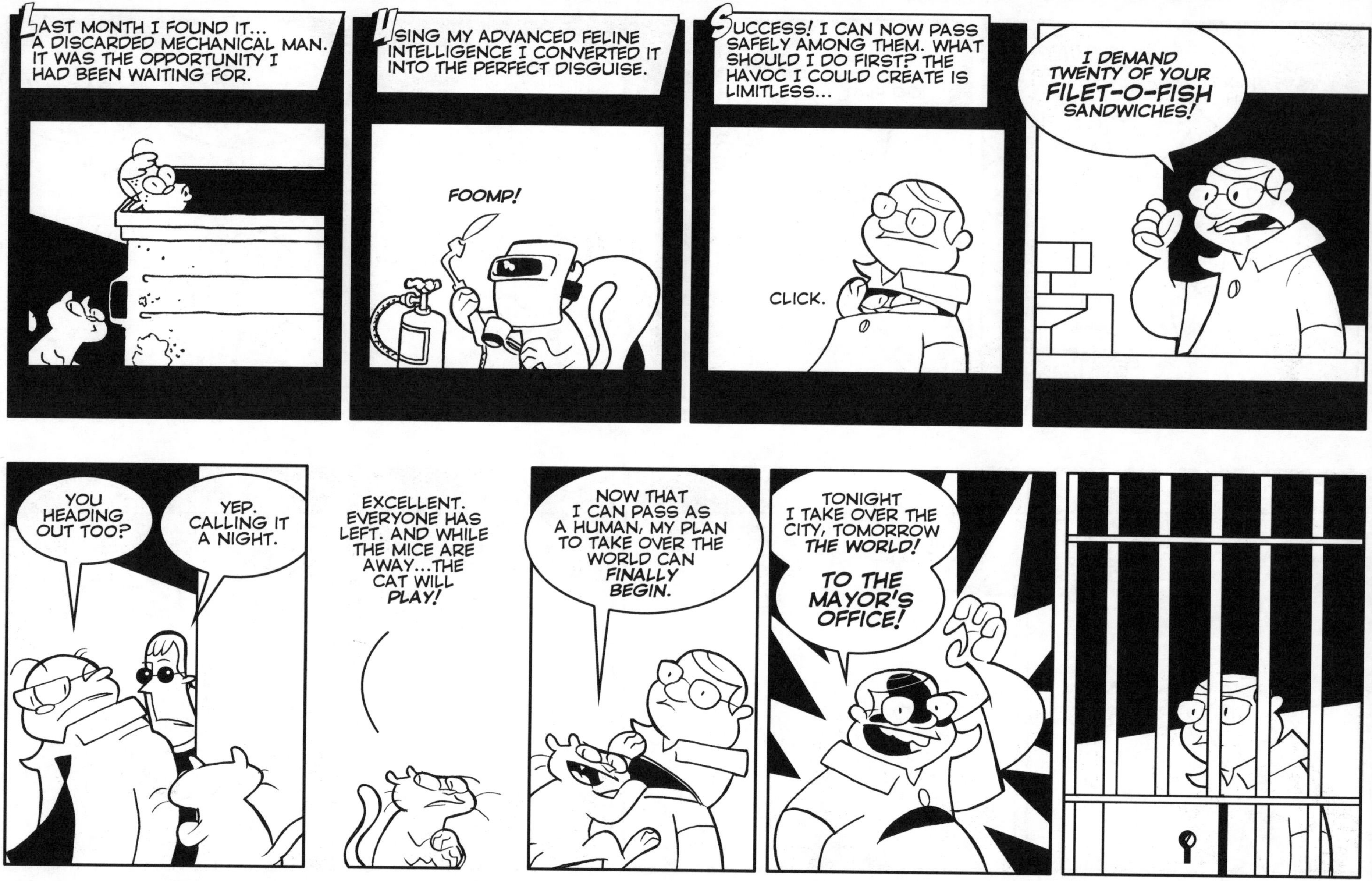
LAST MONTH I FOUND IT... A DISCARDED MECHANICAL MAN. IT WAS THE OPPORTUNITY I HAD BEEN WAITING FOR.
USING MY ADVANCED FELINE INTELLIGENCE I CONVERTED IT INTO THE PERFECT DISGUISE.
FOOMP!
SUCCESS! I CAN NOW PASS SAFELY AMONG THEM. WHAT SHOULD I DO FIRST? THE HAVOC I COULD CREATE IS LIMITLESS...
CLICK.
I DEMAND TWENTY OF YOUR FILET-O-FISH SANDWICHES!
YOU HEADING OUT TOO?
YEP. CALLING IT A NIGHT.
EXCELLENT. EVERYONE HAS LEFT. AND WHILE THE MICE ARE AWAY...THE CAT WILL PLAY!
NOW THAT I CAN PASS AS A HUMAN, MY PLAN TO TAKE OVER THE WORLD CAN FINALLY BEGIN.
TONIGHT I TAKE OVER THE CITY, TOMORROW THE WORLD!
TO THE MAYOR'S OFFICE!

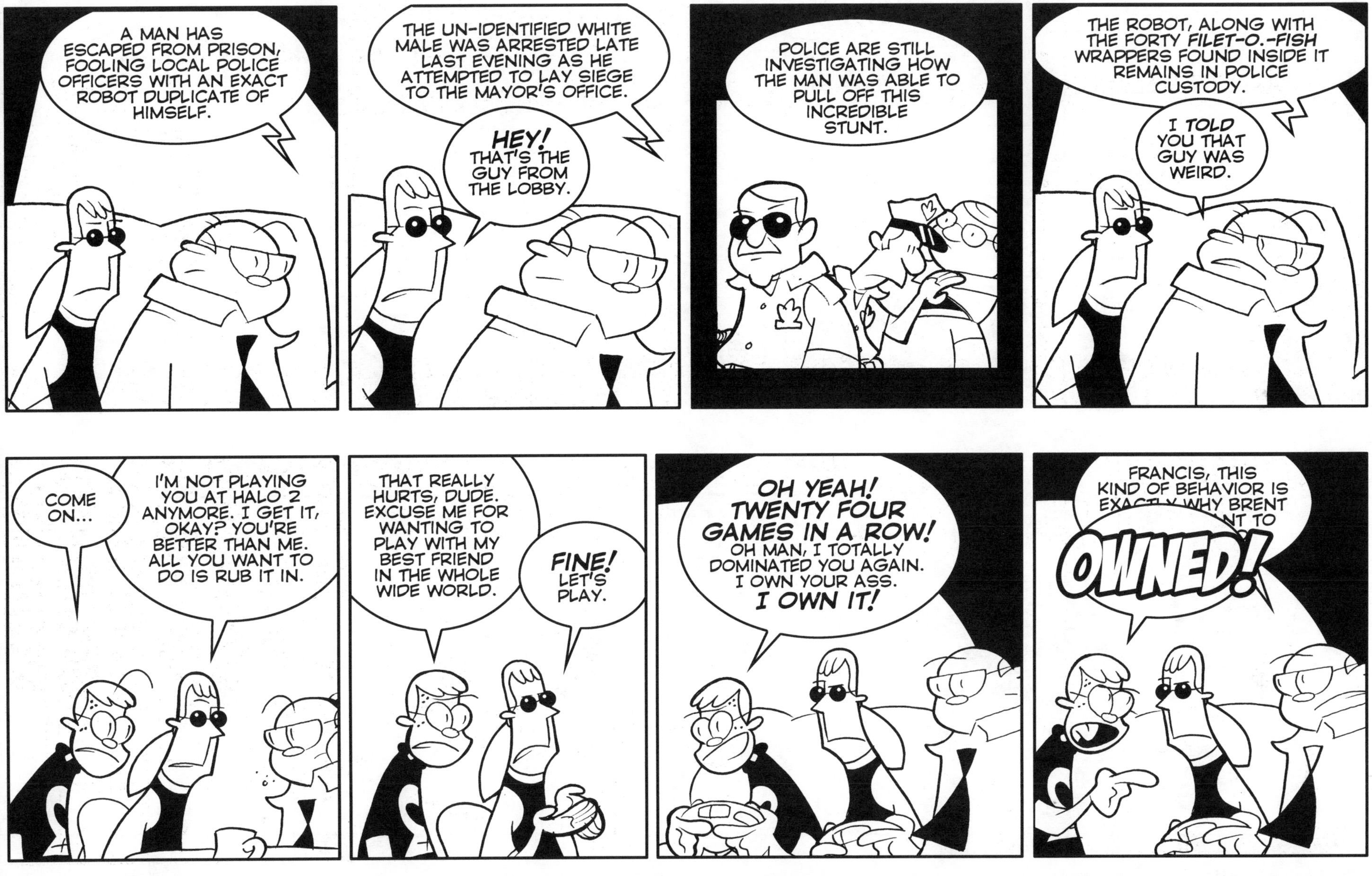
A MAN HAS ESCAPED FROM PRISON, FOOLING LOCAL POLICE OFFICERS WITH AN EXACT ROBOT DUPLICATE OF HIMSELF.
THE UN-IDENTIFIED WHITE MALE WAS ARRESTED LATE LAST EVENING AS HE ATTEMPTED TO LAY SIEGE TO THE MAYOR'S OFFICE.
HEY! THAT'S THE GUY FROM THE LOBBY.
POLICE ARE STILL INVESTIGATING HOW THE MAN WAS ABLE TO PULL OFF THIS INCREDIBLE STUNT.
THE ROBOT, ALONG WITH THE FORTY FILET-O.-FISH WRAPPERS FOUND INSIDE IT REMAINS IN POLICE CUSTODY.
I TOLD YOU THAT GUY WAS WEIRD.
COME ON...
I'M NOT PLAYING YOU AT HALO 2 ANYMORE. I GET IT, OKAY? YOU'RE BETTER THAN ME. ALL YOU WANT TO DO IS RUB IT IN.
THAT REALLY HURTS, DUDE. EXCUSE ME FOR WANTING TO PLAY WITH MY BEST FRIEND IN THE WHOLE WIDE WORLD.
FINE! LET'S PLAY.
OH YEAH! TWENTY FOUR GAMES IN A ROW! OH MAN, I TOTALLY DOMINATED YOU AGAIN. I OWN YOUR ASS. I OWN IT!
FRANCIS, THIS KIND OF BEHAVIOR IS EXACTLY WHY BRENT
OWNED!

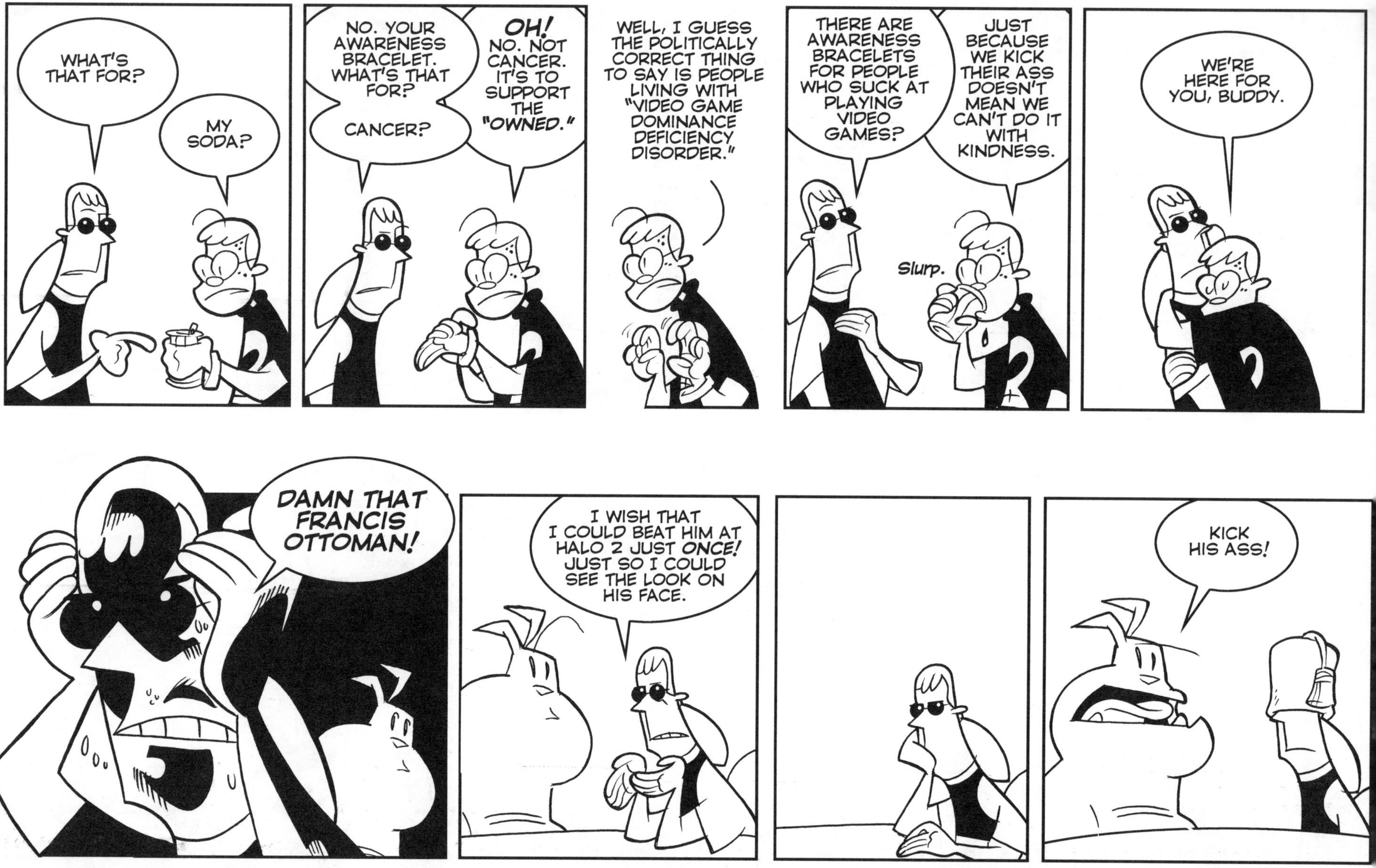
WHAT'S THAT FOR?
MY SODA?
NO. YOUR AWARENESS BRACELET. WHAT'S THAT FOR?
CANCER?
OH! NO. NOT CANCER. IT'S TO SUPPORT THE "OWNED."
WELL, I GUESS THE POLITICALLY CORRECT THING TO SAY IS PEOPLE LIVING WITH "VIDEO GAME DOMINANCE DEFICIENCY DISORDER."
THERE ARE AWARENESS BRACELETS FOR PEOPLE WHO SUCK AT PLAYING VIDEO GAMES?
JUST BECAUSE WE KICK THEIR ASS DOESN'T MEAN WE CAN'T DO IT WITH KINDNESS.
Slurp.
WE'RE HERE FOR YOU, BUDDY.
DAMN THAT FRANCIS OTTOMAN!
I WISH THAT I COULD BEAT HIM AT HALO 2 JUST ONCE! JUST SO I COULD SEE THE LOOK ON HIS FACE.
KICK HIS ASS!

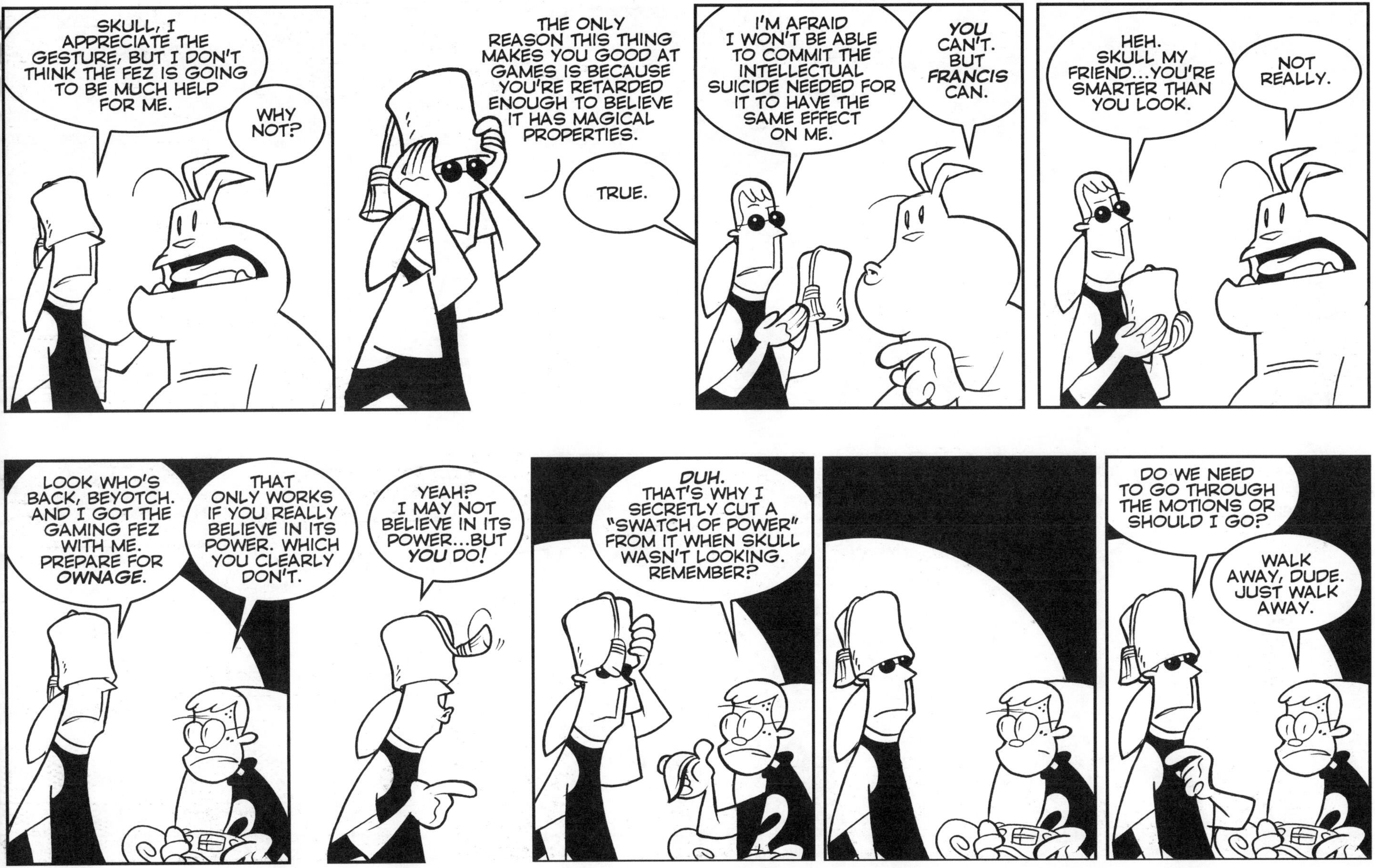

SKULL, I APPRECIATE THE GESTURE, BUT I DON'T THINK THE FEZ IS GOING TO BE MUCH HELP FOR ME.
WHY NOT?
THE ONLY REASON THIS THING MAKES YOU GOOD AT GAMES IS BECAUSE YOU'RE RETARDED ENOUGH TO BELIEVE IT HAS MAGICAL PROPERTIES.
TRUE.
I'M AFRAID I WON'T BE ABLE TO COMMIT THE INTELLECTUAL SUICIDE NEEDED FOR IT TO HAVE THE SAME EFFECT ON ME.
YOU CAN'T. BUT FRANCIS CAN.
HEH. SKULL MY FRIEND...YOU'RE SMARTER THAN YOU LOOK.
NOT REALLY.
LOOK WHO'S BACK, BEYOTCH. AND I GOT THE GAMING FEZ WITH ME. PREPARE FOR OWNAGE.
THAT ONLY WORKS IF YOU REALLY BELIEVE IN ITS POWER. WHICH YOU CLEARLY DON'T.
YEAH? I MAY NOT BELIEVE IN ITS POWER...BUT YOU DO!
DUH. THAT'S WHY I SECRETLY CUT A "SWATCH OF POWER" FROM IT WHEN SKULL WASN'T LOOKING. REMEMBER?
DO WE NEED TO GO THROUGH THE MOTIONS OR SHOULD I GO?
WALK AWAY, DUDE. JUST WALK AWAY.

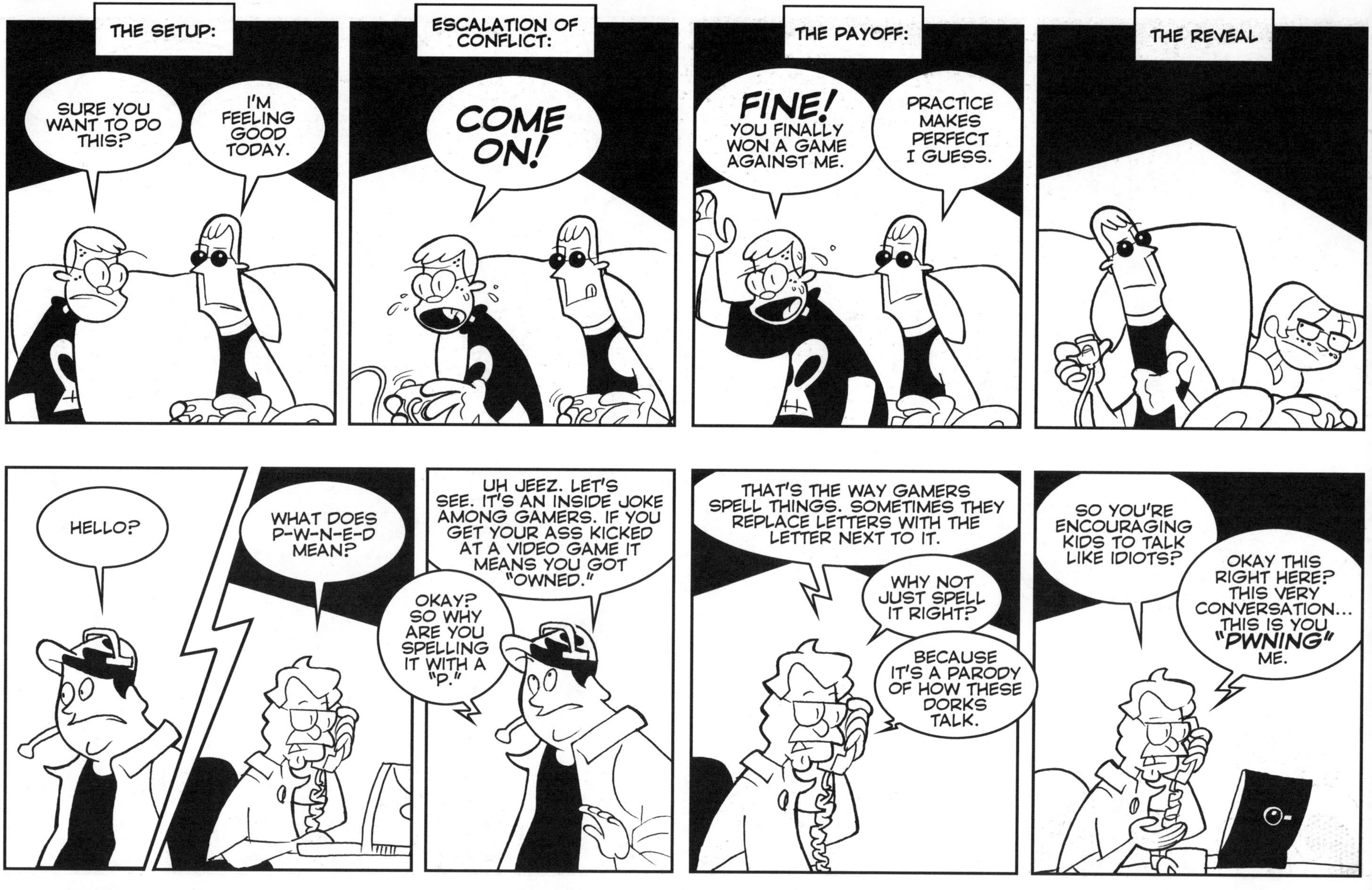

THE SETUP:
SURE YOU WANT TO DO THIS?
I'M FEELING GOOD TODAY.
ESCALATION OF CONFLICT:
COME ON!
THE PAYOFF:
FINE! YOU FINALLY WON A GAME AGAINST ME.
PRACTICE MAKES PERFECT I GUESS.
THE REVEAL
HELLO?
WHAT DOES P-W-N-E-D MEAN?
UH JEEZ. LET'S SEE. IT'S AN INSIDE JOKE AMONG GAMERS. IF YOU GET YOUR ASS KICKED AT A VIDEO GAME IT MEANS YOU GOT "OWNED."
OKAY? SO WHY ARE YOU SPELLING IT WITH A "P."
THAT'S THE WAY GAMERS SPELL THINGS. SOMETIMES THEY REPLACE LETTERS WITH THE LETTER NEXT TO IT.
WHY NOT JUST SPELL IT RIGHT?
BECAUSE IT'S A PARODY OF HOW THESE DORKS TALK.
SO YOU'RE ENCOURAGING KIDS TO TALK LIKE IDIOTS?
OKAY THIS RIGHT HERE? THIS VERY CONVERSATION... THIS IS YOU "PWNING" ME.

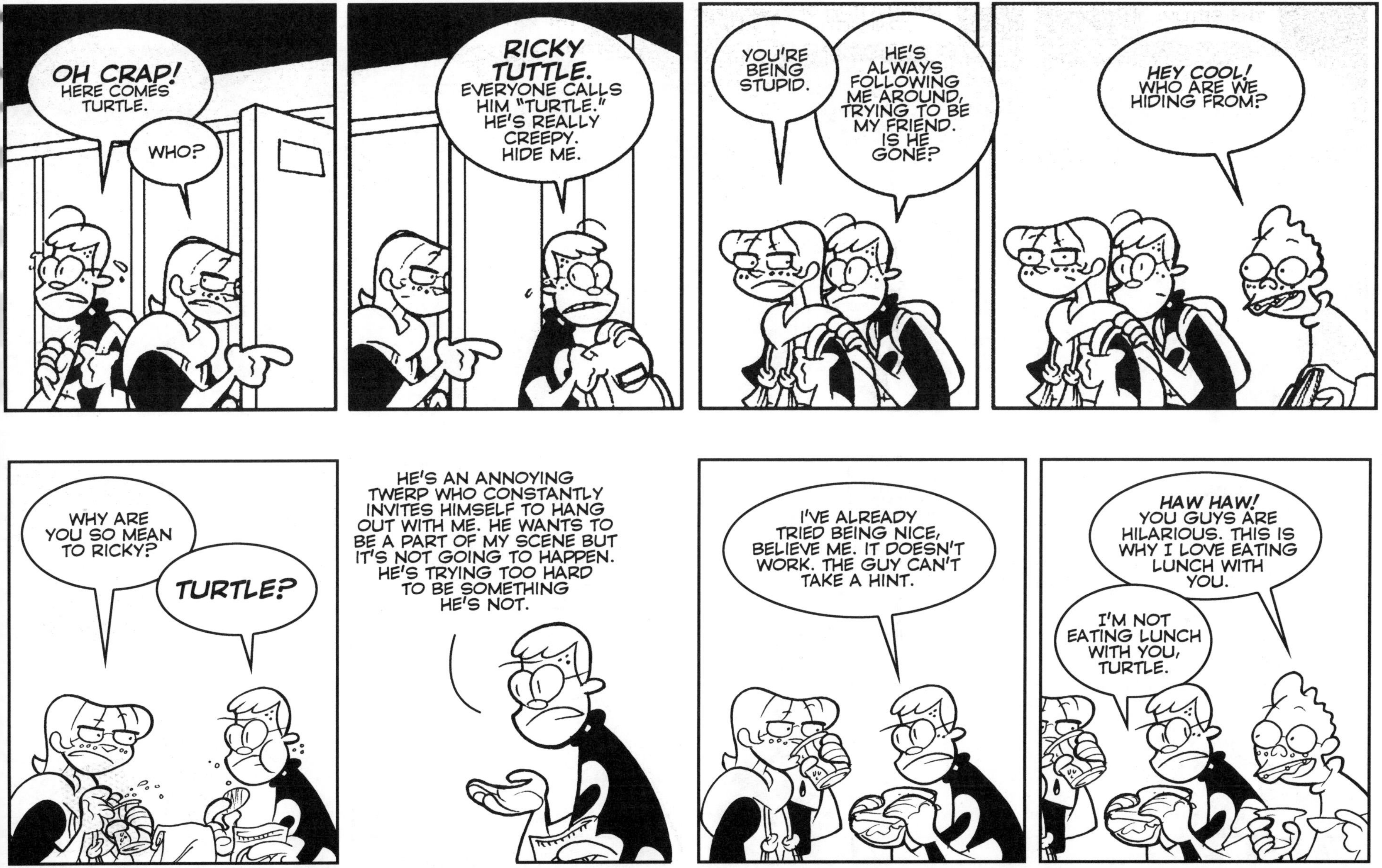
OH CRAP! HERE COMES TURTLE.
WHO?
RICKY TUTTLE. EVERYONE CALLS HIM "TURTLE." HE'S REALLY CREEPY. HIDE ME.
YOU'RE BEING STUPID.
HE'S ALWAYS FOLLOWING ME AROUND, TRYING TO BE MY FRIEND. IS HE GONE?
HEY COOL! WHO ARE WE HIDING FROM?
WHY ARE YOU SO MEAN TO RICKY?
TURTLE?
HE'S AN ANNOYING TWERP WHO CONSTANTLY INVITES HIMSELF TO HANG OUT WITH ME. HE WANTS TO BE A PART OF MY SCENE BUT IT'S NOT GOING TO HAPPEN. HE'S TRYING TOO HARD TO BE SOMETHING HE'S NOT.
I'VE ALREADY TRIED BEING NICE, BELIEVE ME. IT DOESN'T WORK. THE GUY CAN'T TAKE A HINT.
HAW HAW! YOU GUYS ARE HILARIOUS. THIS IS WHY I LOVE EATING LUNCH WITH YOU.
I'M NOT EATING LUNCH WITH YOU, TURTLE.

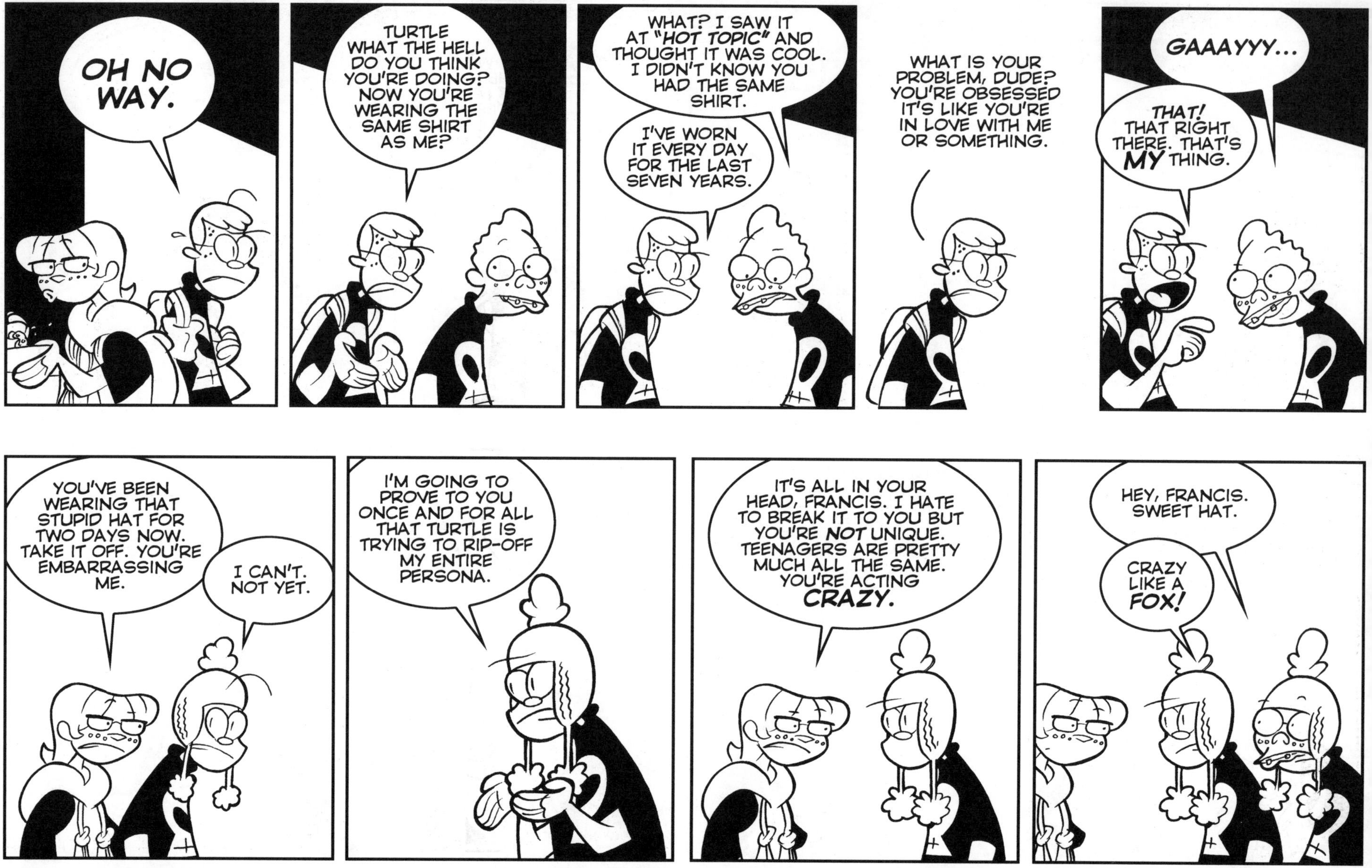
OH NO WAY.
TURTLE WHAT THE HELL DO YOU THINK YOU'RE DOING? NOW YOU'RE WEARING THE SAME SHIRT AS ME?
WHAT? I SAW IT AT "HOT TOPIC" AND THOUGHT IT WAS COOL. I DIDN'T KNOW YOU HAD THE SAME SHIRT.
I'VE WORN IT EVERY DAY FOR THE LAST SEVEN YEARS.
WHAT IS YOUR PROBLEM, DUDE? YOU'RE OBSESSED IT'S LIKE YOU'RE IN LOVE WITH ME OR SOMETHING.
GAAAYYY...
THAT! THAT RIGHT THERE. THAT'S MY THING.
YOU'VE BEEN WEARING THAT STUPID HAT FOR TWO DAYS NOW. TAKE IT OFF. YOU'RE EMBARRASSING ME.
I CAN'T. NOT YET.
I'M GOING TO PROVE TO YOU ONCE AND FOR ALL THAT TURTLE IS TRYING TO RIP-OFF MY ENTIRE PERSONA.
IT'S ALL IN YOUR HEAD, FRANCIS. I HATE TO BREAK IT TO YOU BUT YOU'RE NOT UNIQUE. TEENAGERS ARE PRETTY MUCH ALL THE SAME. YOU'RE ACTING CRAZY.
HEY, FRANCIS. SWEET HAT.
CRAZY LIKE A FOX!

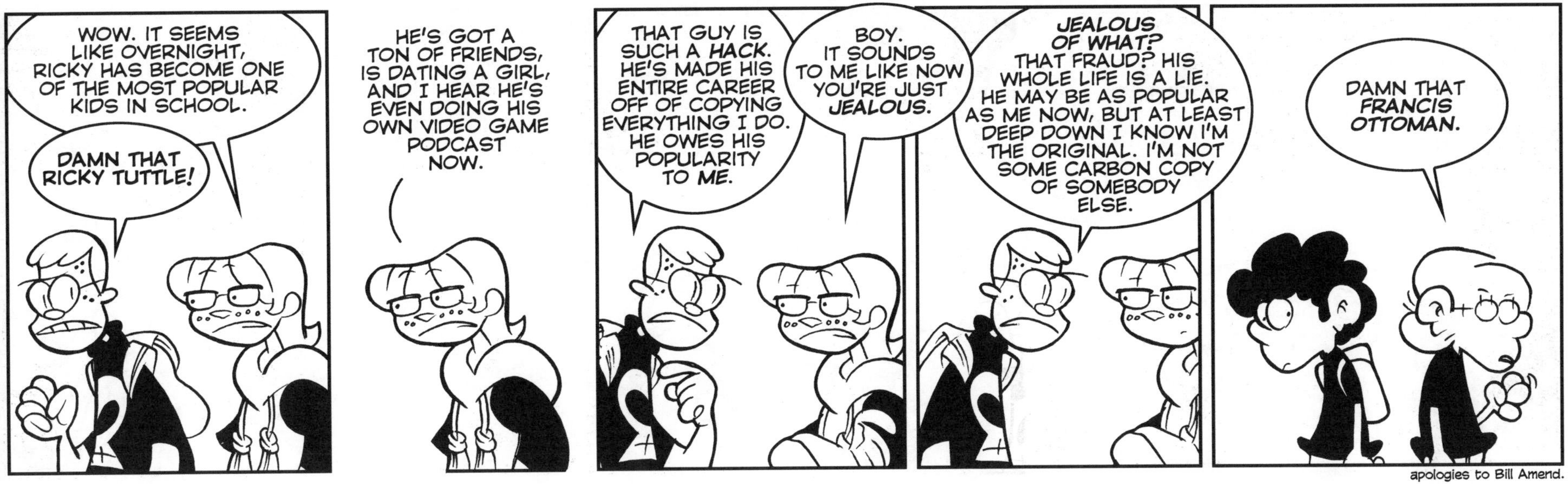
WOW. IT SEEMS LIKE OVERNIGHT, RICKY HAS BECOME ONE OF THE MOST POPULAR KIDS IN SCHOOL.
DAMN THAT RICKY TUTTLE!
HE'S GOT A TON OF FRIENDS, IS DATING A GIRL, AND I HEAR HE'S EVEN DOING HIS OWN VIDEO GAME PODCAST NOW.
THAT GUY IS SUCH A HACK. HE'S MADE HIS ENTIRE CAREER OFF OF COPYING EVERYTHING I DO. HE OWES HIS POPULARITY TO ME.
BOY. IT SOUNDS TO ME LIKE NOW YOU'RE JUST JEALOUS.
JEALOUS OF WHAT? THAT FRAUD? HIS WHOLE LIFE IS A LIE. HE MAY BE AS POPULAR AS ME NOW, BUT AT LEAST DEEP DOWN I KNOW I'M THE ORIGINAL. I'M NOT SOME CARBON COPY OF SOMEBODY ELSE.
DAMN THAT FRANCIS OTTOMAN.

apologies to Bill Amend.

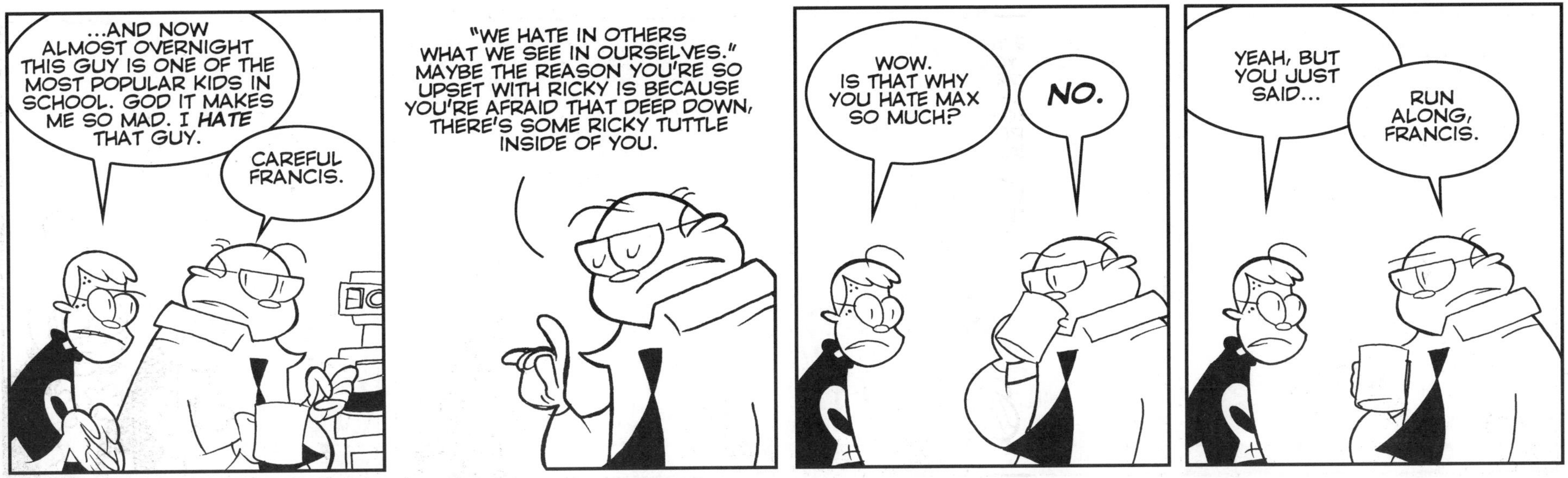
...AND NOW ALMOST OVERNIGHT THIS GUY IS ONE OF THE MOST POPULAR KIDS IN SCHOOL. GOD IT MAKES ME SO MAD. I HATE THAT GUY.
CAREFUL FRANCIS.
"WE HATE IN OTHERS WHAT WE SEE IN OURSELVES." MAYBE THE REASON YOU'RE SO UPSET WITH RICKY IS BECAUSE YOU'RE AFRAID THAT DEEP DOWN, THERE'S SOME RICKY TUTTLE INSIDE OF YOU.
WOW. IS THAT WHY YOU HATE MAX SO MUCH?
NO.
YEAH, BUT YOU JUST SAID...
RUN ALONG, FRANCIS.

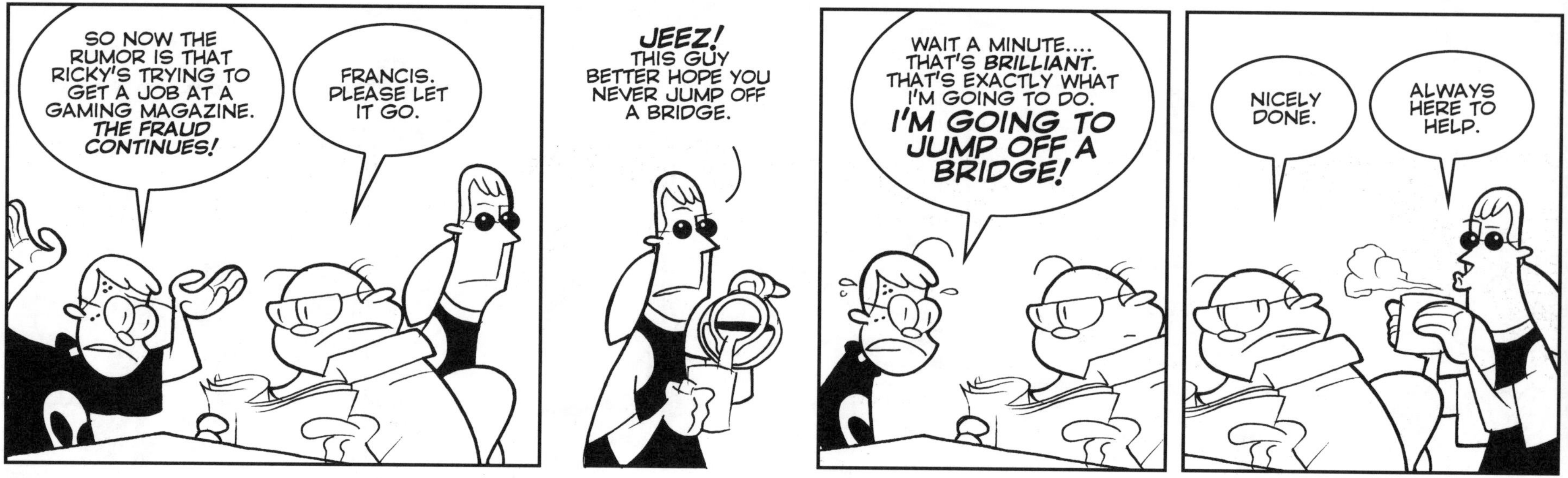
SO NOW THE RUMOR IS THAT RICKY'S TRYING TO GET A JOB AT A GAMING MAGAZINE. *THE FRAUD CONTINUES!*
FRANCIS. PLEASE LET IT GO.
JEEZ! THIS GUY BETTER HOPE YOU NEVER JUMP OFF A BRIDGE.
WAIT A MINUTE.... THAT'S *BRILLIANT*. THAT'S EXACTLY WHAT I'M GOING TO DO. *I'M GOING TO JUMP OFF A BRIDGE!*
NICELY DONE.
ALWAYS HERE TO HELP.

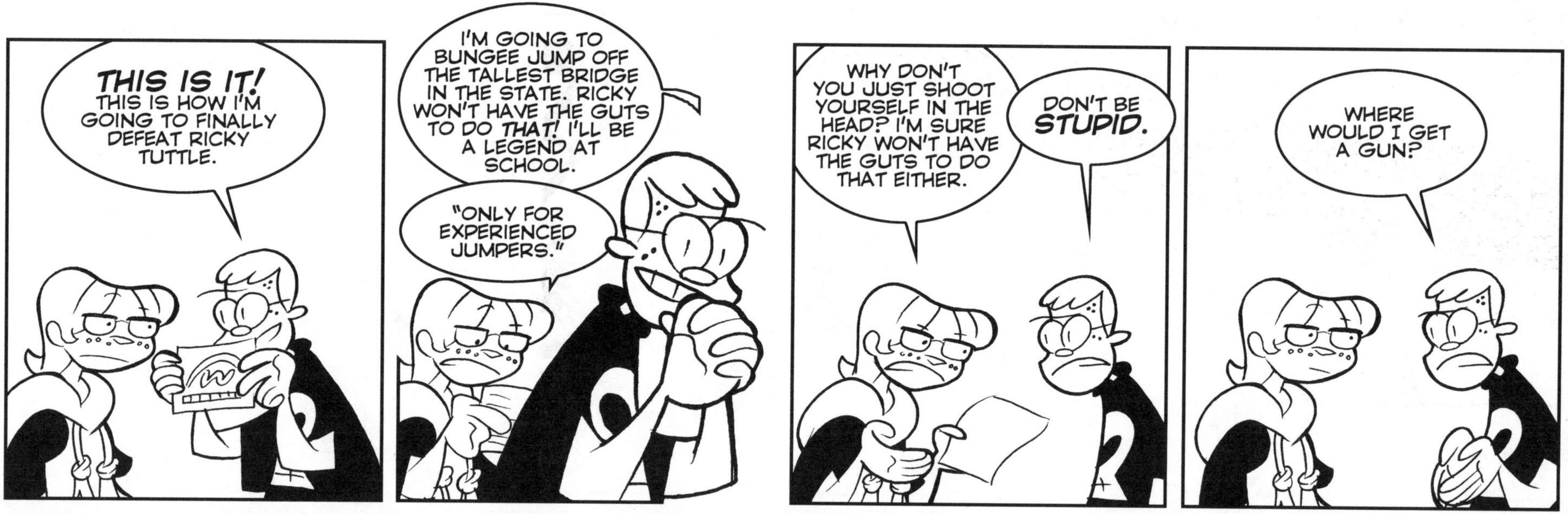
THIS IS IT! THIS IS HOW I'M GOING TO FINALLY DEFEAT RICKY TUTTLE.
I'M GOING TO BUNGEE JUMP OFF THE TALLEST BRIDGE IN THE STATE. RICKY WON'T HAVE THE GUTS TO DO *THAT!* I'LL BE A LEGEND AT SCHOOL.
"ONLY FOR EXPERIENCED JUMPERS."
WHY DON'T YOU JUST SHOOT YOURSELF IN THE HEAD? I'M SURE RICKY WON'T HAVE THE GUTS TO DO THAT EITHER.
DON'T BE *STUPID*.
WHERE WOULD I GET A GUN?

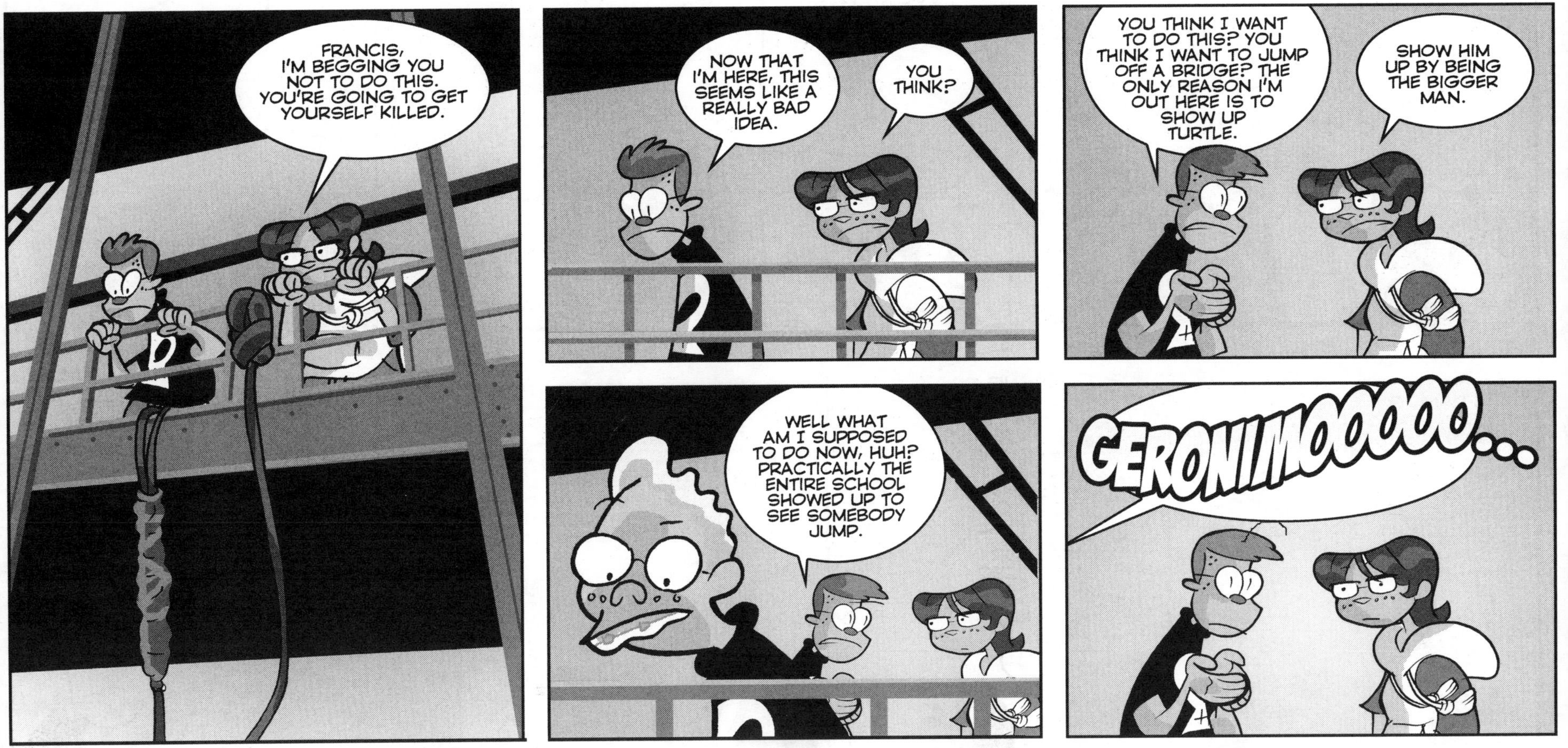
FRANCIS, I'M BEGGING YOU NOT TO DO THIS. YOU'RE GOING TO GET YOURSELF KILLED.
NOW THAT I'M HERE, THIS SEEMS LIKE A REALLY BAD IDEA.
YOU THINK?
YOU THINK I WANT TO DO THIS? YOU THINK I WANT TO JUMP OFF A BRIDGE? THE ONLY REASON I'M OUT HERE IS TO SHOW UP TURTLE.
SHOW HIM UP BY BEING THE BIGGER MAN.
WELL WHAT AM I SUPPOSED TO DO NOW, HUH? PRACTICALLY THE ENTIRE SCHOOL SHOWED UP TO SEE SOMEBODY JUMP.
GERONIIMOOOOO...

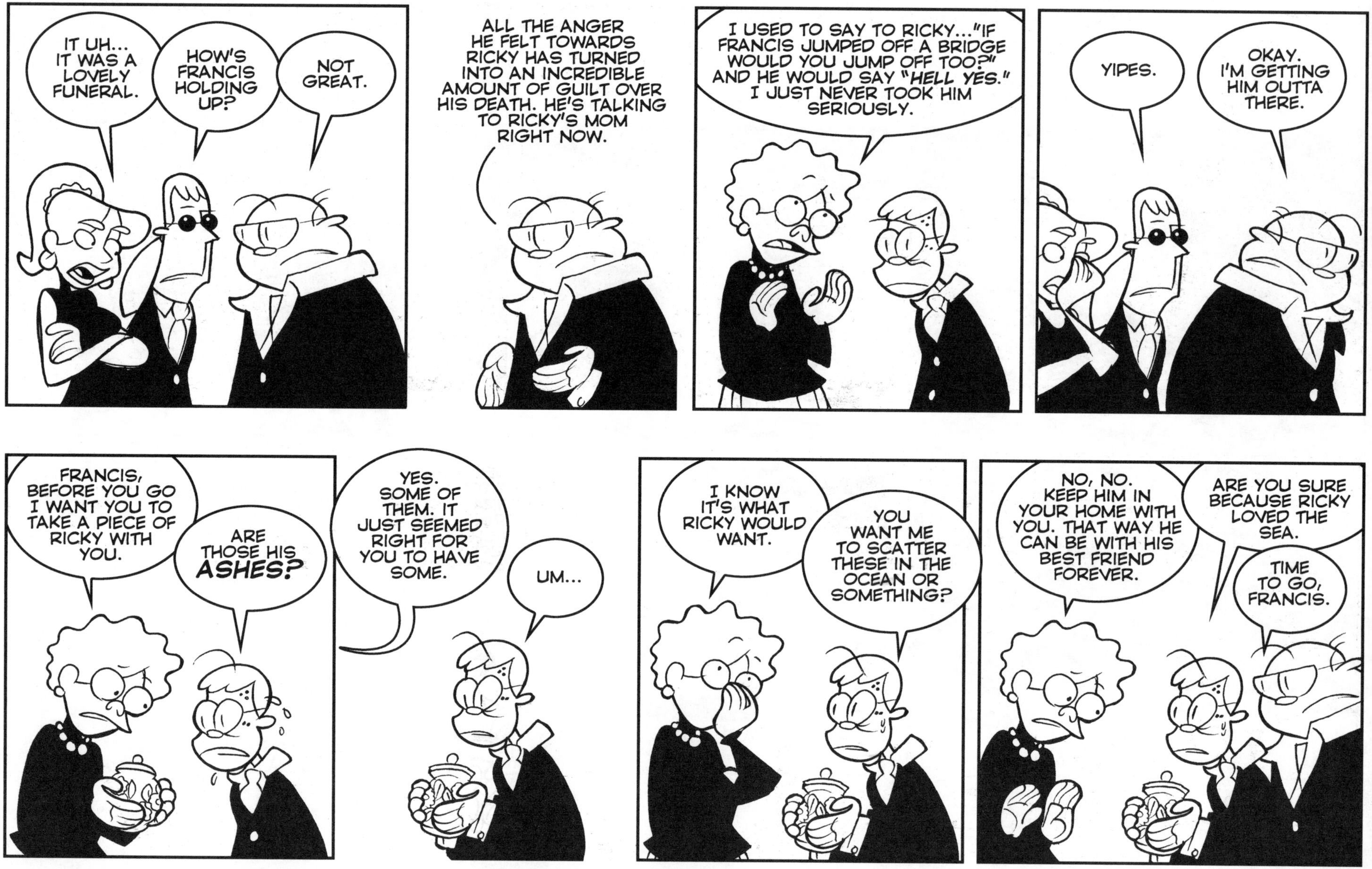
IT UH... IT WAS A LOVELY FUNERAL.
HOW'S FRANCIS HOLDING UP?
NOT GREAT.
ALL THE ANGER HE FELT TOWARDS RICKY HAS TURNED INTO AN INCREDIBLE AMOUNT OF GUILT OVER HIS DEATH. HE'S TALKING TO RICKY'S MOM RIGHT NOW.
I USED TO SAY TO RICKY..."IF FRANCIS JUMPED OFF A BRIDGE WOULD YOU JUMP OFF TOO?" AND HE WOULD SAY "HELL YES." I JUST NEVER TOOK HIM SERIOUSLY.
YIPES.
OKAY. I'M GETTING HIM OUTTA THERE.
FRANCIS, BEFORE YOU GO I WANT YOU TO TAKE A PIECE OF RICKY WITH YOU.
ARE THOSE HIS ASHES?
YES. SOME OF THEM. IT JUST SEEMED RIGHT FOR YOU TO HAVE SOME.
UM...
I KNOW IT'S WHAT RICKY WOULD WANT.
YOU WANT ME TO SCATTER THESE IN THE OCEAN OR SOMETHING?
NO, NO. KEEP HIM IN YOUR HOME WITH YOU. THAT WAY HE CAN BE WITH HIS BEST FRIEND FOREVER.
ARE YOU SURE BECAUSE RICKY LOVED THE SEA.
TIME TO GO, FRANCIS.

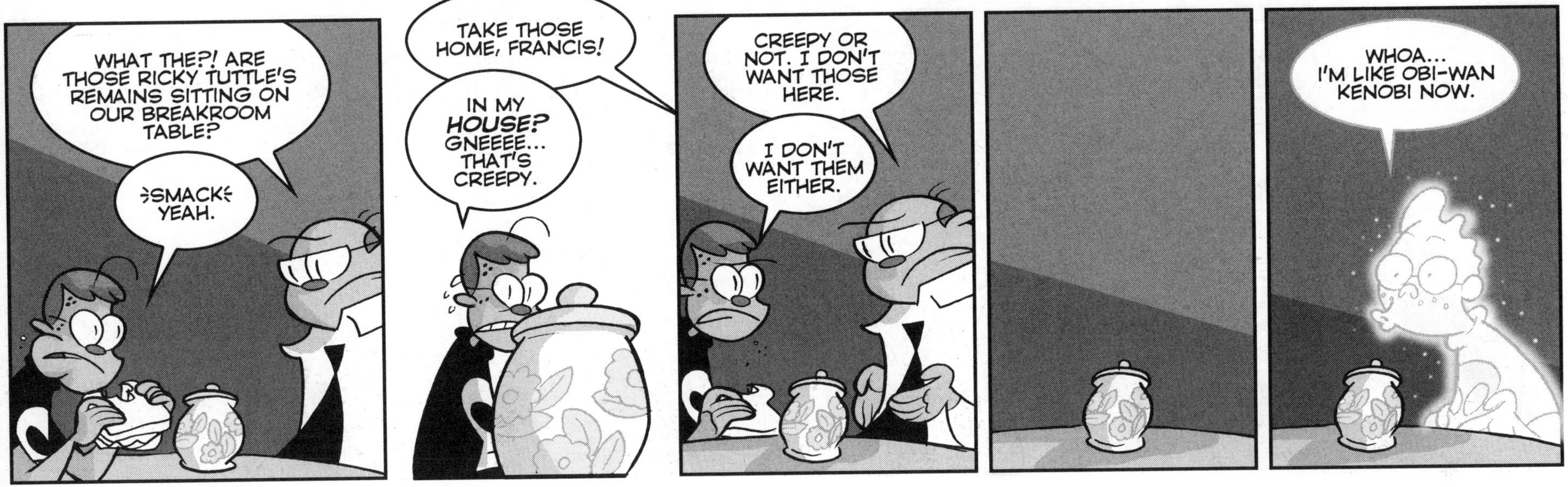
WHAT THE?! ARE THOSE RICKY TUTTLE'S REMAINS SITTING ON OUR BREAKROOM TABLE?
SMACK YEAH.
TAKE THOSE HOME, FRANCIS!
IN MY HOUSE? GNEEEE... THAT'S CREEPY.
CREEPY OR NOT. I DON'T WANT THOSE HERE.
I DON'T WANT THEM EITHER.
WHOA... I'M LIKE OBI-WAN KENOBI NOW.

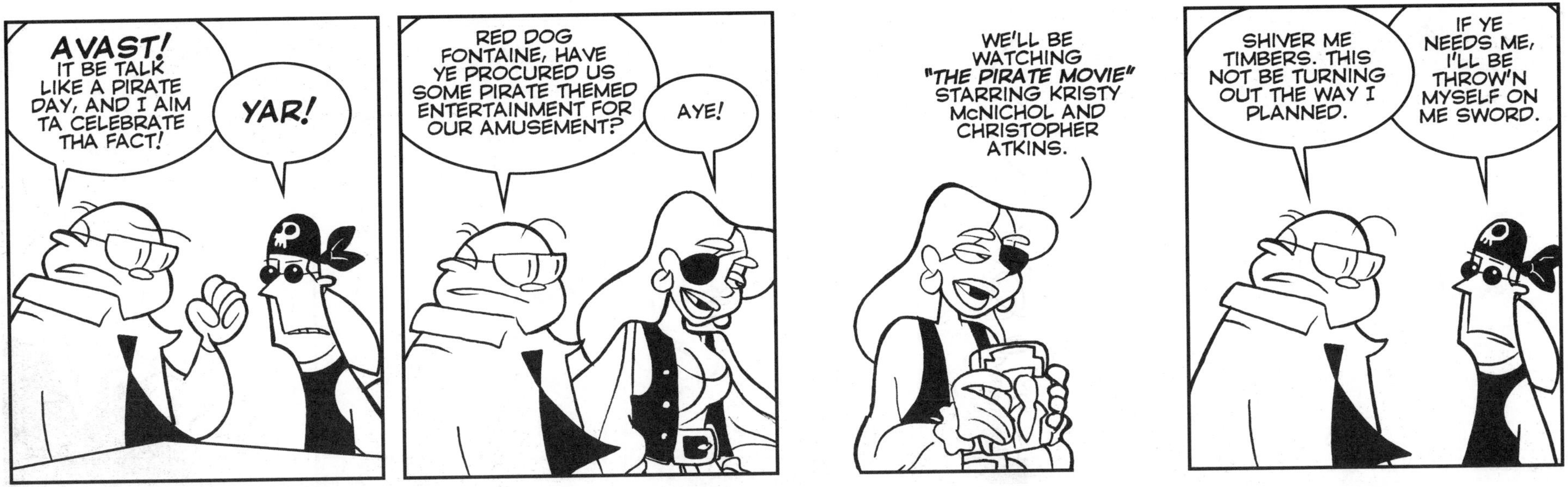
AVAST! IT BE TALK LIKE A PIRATE DAY, AND I AIM TA CELEBRATE THA FACT!
YAR!
RED DOG FONTAINE, HAVE YE PROCURED US SOME PIRATE THEMED ENTERTAINMENT FOR OUR AMUSEMENT?
AYE!
WE'LL BE WATCHING "THE PIRATE MOVIE" STARRING KRISTY McNICHOL AND CHRISTOPHER ATKINS.
SHIVER ME TIMBERS. THIS NOT BE TURNING OUT THE WAY I PLANNED.
IF YE NEEDS ME, I'LL BE THROW'N MYSELF ON ME SWORD.

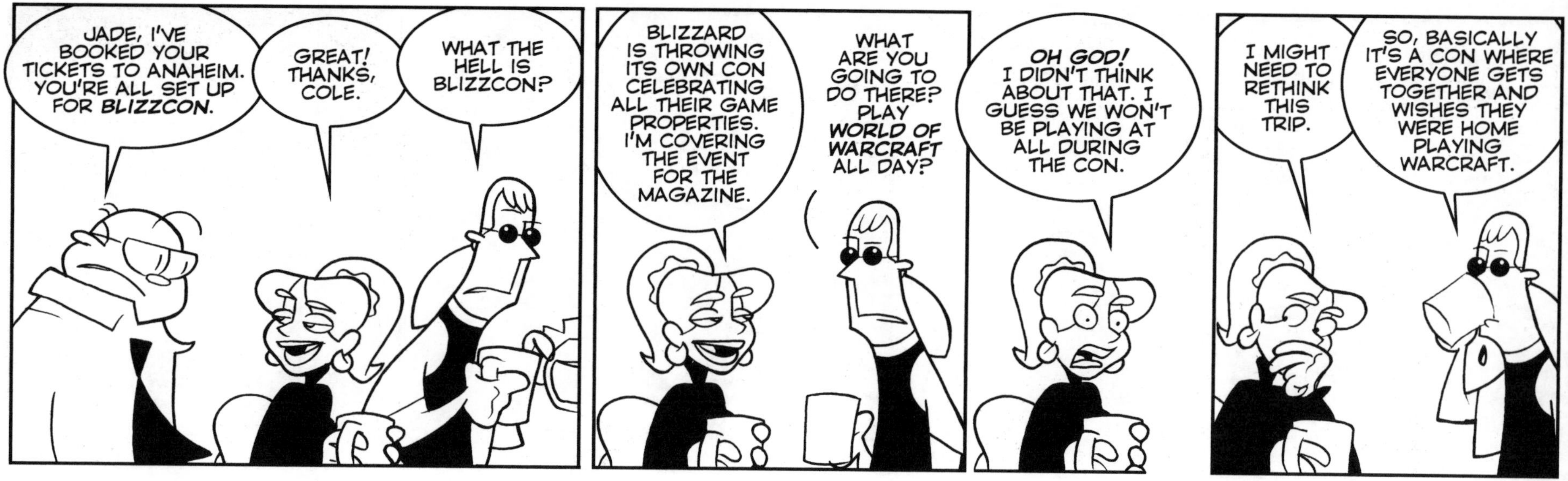
JADE, I'VE BOOKED YOUR TICKETS TO ANAHEIM. YOU'RE ALL SET UP FOR **BLIZZCON**.
GREAT! THANKS, COLE.
WHAT THE HELL IS BLIZZCON?
BLIZZARD IS THROWING ITS OWN CON CELEBRATING ALL THEIR GAME PROPERTIES. I'M COVERING THE EVENT FOR THE MAGAZINE.
WHAT ARE YOU GOING TO DO THERE? PLAY ***WORLD OF WARCRAFT*** ALL DAY?
OH GOD! I DIDN'T THINK ABOUT THAT. I GUESS WE WON'T BE PLAYING AT ALL DURING THE CON.
I MIGHT NEED TO RETHINK THIS TRIP.
SO, BASICALLY IT'S A CON WHERE EVERYONE GETS TOGETHER AND WISHES THEY WERE HOME PLAYING WARCRAFT.

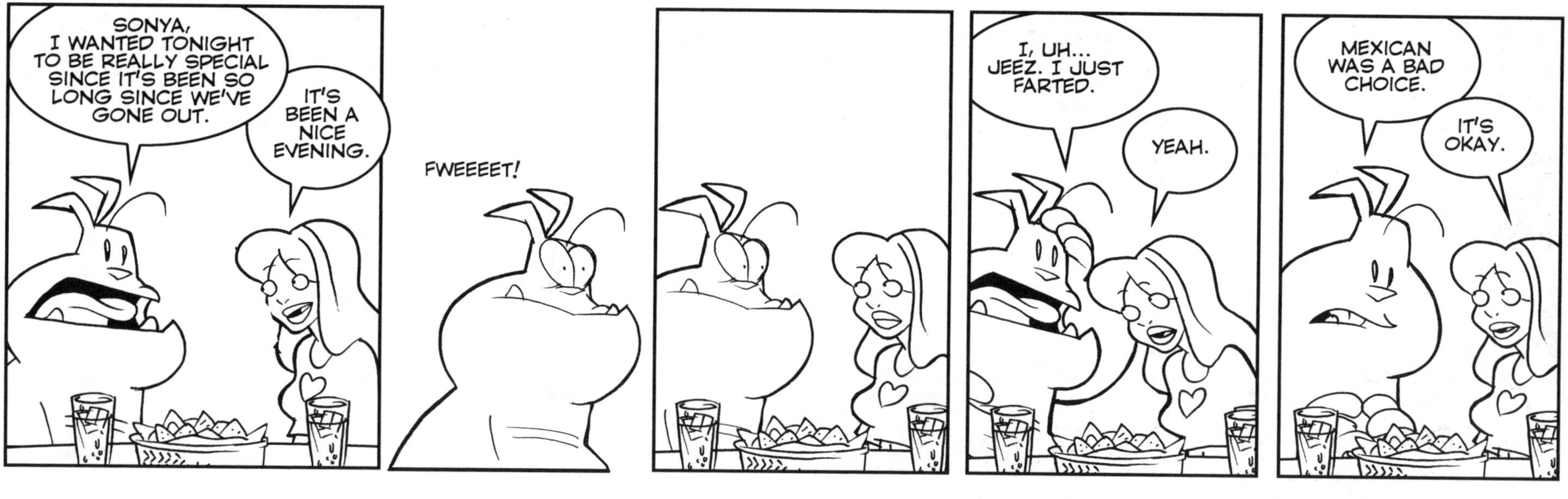
SONYA, I WANTED TONIGHT TO BE REALLY SPECIAL SINCE IT'S BEEN SO LONG SINCE WE'VE GONE OUT.
IT'S BEEN A NICE EVENING.
FWEEEEET!
I, UH... JEEZ. I JUST FARTED.
YEAH.
MEXICAN WAS A BAD CHOICE.
IT'S OKAY.

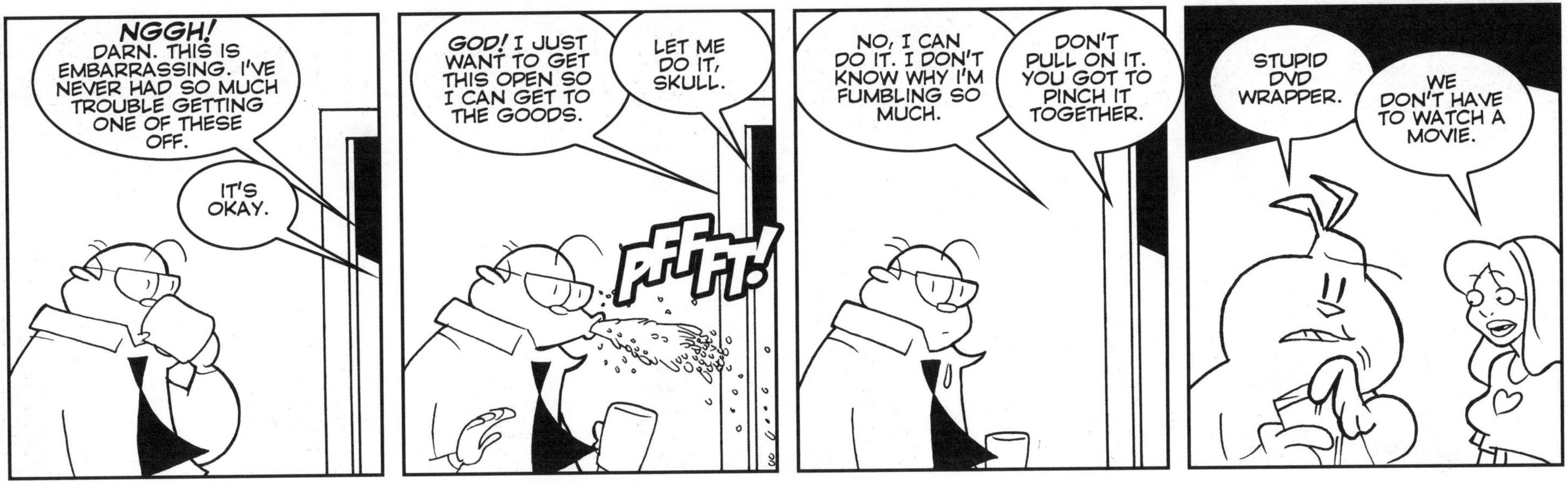
NGGH! DARN. THIS IS EMBARRASSING. I'VE NEVER HAD SO MUCH TROUBLE GETTING ONE OF THESE OFF.
IT'S OKAY.
GOD! I JUST WANT TO GET THIS OPEN SO I CAN GET TO THE GOODS.
LET ME DO IT, SKULL.
PFFFT!
NO, I CAN DO IT. I DON'T KNOW WHY I'M FUMBLING SO MUCH.
DON'T PULL ON IT. YOU GOT TO PINCH IT TOGETHER.
STUPID DVD WRAPPER.
WE DON'T HAVE TO WATCH A MOVIE.

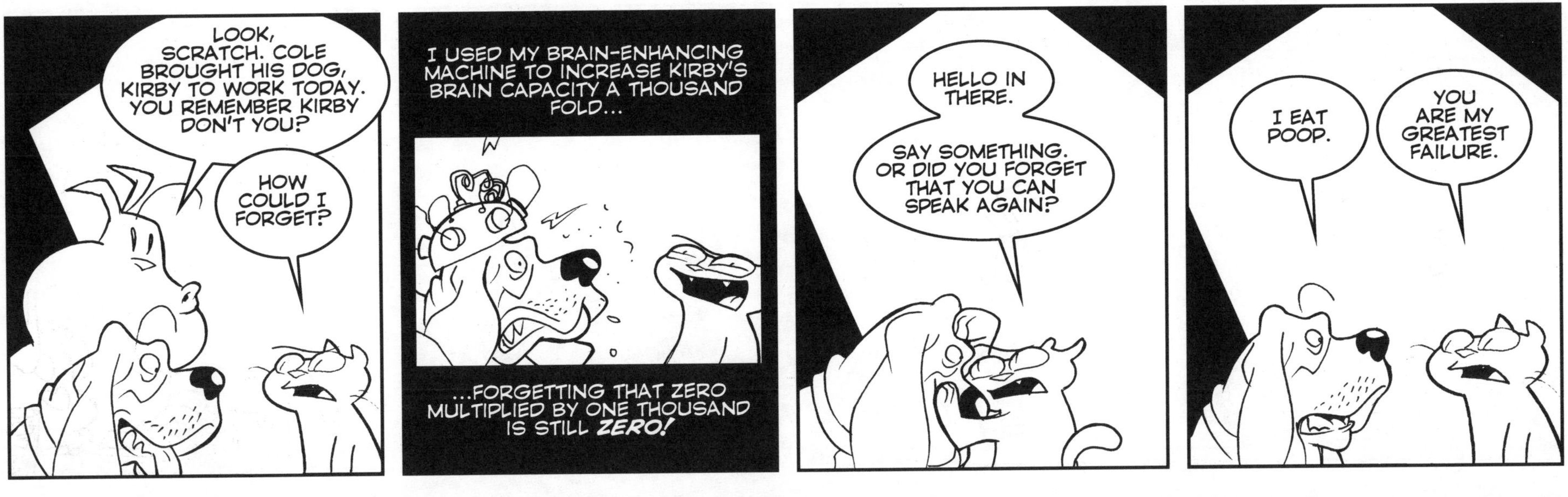
LOOK, SCRATCH. COLE BROUGHT HIS DOG, KIRBY TO WORK TODAY. YOU REMEMBER KIRBY DON'T YOU?
HOW COULD I FORGET?
I USED MY BRAIN-ENHANCING MACHINE TO INCREASE KIRBY'S BRAIN CAPACITY A THOUSAND FOLD...
...FORGETTING THAT ZERO MULTIPLIED BY ONE THOUSAND IS STILL ZERO!
HELLO IN THERE.
SAY SOMETHING. OR DID YOU FORGET THAT YOU CAN SPEAK AGAIN?
I EAT POOP.
YOU ARE MY GREATEST FAILURE.

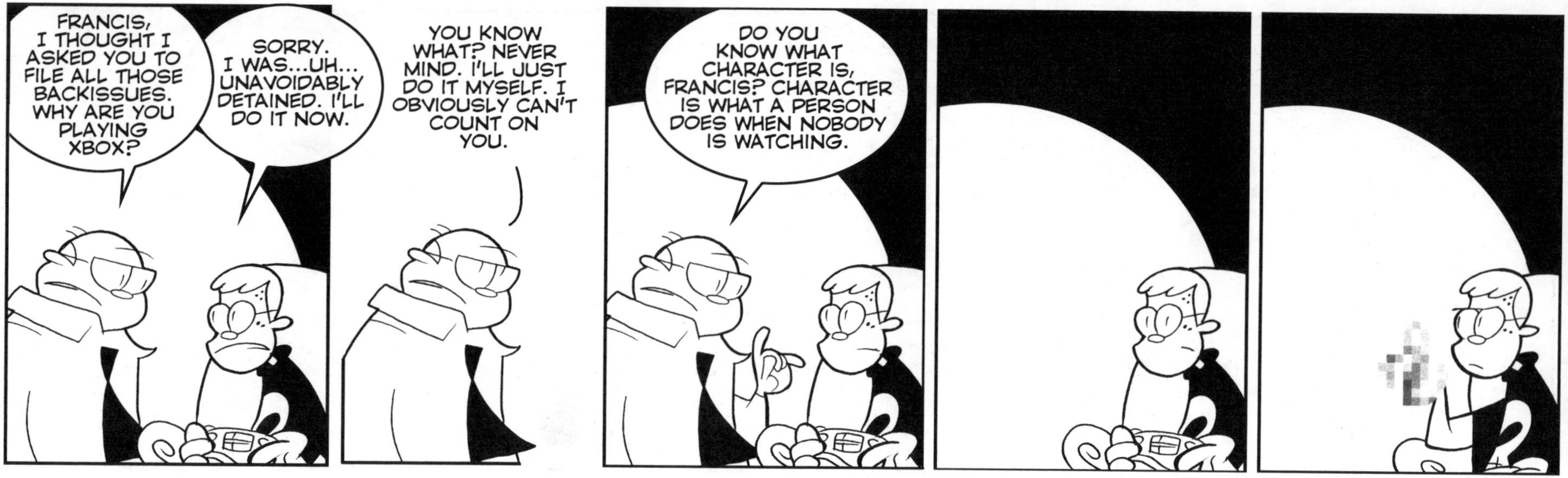
FRANCIS, I THOUGHT I ASKED YOU TO FILE ALL THOSE BACKISSUES. WHY ARE YOU PLAYING XBOX?
SORRY. I WAS...UH... UNAVOIDABLY DETAINED. I'LL DO IT NOW.
YOU KNOW WHAT? NEVER MIND. I'LL JUST DO IT MYSELF. I OBVIOUSLY CAN'T COUNT ON YOU.
DO YOU KNOW WHAT CHARACTER IS, FRANCIS? CHARACTER IS WHAT A PERSON DOES WHEN NOBODY IS WATCHING.

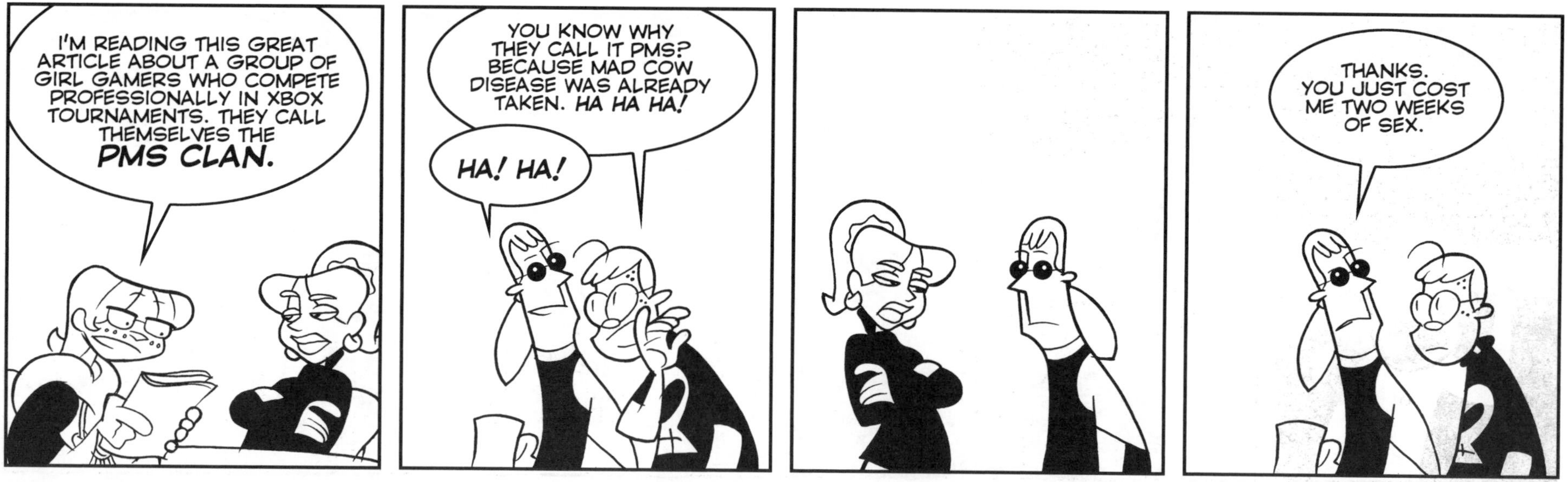
I'M READING THIS GREAT ARTICLE ABOUT A GROUP OF GIRL GAMERS WHO COMPETE PROFESSIONALLY IN XBOX TOURNAMENTS. THEY CALL THEMSELVES THE **PMS CLAN.**
YOU KNOW WHY THEY CALL IT PMS? BECAUSE MAD COW DISEASE WAS ALREADY TAKEN. ***HA HA HA!***
HA! HA!
THANKS. YOU JUST COST ME TWO WEEKS OF SEX.

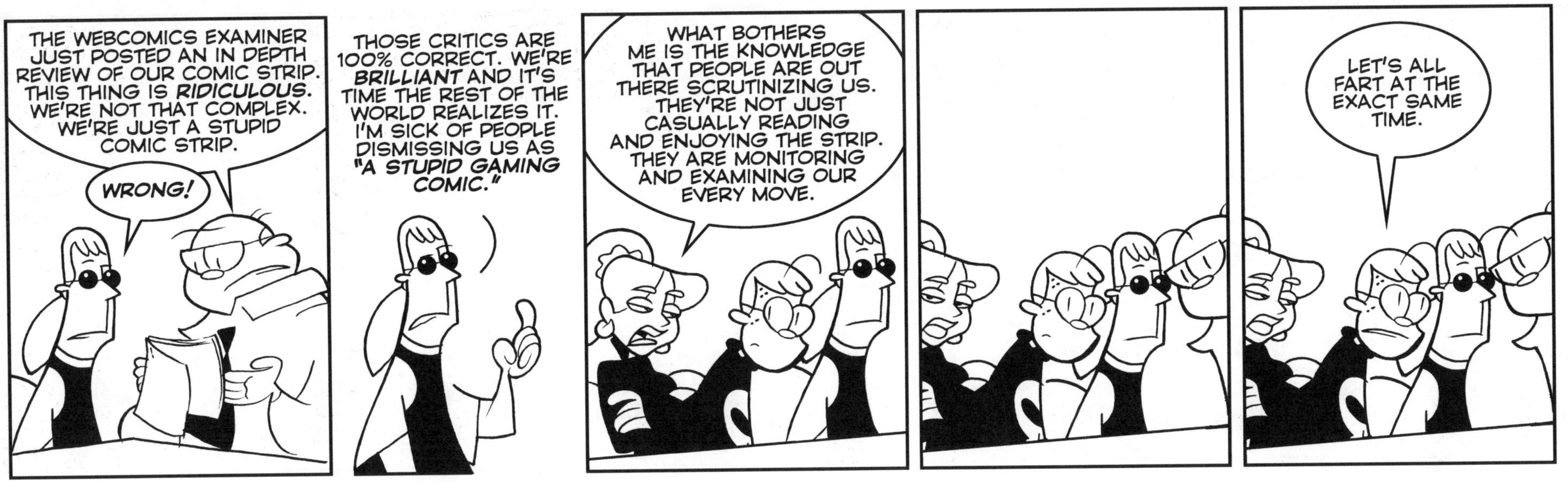
THE WEBCOMICS EXAMINER JUST POSTED AN IN DEPTH REVIEW OF OUR COMIC STRIP. THIS THING IS *RIDICULOUS.* WE'RE NOT THAT COMPLEX. WE'RE JUST A STUPID COMIC STRIP.
WRONG!
THOSE CRITICS ARE 100% CORRECT. WE'RE *BRILLIANT* AND IT'S TIME THE REST OF THE WORLD REALIZES IT. I'M SICK OF PEOPLE DISMISSING US AS ***"A STUPID GAMING COMIC."***
WHAT BOTHERS ME IS THE KNOWLEDGE THAT PEOPLE ARE OUT THERE SCRUTINIZING US. THEY'RE NOT JUST CASUALLY READING AND ENJOYING THE STRIP. THEY ARE MONITORING AND EXAMINING OUR EVERY MOVE.
LET'S ALL FART AT THE EXACT SAME TIME.

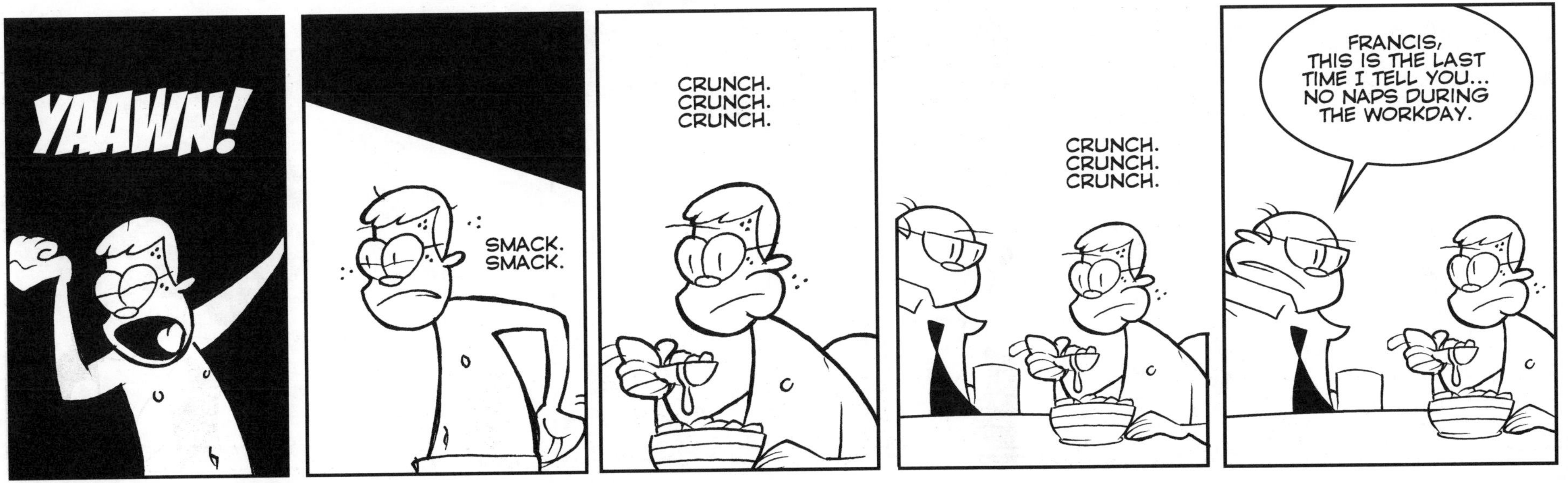
YAAWN!
SMACK. SMACK.
CRUNCH. CRUNCH. CRUNCH.
CRUNCH. CRUNCH. CRUNCH.
FRANCIS, THIS IS THE LAST TIME I TELL YOU... NO NAPS DURING THE WORKDAY.

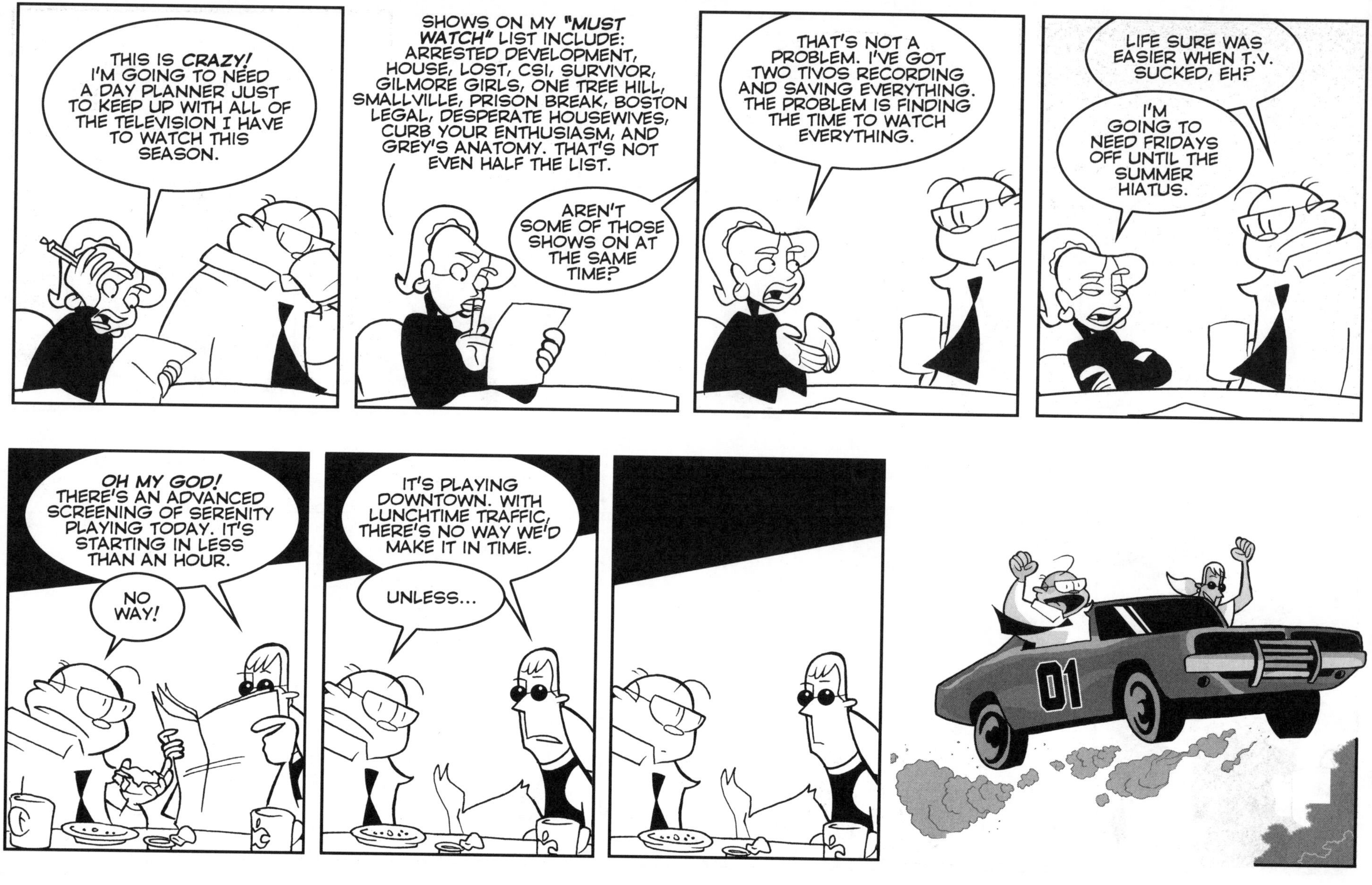
THIS IS *CRAZY!* I'M GOING TO NEED A DAY PLANNER JUST TO KEEP UP WITH ALL OF THE TELEVISION I HAVE TO WATCH THIS SEASON.
SHOWS ON MY *"MUST WATCH"* LIST INCLUDE: ARRESTED DEVELOPMENT, HOUSE, LOST, CSI, SURVIVOR, GILMORE GIRLS, ONE TREE HILL, SMALLVILLE, PRISON BREAK, BOSTON LEGAL, DESPERATE HOUSEWIVES, CURB YOUR ENTHUSIASM, AND GREY'S ANATOMY. THAT'S NOT EVEN HALF THE LIST.
AREN'T SOME OF THOSE SHOWS ON AT THE SAME TIME?
THAT'S NOT A PROBLEM. I'VE GOT TWO TIVOS RECORDING AND SAVING EVERYTHING. THE PROBLEM IS FINDING THE TIME TO WATCH EVERYTHING.
LIFE SURE WAS EASIER WHEN T.V. SUCKED, EH?
I'M GOING TO NEED FRIDAYS OFF UNTIL THE SUMMER HIATUS.
OH MY GOD! THERE'S AN ADVANCED SCREENING OF SERENITY PLAYING TODAY. IT'S STARTING IN LESS THAN AN HOUR.
NO WAY!
IT'S PLAYING DOWNTOWN. WITH LUNCHTIME TRAFFIC, THERE'S NO WAY WE'D MAKE IT IN TIME.
UNLESS...
01

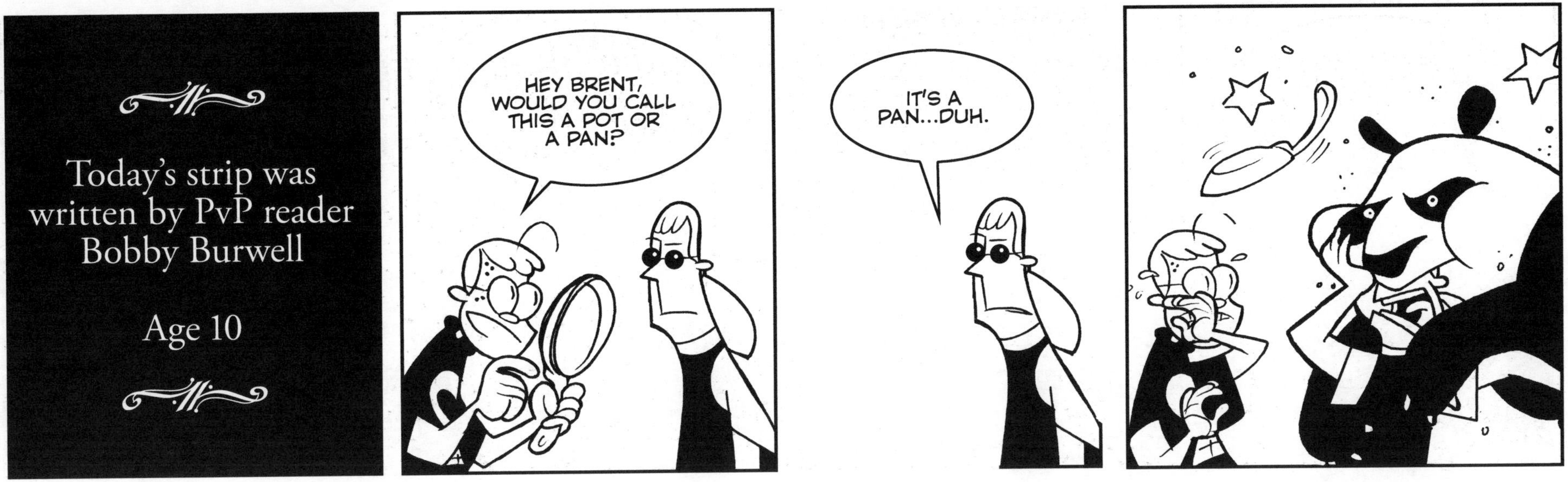
Today's strip was written by PvP reader Bobby Burwell
Age 10
HEY BRENT, WOULD YOU CALL THIS A POT OR A PAN?
IT'S A PAN...DUH.

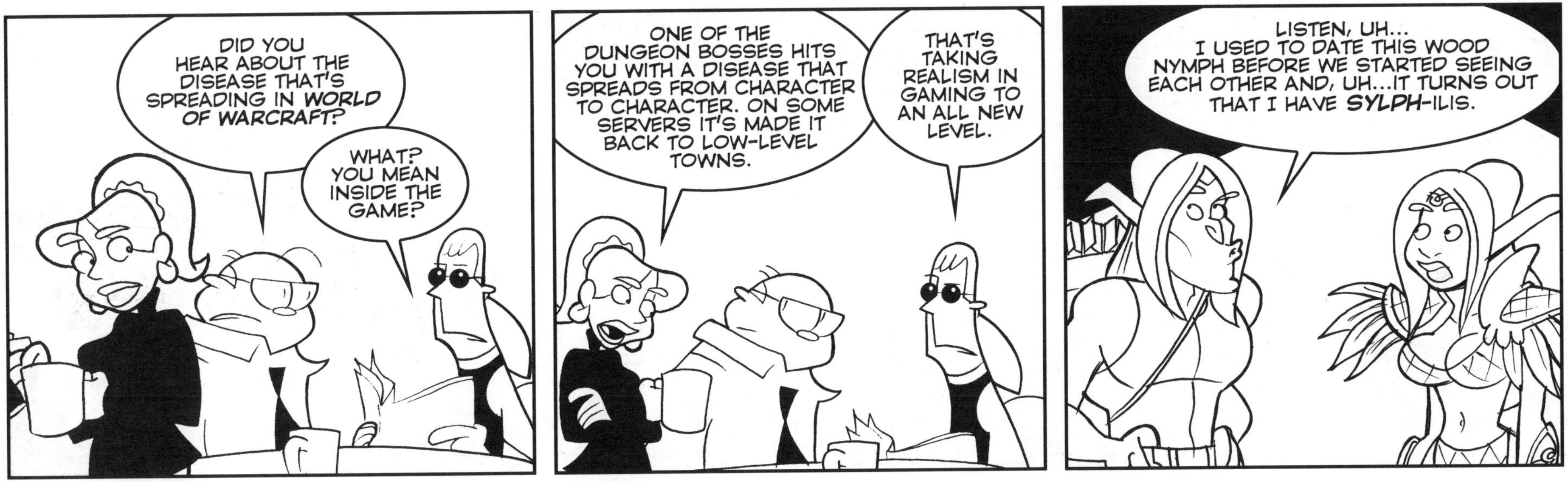
DID YOU HEAR ABOUT THE DISEASE THAT'S SPREADING IN *WORLD OF WARCRAFT*?
WHAT? YOU MEAN INSIDE THE GAME?
ONE OF THE DUNGEON BOSSES HITS YOU WITH A DISEASE THAT SPREADS FROM CHARACTER TO CHARACTER. ON SOME SERVERS IT'S MADE IT BACK TO LOW-LEVEL TOWNS.
THAT'S TAKING REALISM IN GAMING TO AN ALL NEW LEVEL.
LISTEN, UH... I USED TO DATE THIS WOOD NYMPH BEFORE WE STARTED SEEING EACH OTHER AND, UH...IT TURNS OUT THAT I HAVE ***SYLPH***-ILIS.

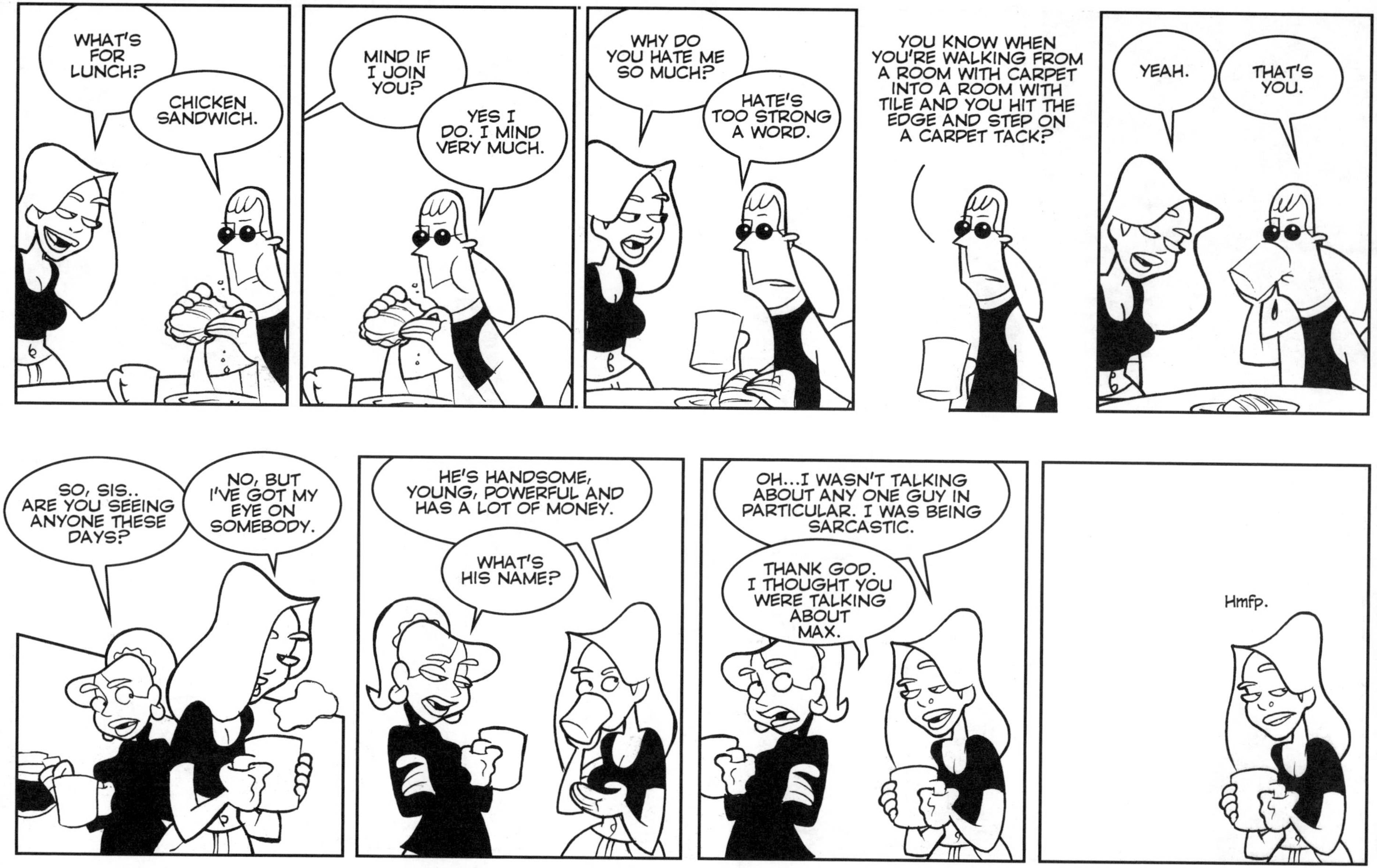
WHAT'S FOR LUNCH?
CHICKEN SANDWICH.
MIND IF I JOIN YOU?
YES I DO. I MIND VERY MUCH.
WHY DO YOU HATE ME SO MUCH?
HATE'S TOO STRONG A WORD.
YOU KNOW WHEN YOU'RE WALKING FROM A ROOM WITH CARPET INTO A ROOM WITH TILE AND YOU HIT THE EDGE AND STEP ON A CARPET TACK?
YEAH.
THAT'S YOU.
SO, SIS.. ARE YOU SEEING ANYONE THESE DAYS?
NO, BUT I'VE GOT MY EYE ON SOMEBODY.
HE'S HANDSOME, YOUNG, POWERFUL AND HAS A LOT OF MONEY.
WHAT'S HIS NAME?
OH...I WASN'T TALKING ABOUT ANY ONE GUY IN PARTICULAR. I WAS BEING SARCASTIC.
THANK GOD. I THOUGHT YOU WERE TALKING ABOUT MAX.
Hmfp.

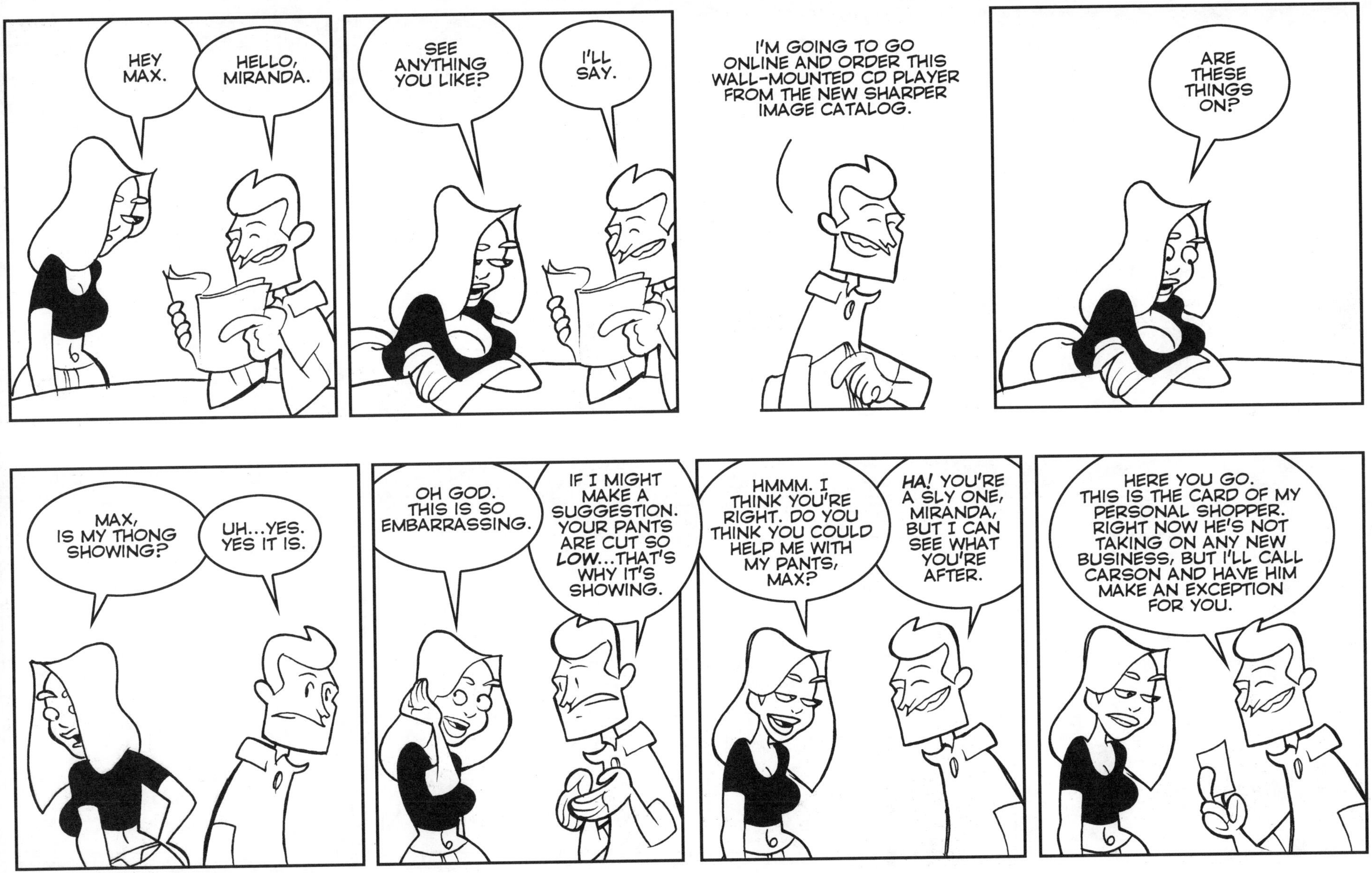
HEY MAX.
HELLO, MIRANDA.
SEE ANYTHING YOU LIKE?
I'LL SAY.
I'M GOING TO GO ONLINE AND ORDER THIS WALL-MOUNTED CD PLAYER FROM THE NEW SHARPER IMAGE CATALOG.
ARE THESE THINGS ON?
MAX, IS MY THONG SHOWING?
UH...YES. YES IT IS.
OH GOD. THIS IS SO EMBARRASSING.
IF I MIGHT MAKE A SUGGESTION. YOUR PANTS ARE CUT SO *LOW*...THAT'S WHY IT'S SHOWING.
HMMM. I THINK YOU'RE RIGHT. DO YOU THINK YOU COULD HELP ME WITH MY PANTS, MAX?
HA! YOU'RE A SLY ONE, MIRANDA, BUT I CAN SEE WHAT YOU'RE AFTER.
HERE YOU GO. THIS IS THE CARD OF MY PERSONAL SHOPPER. RIGHT NOW HE'S NOT TAKING ON ANY NEW BUSINESS, BUT I'LL CALL CARSON AND HAVE HIM MAKE AN EXCEPTION FOR YOU.

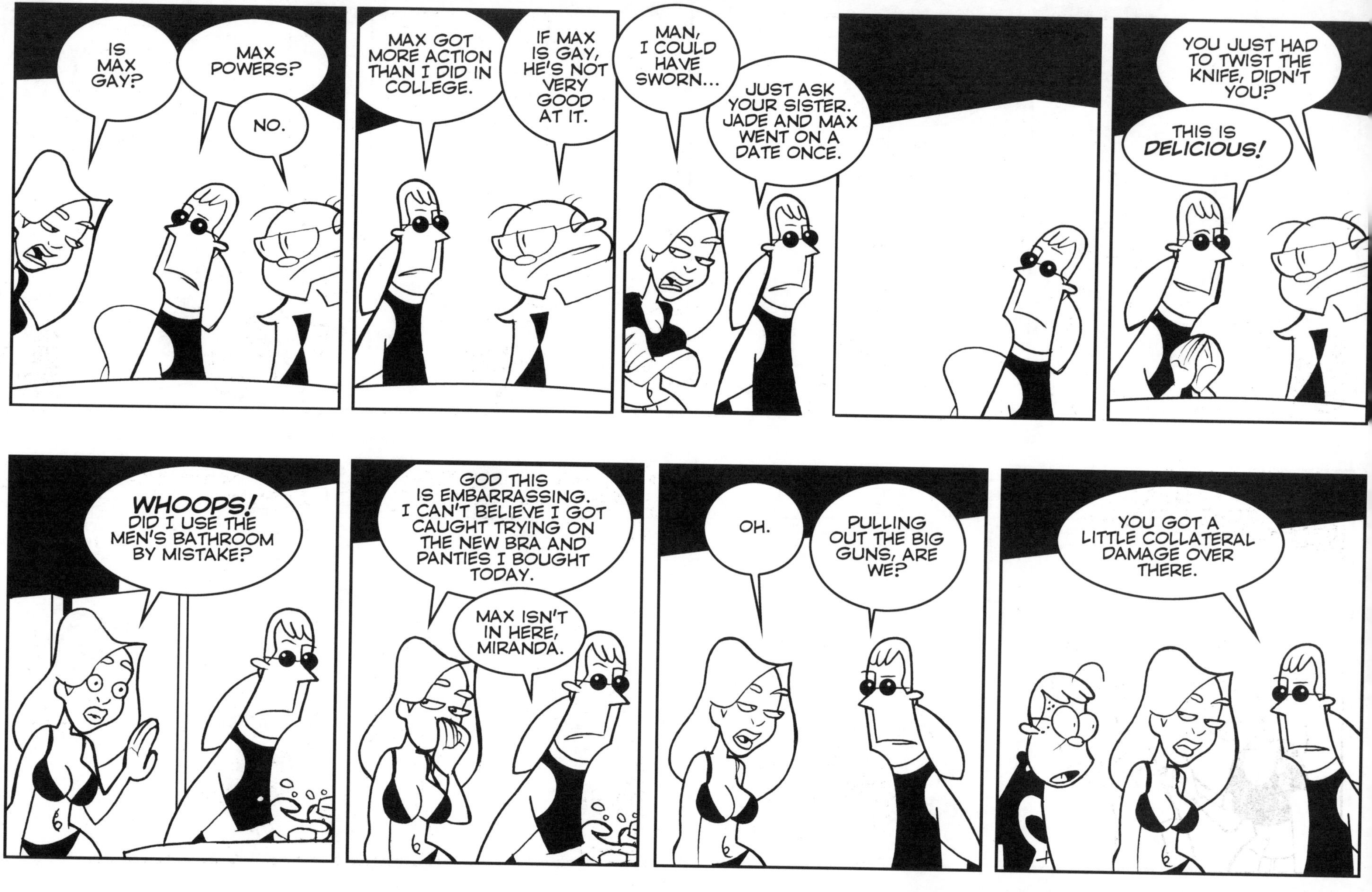
IS MAX GAY?
MAX POWERS?
NO.
MAX GOT MORE ACTION THAN I DID IN COLLEGE.
IF MAX IS GAY, HE'S NOT VERY GOOD AT IT.
MAN, I COULD HAVE SWORN...
JUST ASK YOUR SISTER. JADE AND MAX WENT ON A DATE ONCE.
YOU JUST HAD TO TWIST THE KNIFE, DIDN'T YOU?
THIS IS DELICIOUS!
WHOOPS! DID I USE THE MEN'S BATHROOM BY MISTAKE?
GOD THIS IS EMBARRASSING. I CAN'T BELIEVE I GOT CAUGHT TRYING ON THE NEW BRA AND PANTIES I BOUGHT TODAY.
MAX ISN'T IN HERE, MIRANDA.
OH.
PULLING OUT THE BIG GUNS, ARE WE?
YOU GOT A LITTLE COLLATERAL DAMAGE OVER THERE.

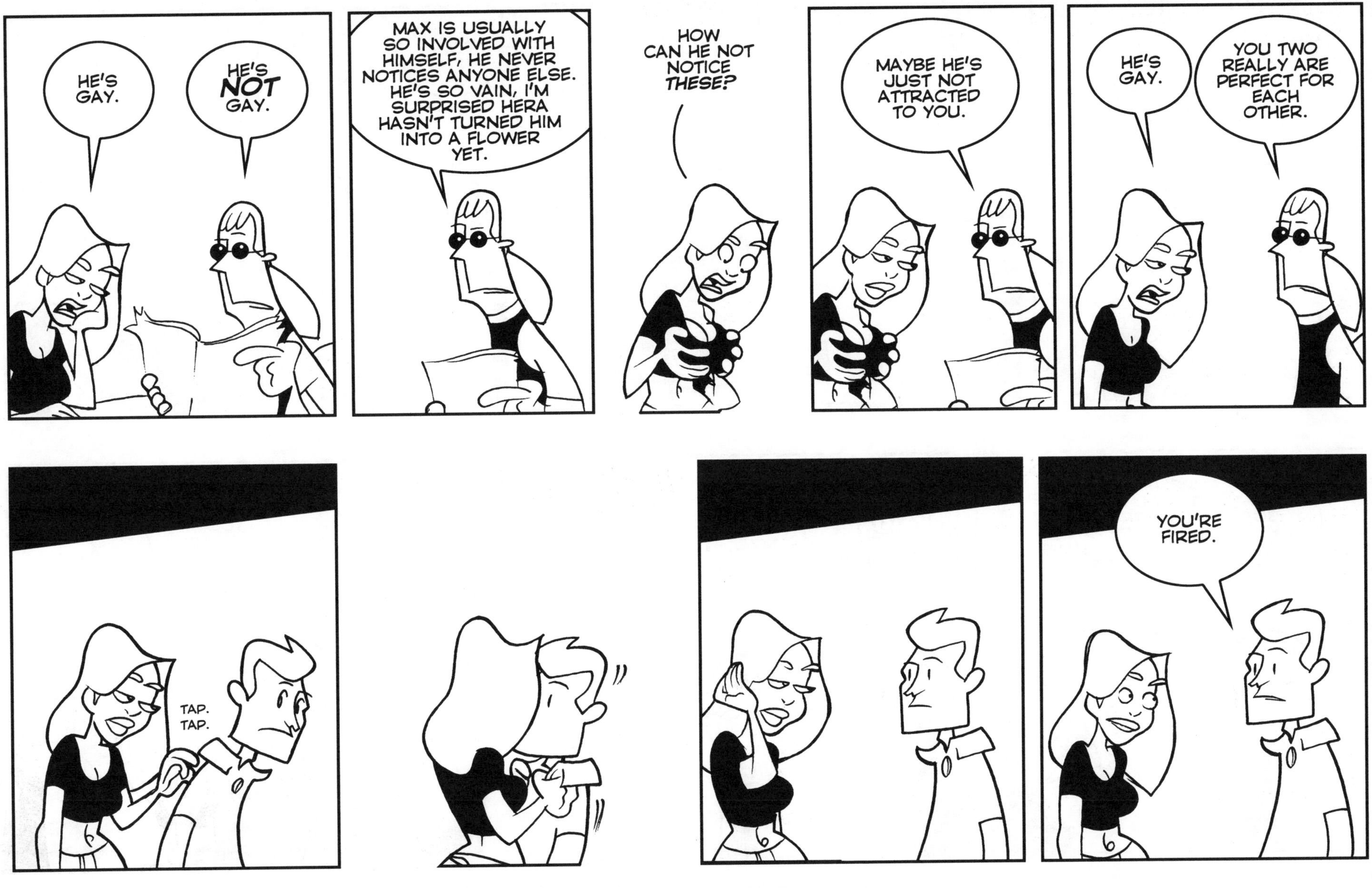
HE'S GAY.
HE'S NOT GAY.
MAX IS USUALLY SO INVOLVED WITH HIMSELF, HE NEVER NOTICES ANYONE ELSE. HE'S SO VAIN, I'M SURPRISED HERA HASN'T TURNED HIM INTO A FLOWER YET.
HOW CAN HE NOT NOTICE THESE?
MAYBE HE'S JUST NOT ATTRACTED TO YOU.
HE'S GAY.
YOU TWO REALLY ARE PERFECT FOR EACH OTHER.
TAP. TAP.
YOU'RE FIRED.

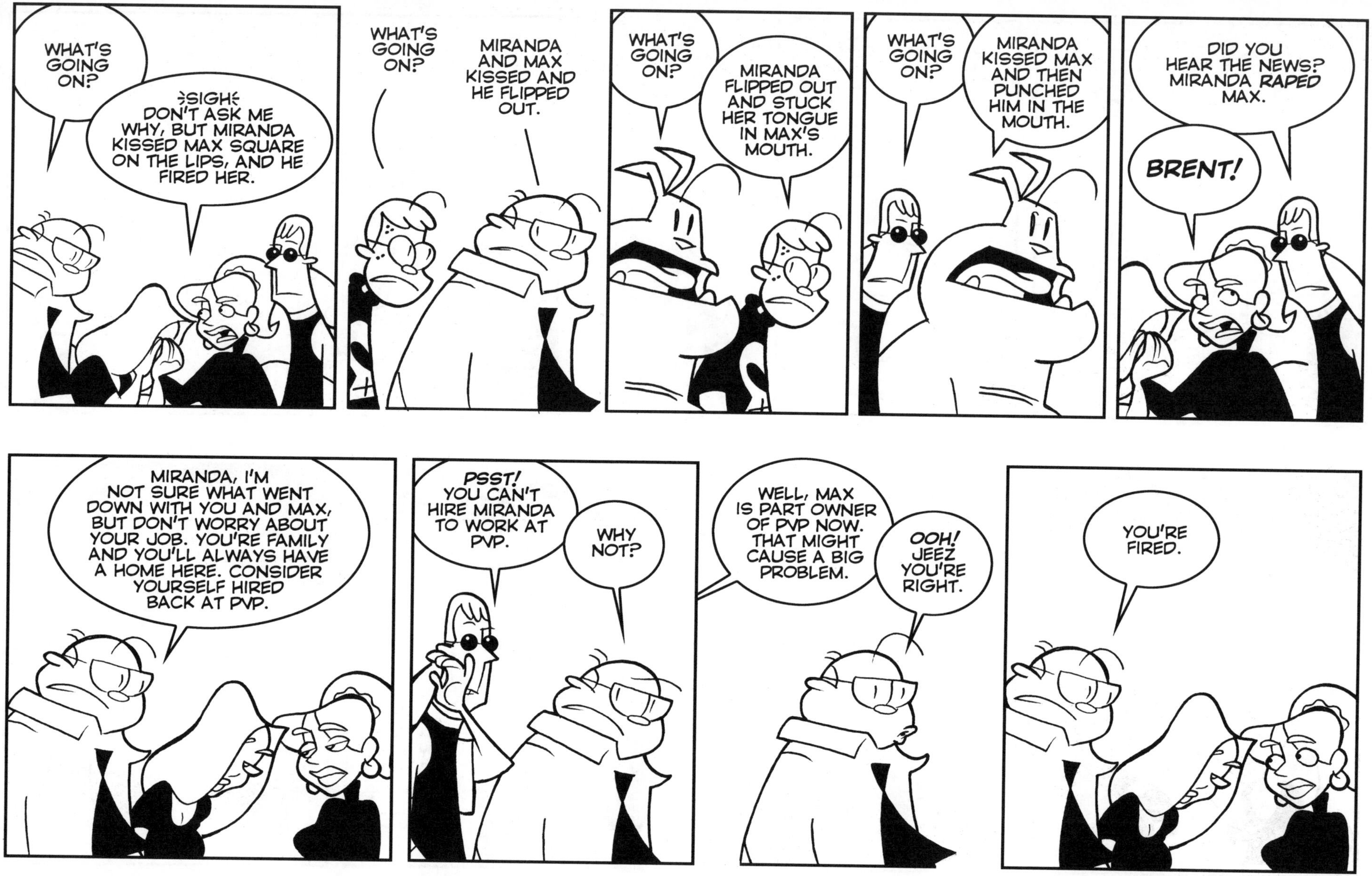

WHAT'S GOING ON?
SIGH DON'T ASK ME WHY, BUT MIRANDA KISSED MAX SQUARE ON THE LIPS, AND HE FIRED HER.
WHAT'S GOING ON?
MIRANDA AND MAX KISSED AND HE FLIPPED OUT.
WHAT'S GOING ON?
MIRANDA FLIPPED OUT AND STUCK HER TONGUE IN MAX'S MOUTH.
WHAT'S GOING ON?
MIRANDA KISSED MAX AND THEN PUNCHED HIM IN THE MOUTH.
DID YOU HEAR THE NEWS? MIRANDA *RAPED* MAX.
BRENT!
MIRANDA, I'M NOT SURE WHAT WENT DOWN WITH YOU AND MAX, BUT DON'T WORRY ABOUT YOUR JOB. YOU'RE FAMILY AND YOU'LL ALWAYS HAVE A HOME HERE. CONSIDER YOURSELF HIRED BACK AT PVP.
PSST! YOU CAN'T HIRE MIRANDA TO WORK AT PVP.
WHY NOT?
WELL, MAX IS PART OWNER OF PVP NOW. THAT MIGHT CAUSE A BIG PROBLEM.
OOH! JEEZ YOU'RE RIGHT.
YOU'RE FIRED.

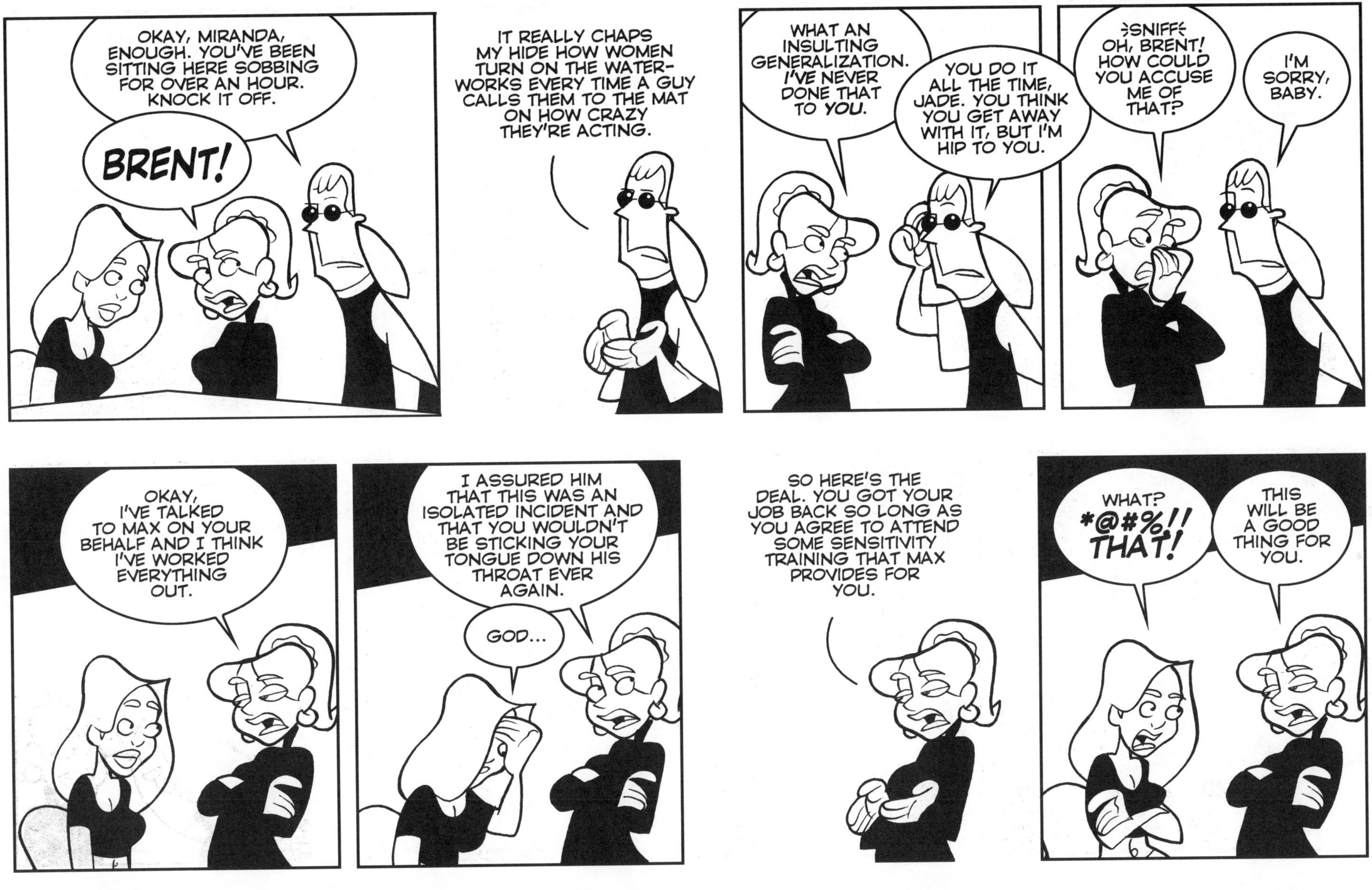
OKAY, MIRANDA, ENOUGH. YOU'VE BEEN SITTING HERE SOBBING FOR OVER AN HOUR. KNOCK IT OFF.
BRENT!
IT REALLY CHAPS MY HIDE HOW WOMEN TURN ON THE WATER-WORKS EVERY TIME A GUY CALLS THEM TO THE MAT ON HOW CRAZY THEY'RE ACTING.
WHAT AN INSULTING GENERALIZATION. I'VE NEVER DONE THAT TO YOU.
YOU DO IT ALL THE TIME, JADE. YOU THINK YOU GET AWAY WITH IT, BUT I'M HIP TO YOU.
SNIFF OH, BRENT! HOW COULD YOU ACCUSE ME OF THAT?
I'M SORRY, BABY.
OKAY, I'VE TALKED TO MAX ON YOUR BEHALF AND I THINK I'VE WORKED EVERYTHING OUT.
I ASSURED HIM THAT THIS WAS AN ISOLATED INCIDENT AND THAT YOU WOULDN'T BE STICKING YOUR TONGUE DOWN HIS THROAT EVER AGAIN.
GOD...
SO HERE'S THE DEAL. YOU GOT YOUR JOB BACK SO LONG AS YOU AGREE TO ATTEND SOME SENSITIVITY TRAINING THAT MAX PROVIDES FOR YOU.
WHAT? *@#%!! THAT!
THIS WILL BE A GOOD THING FOR YOU.

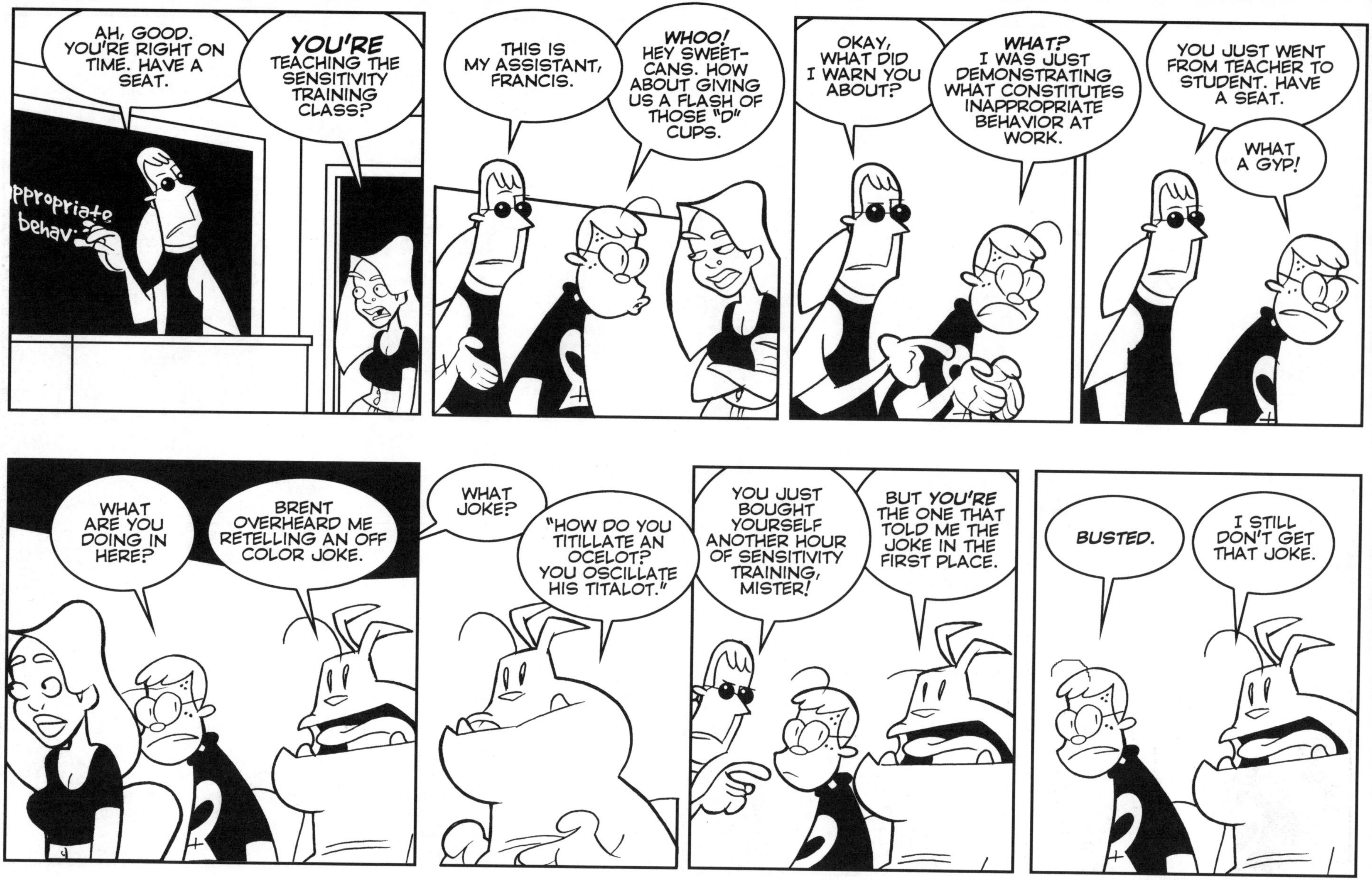
AH, GOOD. YOU'RE RIGHT ON TIME. HAVE A SEAT.
YOU'RE TEACHING THE SENSITIVITY TRAINING CLASS?
ppropriate behav:
THIS IS MY ASSISTANT, FRANCIS.
WHOO! HEY SWEET-CANS. HOW ABOUT GIVING US A FLASH OF THOSE "D" CUPS.
OKAY, WHAT DID I WARN YOU ABOUT?
WHAT? I WAS JUST DEMONSTRATING WHAT CONSTITUTES INAPPROPRIATE BEHAVIOR AT WORK.
YOU JUST WENT FROM TEACHER TO STUDENT. HAVE A SEAT.
WHAT A GYP!
WHAT ARE YOU DOING IN HERE?
BRENT OVERHEARD ME RETELLING AN OFF COLOR JOKE.
WHAT JOKE?
"HOW DO YOU TITILLATE AN OCELOT? YOU OSCILLATE HIS TITALOT."
YOU JUST BOUGHT YOURSELF ANOTHER HOUR OF SENSITIVITY TRAINING, MISTER!
BUT *YOU'RE* THE ONE THAT TOLD ME THE JOKE IN THE FIRST PLACE.
BUSTED.
I STILL DON'T GET THAT JOKE.

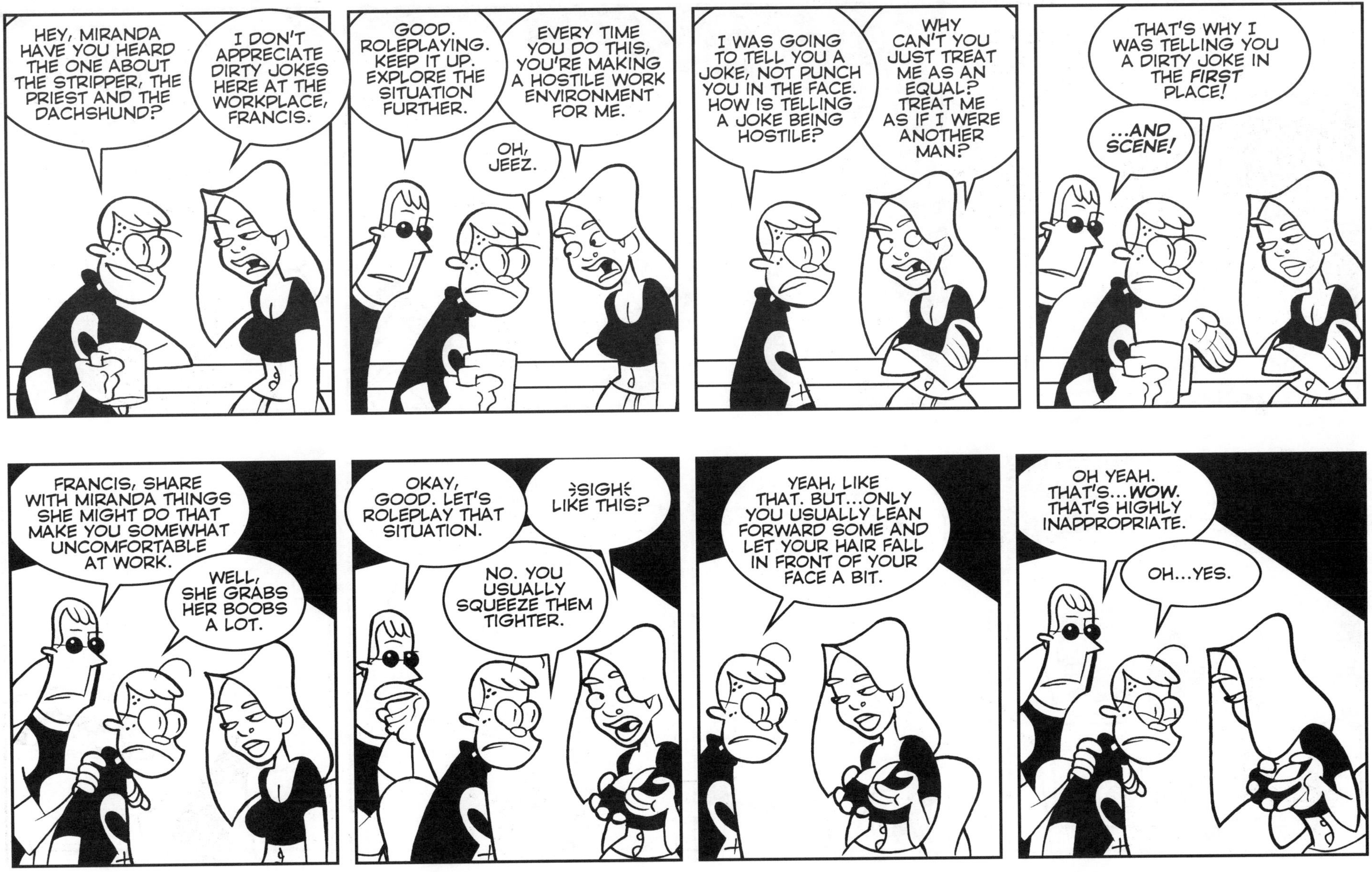
HEY, MIRANDA HAVE YOU HEARD THE ONE ABOUT THE STRIPPER, THE PRIEST AND THE DACHSHUND?
I DON'T APPRECIATE DIRTY JOKES HERE AT THE WORKPLACE, FRANCIS.
GOOD. ROLEPLAYING. KEEP IT UP. EXPLORE THE SITUATION FURTHER.
EVERY TIME YOU DO THIS, YOU'RE MAKING A HOSTILE WORK ENVIRONMENT FOR ME.
OH, JEEZ.
I WAS GOING TO TELL YOU A JOKE, NOT PUNCH YOU IN THE FACE. HOW IS TELLING A JOKE BEING HOSTILE?
WHY CAN'T YOU JUST TREAT ME AS AN EQUAL? TREAT ME AS IF I WERE ANOTHER MAN?
THAT'S WHY I WAS TELLING YOU A DIRTY JOKE IN THE *FIRST* PLACE!
...**AND SCENE!**
FRANCIS, SHARE WITH MIRANDA THINGS SHE MIGHT DO THAT MAKE YOU SOMEWHAT UNCOMFORTABLE AT WORK.
WELL, SHE GRABS HER BOOBS A LOT.
OKAY, GOOD. LET'S ROLEPLAY THAT SITUATION.
SIGH LIKE THIS?
NO. YOU USUALLY SQUEEZE THEM TIGHTER.
YEAH, LIKE THAT. BUT...ONLY YOU USUALLY LEAN FORWARD SOME AND LET YOUR HAIR FALL IN FRONT OF YOUR FACE A BIT.
OH YEAH. THAT'S...**WOW**. THAT'S HIGHLY INAPPROPRIATE.
OH...YES.

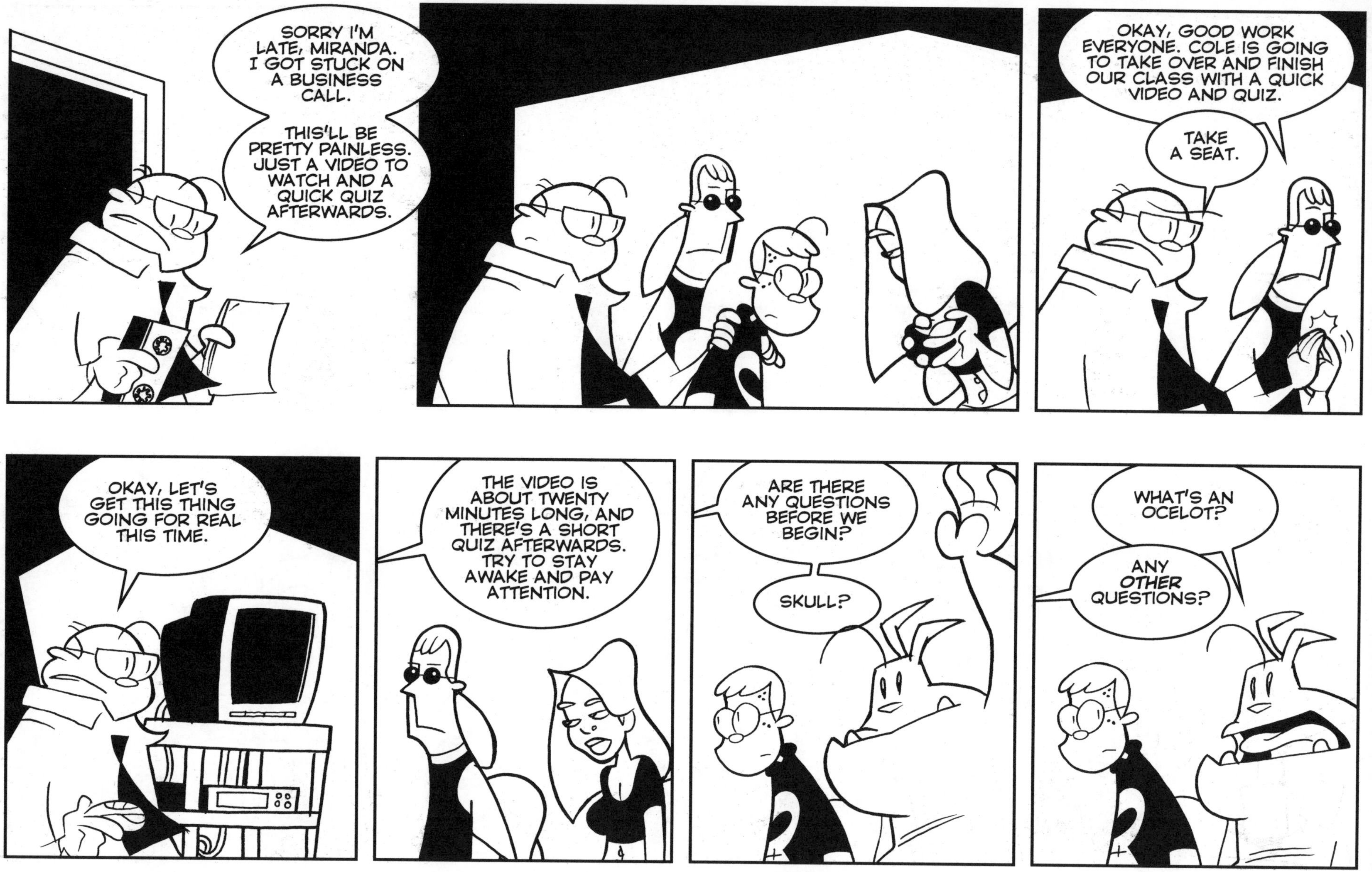
SORRY I'M LATE, MIRANDA. I GOT STUCK ON A BUSINESS CALL.
THIS'LL BE PRETTY PAINLESS. JUST A VIDEO TO WATCH AND A QUICK QUIZ AFTERWARDS.
OKAY, GOOD WORK EVERYONE. COLE IS GOING TO TAKE OVER AND FINISH OUR CLASS WITH A QUICK VIDEO AND QUIZ.
TAKE A SEAT.
OKAY, LET'S GET THIS THING GOING FOR REAL THIS TIME.
THE VIDEO IS ABOUT TWENTY MINUTES LONG, AND THERE'S A SHORT QUIZ AFTERWARDS. TRY TO STAY AWAKE AND PAY ATTENTION.
ARE THERE ANY QUESTIONS BEFORE WE BEGIN?
SKULL?
WHAT'S AN OCELOT?
ANY *OTHER* QUESTIONS?

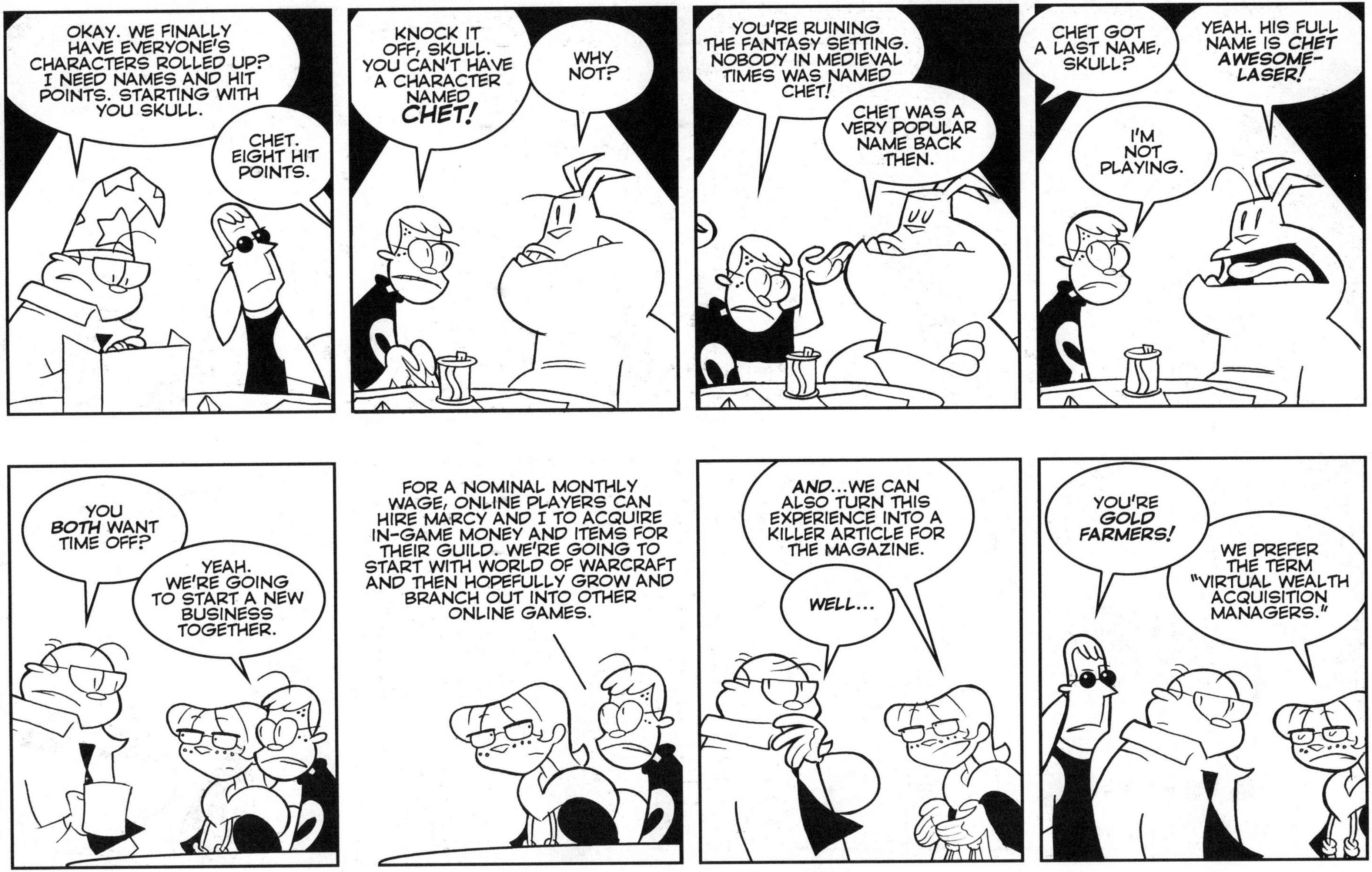
OKAY. WE FINALLY HAVE EVERYONE'S CHARACTERS ROLLED UP? I NEED NAMES AND HIT POINTS. STARTING WITH YOU SKULL.
CHET. EIGHT HIT POINTS.
KNOCK IT OFF, SKULL. YOU CAN'T HAVE A CHARACTER NAMED CHET!
WHY NOT?
YOU'RE RUINING THE FANTASY SETTING. NOBODY IN MEDIEVAL TIMES WAS NAMED CHET!
CHET WAS A VERY POPULAR NAME BACK THEN.
CHET GOT A LAST NAME, SKULL?
YEAH. HIS FULL NAME IS CHET AWESOME-LASER!
I'M NOT PLAYING.
YOU BOTH WANT TIME OFF?
YEAH. WE'RE GOING TO START A NEW BUSINESS TOGETHER.
FOR A NOMINAL MONTHLY WAGE, ONLINE PLAYERS CAN HIRE MARCY AND I TO ACQUIRE IN-GAME MONEY AND ITEMS FOR THEIR GUILD. WE'RE GOING TO START WITH WORLD OF WARCRAFT AND THEN HOPEFULLY GROW AND BRANCH OUT INTO OTHER ONLINE GAMES.
AND...WE CAN ALSO TURN THIS EXPERIENCE INTO A KILLER ARTICLE FOR THE MAGAZINE.
WELL...
YOU'RE GOLD FARMERS!
WE PREFER THE TERM "VIRTUAL WEALTH ACQUISITION MANAGERS."

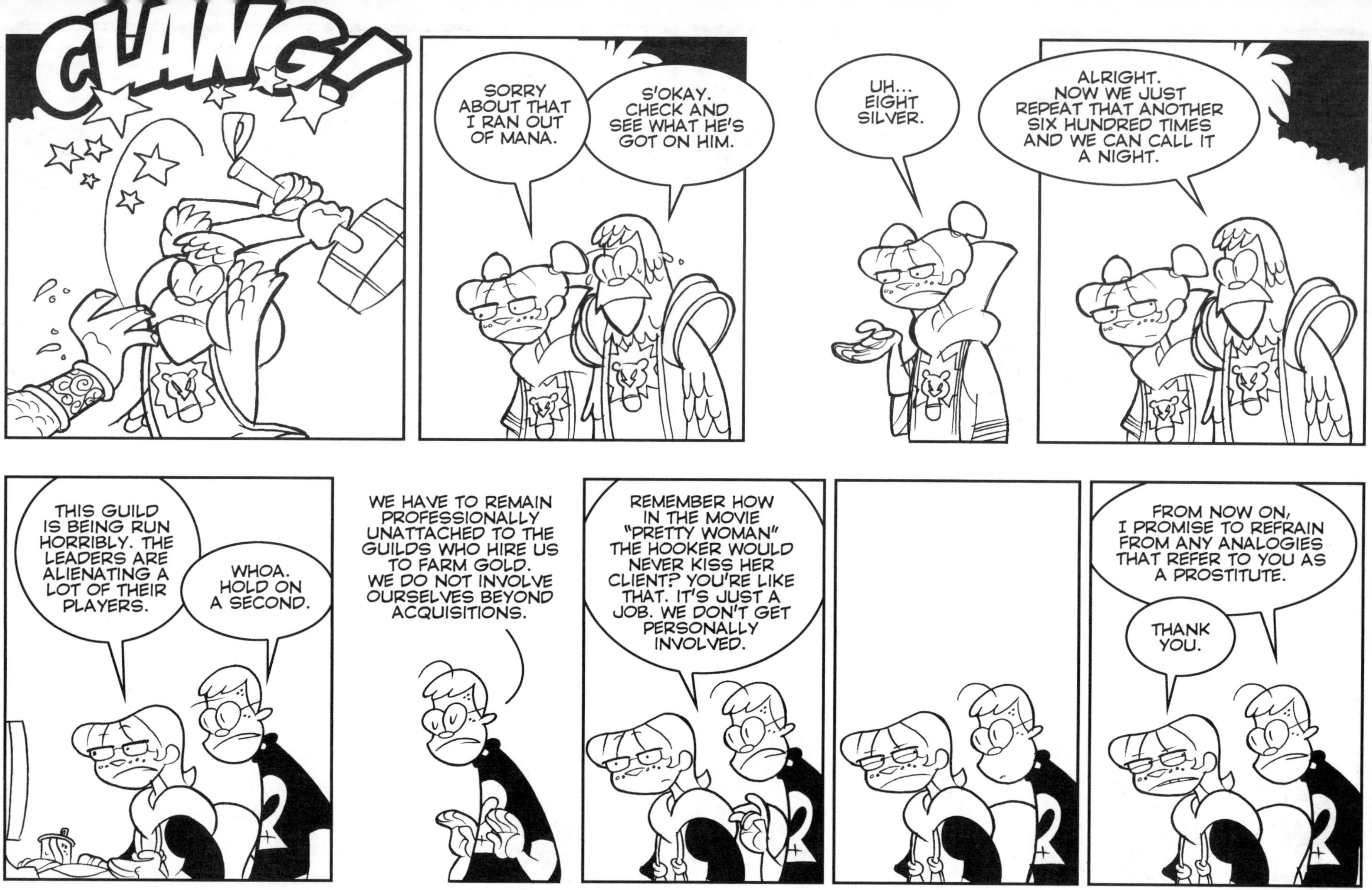
CLANG!
SORRY ABOUT THAT I RAN OUT OF MANA.
S'OKAY. CHECK AND SEE WHAT HE'S GOT ON HIM.
UH... EIGHT SILVER.
ALRIGHT. NOW WE JUST REPEAT THAT ANOTHER SIX HUNDRED TIMES AND WE CAN CALL IT A NIGHT.
THIS GUILD IS BEING RUN HORRIBLY. THE LEADERS ARE ALIENATING A LOT OF THEIR PLAYERS.
WHOA. HOLD ON A SECOND.
WE HAVE TO REMAIN PROFESSIONALLY UNATTACHED TO THE GUILDS WHO HIRE US TO FARM GOLD. WE DO NOT INVOLVE OURSELVES BEYOND ACQUISITIONS.
REMEMBER HOW IN THE MOVIE "PRETTY WOMAN" THE HOOKER WOULD NEVER KISS HER CLIENT? YOU'RE LIKE THAT. IT'S JUST A JOB. WE DON'T GET PERSONALLY INVOLVED.
FROM NOW ON, I PROMISE TO REFRAIN FROM ANY ANALOGIES THAT REFER TO YOU AS A PROSTITUTE.
THANK YOU.

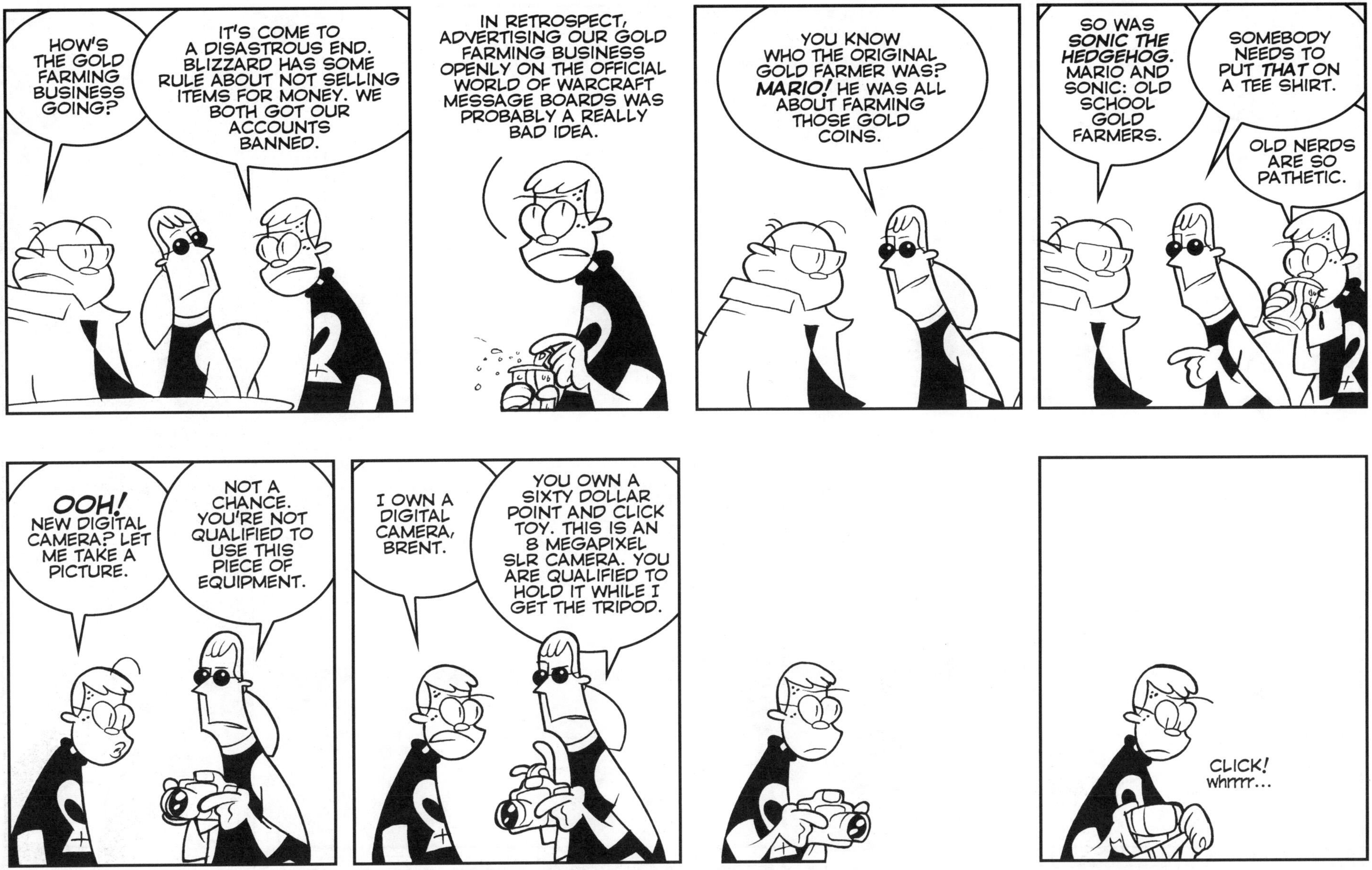
HOW'S THE GOLD FARMING BUSINESS GOING?
IT'S COME TO A DISASTROUS END. BLIZZARD HAS SOME RULE ABOUT NOT SELLING ITEMS FOR MONEY. WE BOTH GOT OUR ACCOUNTS BANNED.
IN RETROSPECT, ADVERTISING OUR GOLD FARMING BUSINESS OPENLY ON THE OFFICIAL WORLD OF WARCRAFT MESSAGE BOARDS WAS PROBABLY A REALLY BAD IDEA.
YOU KNOW WHO THE ORIGINAL GOLD FARMER WAS? MARIO! HE WAS ALL ABOUT FARMING THOSE GOLD COINS.
SO WAS SONIC THE HEDGEHOG. MARIO AND SONIC: OLD SCHOOL GOLD FARMERS.
SOMEBODY NEEDS TO PUT THAT ON A TEE SHIRT.
OLD NERDS ARE SO PATHETIC.
OOH! NEW DIGITAL CAMERA? LET ME TAKE A PICTURE.
NOT A CHANCE. YOU'RE NOT QUALIFIED TO USE THIS PIECE OF EQUIPMENT.
I OWN A DIGITAL CAMERA, BRENT.
YOU OWN A SIXTY DOLLAR POINT AND CLICK TOY. THIS IS AN 8 MEGAPIXEL SLR CAMERA. YOU ARE QUALIFIED TO HOLD IT WHILE I GET THE TRIPOD.
CLICK! whrrrr...

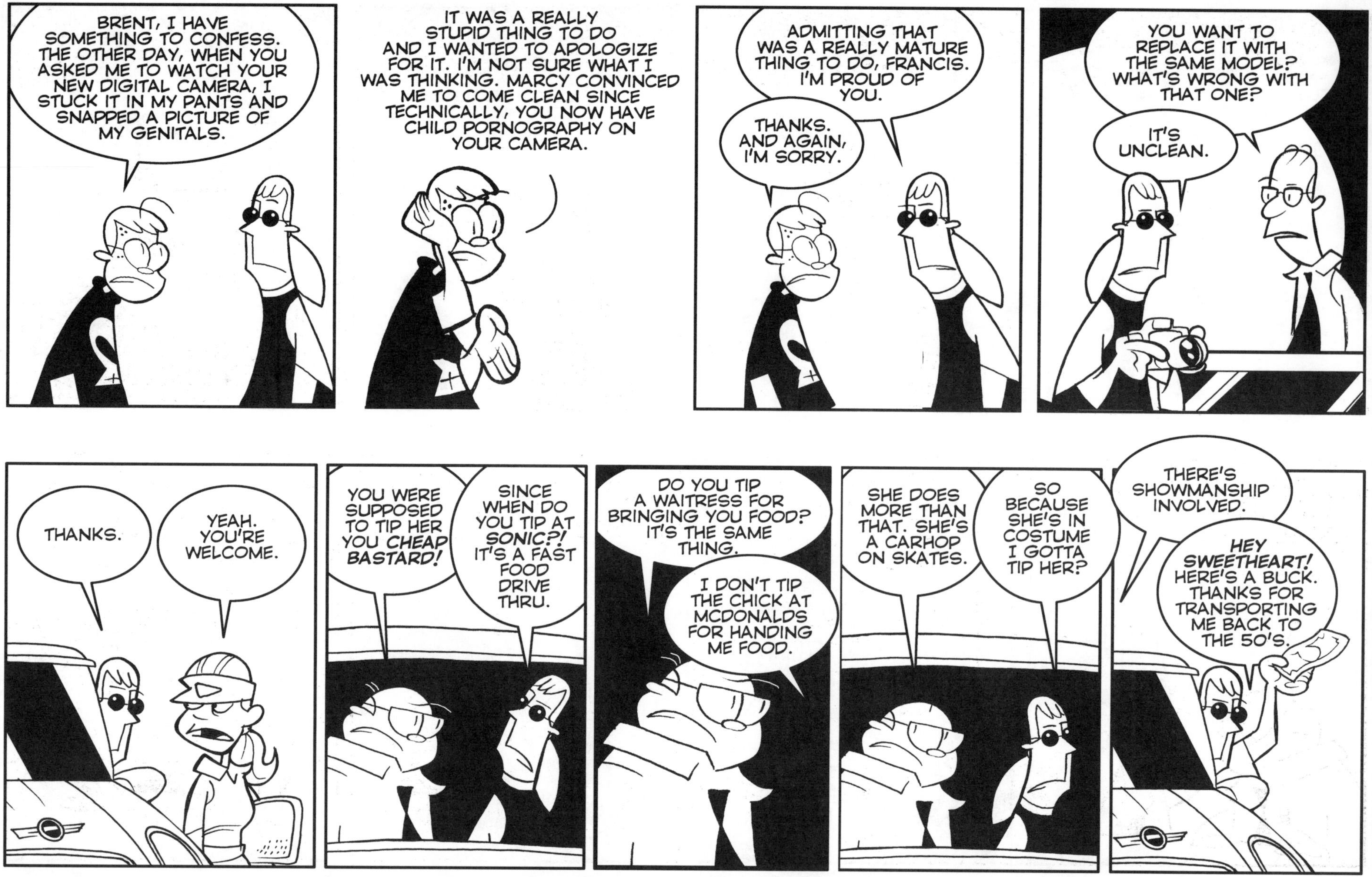

BRENT, I HAVE SOMETHING TO CONFESS. THE OTHER DAY, WHEN YOU ASKED ME TO WATCH YOUR NEW DIGITAL CAMERA, I STUCK IT IN MY PANTS AND SNAPPED A PICTURE OF MY GENITALS.
IT WAS A REALLY STUPID THING TO DO AND I WANTED TO APOLOGIZE FOR IT. I'M NOT SURE WHAT I WAS THINKING. MARCY CONVINCED ME TO COME CLEAN SINCE TECHNICALLY, YOU NOW HAVE CHILD PORNOGRAPHY ON YOUR CAMERA.
ADMITTING THAT WAS A REALLY MATURE THING TO DO, FRANCIS. I'M PROUD OF YOU.
THANKS. AND AGAIN, I'M SORRY.
YOU WANT TO REPLACE IT WITH THE SAME MODEL? WHAT'S WRONG WITH THAT ONE?
IT'S UNCLEAN.
THANKS.
YEAH. YOU'RE WELCOME.
YOU WERE SUPPOSED TO TIP HER YOU *CHEAP BASTARD!*
SINCE WHEN DO YOU TIP AT *SONIC?!* IT'S A FAST FOOD DRIVE THRU.
DO YOU TIP A WAITRESS FOR BRINGING YOU FOOD? IT'S THE SAME THING.
I DON'T TIP THE CHICK AT MCDONALDS FOR HANDING ME FOOD.
SHE DOES MORE THAN THAT. SHE'S A CARHOP ON SKATES.
SO BECAUSE SHE'S IN COSTUME I GOTTA TIP HER?
THERE'S SHOWMANSHIP INVOLVED.
HEY SWEETHEART! HERE'S A BUCK. THANKS FOR TRANSPORTING ME BACK TO THE 50'S.

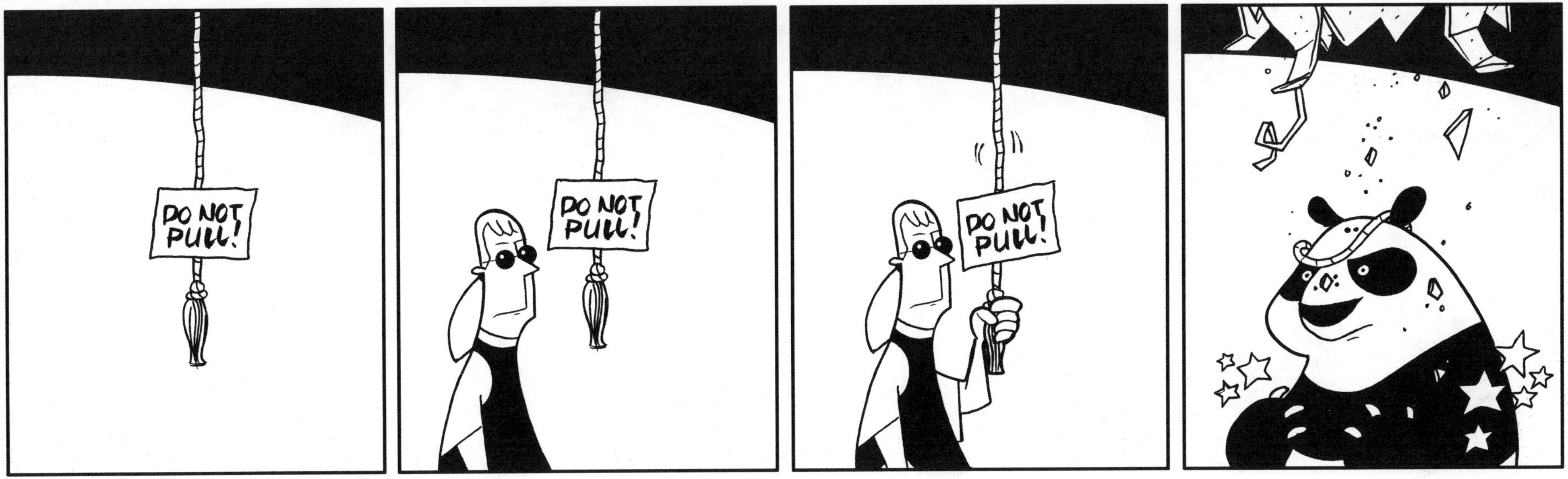
DO NOT PULL!
DO NOT PULL!
DO NOT PULL!

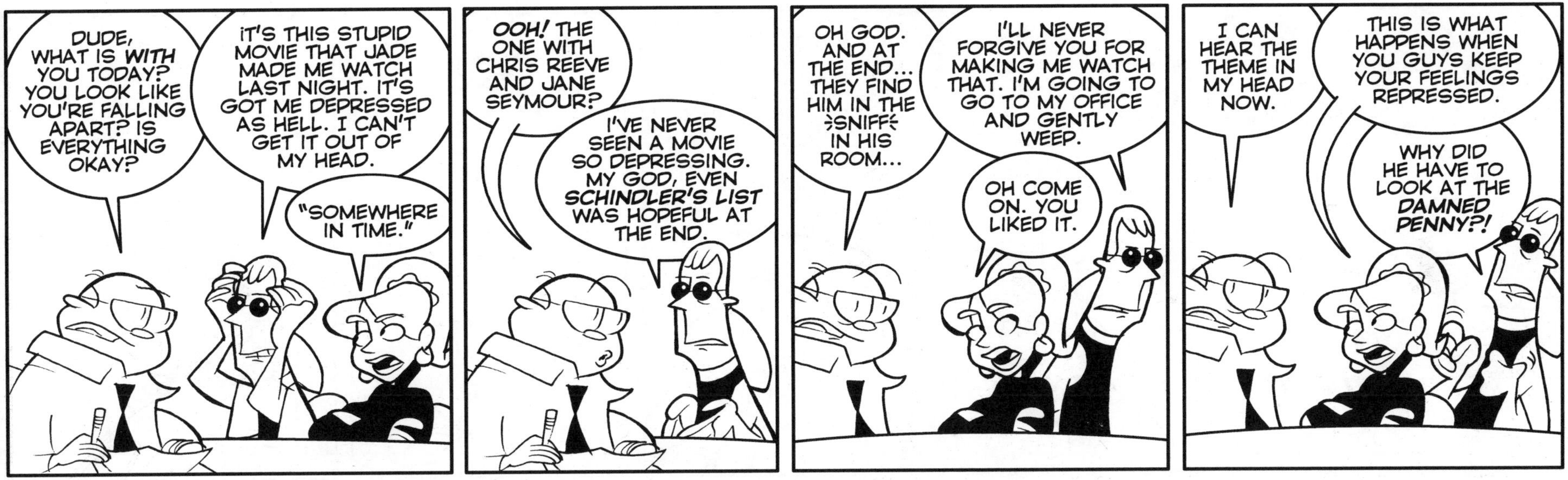
DUDE, WHAT IS WITH YOU TODAY? YOU LOOK LIKE YOU'RE FALLING APART? IS EVERYTHING OKAY?
IT'S THIS STUPID MOVIE THAT JADE MADE ME WATCH LAST NIGHT. IT'S GOT ME DEPRESSED AS HELL. I CAN'T GET IT OUT OF MY HEAD.
"SOMEWHERE IN TIME."
OOH! THE ONE WITH CHRIS REEVE AND JANE SEYMOUR?
I'VE NEVER SEEN A MOVIE SO DEPRESSING. MY GOD, EVEN SCHINDLER'S LIST WAS HOPEFUL AT THE END.
OH GOD. AND AT THE END... THEY FIND HIM IN THE SNIFF IN HIS ROOM...
I'LL NEVER FORGIVE YOU FOR MAKING ME WATCH THAT. I'M GOING TO GO TO MY OFFICE AND GENTLY WEEP.
OH COME ON. YOU LIKED IT.
I CAN HEAR THE THEME IN MY HEAD NOW.
THIS IS WHAT HAPPENS WHEN YOU GUYS KEEP YOUR FEELINGS REPRESSED.
WHY DID HE HAVE TO LOOK AT THE DAMNED PENNY?!

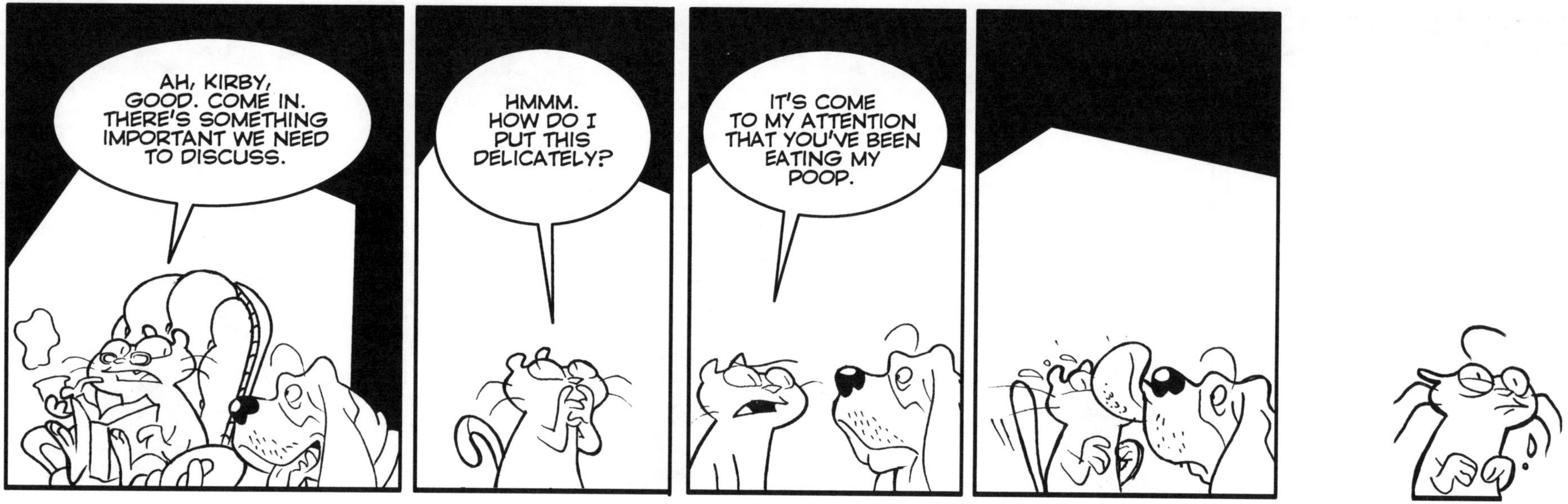
AH, KIRBY, GOOD. COME IN. THERE'S SOMETHING IMPORTANT WE NEED TO DISCUSS.
HMMM. HOW DO I PUT THIS DELICATELY?
IT'S COME TO MY ATTENTION THAT YOU'VE BEEN EATING MY POOP.

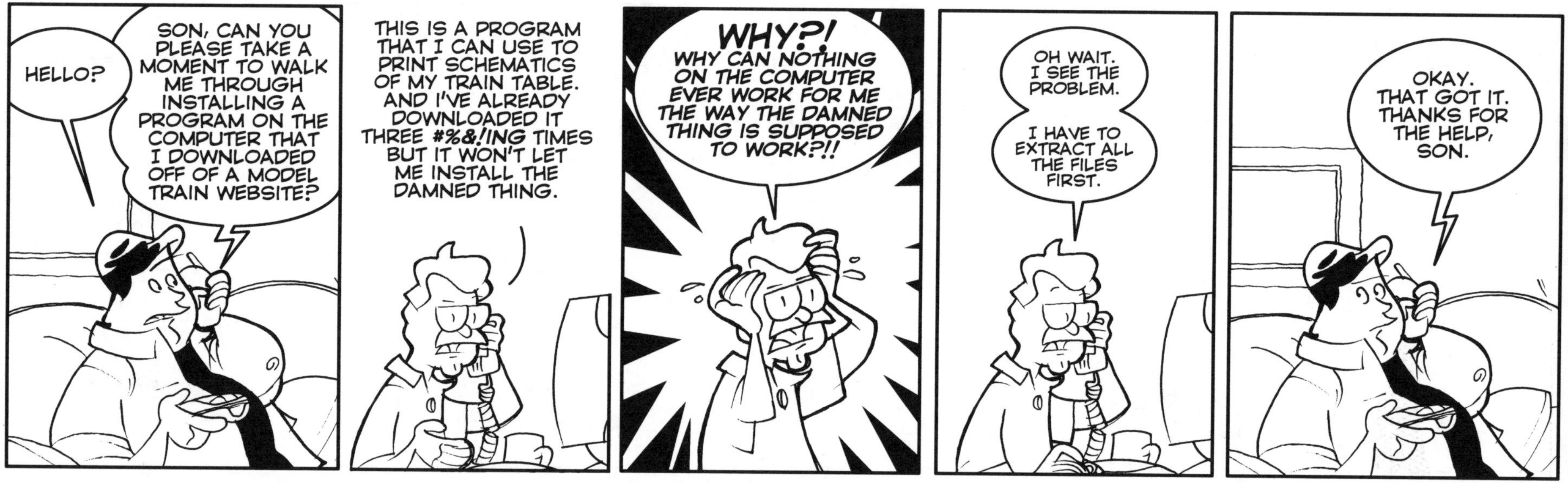
HELLO?
SON, CAN YOU PLEASE TAKE A MOMENT TO WALK ME THROUGH INSTALLING A PROGRAM ON THE COMPUTER THAT I DOWNLOADED OFF OF A MODEL TRAIN WEBSITE?
THIS IS A PROGRAM THAT I CAN USE TO PRINT SCHEMATICS OF MY TRAIN TABLE. AND I'VE ALREADY DOWNLOADED IT THREE #%&!ING TIMES BUT IT WON'T LET ME INSTALL THE DAMNED THING.
WHY?! WHY CAN NOTHING ON THE COMPUTER EVER WORK FOR ME THE WAY THE DAMNED THING IS SUPPOSED TO WORK?!!
OH WAIT. I SEE THE PROBLEM.
I HAVE TO EXTRACT ALL THE FILES FIRST.
OKAY. THAT GOT IT. THANKS FOR THE HELP, SON.

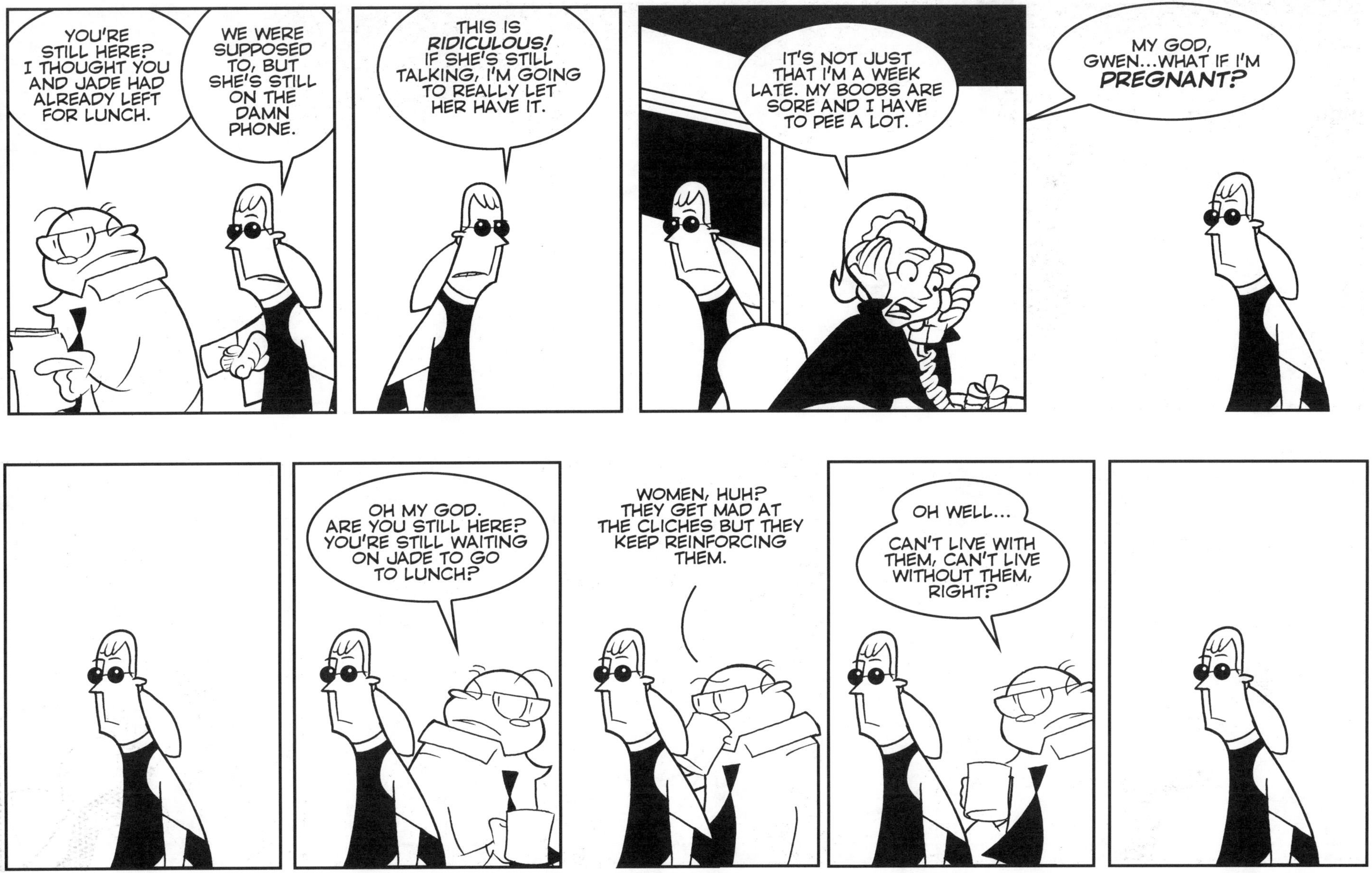
YOU'RE STILL HERE? I THOUGHT YOU AND JADE HAD ALREADY LEFT FOR LUNCH.
WE WERE SUPPOSED TO, BUT SHE'S STILL ON THE DAMN PHONE.
THIS IS *RIDICULOUS!* IF SHE'S STILL TALKING, I'M GOING TO REALLY LET HER HAVE IT.
IT'S NOT JUST THAT I'M A WEEK LATE. MY BOOBS ARE SORE AND I HAVE TO PEE A LOT.
MY GOD, GWEN...WHAT IF I'M ***PREGNANT?***
OH MY GOD. ARE YOU STILL HERE? YOU'RE STILL WAITING ON JADE TO GO TO LUNCH?
WOMEN, HUH? THEY GET MAD AT THE CLICHES BUT THEY KEEP REINFORCING THEM.
OH WELL...
CAN'T LIVE WITH THEM, CAN'T LIVE WITHOUT THEM, RIGHT?

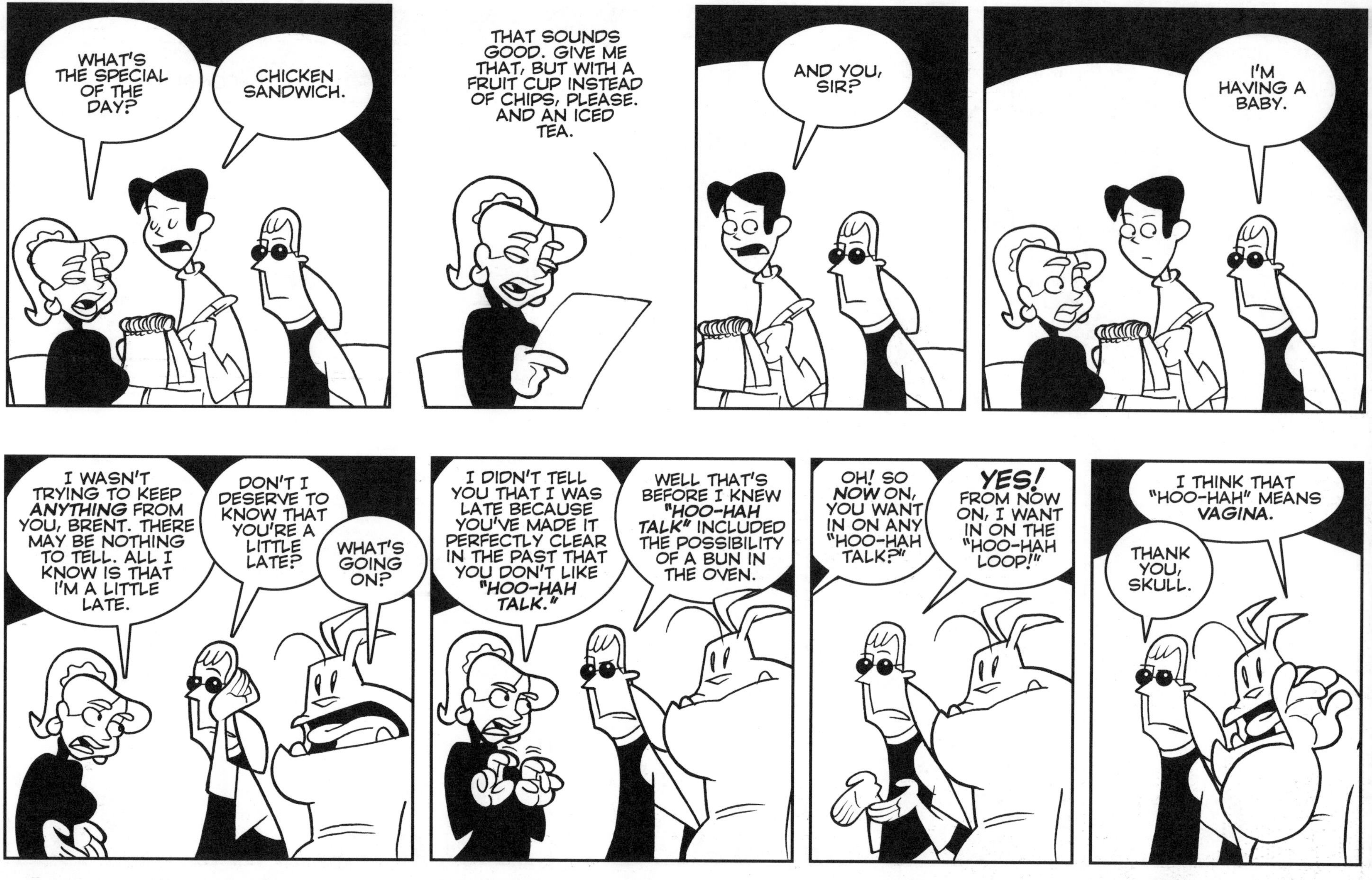
WHAT'S THE SPECIAL OF THE DAY?
CHICKEN SANDWICH.
THAT SOUNDS GOOD. GIVE ME THAT, BUT WITH A FRUIT CUP INSTEAD OF CHIPS, PLEASE. AND AN ICED TEA.
AND YOU, SIR?
I'M HAVING A BABY.
I WASN'T TRYING TO KEEP **ANYTHING** FROM YOU, BRENT. THERE MAY BE NOTHING TO TELL. ALL I KNOW IS THAT I'M A LITTLE LATE.
DON'T I DESERVE TO KNOW THAT YOU'RE A LITTLE LATE?
WHAT'S GOING ON?
I DIDN'T TELL YOU THAT I WAS LATE BECAUSE YOU'VE MADE IT PERFECTLY CLEAR IN THE PAST THAT YOU DON'T LIKE ***"HOO-HAH TALK."***
WELL THAT'S BEFORE I KNEW ***"HOO-HAH TALK"*** INCLUDED THE POSSIBILITY OF A BUN IN THE OVEN.
OH! SO **NOW** ON, YOU WANT IN ON ANY "HOO-HAH TALK?"
YES! FROM NOW ON, I WANT IN ON THE "HOO-HAH LOOP!"
I THINK THAT "HOO-HAH" MEANS **VAGINA**.
THANK YOU, SKULL.

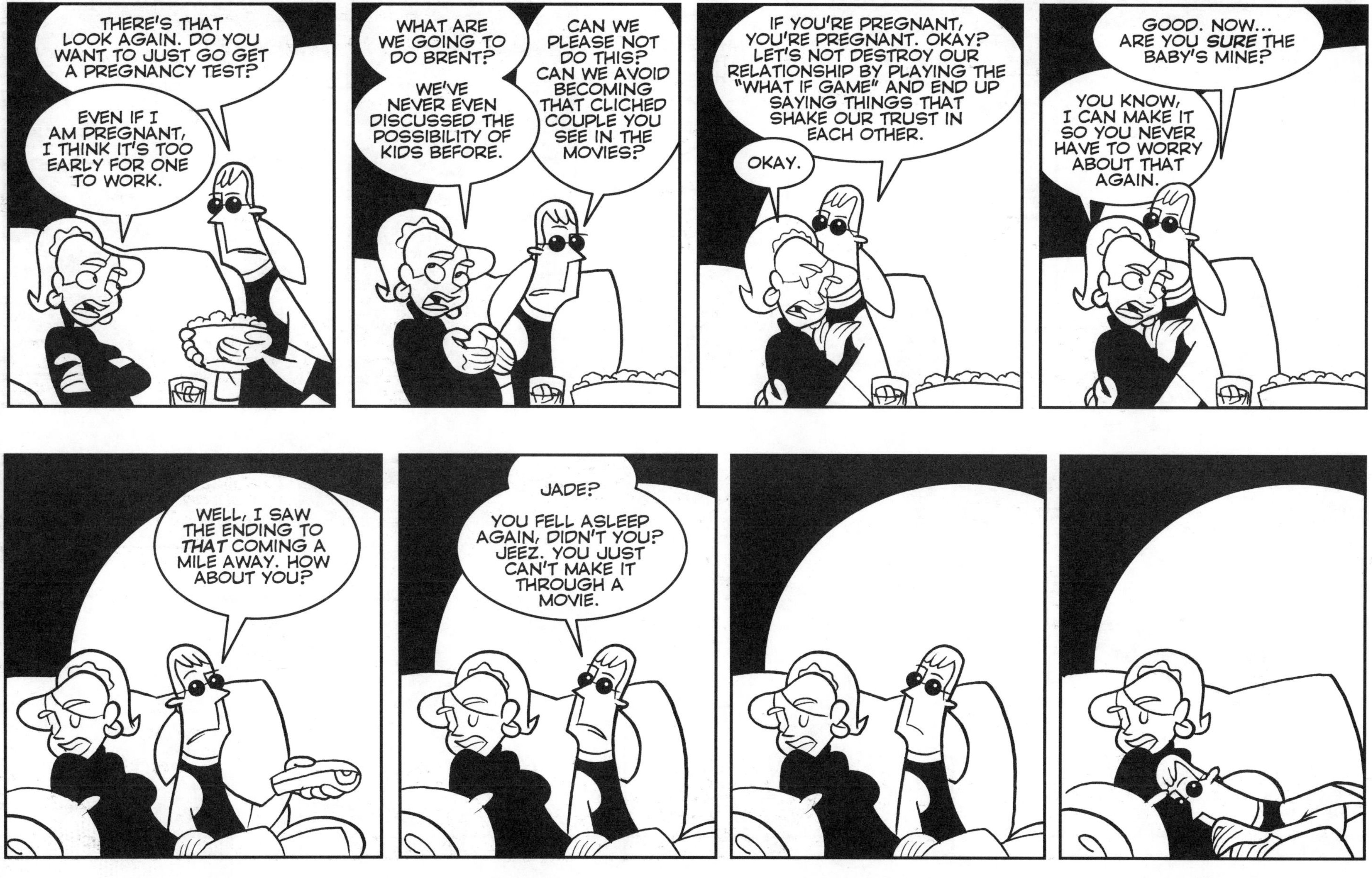
THERE'S THAT LOOK AGAIN. DO YOU WANT TO JUST GO GET A PREGNANCY TEST?
EVEN IF I AM PREGNANT, I THINK IT'S TOO EARLY FOR ONE TO WORK.
WHAT ARE WE GOING TO DO BRENT?
WE'VE NEVER EVEN DISCUSSED THE POSSIBILITY OF KIDS BEFORE.
CAN WE PLEASE NOT DO THIS? CAN WE AVOID BECOMING THAT CLICHED COUPLE YOU SEE IN THE MOVIES?
IF YOU'RE PREGNANT, YOU'RE PREGNANT. OKAY? LET'S NOT DESTROY OUR RELATIONSHIP BY PLAYING THE "WHAT IF GAME" AND END UP SAYING THINGS THAT SHAKE OUR TRUST IN EACH OTHER.
OKAY.
GOOD. NOW... ARE YOU SURE THE BABY'S MINE?
YOU KNOW, I CAN MAKE IT SO YOU NEVER HAVE TO WORRY ABOUT THAT AGAIN.
WELL, I SAW THE ENDING TO THAT COMING A MILE AWAY. HOW ABOUT YOU?
JADE?
YOU FELL ASLEEP AGAIN, DIDN'T YOU? JEEZ. YOU JUST CAN'T MAKE IT THROUGH A MOVIE.

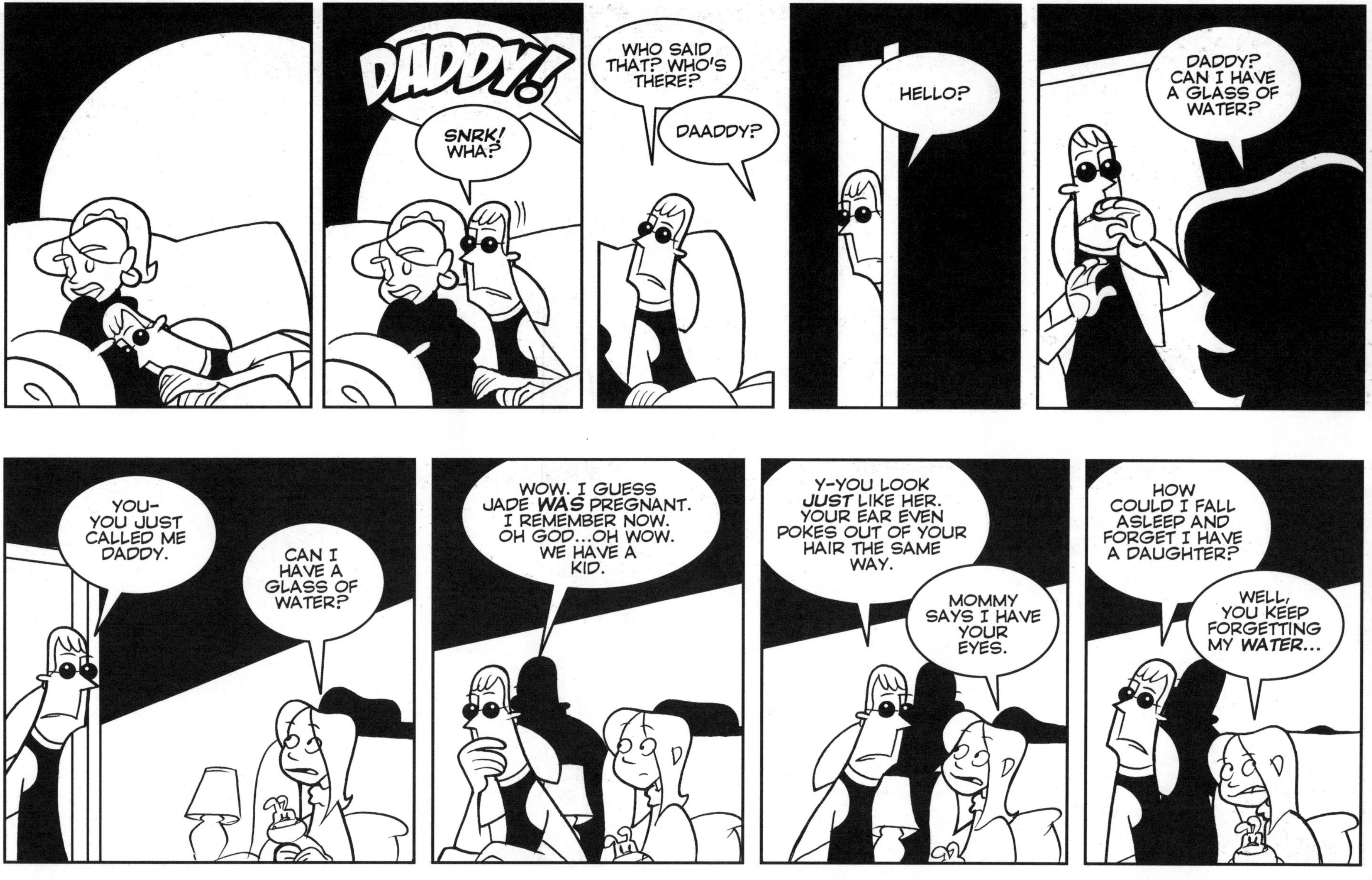
DADDY!
SNRK! WHA?
WHO SAID THAT? WHO'S THERE?
DAADDY?
HELLO?
DADDY? CAN I HAVE A GLASS OF WATER?
YOU- YOU JUST CALLED ME DADDY.
CAN I HAVE A GLASS OF WATER?
WOW. I GUESS JADE WAS PREGNANT. I REMEMBER NOW. OH GOD...OH WOW. WE HAVE A KID.
Y-YOU LOOK JUST LIKE HER. YOUR EAR EVEN POKES OUT OF YOUR HAIR THE SAME WAY.
MOMMY SAYS I HAVE YOUR EYES.
HOW COULD I FALL ASLEEP AND FORGET I HAVE A DAUGHTER?
WELL, YOU KEEP FORGETTING MY WATER...

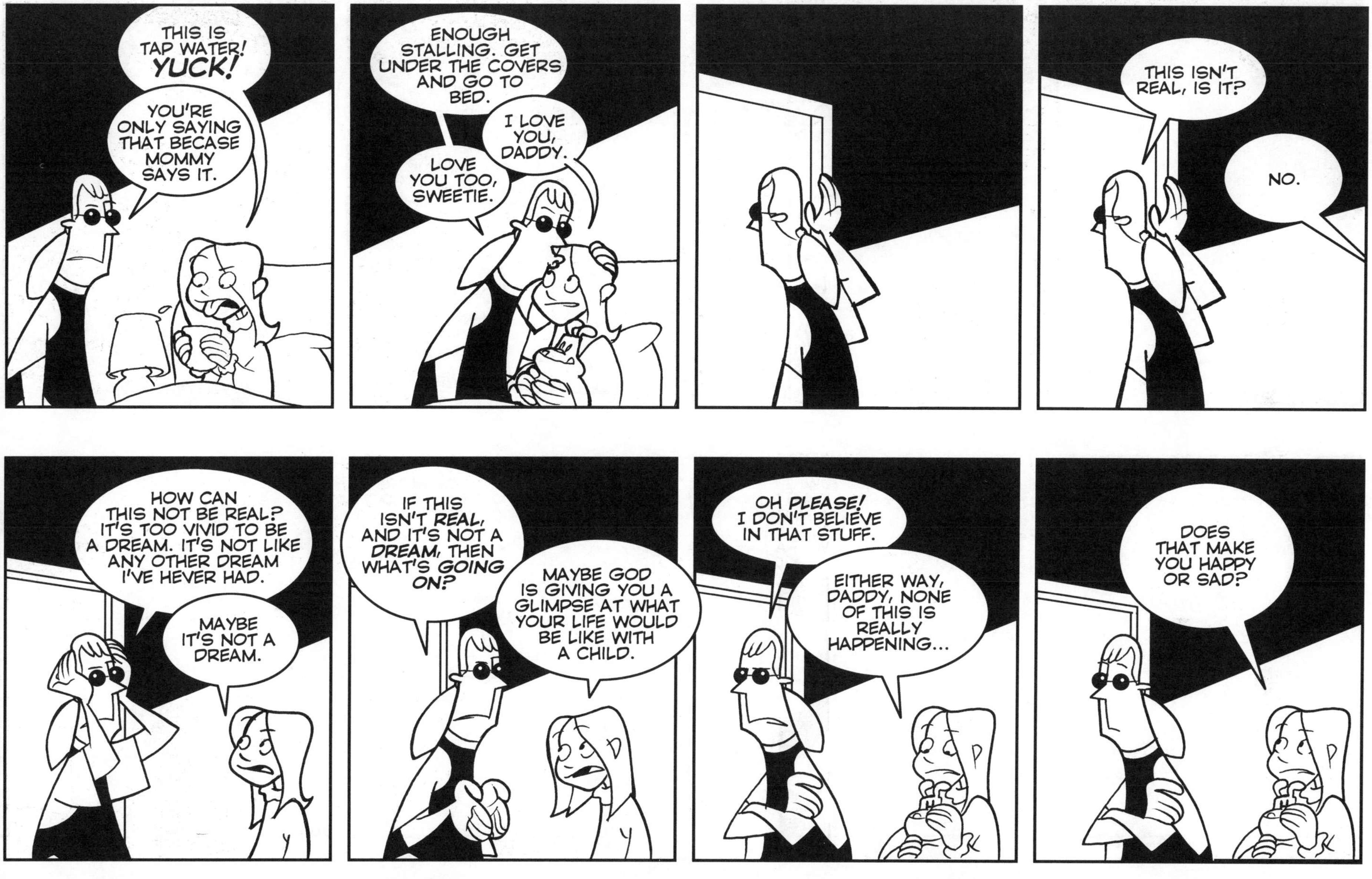
THIS IS TAP WATER! YUCK!
YOU'RE ONLY SAYING THAT BECASE MOMMY SAYS IT.
ENOUGH STALLING. GET UNDER THE COVERS AND GO TO BED.
I LOVE YOU, DADDY.
LOVE YOU TOO, SWEETIE.
THIS ISN'T REAL, IS IT?
NO.
HOW CAN THIS NOT BE REAL? IT'S TOO VIVID TO BE A DREAM. IT'S NOT LIKE ANY OTHER DREAM I'VE HEVER HAD.
MAYBE IT'S NOT A DREAM.
IF THIS ISN'T REAL, AND IT'S NOT A DREAM, THEN WHAT'S GOING ON?
MAYBE GOD IS GIVING YOU A GLIMPSE AT WHAT YOUR LIFE WOULD BE LIKE WITH A CHILD.
OH PLEASE! I DON'T BELIEVE IN THAT STUFF.
EITHER WAY, DADDY, NONE OF THIS IS REALLY HAPPENING...
DOES THAT MAKE YOU HAPPY OR SAD?

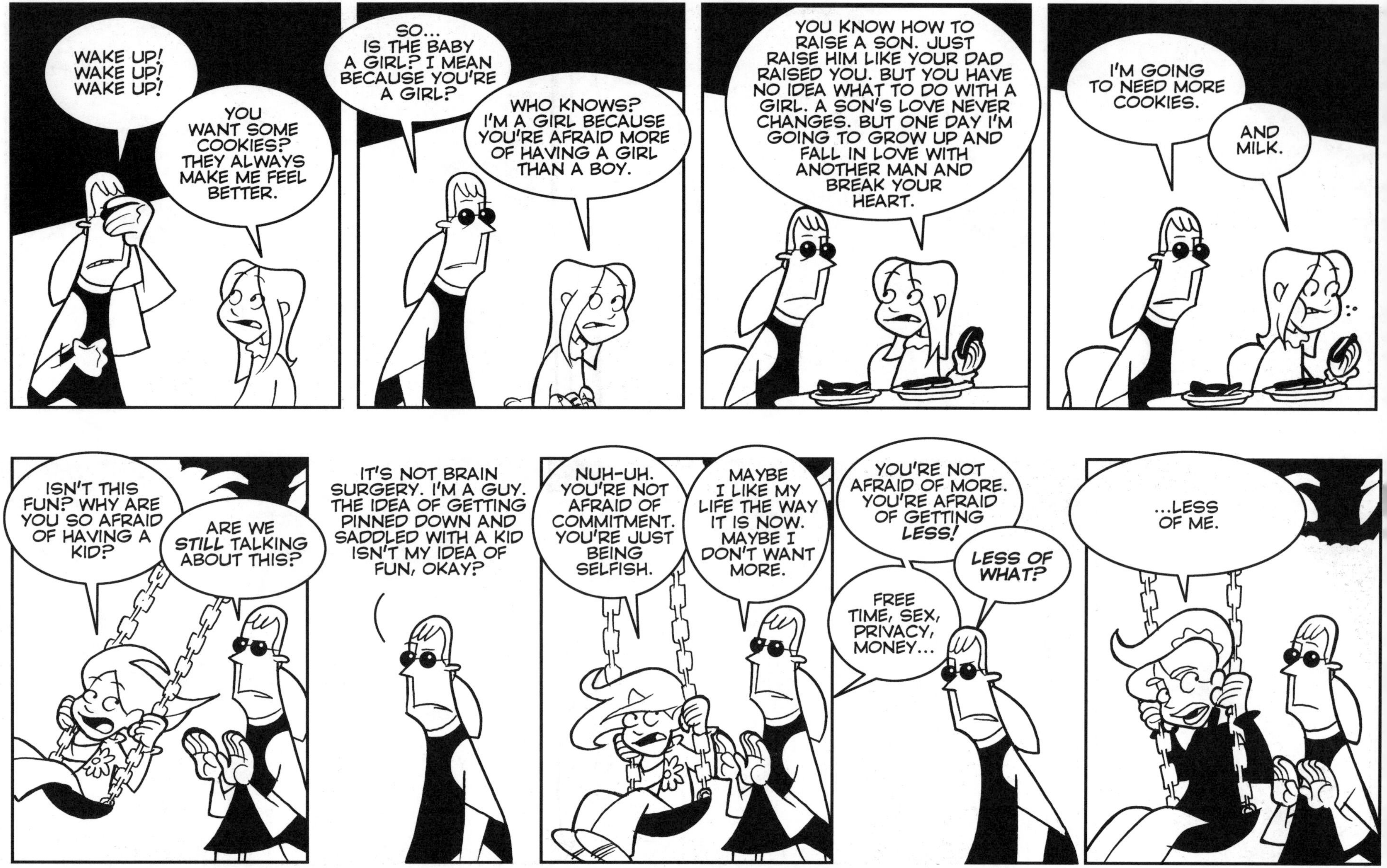
WAKE UP! WAKE UP! WAKE UP!
YOU WANT SOME COOKIES? THEY ALWAYS MAKE ME FEEL BETTER.
SO... IS THE BABY A GIRL? I MEAN BECAUSE YOU'RE A GIRL?
WHO KNOWS? I'M A GIRL BECAUSE YOU'RE AFRAID MORE OF HAVING A GIRL THAN A BOY.
YOU KNOW HOW TO RAISE A SON. JUST RAISE HIM LIKE YOUR DAD RAISED YOU. BUT YOU HAVE NO IDEA WHAT TO DO WITH A GIRL. A SON'S LOVE NEVER CHANGES. BUT ONE DAY I'M GOING TO GROW UP AND FALL IN LOVE WITH ANOTHER MAN AND BREAK YOUR HEART.
I'M GOING TO NEED MORE COOKIES.
AND MILK.
ISN'T THIS FUN? WHY ARE YOU SO AFRAID OF HAVING A KID?
ARE WE STILL TALKING ABOUT THIS?
IT'S NOT BRAIN SURGERY. I'M A GUY. THE IDEA OF GETTING PINNED DOWN AND SADDLED WITH A KID ISN'T MY IDEA OF FUN, OKAY?
NUH-UH. YOU'RE NOT AFRAID OF COMMITMENT. YOU'RE JUST BEING SELFISH.
MAYBE I LIKE MY LIFE THE WAY IT IS NOW. MAYBE I DON'T WANT MORE.
YOU'RE NOT AFRAID OF MORE. YOU'RE AFRAID OF GETTING LESS!
LESS OF WHAT?
FREE TIME, SEX, PRIVACY, MONEY...
...LESS OF ME.

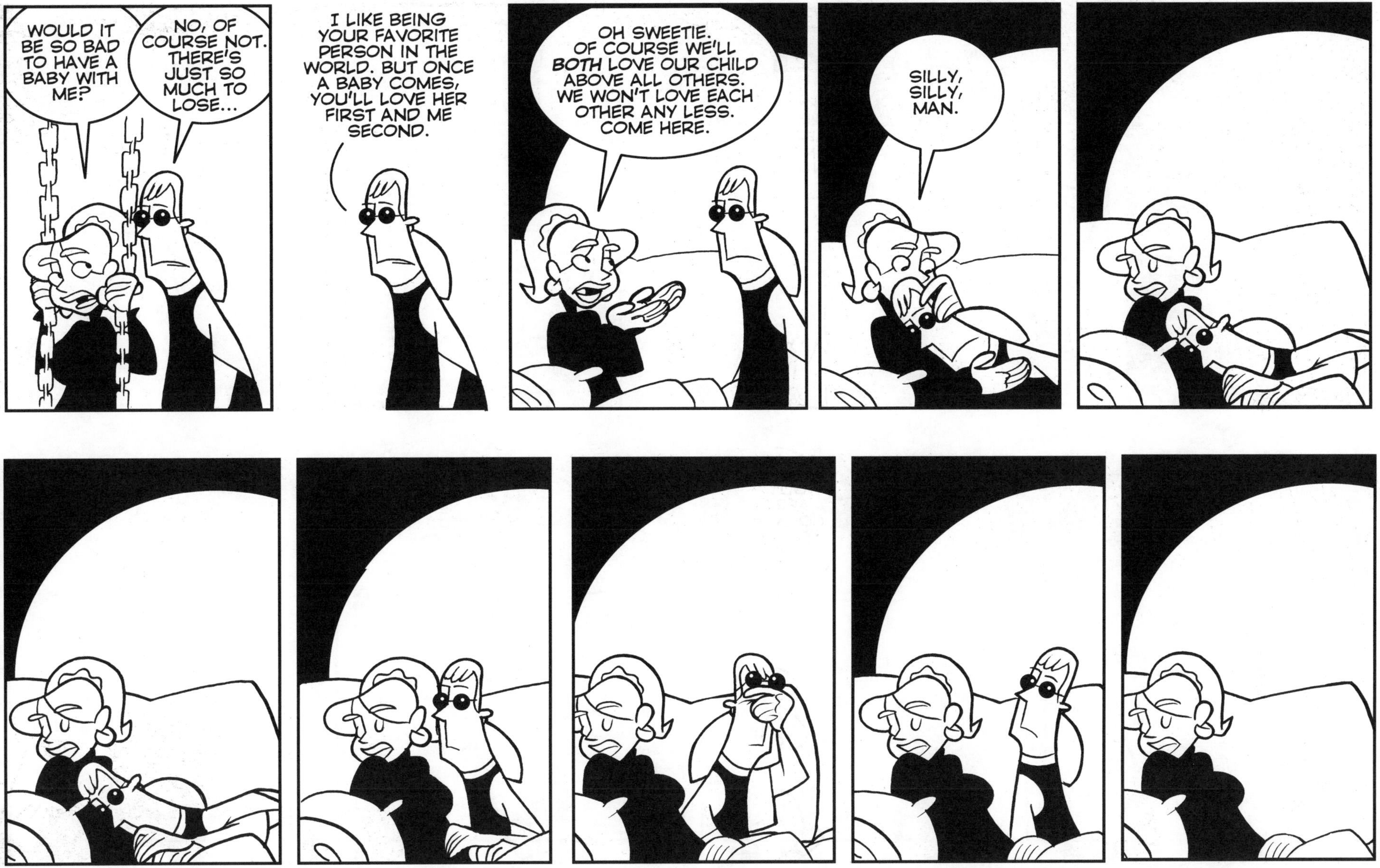
WOULD IT BE SO BAD TO HAVE A BABY WITH ME?
NO, OF COURSE NOT. THERE'S JUST SO MUCH TO LOSE...
I LIKE BEING YOUR FAVORITE PERSON IN THE WORLD. BUT ONCE A BABY COMES, YOU'LL LOVE HER FIRST AND ME SECOND.
OH SWEETIE. OF COURSE WE'LL *BOTH* LOVE OUR CHILD ABOVE ALL OTHERS. WE WON'T LOVE EACH OTHER ANY LESS. COME HERE.
SILLY, SILLY, MAN.

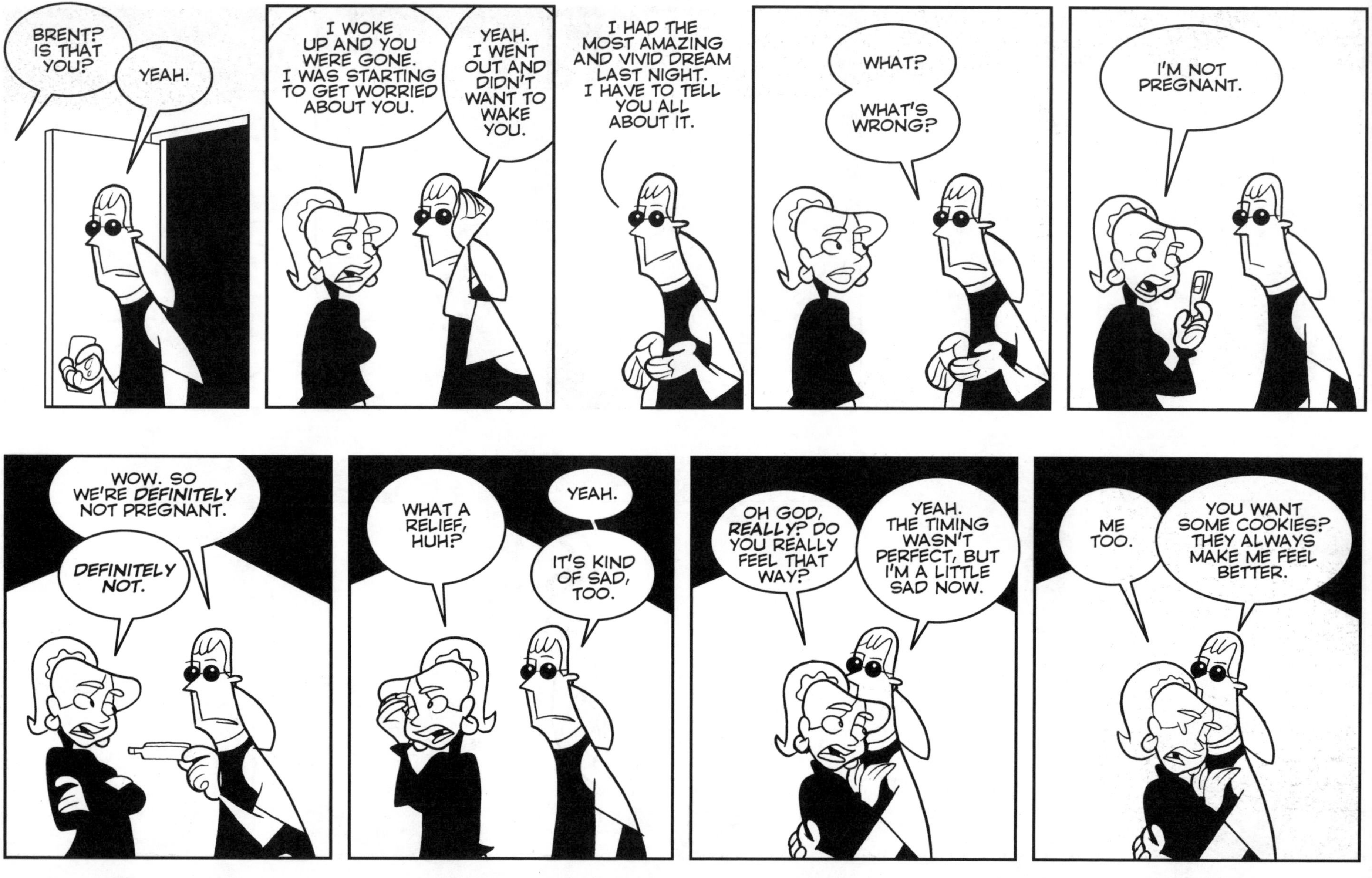
BRENT? IS THAT YOU?
YEAH.
I WOKE UP AND YOU WERE GONE. I WAS STARTING TO GET WORRIED ABOUT YOU.
YEAH. I WENT OUT AND DIDN'T WANT TO WAKE YOU.
I HAD THE MOST AMAZING AND VIVID DREAM LAST NIGHT. I HAVE TO TELL YOU ALL ABOUT IT.
WHAT?
WHAT'S WRONG?
I'M NOT PREGNANT.
WOW. SO WE'RE *DEFINITELY* NOT PREGNANT.
DEFINITELY NOT.
WHAT A RELIEF, HUH?
YEAH.
IT'S KIND OF SAD, TOO.
OH GOD, ***REALLY***? DO YOU REALLY FEEL THAT WAY?
YEAH. THE TIMING WASN'T PERFECT, BUT I'M A LITTLE SAD NOW.
ME TOO.
YOU WANT SOME COOKIES? THEY ALWAYS MAKE ME FEEL BETTER.

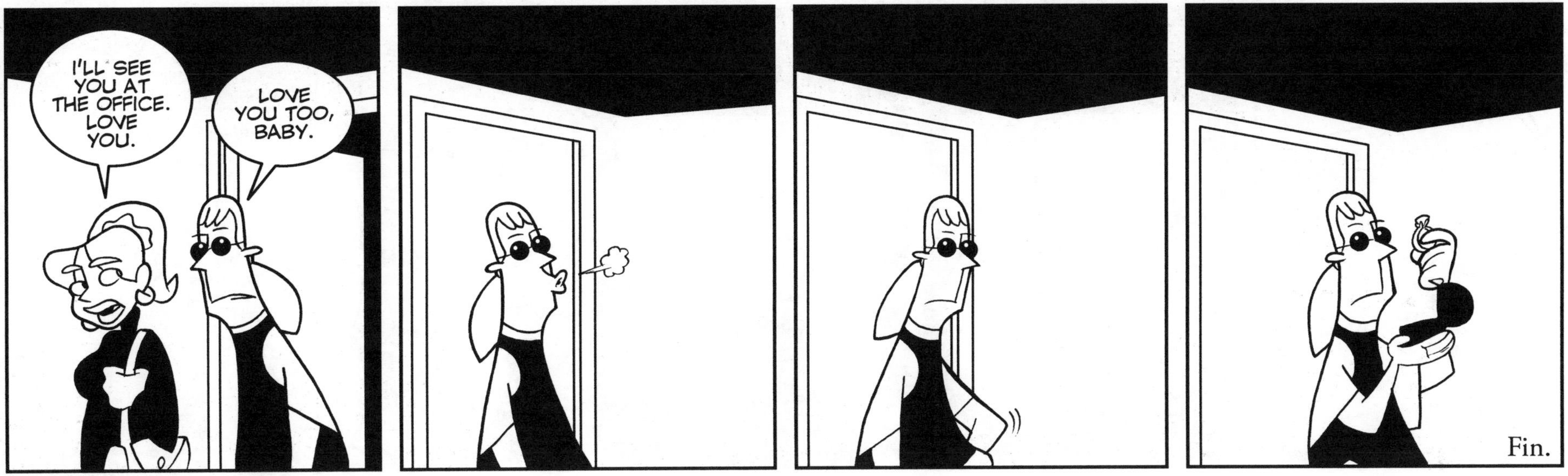
I'LL SEE YOU AT THE OFFICE. LOVE YOU.
LOVE YOU TOO, BABY.
Fin.

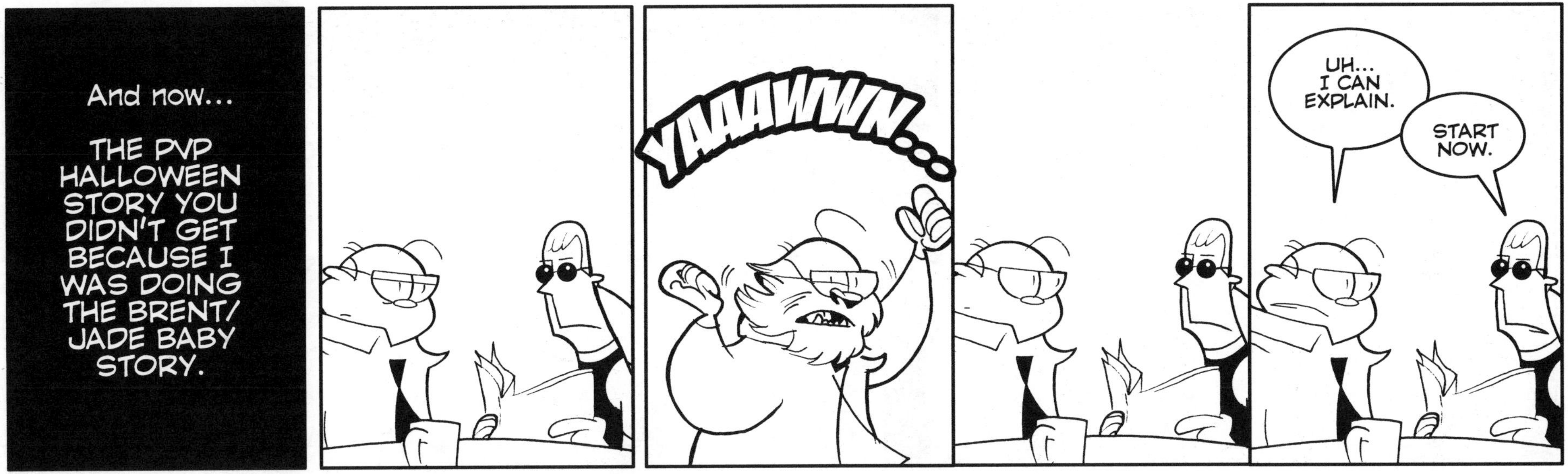
And now...
THE PVP HALLOWEEN STORY YOU DIDN'T GET BECAUSE I WAS DOING THE BRENT/JADE BABY STORY.
YAAAWWN...
UH... I CAN EXPLAIN.
START NOW.

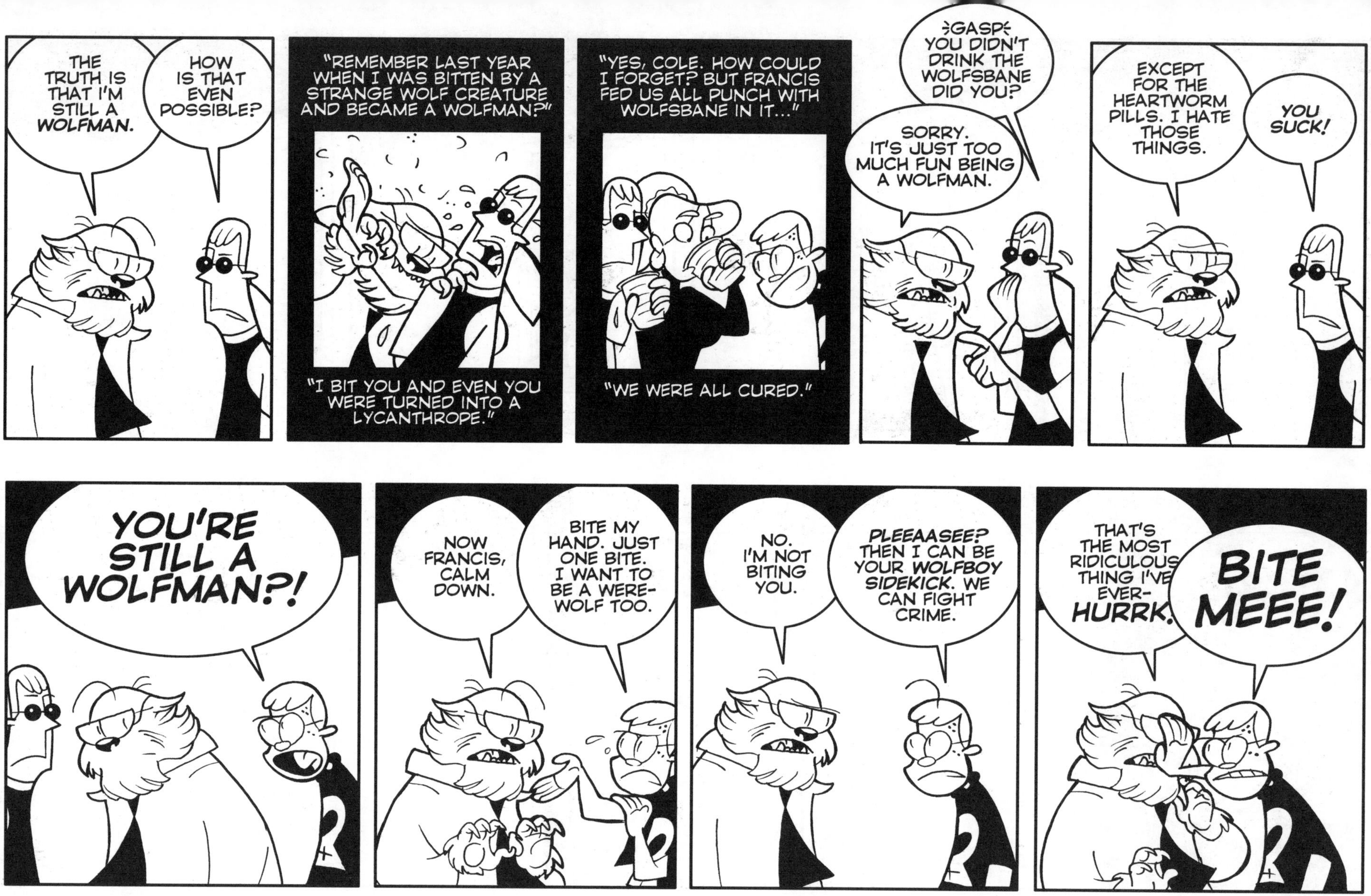
THE TRUTH IS THAT I'M STILL A WOLFMAN.
HOW IS THAT EVEN POSSIBLE?
"REMEMBER LAST YEAR WHEN I WAS BITTEN BY A STRANGE WOLF CREATURE AND BECAME A WOLFMAN?"
"I BIT YOU AND EVEN YOU WERE TURNED INTO A LYCANTHROPE."
"YES, COLE. HOW COULD I FORGET? BUT FRANCIS FED US ALL PUNCH WITH WOLFSBANE IN IT..."
"WE WERE ALL CURED."
GASP YOU DIDN'T DRINK THE WOLFSBANE DID YOU?
SORRY. IT'S JUST TOO MUCH FUN BEING A WOLFMAN.
EXCEPT FOR THE HEARTWORM PILLS. I HATE THOSE THINGS.
YOU SUCK!
YOU'RE STILL A WOLFMAN?!
NOW FRANCIS, CALM DOWN.
BITE MY HAND. JUST ONE BITE. I WANT TO BE A WERE-WOLF TOO.
NO. I'M NOT BITING YOU.
PLEEAASEE? THEN I CAN BE YOUR WOLFBOY SIDEKICK. WE CAN FIGHT CRIME.
THAT'S THE MOST RIDICULOUS THING I'VE EVER-HURRK.
BITE MEEE!

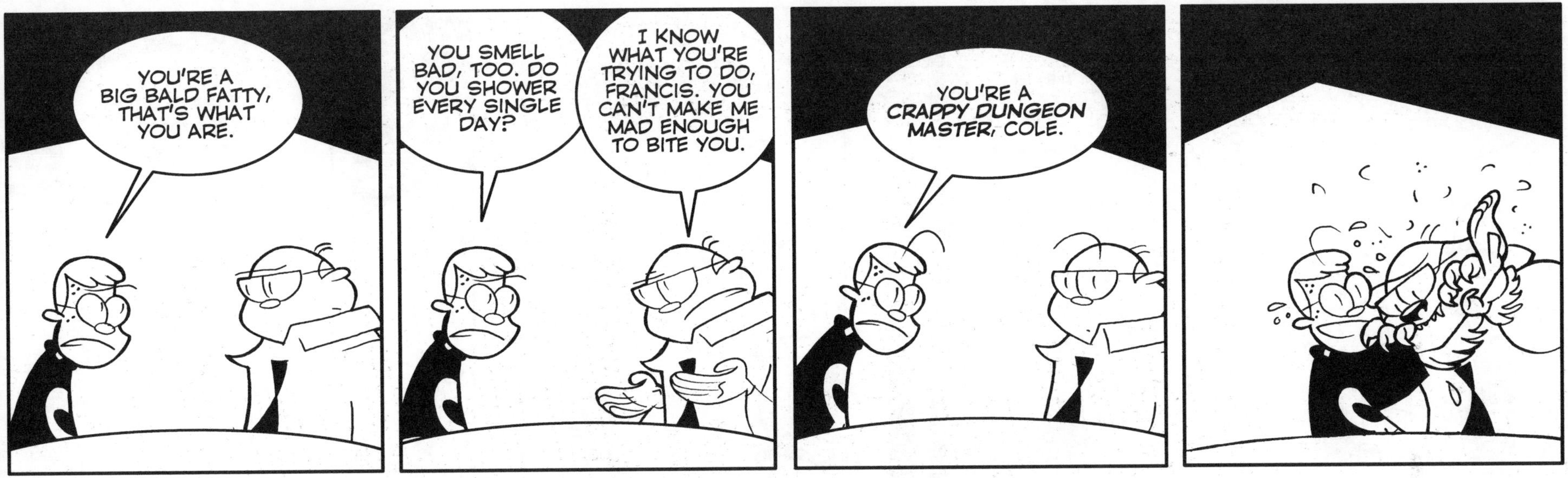
YOU'RE A BIG BALD FATTY, THAT'S WHAT YOU ARE.
YOU SMELL BAD, TOO. DO YOU SHOWER EVERY SINGLE DAY?
I KNOW WHAT YOU'RE TRYING TO DO, FRANCIS. YOU CAN'T MAKE ME MAD ENOUGH TO BITE YOU.
YOU'RE A CRAPPY DUNGEON MASTER, COLE.

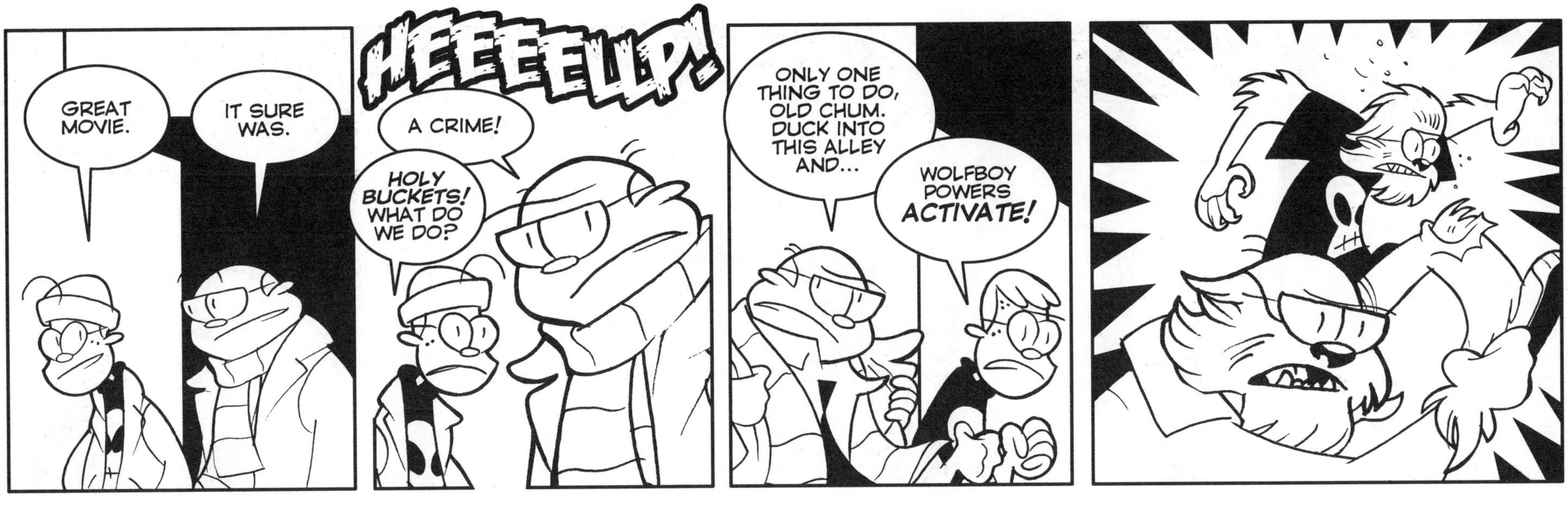
GREAT MOVIE.
IT SURE WAS.
HEEEELLP!
A CRIME!
HOLY BUCKETS! WHAT DO WE DO?
ONLY ONE THING TO DO, OLD CHUM. DUCK INTO THIS ALLEY AND...
WOLFBOY POWERS ACTIVATE!

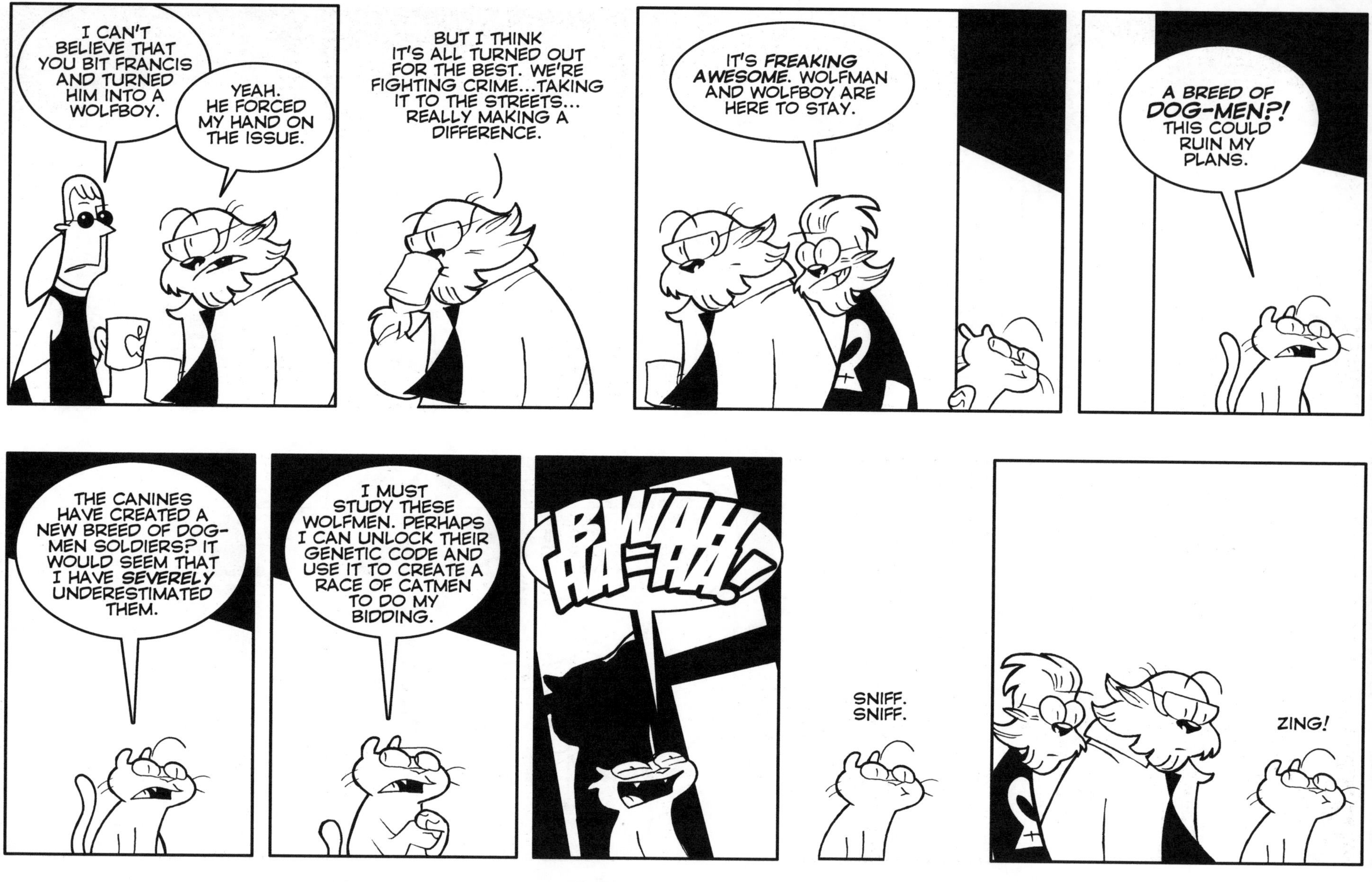
I CAN'T BELIEVE THAT YOU BIT FRANCIS AND TURNED HIM INTO A WOLFBOY.
YEAH. HE FORCED MY HAND ON THE ISSUE.
BUT I THINK IT'S ALL TURNED OUT FOR THE BEST. WE'RE FIGHTING CRIME...TAKING IT TO THE STREETS... REALLY MAKING A DIFFERENCE.
IT'S *FREAKING AWESOME*. WOLFMAN AND WOLFBOY ARE HERE TO STAY.
A BREED OF *DOG-MEN?!* THIS COULD RUIN MY PLANS.
THE CANINES HAVE CREATED A NEW BREED OF DOG-MEN SOLDIERS? IT WOULD SEEM THAT I HAVE *SEVERELY* UNDERESTIMATED THEM.
I MUST STUDY THESE WOLFMEN. PERHAPS I CAN UNLOCK THEIR GENETIC CODE AND USE IT TO CREATE A RACE OF CATMEN TO DO MY BIDDING.
BWAH HA-HA!
SNIFF. SNIFF.
ZING!

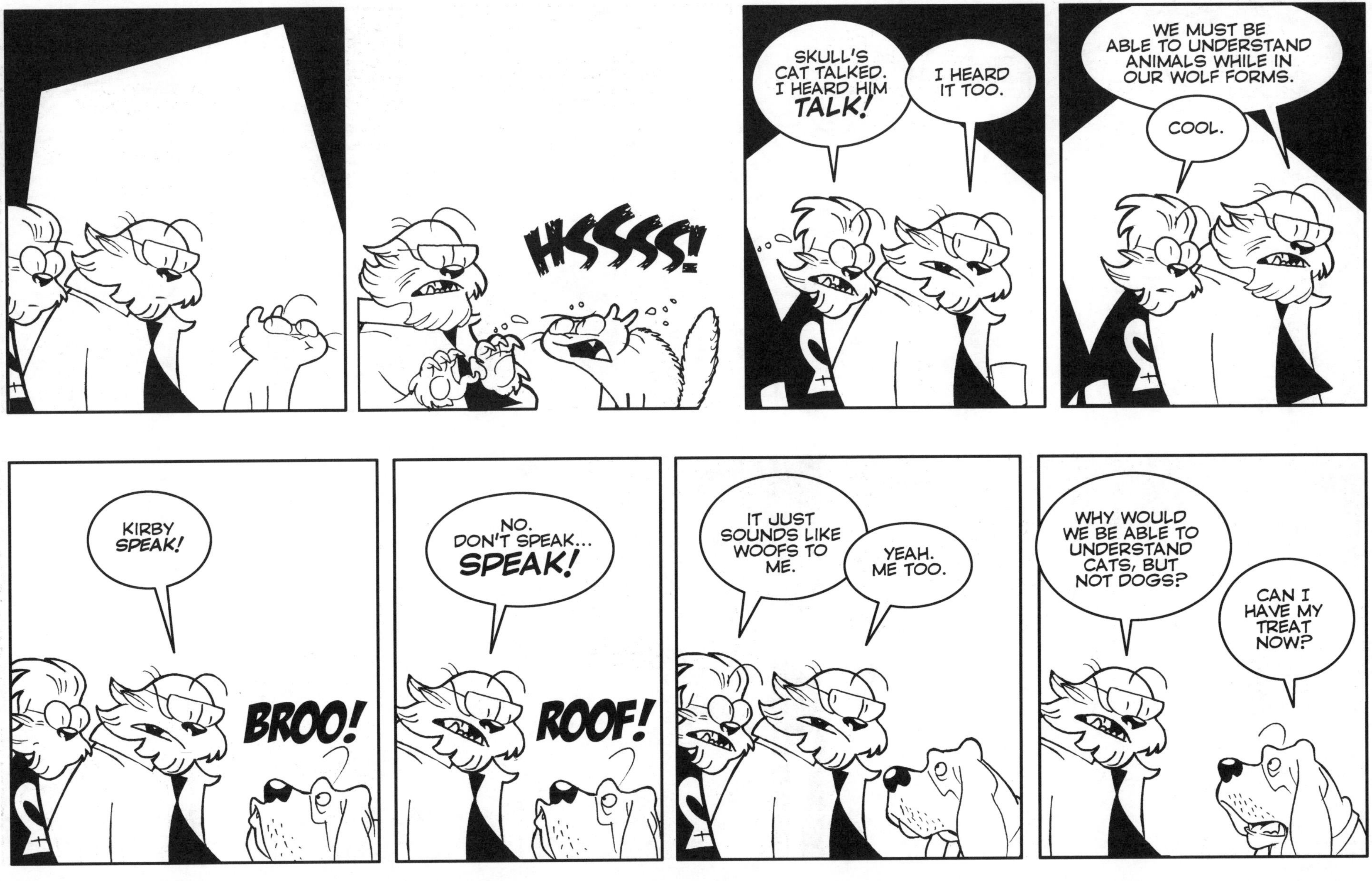
HSSSS!
SKULL'S CAT TALKED. I HEARD HIM TALK!
I HEARD IT TOO.
WE MUST BE ABLE TO UNDERSTAND ANIMALS WHILE IN OUR WOLF FORMS.
COOL.
KIRBY SPEAK!
BROO!
NO. DON'T SPEAK... SPEAK!
ROOF!
IT JUST SOUNDS LIKE WOOFS TO ME.
YEAH. ME TOO.
WHY WOULD WE BE ABLE TO UNDERSTAND CATS, BUT NOT DOGS?
CAN I HAVE MY TREAT NOW?

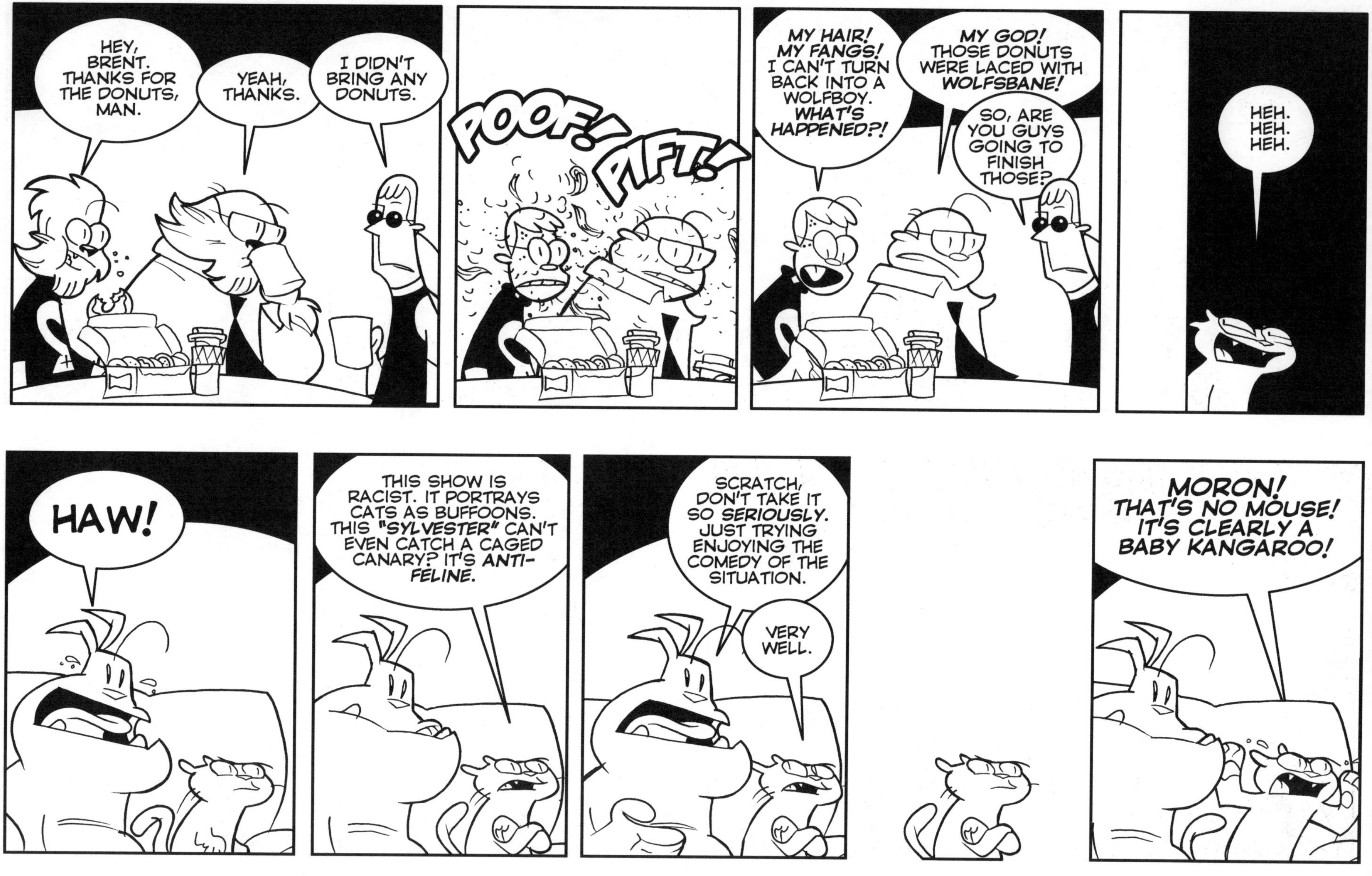

HEY, BRENT. THANKS FOR THE DONUTS, MAN.
YEAH, THANKS.
I DIDN'T BRING ANY DONUTS.
POOF!
PIFT!
MY HAIR! MY FANGS! I CAN'T TURN BACK INTO A WOLFBOY. WHAT'S HAPPENED?!
MY GOD! THOSE DONUTS WERE LACED WITH WOLFSBANE!
SO, ARE YOU GUYS GOING TO FINISH THOSE?
HEH. HEH. HEH.
HAW!
THIS SHOW IS RACIST. IT PORTRAYS CATS AS BUFFOONS. THIS "SYLVESTER" CAN'T EVEN CATCH A CAGED CANARY? IT'S ANTI-FELINE.
SCRATCH, DON'T TAKE IT SO SERIOUSLY. JUST TRYING ENJOYING THE COMEDY OF THE SITUATION.
VERY WELL.
MORON! THAT'S NO MOUSE! IT'S CLEARLY A BABY KANGAROO!

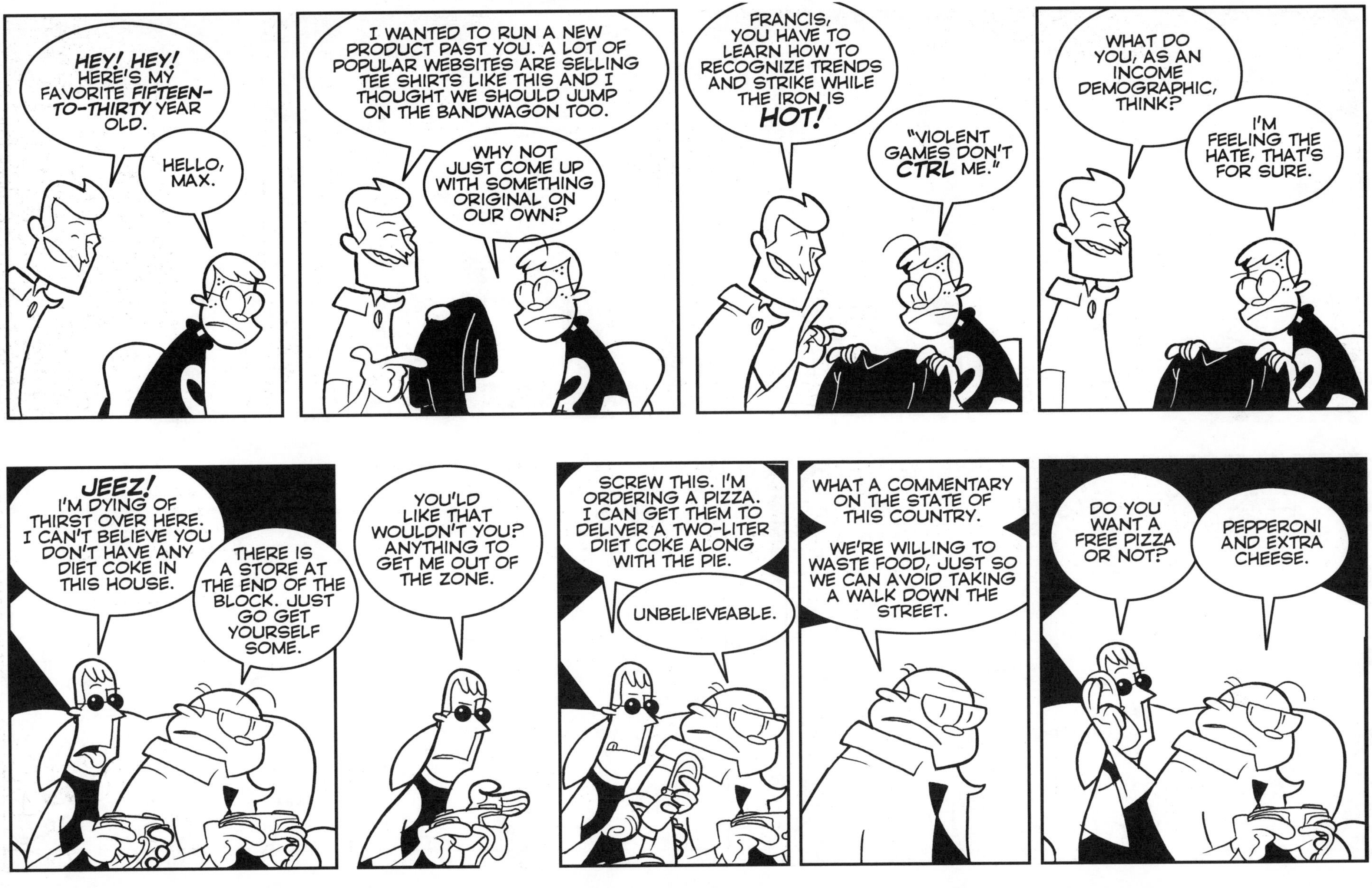

HEY! HEY! HERE'S MY FAVORITE FIFTEEN-TO-THIRTY YEAR OLD.
HELLO, MAX.
I WANTED TO RUN A NEW PRODUCT PAST YOU. A LOT OF POPULAR WEBSITES ARE SELLING TEE SHIRTS LIKE THIS AND I THOUGHT WE SHOULD JUMP ON THE BANDWAGON TOO.
WHY NOT JUST COME UP WITH SOMETHING ORIGINAL ON OUR OWN?
FRANCIS, YOU HAVE TO LEARN HOW TO RECOGNIZE TRENDS AND STRIKE WHILE THE IRON IS HOT!
"VIOLENT GAMES DON'T CTRL ME."
WHAT DO YOU, AS AN INCOME DEMOGRAPHIC, THINK?
I'M FEELING THE HATE, THAT'S FOR SURE.
JEEZ! I'M DYING OF THIRST OVER HERE. I CAN'T BELIEVE YOU DON'T HAVE ANY DIET COKE IN THIS HOUSE.
THERE IS A STORE AT THE END OF THE BLOCK. JUST GO GET YOURSELF SOME.
YOU'LD LIKE THAT WOULDN'T YOU? ANYTHING TO GET ME OUT OF THE ZONE.
SCREW THIS. I'M ORDERING A PIZZA. I CAN GET THEM TO DELIVER A TWO-LITER DIET COKE ALONG WITH THE PIE.
UNBELIEVEABLE.
WHAT A COMMENTARY ON THE STATE OF THIS COUNTRY.
WE'RE WILLING TO WASTE FOOD, JUST SO WE CAN AVOID TAKING A WALK DOWN THE STREET.
DO YOU WANT A FREE PIZZA OR NOT?
PEPPERONI AND EXTRA CHEESE.

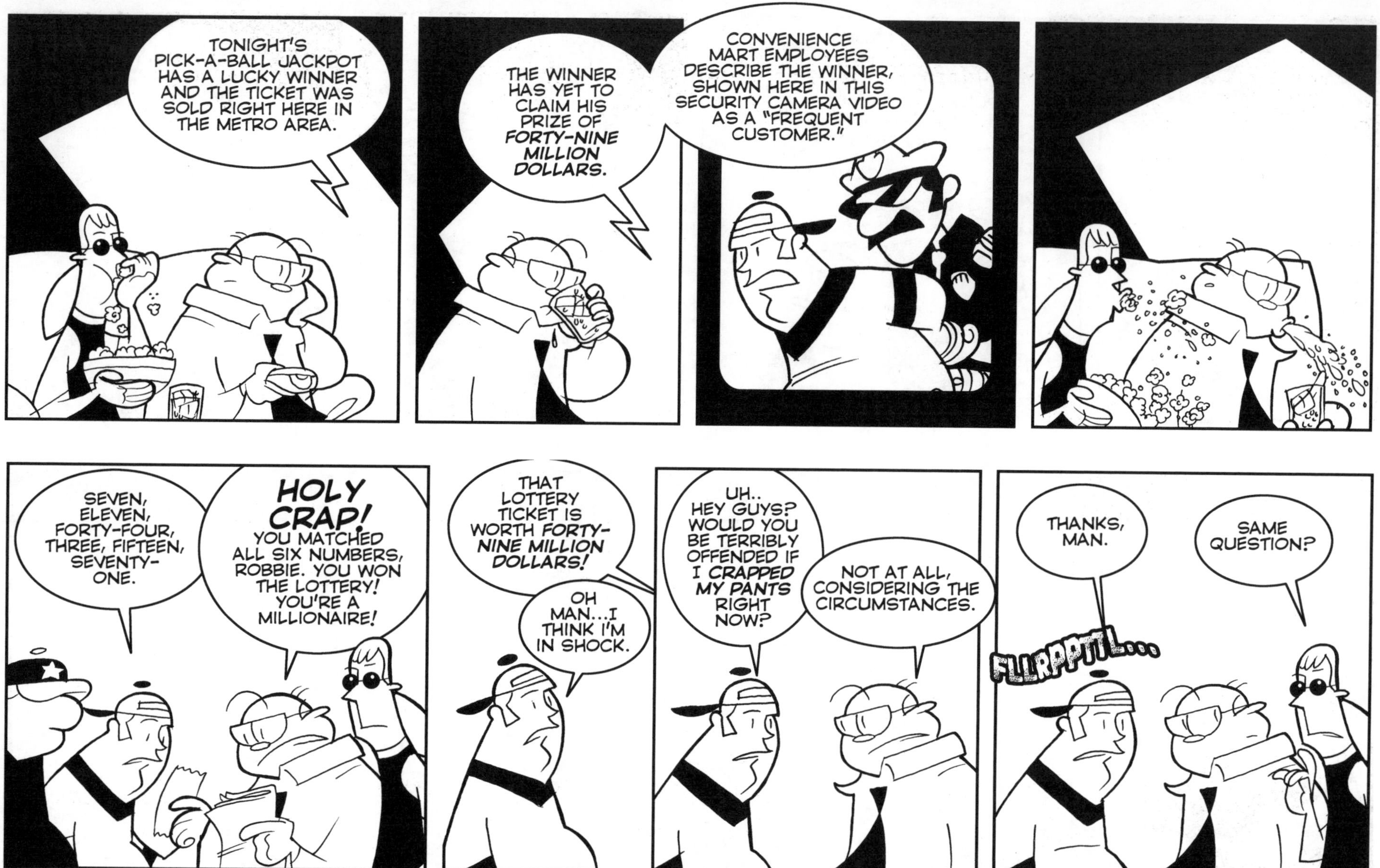
TONIGHT'S PICK-A-BALL JACKPOT HAS A LUCKY WINNER AND THE TICKET WAS SOLD RIGHT HERE IN THE METRO AREA.
THE WINNER HAS YET TO CLAIM HIS PRIZE OF *FORTY-NINE MILLION DOLLARS*.
CONVENIENCE MART EMPLOYEES DESCRIBE THE WINNER, SHOWN HERE IN THIS SECURITY CAMERA VIDEO AS A "FREQUENT CUSTOMER."
SEVEN, ELEVEN, FORTY-FOUR, THREE, FIFTEEN, SEVENTY-ONE.
HOLY CRAP! YOU MATCHED ALL SIX NUMBERS, ROBBIE. YOU WON THE LOTTERY! YOU'RE A MILLIONAIRE!
THAT LOTTERY TICKET IS WORTH *FORTY-NINE MILLION DOLLARS!*
OH MAN...I THINK I'M IN SHOCK.
UH.. HEY GUYS? WOULD YOU BE TERRIBLY OFFENDED IF I *CRAPPED MY PANTS* RIGHT NOW?
NOT AT ALL, CONSIDERING THE CIRCUMSTANCES.
FLLRPPTTL...
THANKS, MAN.
SAME QUESTION?

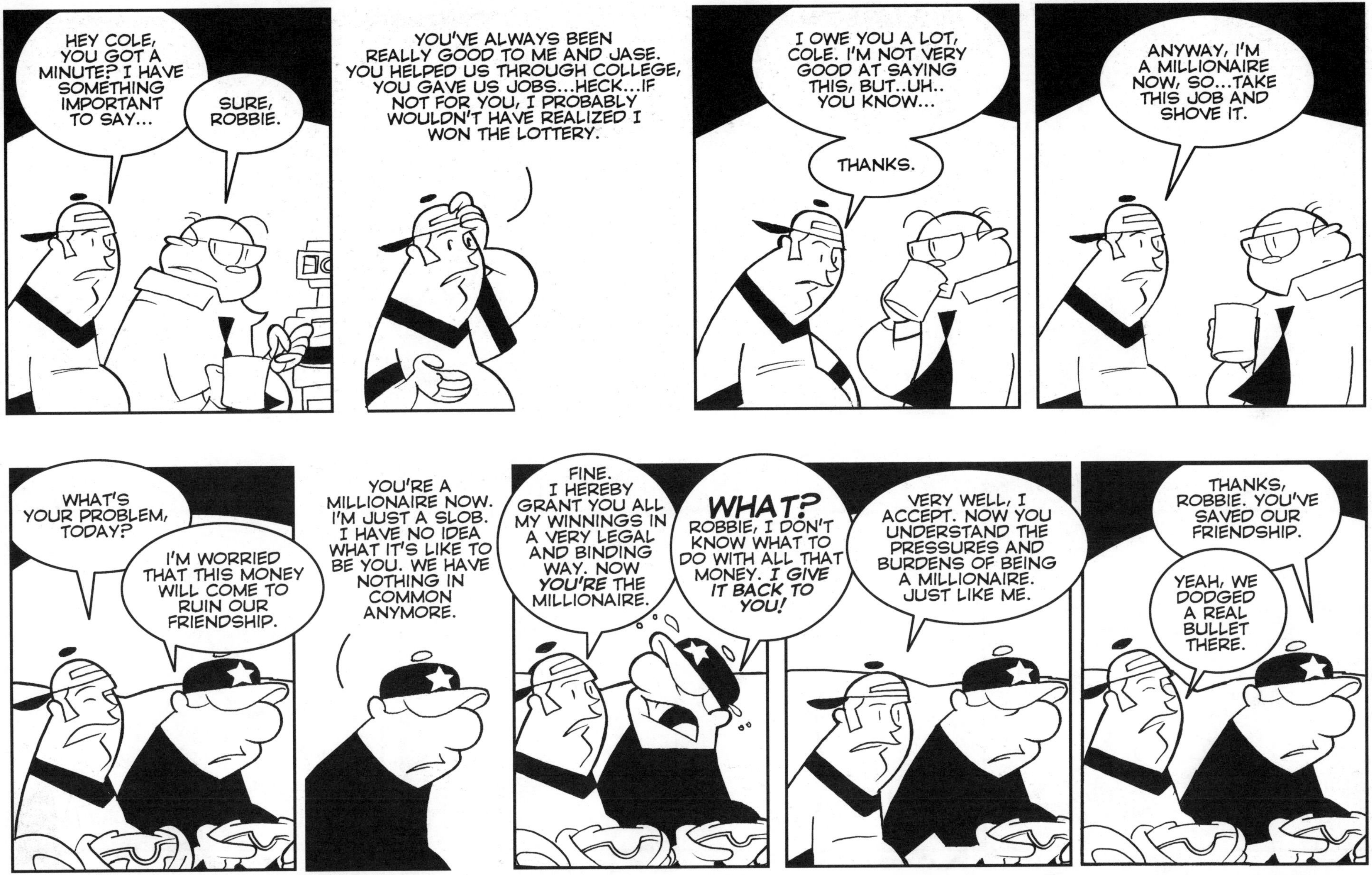
HEY COLE, YOU GOT A MINUTE? I HAVE SOMETHING IMPORTANT TO SAY...
SURE, ROBBIE.
YOU'VE ALWAYS BEEN REALLY GOOD TO ME AND JASE. YOU HELPED US THROUGH COLLEGE, YOU GAVE US JOBS...HECK...IF NOT FOR YOU, I PROBABLY WOULDN'T HAVE REALIZED I WON THE LOTTERY.
I OWE YOU A LOT, COLE. I'M NOT VERY GOOD AT SAYING THIS, BUT..UH.. YOU KNOW...
THANKS.
ANYWAY, I'M A MILLIONAIRE NOW, SO...TAKE THIS JOB AND SHOVE IT.
WHAT'S YOUR PROBLEM, TODAY?
I'M WORRIED THAT THIS MONEY WILL COME TO RUIN OUR FRIENDSHIP.
YOU'RE A MILLIONAIRE NOW. I'M JUST A SLOB. I HAVE NO IDEA WHAT IT'S LIKE TO BE YOU. WE HAVE NOTHING IN COMMON ANYMORE.
FINE. I HEREBY GRANT YOU ALL MY WINNINGS IN A VERY LEGAL AND BINDING WAY. NOW *YOU'RE* THE MILLIONAIRE.
WHAT? ROBBIE, I DON'T KNOW WHAT TO DO WITH ALL THAT MONEY. *I GIVE IT BACK TO YOU!*
VERY WELL, I ACCEPT. NOW YOU UNDERSTAND THE PRESSURES AND BURDENS OF BEING A MILLIONAIRE. JUST LIKE ME.
THANKS, ROBBIE. YOU'VE SAVED OUR FRIENDSHIP.
YEAH, WE DODGED A REAL BULLET THERE.

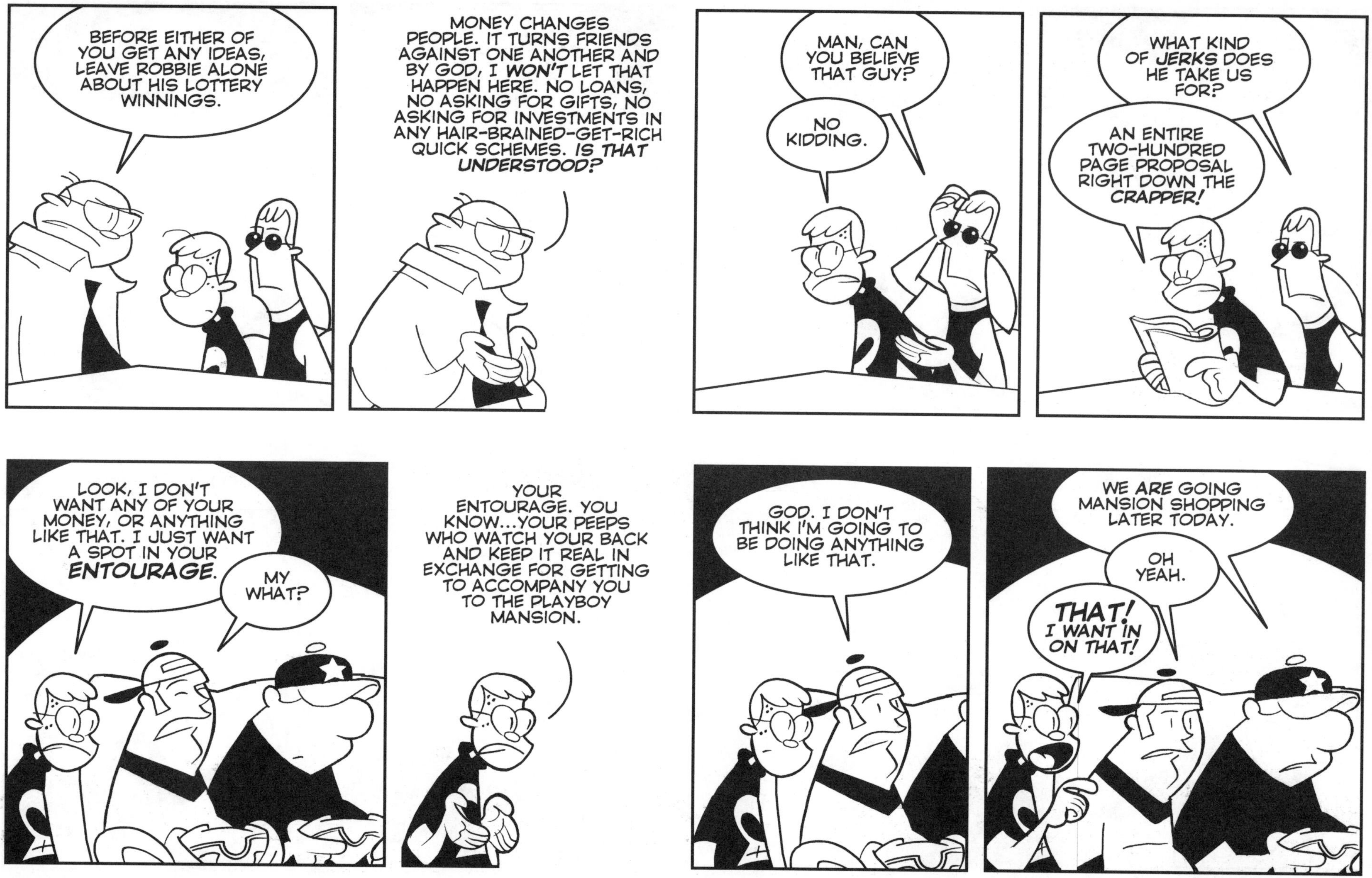
BEFORE EITHER OF YOU GET ANY IDEAS, LEAVE ROBBIE ALONE ABOUT HIS LOTTERY WINNINGS.
MONEY CHANGES PEOPLE. IT TURNS FRIENDS AGAINST ONE ANOTHER AND BY GOD, I ***WON'T*** LET THAT HAPPEN HERE. NO LOANS, NO ASKING FOR GIFTS, NO ASKING FOR INVESTMENTS IN ANY HAIR-BRAINED-GET-RICH QUICK SCHEMES. ***IS THAT UNDERSTOOD?***
MAN, CAN YOU BELIEVE THAT GUY?
NO KIDDING.
WHAT KIND OF ***JERKS*** DOES HE TAKE US FOR?
AN ENTIRE TWO-HUNDRED PAGE PROPOSAL RIGHT DOWN THE ***CRAPPER!***
LOOK, I DON'T WANT ANY OF YOUR MONEY, OR ANYTHING LIKE THAT. I JUST WANT A SPOT IN YOUR ***ENTOURAGE***.
MY WHAT?
YOUR ENTOURAGE. YOU KNOW...YOUR PEEPS WHO WATCH YOUR BACK AND KEEP IT REAL IN EXCHANGE FOR GETTING TO ACCOMPANY YOU TO THE PLAYBOY MANSION.
GOD. I DON'T THINK I'M GOING TO BE DOING ANYTHING LIKE THAT.
WE ***ARE*** GOING MANSION SHOPPING LATER TODAY.
OH YEAH.
THAT! I WANT IN ON THAT!

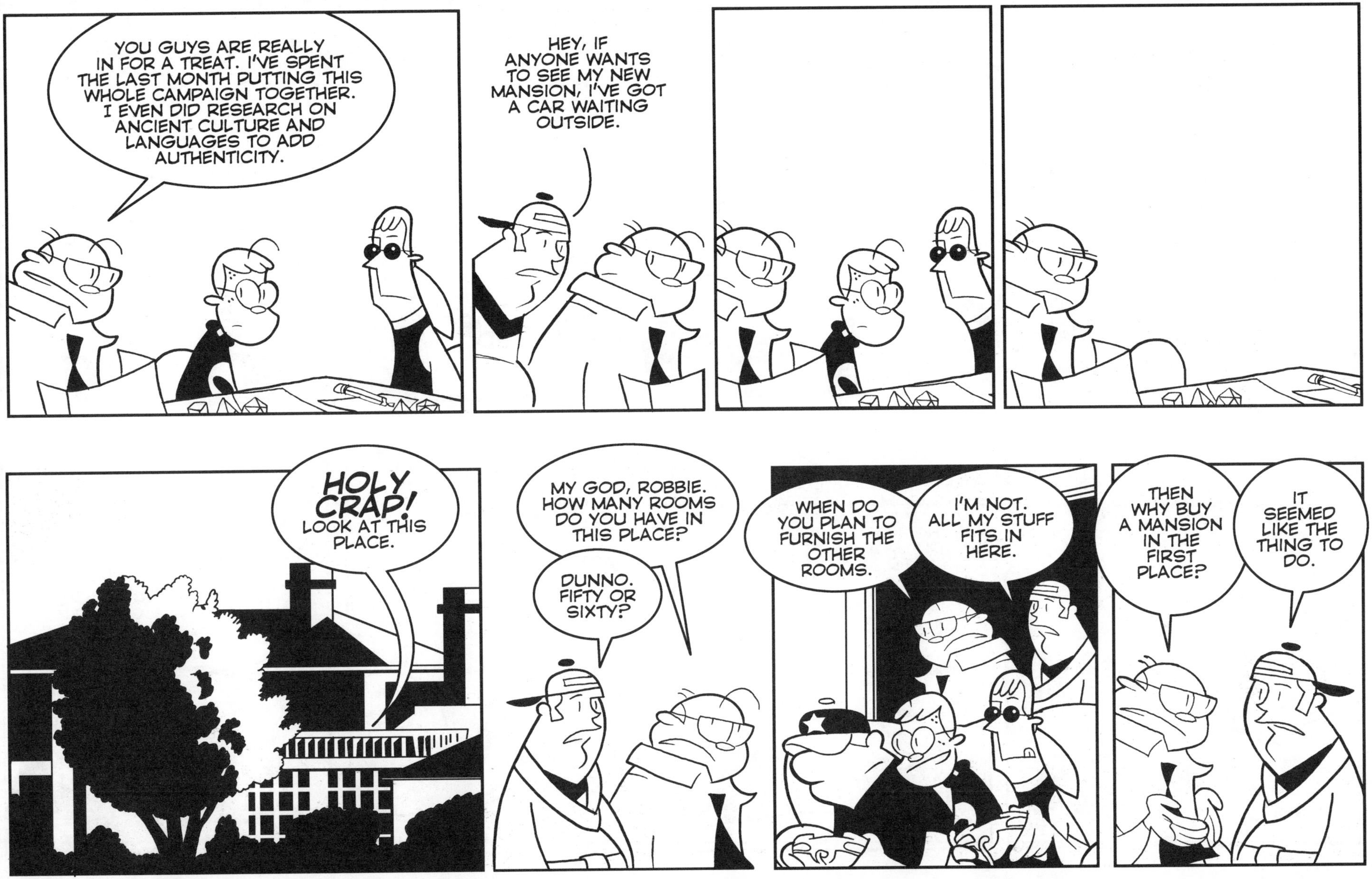
YOU GUYS ARE REALLY IN FOR A TREAT. I'VE SPENT THE LAST MONTH PUTTING THIS WHOLE CAMPAIGN TOGETHER. I EVEN DID RESEARCH ON ANCIENT CULTURE AND LANGUAGES TO ADD AUTHENTICITY.
HEY, IF ANYONE WANTS TO SEE MY NEW MANSION, I'VE GOT A CAR WAITING OUTSIDE.
HOLY CRAP! LOOK AT THIS PLACE.
MY GOD, ROBBIE. HOW MANY ROOMS DO YOU HAVE IN THIS PLACE?
DUNNO. FIFTY OR SIXTY?
WHEN DO YOU PLAN TO FURNISH THE OTHER ROOMS.
I'M NOT. ALL MY STUFF FITS IN HERE.
THEN WHY BUY A MANSION IN THE FIRST PLACE?
IT SEEMED LIKE THE THING TO DO.

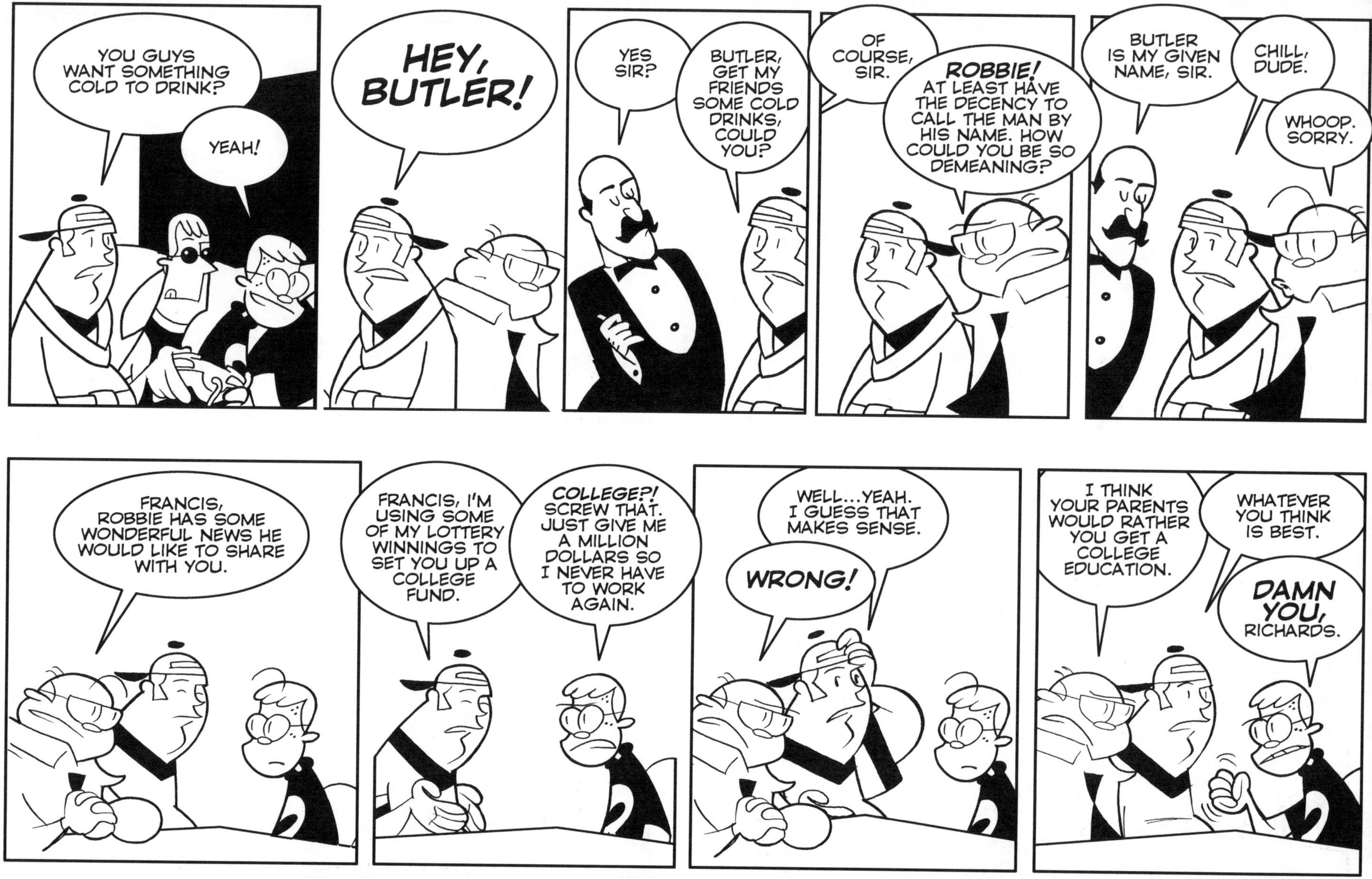
YOU GUYS WANT SOMETHING COLD TO DRINK?
YEAH!
HEY, BUTLER!
YES SIR?
BUTLER, GET MY FRIENDS SOME COLD DRINKS, COULD YOU?
OF COURSE, SIR.
ROBBIE! AT LEAST HAVE THE DECENCY TO CALL THE MAN BY HIS NAME. HOW COULD YOU BE SO DEMEANING?
BUTLER IS MY GIVEN NAME, SIR.
CHILL, DUDE.
WHOOP. SORRY.
FRANCIS, ROBBIE HAS SOME WONDERFUL NEWS HE WOULD LIKE TO SHARE WITH YOU.
FRANCIS, I'M USING SOME OF MY LOTTERY WINNINGS TO SET YOU UP A COLLEGE FUND.
COLLEGE?! SCREW THAT. JUST GIVE ME A MILLION DOLLARS SO I NEVER HAVE TO WORK AGAIN.
WELL...YEAH. I GUESS THAT MAKES SENSE.
WRONG!
I THINK YOUR PARENTS WOULD RATHER YOU GET A COLLEGE EDUCATION.
WHATEVER YOU THINK IS BEST.
DAMN YOU, RICHARDS.

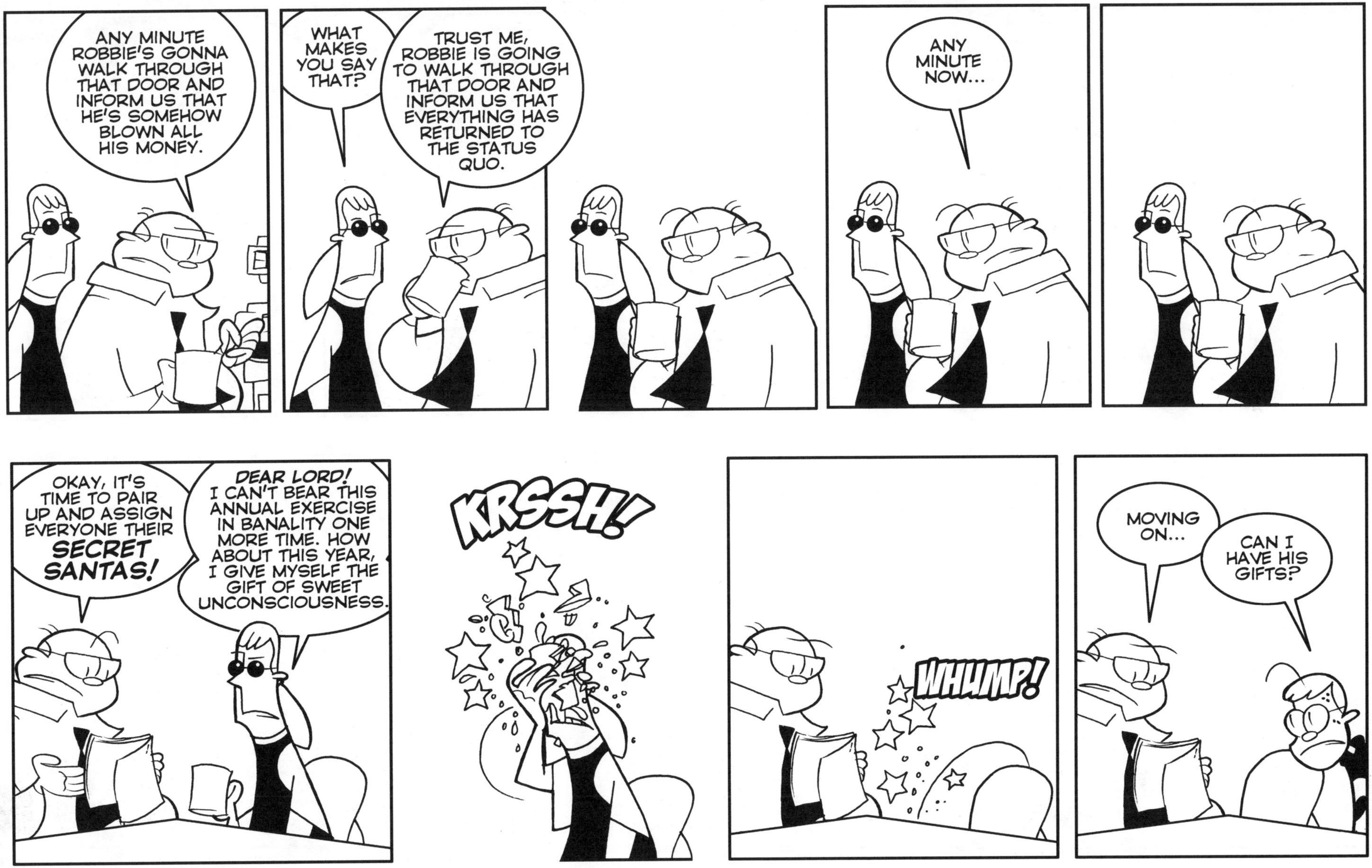
ANY MINUTE ROBBIE'S GONNA WALK THROUGH THAT DOOR AND INFORM US THAT HE'S SOMEHOW BLOWN ALL HIS MONEY.
WHAT MAKES YOU SAY THAT?
TRUST ME, ROBBIE IS GOING TO WALK THROUGH THAT DOOR AND INFORM US THAT EVERYTHING HAS RETURNED TO THE STATUS QUO.
ANY MINUTE NOW...
OKAY, IT'S TIME TO PAIR UP AND ASSIGN EVERYONE THEIR SECRET SANTAS!
DEAR LORD! I CAN'T BEAR THIS ANNUAL EXERCISE IN BANALITY ONE MORE TIME. HOW ABOUT THIS YEAR, I GIVE MYSELF THE GIFT OF SWEET UNCONSCIOUSNESS.
KRSSH!
WHUMP!
MOVING ON...
CAN I HAVE HIS GIFTS?

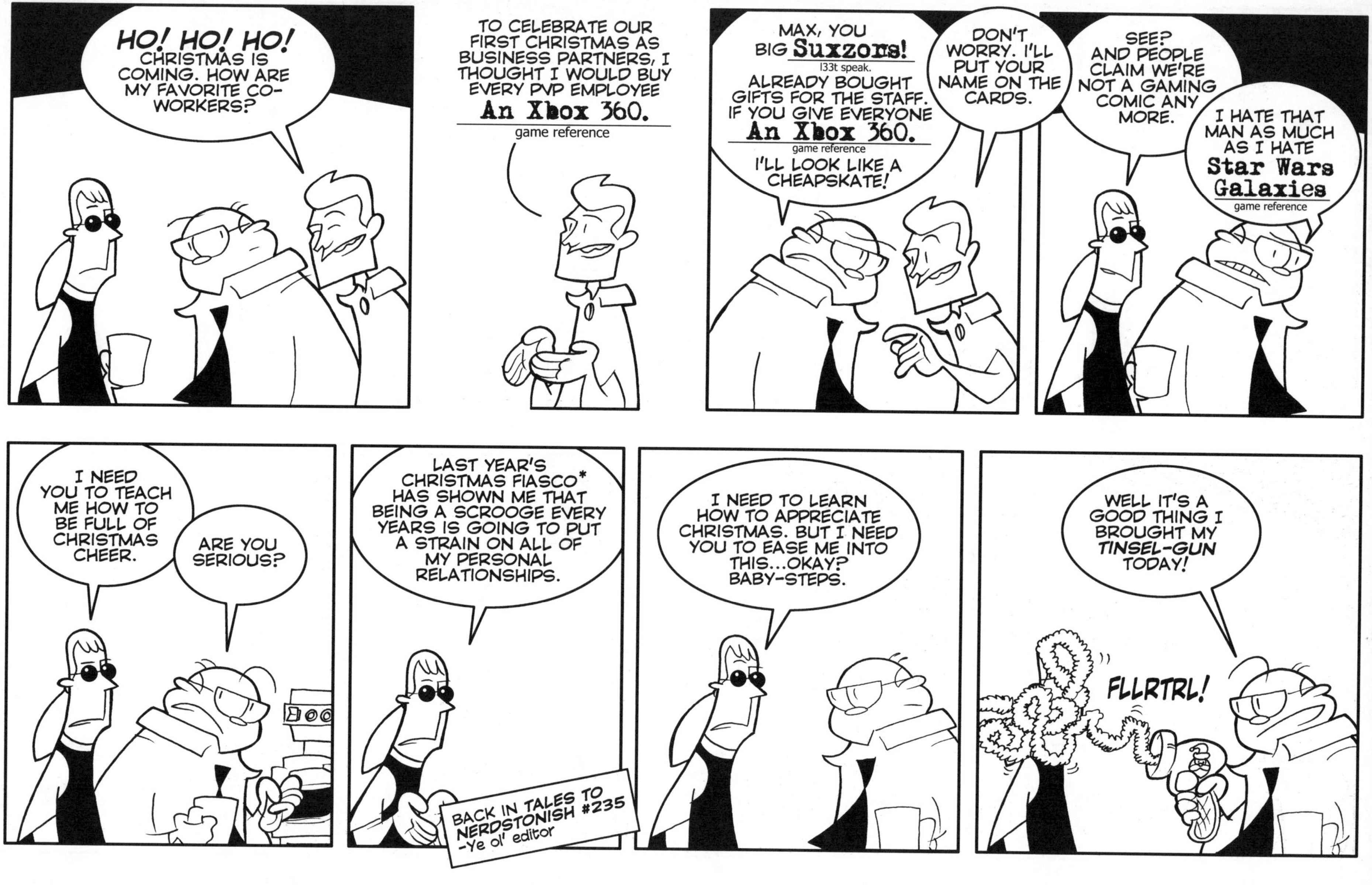
HO! HO! HO! CHRISTMAS IS COMING. HOW ARE MY FAVORITE CO-WORKERS?
TO CELEBRATE OUR FIRST CHRISTMAS AS BUSINESS PARTNERS, I THOUGHT I WOULD BUY EVERY PVP EMPLOYEE An Xbox 360.
game reference
MAX, YOU BIG Suxzors!
l33t speak.
ALREADY BOUGHT GIFTS FOR THE STAFF. IF YOU GIVE EVERYONE An Xbox 360.
game reference
I'LL LOOK LIKE A CHEAPSKATE!
DON'T WORRY. I'LL PUT YOUR NAME ON THE CARDS.
SEE? AND PEOPLE CLAIM WE'RE NOT A GAMING COMIC ANY MORE.
I HATE THAT MAN AS MUCH AS I HATE Star Wars Galaxies
game reference
I NEED YOU TO TEACH ME HOW TO BE FULL OF CHRISTMAS CHEER.
ARE YOU SERIOUS?
LAST YEAR'S CHRISTMAS FIASCO* HAS SHOWN ME THAT BEING A SCROOGE EVERY YEARS IS GOING TO PUT A STRAIN ON ALL OF MY PERSONAL RELATIONSHIPS.
BACK IN TALES TO NERDSTONISH #235 -Ye ol' editor
I NEED TO LEARN HOW TO APPRECIATE CHRISTMAS. BUT I NEED YOU TO EASE ME INTO THIS...OKAY? BABY-STEPS.
WELL IT'S A GOOD THING I BROUGHT MY TINSEL-GUN TODAY!
FLLRTRL!

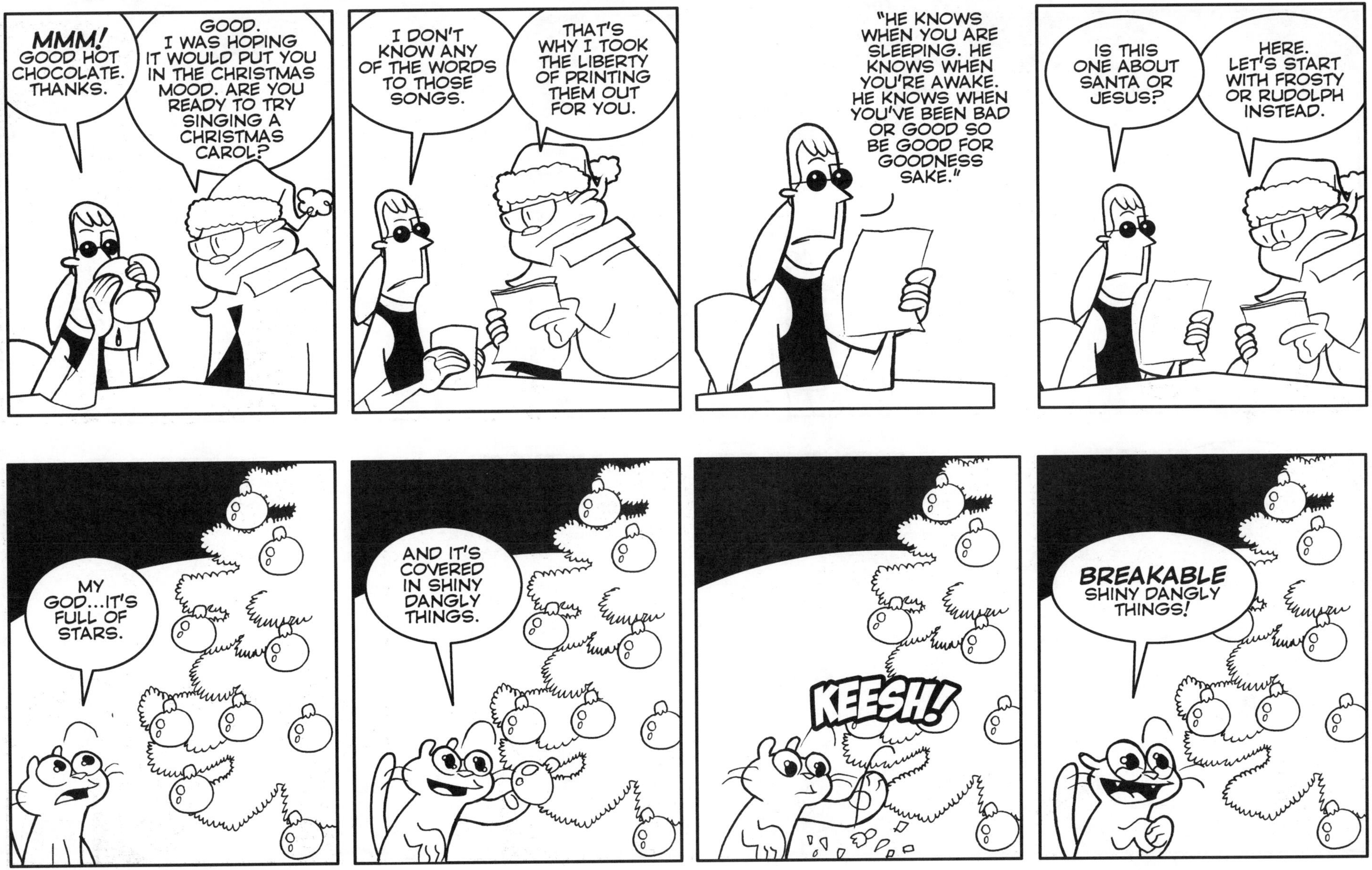
MMM! GOOD HOT CHOCOLATE. THANKS.
GOOD. I WAS HOPING IT WOULD PUT YOU IN THE CHRISTMAS MOOD. ARE YOU READY TO TRY SINGING A CHRISTMAS CAROL?
I DON'T KNOW ANY OF THE WORDS TO THOSE SONGS.
THAT'S WHY I TOOK THE LIBERTY OF PRINTING THEM OUT FOR YOU.
"HE KNOWS WHEN YOU ARE SLEEPING. HE KNOWS WHEN YOU'RE AWAKE. HE KNOWS WHEN YOU'VE BEEN BAD OR GOOD SO BE GOOD FOR GOODNESS SAKE."
IS THIS ONE ABOUT SANTA OR JESUS?
HERE. LET'S START WITH FROSTY OR RUDOLPH INSTEAD.
MY GOD...IT'S FULL OF STARS.
AND IT'S COVERED IN SHINY DANGLY THINGS.
KEESH!
BREAKABLE SHINY DANGLY THINGS!

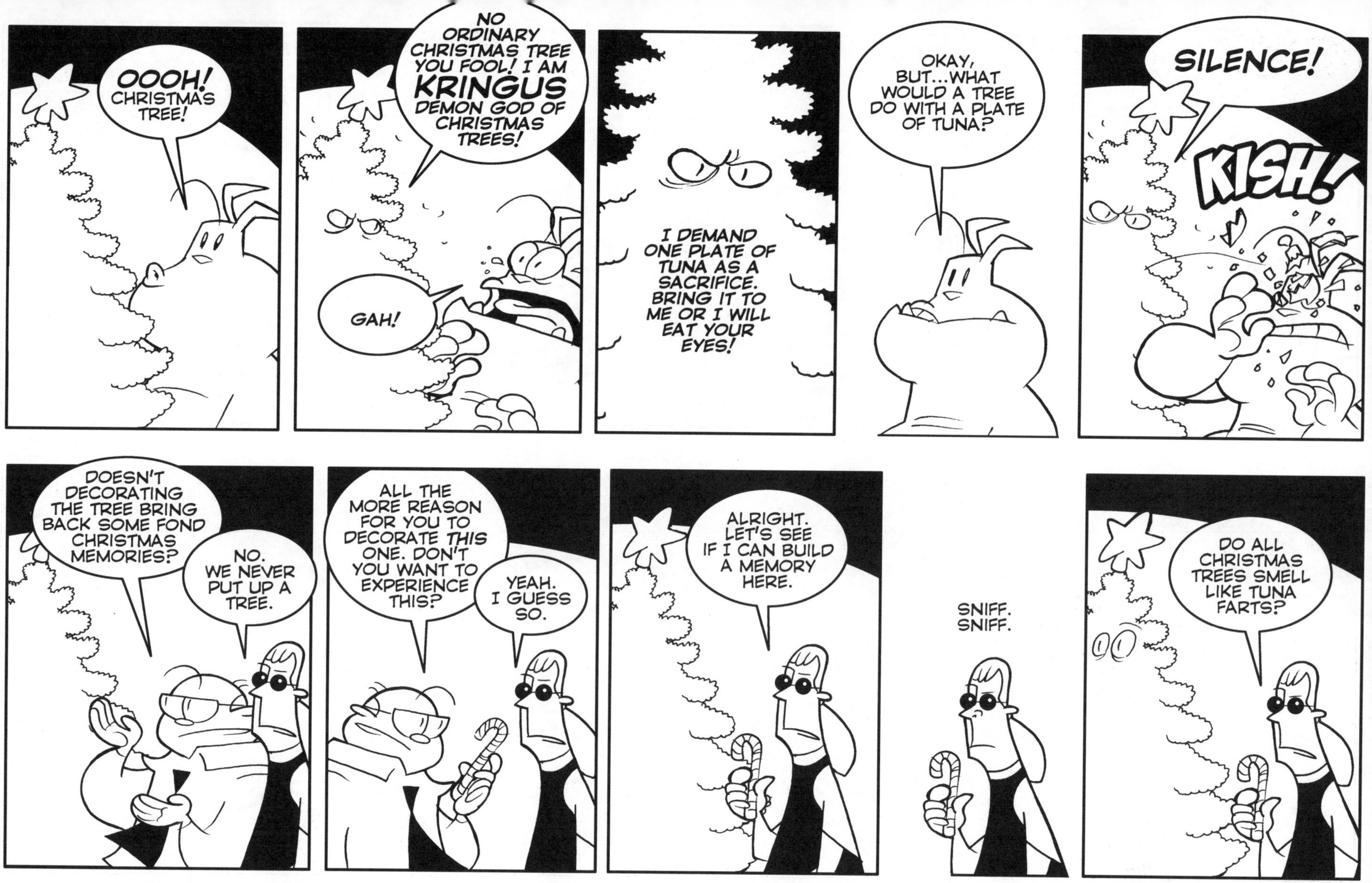
OOOH! CHRISTMAS TREE!
NO ORDINARY CHRISTMAS TREE YOU FOOL! I AM KRINGUS DEMON GOD OF CHRISTMAS TREES!
GAH!
I DEMAND ONE PLATE OF TUNA AS A SACRIFICE. BRING IT TO ME OR I WILL EAT YOUR EYES!
OKAY, BUT...WHAT WOULD A TREE DO WITH A PLATE OF TUNA?
SILENCE!
KISH!
DOESN'T DECORATING THE TREE BRING BACK SOME FOND CHRISTMAS MEMORIES?
NO. WE NEVER PUT UP A TREE.
ALL THE MORE REASON FOR YOU TO DECORATE THIS ONE. DON'T YOU WANT TO EXPERIENCE THIS?
YEAH. I GUESS SO.
ALRIGHT. LET'S SEE IF I CAN BUILD A MEMORY HERE.
SNIFF. SNIFF.
DO ALL CHRISTMAS TREES SMELL LIKE TUNA FARTS?

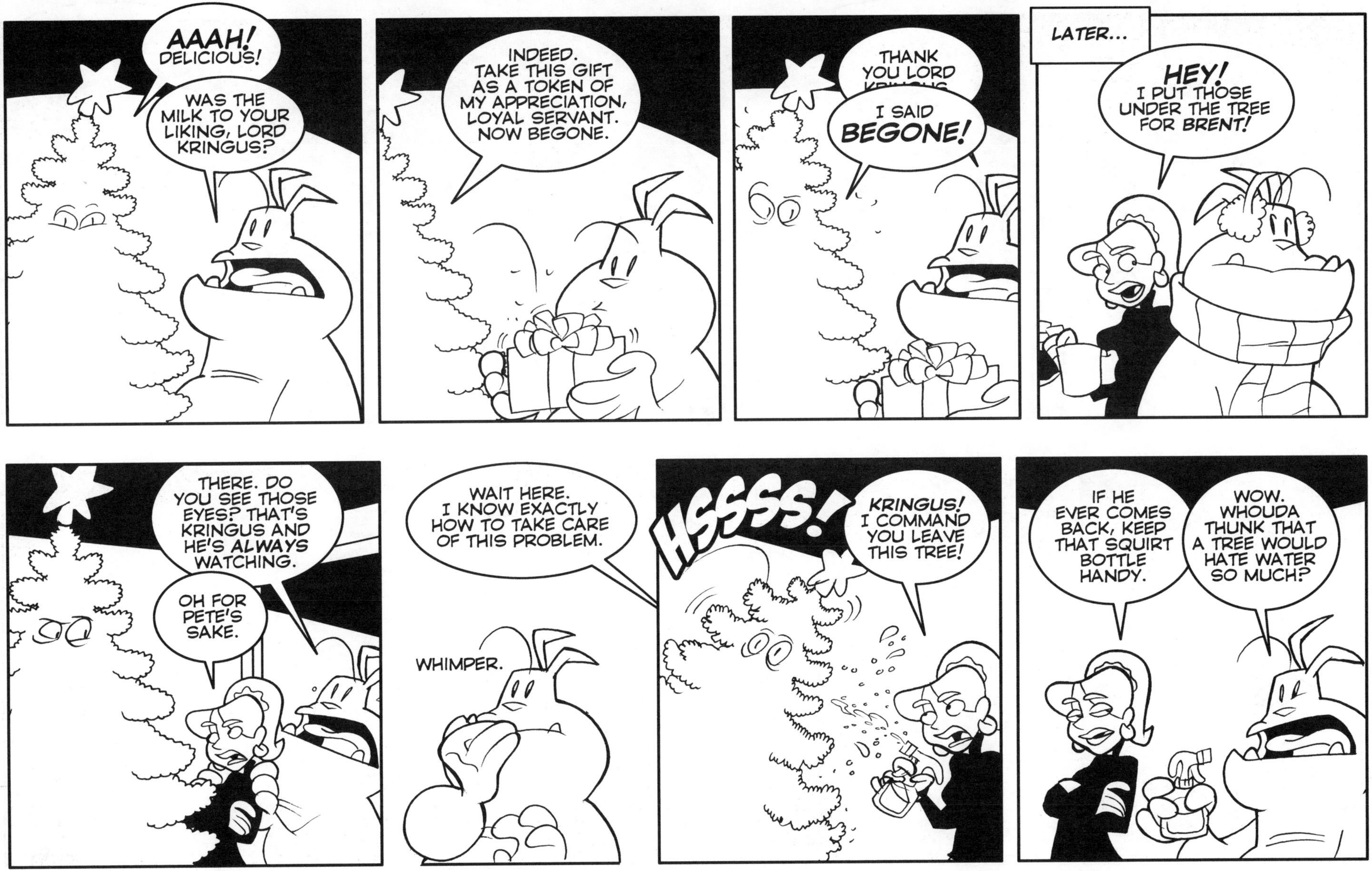
AAAH! DELICIOUS!
WAS THE MILK TO YOUR LIKING, LORD KRINGUS?
INDEED. TAKE THIS GIFT AS A TOKEN OF MY APPRECIATION, LOYAL SERVANT. NOW BEGONE.
THANK YOU LORD
I SAID BEGONE!
LATER...
HEY! I PUT THOSE UNDER THE TREE FOR BRENT!
THERE. DO YOU SEE THOSE EYES? THAT'S KRINGUS AND HE'S ALWAYS WATCHING.
OH FOR PETE'S SAKE.
WAIT HERE. I KNOW EXACTLY HOW TO TAKE CARE OF THIS PROBLEM.
WHIMPER.
HSSSS!
KRINGUS! I COMMAND YOU LEAVE THIS TREE!
IF HE EVER COMES BACK, KEEP THAT SQUIRT BOTTLE HANDY.
WOW. WHOUDA THUNK THAT A TREE WOULD HATE WATER SO MUCH?

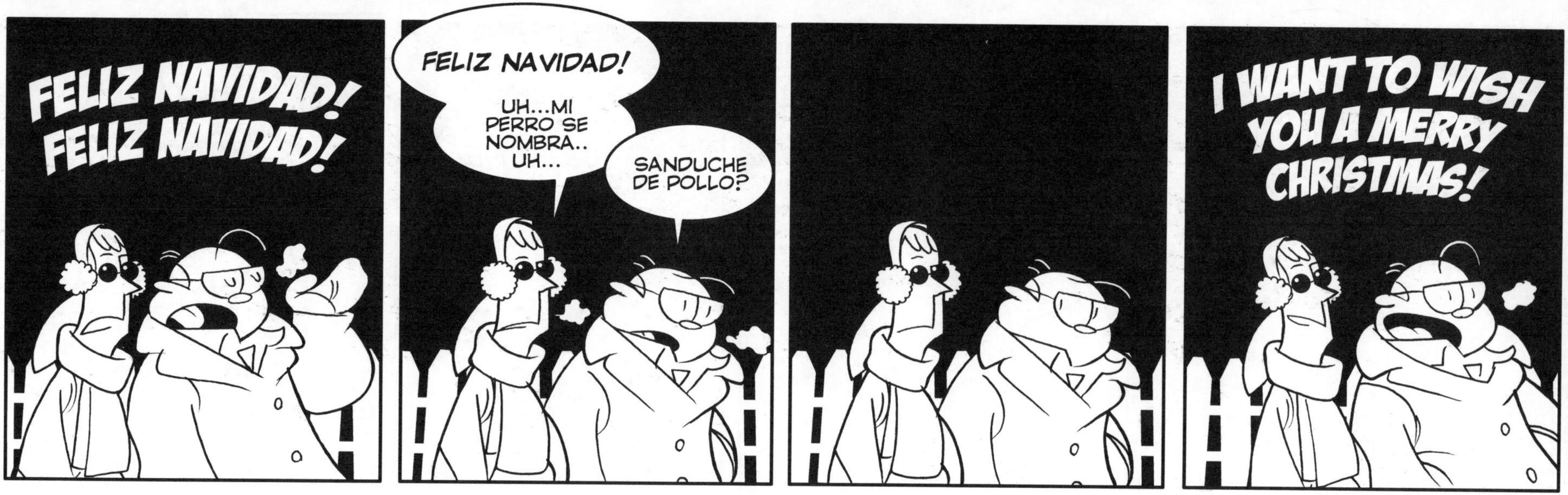
FELIZ NAVIDAD! FELIZ NAVIDAD!
FELIZ NAVIDAD!
UH...MI PERRO SE NOMBRA.. UH...
SANDUCHE DE POLLO?
I WANT TO WISH YOU A MERRY CHRISTMAS!

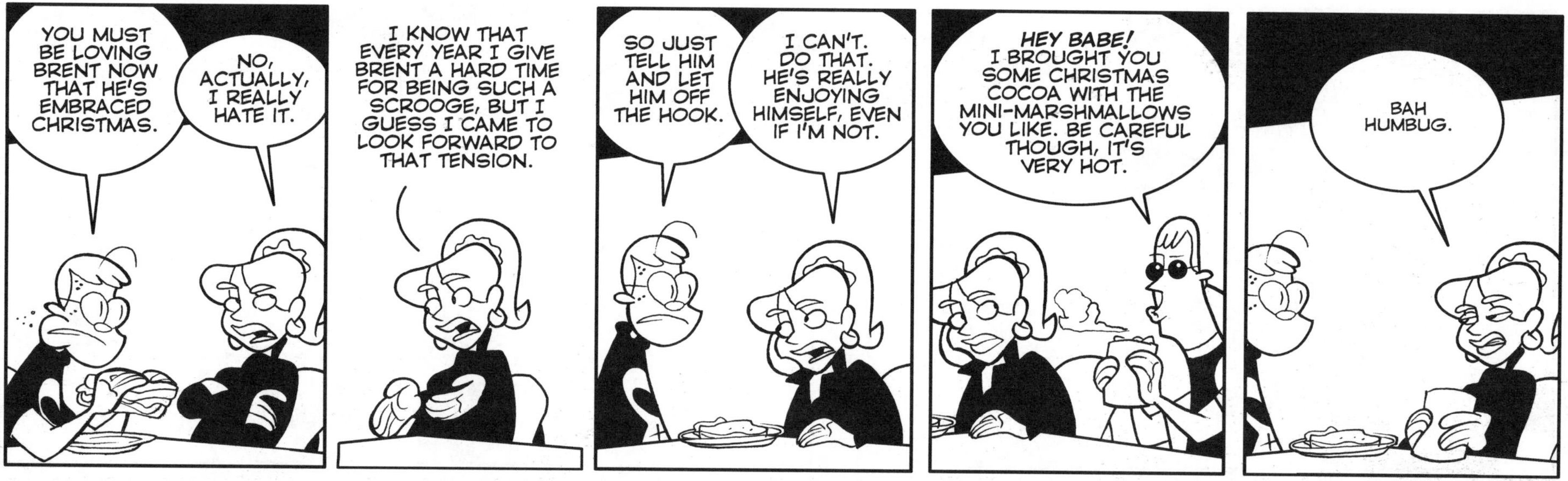
YOU MUST BE LOVING BRENT NOW THAT HE'S EMBRACED CHRISTMAS.
NO, ACTUALLY, I REALLY HATE IT.
I KNOW THAT EVERY YEAR I GIVE BRENT A HARD TIME FOR BEING SUCH A SCROOGE, BUT I GUESS I CAME TO LOOK FORWARD TO THAT TENSION.
SO JUST TELL HIM AND LET HIM OFF THE HOOK.
I CAN'T. DO THAT. HE'S REALLY ENJOYING HIMSELF, EVEN IF I'M NOT.
HEY BABE! I BROUGHT YOU SOME CHRISTMAS COCOA WITH THE MINI-MARSHMALLOWS YOU LIKE. BE CAREFUL THOUGH, IT'S VERY HOT.
BAH HUMBUG.

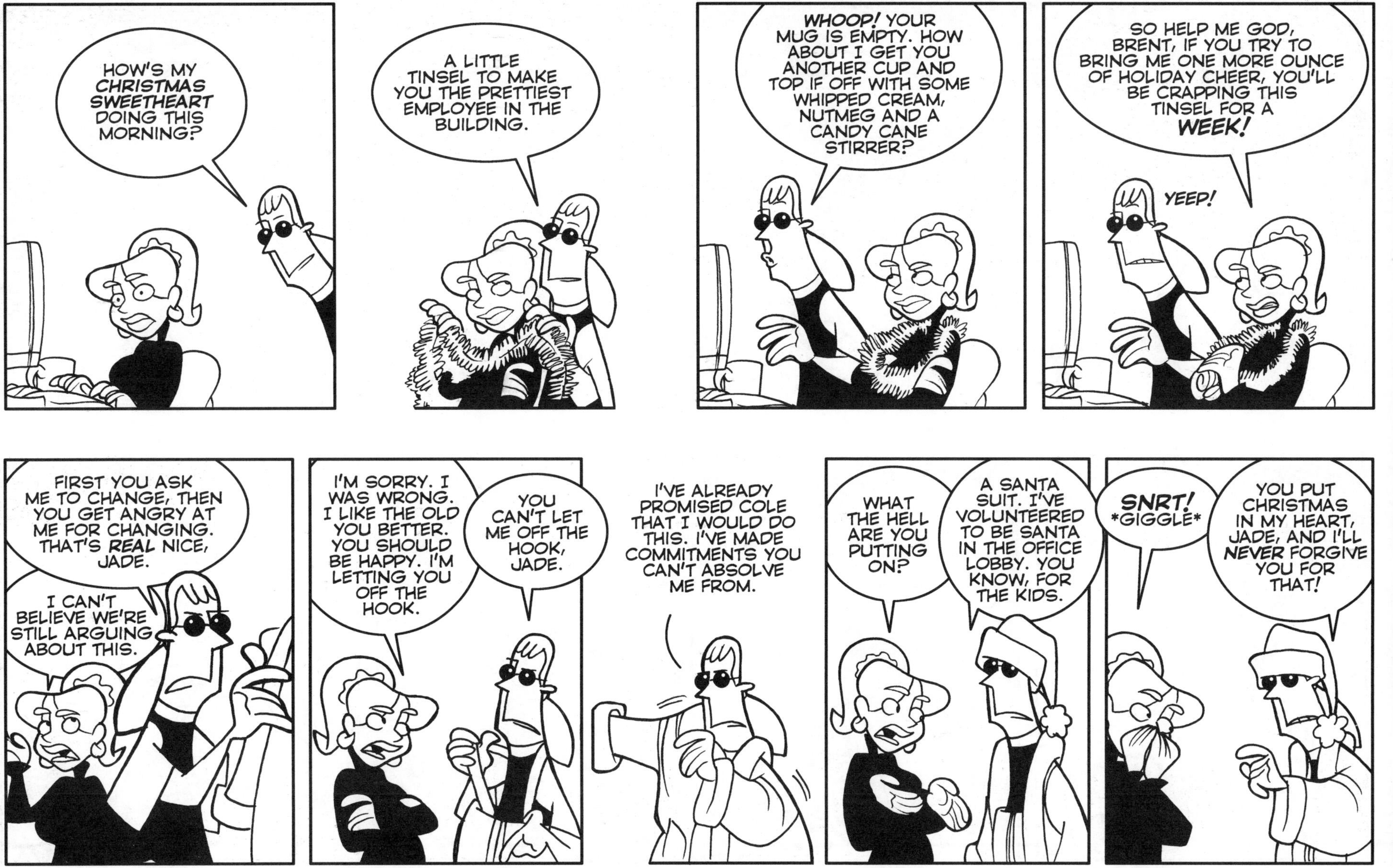
HOW'S MY CHRISTMAS SWEETHEART DOING THIS MORNING?
A LITTLE TINSEL TO MAKE YOU THE PRETTIEST EMPLOYEE IN THE BUILDING.
WHOOP! YOUR MUG IS EMPTY. HOW ABOUT I GET YOU ANOTHER CUP AND TOP IF OFF WITH SOME WHIPPED CREAM, NUTMEG AND A CANDY CANE STIRRER?
SO HELP ME GOD, BRENT, IF YOU TRY TO BRING ME ONE MORE OUNCE OF HOLIDAY CHEER, YOU'LL BE CRAPPING THIS TINSEL FOR A WEEK!
YEEP!
FIRST YOU ASK ME TO CHANGE, THEN YOU GET ANGRY AT ME FOR CHANGING. THAT'S REAL NICE, JADE.
I CAN'T BELIEVE WE'RE STILL ARGUING ABOUT THIS.
I'M SORRY. I WAS WRONG. I LIKE THE OLD YOU BETTER. YOU SHOULD BE HAPPY. I'M LETTING YOU OFF THE HOOK.
YOU CAN'T LET ME OFF THE HOOK, JADE.
I'VE ALREADY PROMISED COLE THAT I WOULD DO THIS. I'VE MADE COMMITMENTS YOU CAN'T ABSOLVE ME FROM.
WHAT THE HELL ARE YOU PUTTING ON?
A SANTA SUIT. I'VE VOLUNTEERED TO BE SANTA IN THE OFFICE LOBBY. YOU KNOW, FOR THE KIDS.
SNRT! *GIGGLE*
YOU PUT CHRISTMAS IN MY HEART, JADE, AND I'LL NEVER FORGIVE YOU FOR THAT!

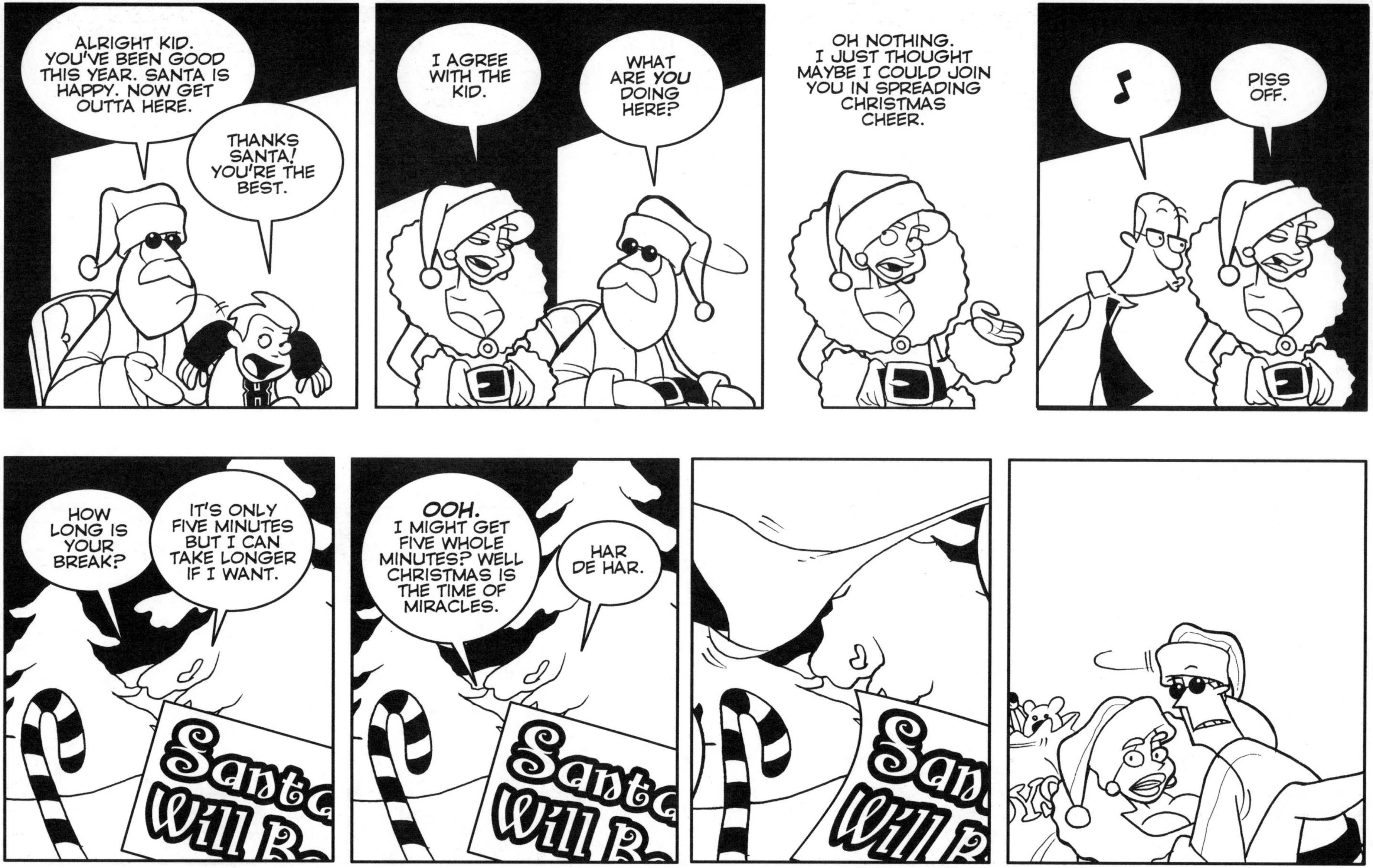
ALRIGHT KID. YOU'VE BEEN GOOD THIS YEAR. SANTA IS HAPPY. NOW GET OUTTA HERE.
THANKS SANTA! YOU'RE THE BEST.
I AGREE WITH THE KID.
WHAT ARE *YOU* DOING HERE?
OH NOTHING. I JUST THOUGHT MAYBE I COULD JOIN YOU IN SPREADING CHRISTMAS CHEER.
♪
PISS OFF.
HOW LONG IS YOUR BREAK?
IT'S ONLY FIVE MINUTES BUT I CAN TAKE LONGER IF I WANT.
OOH. I MIGHT GET FIVE WHOLE MINUTES? WELL CHRISTMAS IS THE TIME OF MIRACLES.
HAR DE HAR.

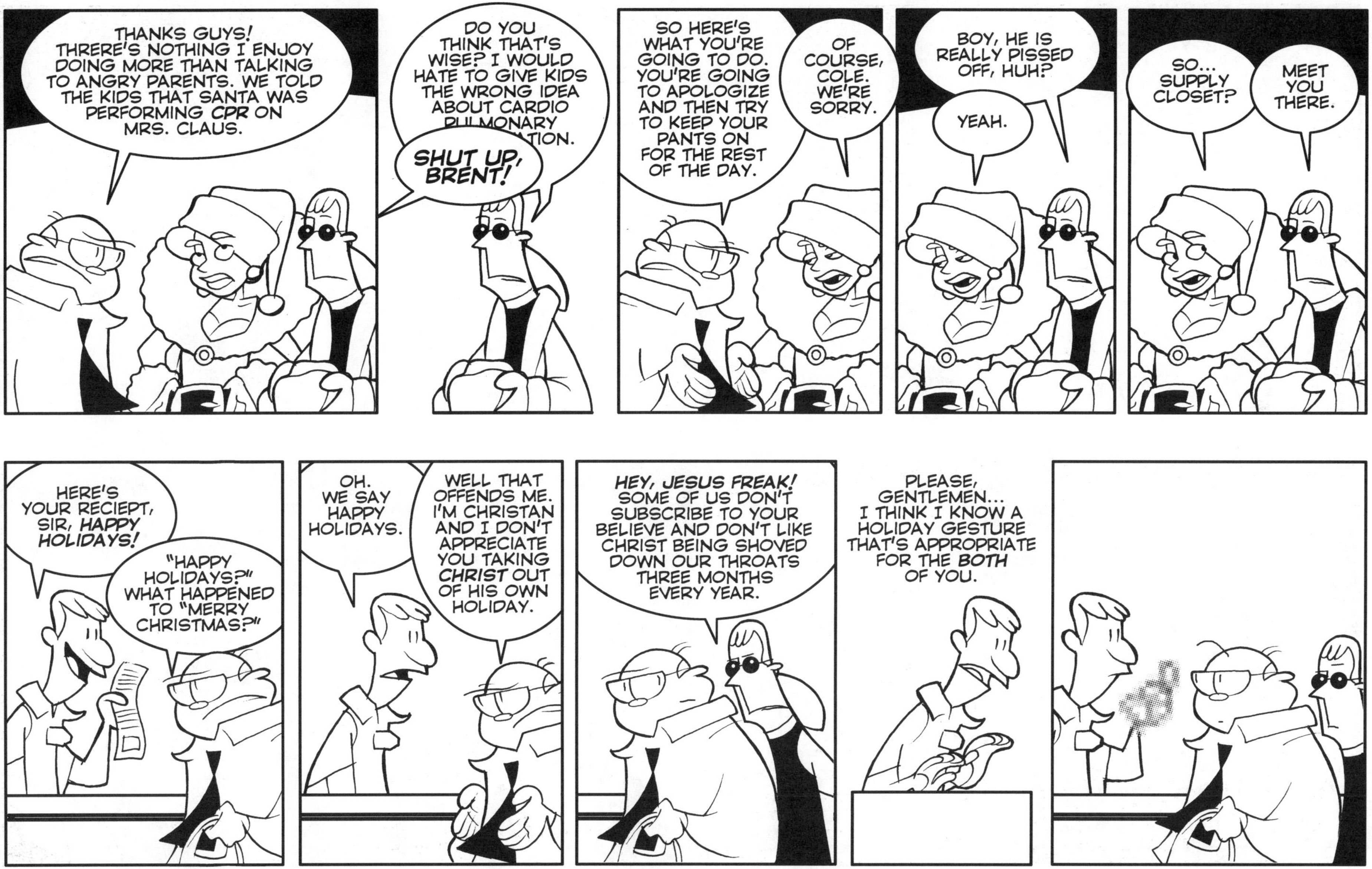

THANKS GUYS! THRERE'S NOTHING I ENJOY DOING MORE THAN TALKING TO ANGRY PARENTS. WE TOLD THE KIDS THAT SANTA WAS PERFORMING **CPR** ON MRS. CLAUS.
DO YOU THINK THAT'S WISE? I WOULD HATE TO GIVE KIDS THE WRONG IDEA ABOUT CARDIO PULMONARY
SHUT UP, BRENT!
SO HERE'S WHAT YOU'RE GOING TO DO. YOU'RE GOING TO APOLOGIZE AND THEN TRY TO KEEP YOUR PANTS ON FOR THE REST OF THE DAY.
OF COURSE, COLE. WE'RE SORRY.
BOY, HE IS REALLY PISSED OFF, HUH?
YEAH.
SO... SUPPLY CLOSET?
MEET YOU THERE.
HERE'S YOUR RECIEPT, SIR, **HAPPY HOLIDAYS!**
"HAPPY HOLIDAYS?" WHAT HAPPENED TO "MERRY CHRISTMAS?"
OH. WE SAY HAPPY HOLIDAYS.
WELL THAT OFFENDS ME. I'M CHRISTAN AND I DON'T APPRECIATE YOU TAKING **CHRIST** OUT OF HIS OWN HOLIDAY.
HEY, JESUS FREAK! SOME OF US DON'T SUBSCRIBE TO YOUR BELIEVE AND DON'T LIKE CHRIST BEING SHOVED DOWN OUR THROATS THREE MONTHS EVERY YEAR.
PLEASE, GENTLEMEN... I THINK I KNOW A HOLIDAY GESTURE THAT'S APPROPRIATE FOR THE **BOTH** OF YOU.

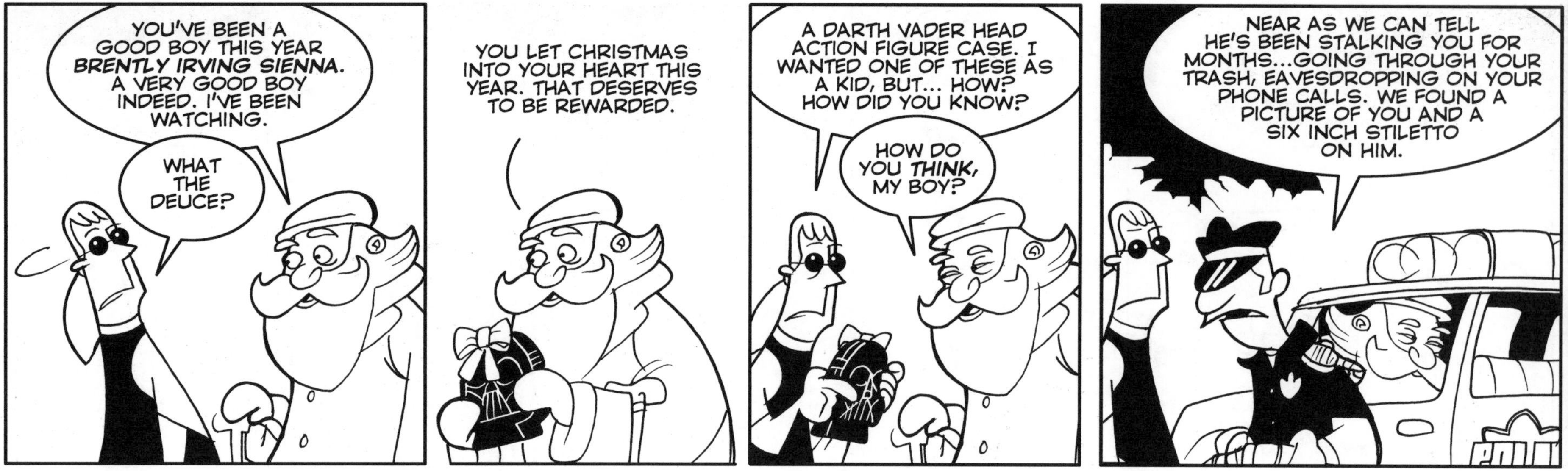
YOU'VE BEEN A GOOD BOY THIS YEAR BRENTLY IRVING SIENNA. A VERY GOOD BOY INDEED. I'VE BEEN WATCHING.
WHAT THE DEUCE?
YOU LET CHRISTMAS INTO YOUR HEART THIS YEAR. THAT DESERVES TO BE REWARDED.
A DARTH VADER HEAD ACTION FIGURE CASE. I WANTED ONE OF THESE AS A KID, BUT... HOW? HOW DID YOU KNOW?
HOW DO YOU THINK, MY BOY?
NEAR AS WE CAN TELL HE'S BEEN STALKING YOU FOR MONTHS...GOING THROUGH YOUR TRASH, EAVESDROPPING ON YOUR PHONE CALLS. WE FOUND A PICTURE OF YOU AND A SIX INCH STILETTO ON HIM.

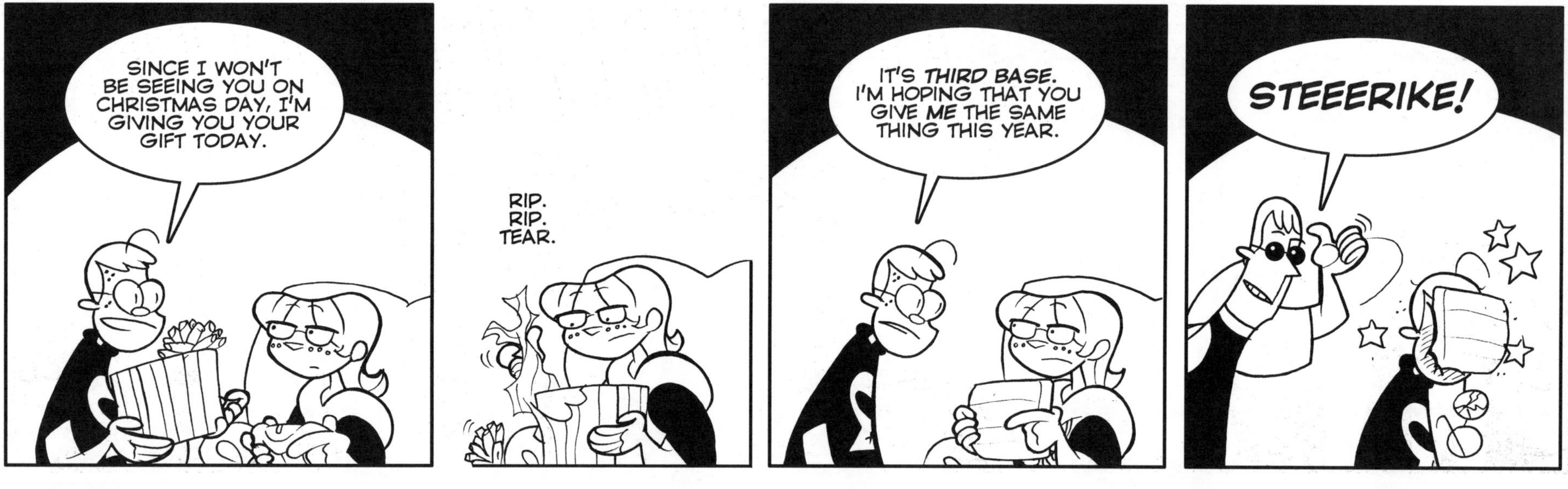
SINCE I WON'T BE SEEING YOU ON CHRISTMAS DAY, I'M GIVING YOU YOUR GIFT TODAY.
RIP. RIP. TEAR.
IT'S THIRD BASE. I'M HOPING THAT YOU GIVE ME THE SAME THING THIS YEAR.
STEEERIKE!

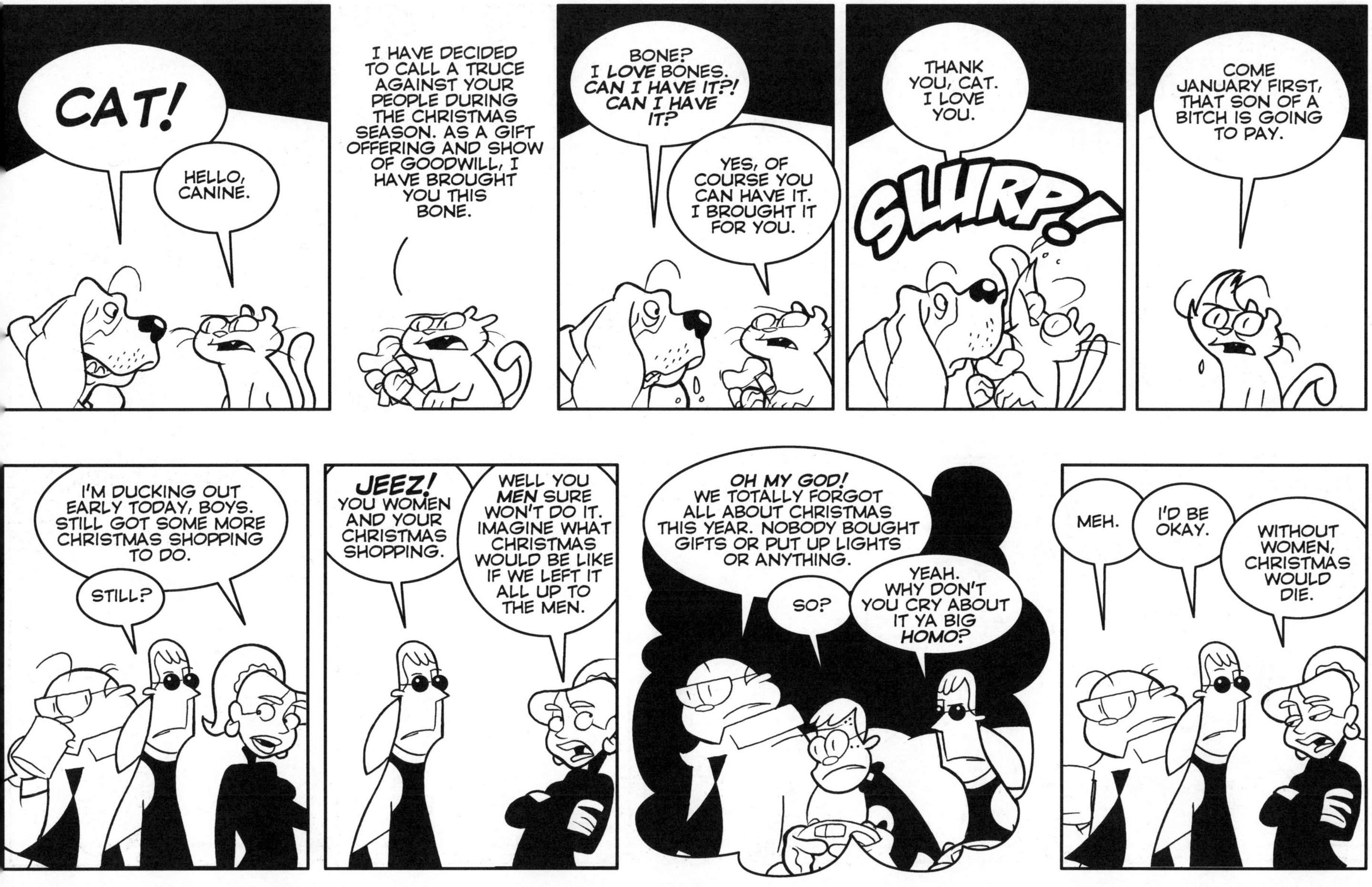
CAT!
HELLO, CANINE.
I HAVE DECIDED TO CALL A TRUCE AGAINST YOUR PEOPLE DURING THE CHRISTMAS SEASON. AS A GIFT OFFERING AND SHOW OF GOODWILL, I HAVE BROUGHT YOU THIS BONE.
BONE? I LOVE BONES. CAN I HAVE IT?! CAN I HAVE IT?
YES, OF COURSE YOU CAN HAVE IT. I BROUGHT IT FOR YOU.
THANK YOU, CAT. I LOVE YOU.
SLURP!
COME JANUARY FIRST, THAT SON OF A BITCH IS GOING TO PAY.
I'M DUCKING OUT EARLY TODAY, BOYS. STILL GOT SOME MORE CHRISTMAS SHOPPING TO DO.
STILL?
JEEZ! YOU WOMEN AND YOUR CHRISTMAS SHOPPING.
WELL YOU MEN SURE WON'T DO IT. IMAGINE WHAT CHRISTMAS WOULD BE LIKE IF WE LEFT IT ALL UP TO THE MEN.
OH MY GOD! WE TOTALLY FORGOT ALL ABOUT CHRISTMAS THIS YEAR. NOBODY BOUGHT GIFTS OR PUT UP LIGHTS OR ANYTHING.
SO?
YEAH. WHY DON'T YOU CRY ABOUT IT YA BIG HOMO?
MEH.
I'D BE OKAY.
WITHOUT WOMEN, CHRISTMAS WOULD DIE.

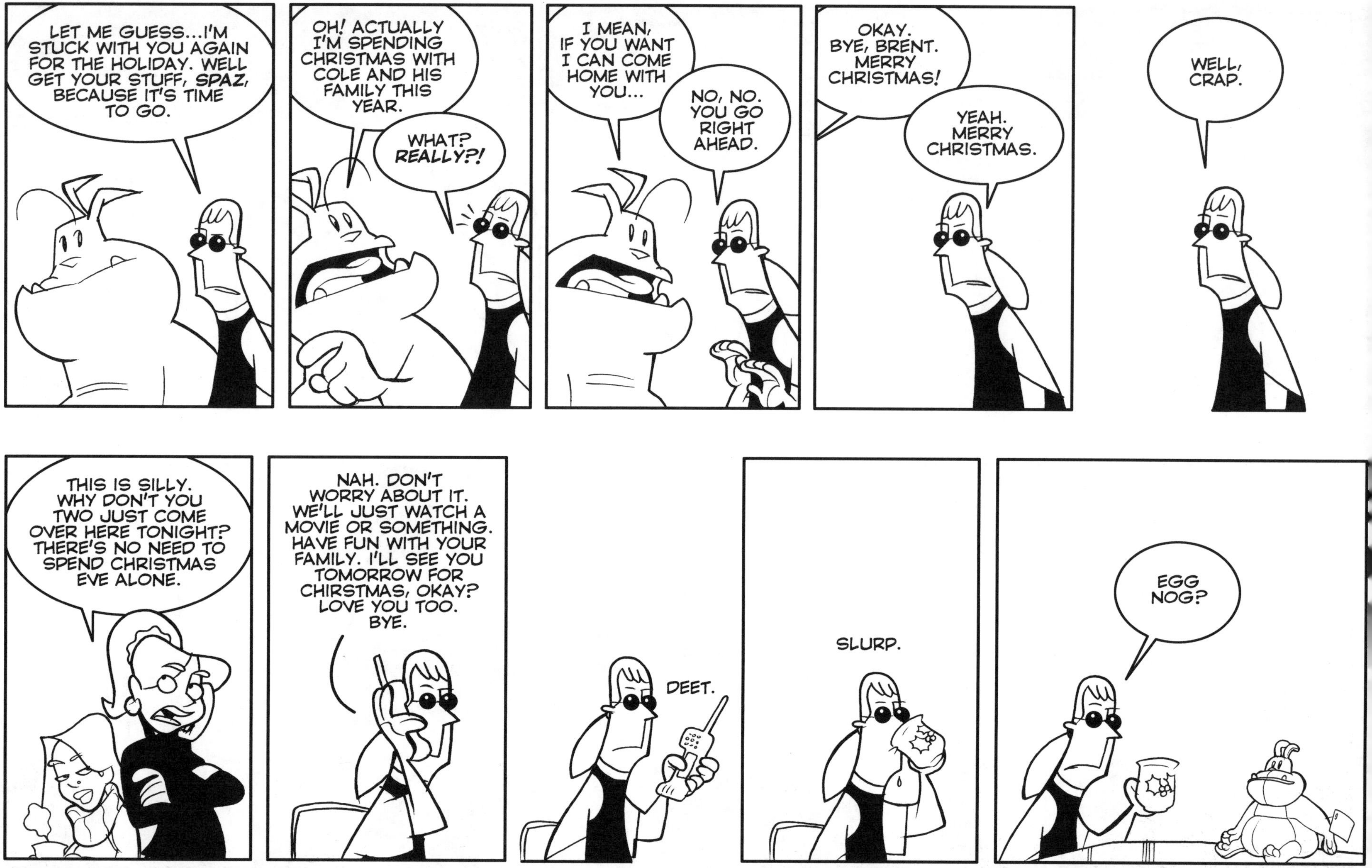
LET ME GUESS...I'M STUCK WITH YOU AGAIN FOR THE HOLIDAY. WELL GET YOUR STUFF, **SPAZ**, BECAUSE IT'S TIME TO GO.
OH! ACTUALLY I'M SPENDING CHRISTMAS WITH COLE AND HIS FAMILY THIS YEAR.
WHAT? ***REALLY?!***
I MEAN, IF YOU WANT I CAN COME HOME WITH YOU...
NO, NO. YOU GO RIGHT AHEAD.
OKAY. BYE, BRENT. MERRY CHRISTMAS!
YEAH. MERRY CHRISTMAS.
WELL, CRAP.
THIS IS SILLY. WHY DON'T YOU TWO JUST COME OVER HERE TONIGHT? THERE'S NO NEED TO SPEND CHRISTMAS EVE ALONE.
NAH. DON'T WORRY ABOUT IT. WE'LL JUST WATCH A MOVIE OR SOMETHING. HAVE FUN WITH YOUR FAMILY. I'LL SEE YOU TOMORROW FOR CHIRSTMAS, OKAY? LOVE YOU TOO. BYE.
DEET.
SLURP.
EGG NOG?

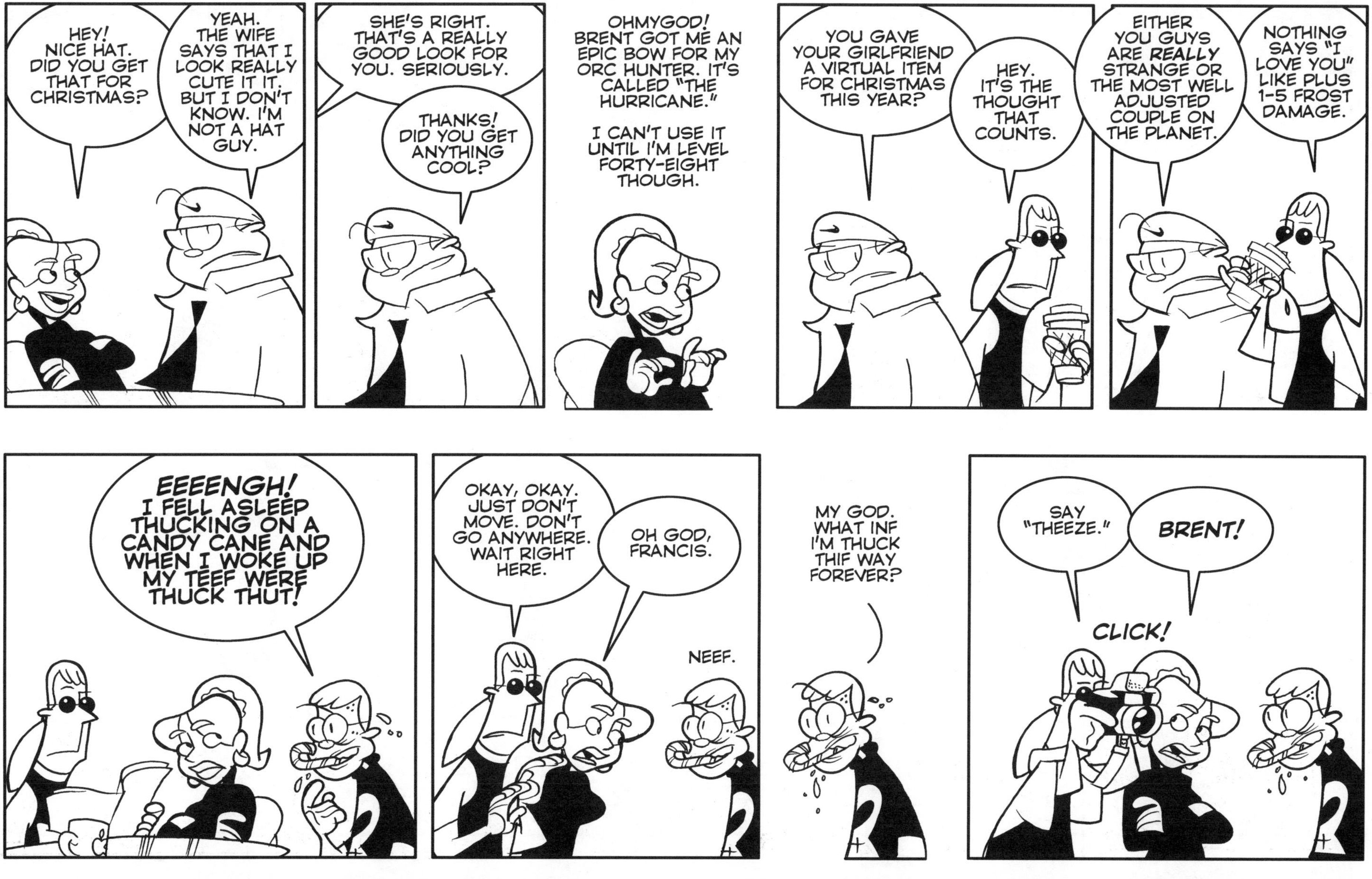
HEY! NICE HAT. DID YOU GET THAT FOR CHRISTMAS?
YEAH. THE WIFE SAYS THAT I LOOK REALLY CUTE IT IT. BUT I DON'T KNOW. I'M NOT A HAT GUY.
SHE'S RIGHT. THAT'S A REALLY GOOD LOOK FOR YOU. SERIOUSLY.
THANKS! DID YOU GET ANYTHING COOL?
OHMYGOD! BRENT GOT ME AN EPIC BOW FOR MY ORC HUNTER. IT'S CALLED "THE HURRICANE."
I CAN'T USE IT UNTIL I'M LEVEL FORTY-EIGHT THOUGH.
YOU GAVE YOUR GIRLFRIEND A VIRTUAL ITEM FOR CHRISTMAS THIS YEAR?
HEY. IT'S THE THOUGHT THAT COUNTS.
EITHER YOU GUYS ARE **REALLY** STRANGE OR THE MOST WELL ADJUSTED COUPLE ON THE PLANET.
NOTHING SAYS "I LOVE YOU" LIKE PLUS 1-5 FROST DAMAGE.
EEEENGH! I FELL ASLEEP THUCKING ON A CANDY CANE AND WHEN I WOKE UP MY TEEF WERE THUCK THUT!
OKAY, OKAY. JUST DON'T MOVE. DON'T GO ANYWHERE. WAIT RIGHT HERE.
OH GOD, FRANCIS.
NEEF.
MY GOD. WHAT INF I'M THUCK THIF WAY FOREVER?
SAY "THEEZE."
BRENT!
CLICK!

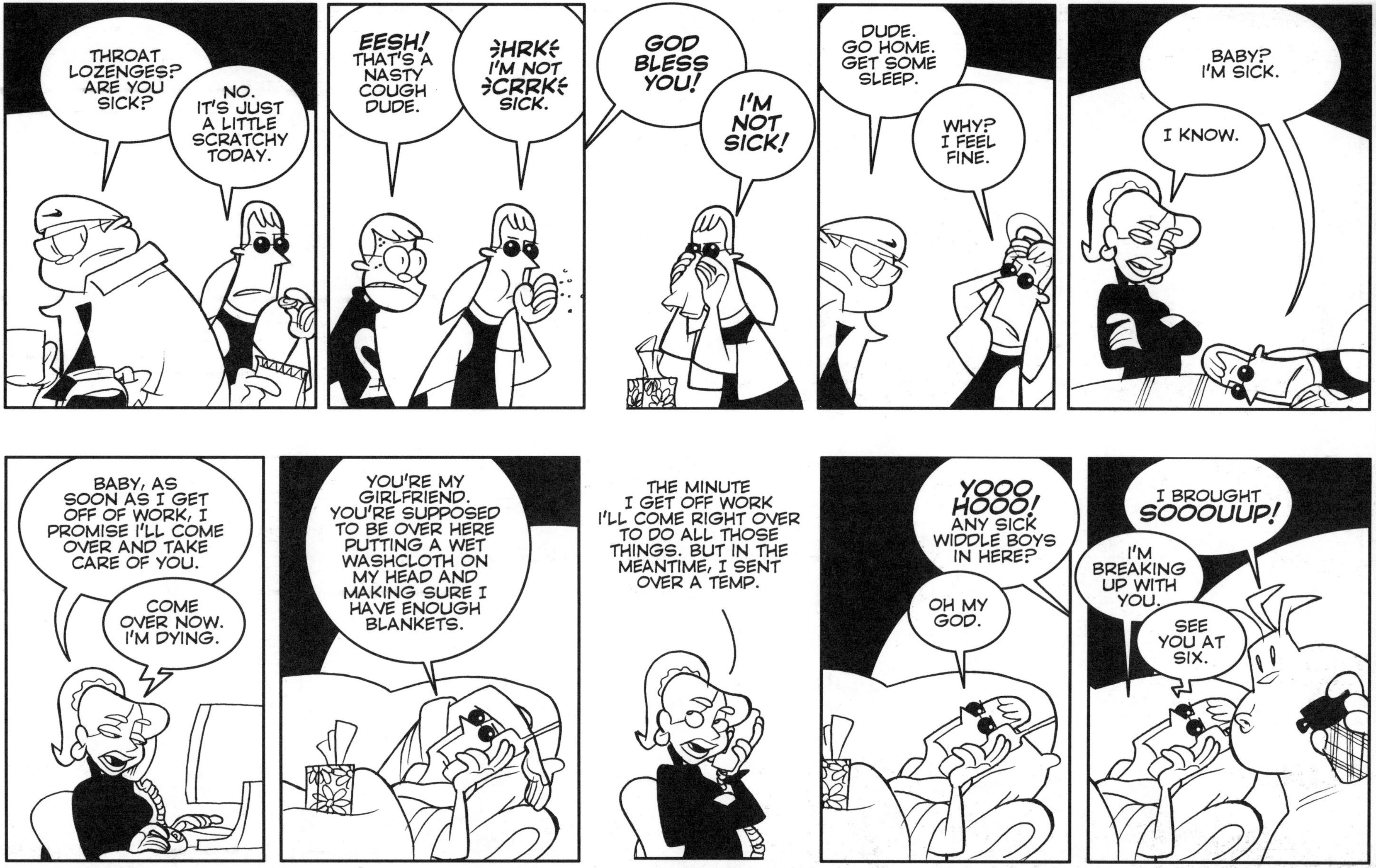
THROAT LOZENGES? ARE YOU SICK?
NO. IT'S JUST A LITTLE SCRATCHY TODAY.
EESH! THAT'S A NASTY COUGH DUDE.
HRK I'M NOT CRRK SICK.
GOD BLESS YOU!
I'M NOT SICK!
DUDE. GO HOME. GET SOME SLEEP.
WHY? I FEEL FINE.
BABY? I'M SICK.
I KNOW.
BABY, AS SOON AS I GET OFF OF WORK, I PROMISE I'LL COME OVER AND TAKE CARE OF YOU.
COME OVER NOW. I'M DYING.
YOU'RE MY GIRLFRIEND. YOU'RE SUPPOSED TO BE OVER HERE PUTTING A WET WASHCLOTH ON MY HEAD AND MAKING SURE I HAVE ENOUGH BLANKETS.
THE MINUTE I GET OFF WORK I'LL COME RIGHT OVER TO DO ALL THOSE THINGS. BUT IN THE MEANTIME, I SENT OVER A TEMP.
YOOO HOOO! ANY SICK WIDDLE BOYS IN HERE?
OH MY GOD.
I BROUGHT SOOOUUP!
I'M BREAKING UP WITH YOU.
SEE YOU AT SIX.

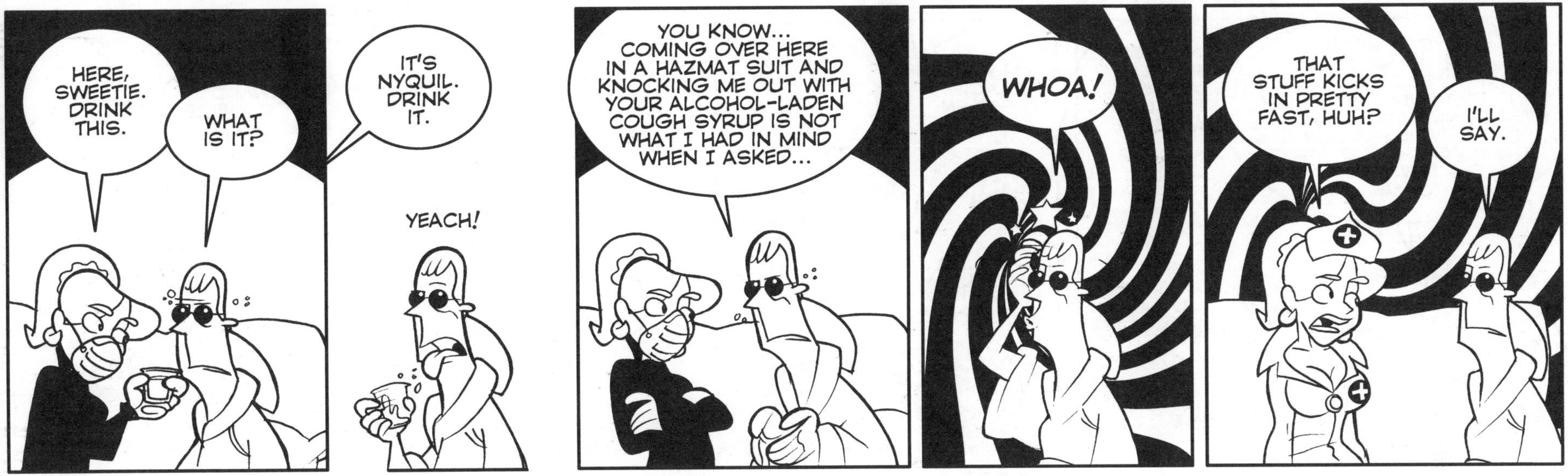
HERE, SWEETIE. DRINK THIS.
WHAT IS IT?
IT'S NYQUIL. DRINK IT.
YEACH!
YOU KNOW... COMING OVER HERE IN A HAZMAT SUIT AND KNOCKING ME OUT WITH YOUR ALCOHOL-LADEN COUGH SYRUP IS NOT WHAT I HAD IN MIND WHEN I ASKED...
WHOA!
THAT STUFF KICKS IN PRETTY FAST, HUH?
I'LL SAY.

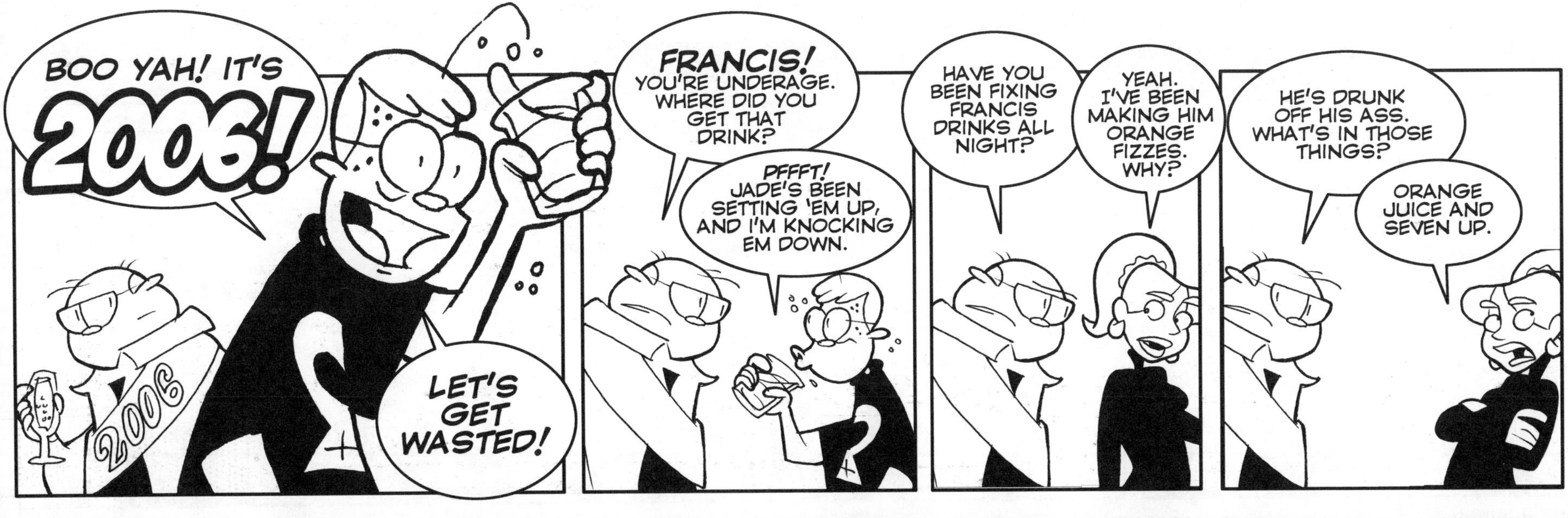
BOO YAH! IT'S 2006!
LET'S GET WASTED!
2006
FRANCIS! YOU'RE UNDERAGE. WHERE DID YOU GET THAT DRINK?
PFFFT! JADE'S BEEN SETTING 'EM UP, AND I'M KNOCKING EM DOWN.
HAVE YOU BEEN FIXING FRANCIS DRINKS ALL NIGHT?
YEAH. I'VE BEEN MAKING HIM ORANGE FIZZES. WHY?
HE'S DRUNK OFF HIS ASS. WHAT'S IN THOSE THINGS?
ORANGE JUICE AND SEVEN UP.

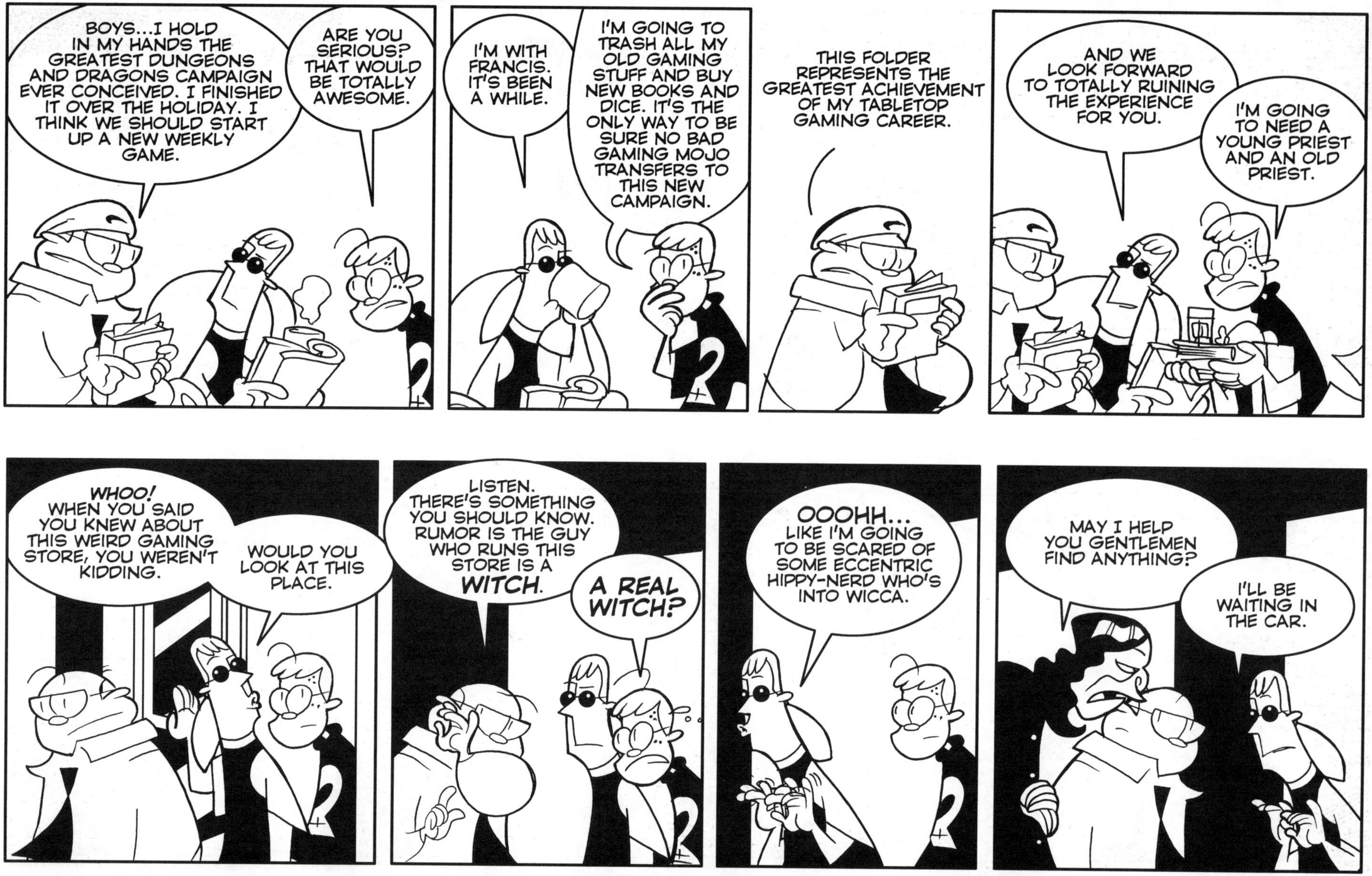
BOYS...I HOLD IN MY HANDS THE GREATEST DUNGEONS AND DRAGONS CAMPAIGN EVER CONCEIVED. I FINISHED IT OVER THE HOLIDAY. I THINK WE SHOULD START UP A NEW WEEKLY GAME.
ARE YOU SERIOUS? THAT WOULD BE TOTALLY AWESOME.
I'M WITH FRANCIS. IT'S BEEN A WHILE.
I'M GOING TO TRASH ALL MY OLD GAMING STUFF AND BUY NEW BOOKS AND DICE. IT'S THE ONLY WAY TO BE SURE NO BAD GAMING MOJO TRANSFERS TO THIS NEW CAMPAIGN.
THIS FOLDER REPRESENTS THE GREATEST ACHIEVEMENT OF MY TABLETOP GAMING CAREER.
AND WE LOOK FORWARD TO TOTALLY RUINING THE EXPERIENCE FOR YOU.
I'M GOING TO NEED A YOUNG PRIEST AND AN OLD PRIEST.
WHOO! WHEN YOU SAID YOU KNEW ABOUT THIS WEIRD GAMING STORE, YOU WEREN'T KIDDING.
WOULD YOU LOOK AT THIS PLACE.
LISTEN. THERE'S SOMETHING YOU SHOULD KNOW. RUMOR IS THE GUY WHO RUNS THIS STORE IS A WITCH.
A REAL WITCH?
OOOHH... LIKE I'M GOING TO BE SCARED OF SOME ECCENTRIC HIPPY-NERD WHO'S INTO WICCA.
MAY I HELP YOU GENTLEMEN FIND ANYTHING?
I'LL BE WAITING IN THE CAR.

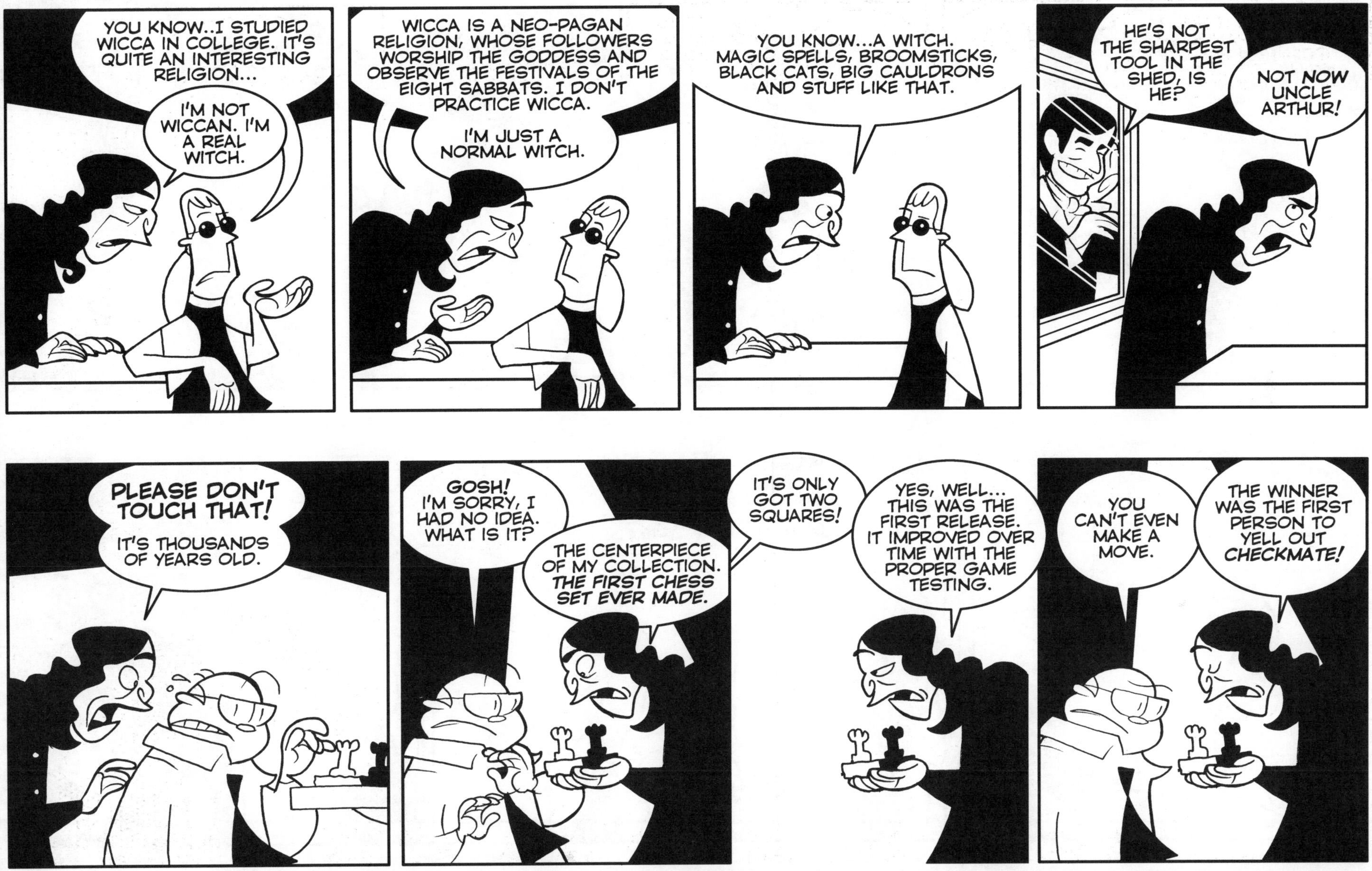

YOU KNOW..I STUDIED WICCA IN COLLEGE. IT'S QUITE AN INTERESTING RELIGION...
I'M NOT WICCAN. I'M A REAL WITCH.
WICCA IS A NEO-PAGAN RELIGION, WHOSE FOLLOWERS WORSHIP THE GODDESS AND OBSERVE THE FESTIVALS OF THE EIGHT SABBATS. I DON'T PRACTICE WICCA.
I'M JUST A NORMAL WITCH.
YOU KNOW...A WITCH. MAGIC SPELLS, BROOMSTICKS, BLACK CATS, BIG CAULDRONS AND STUFF LIKE THAT.
HE'S NOT THE SHARPEST TOOL IN THE SHED, IS HE?
NOT **NOW** UNCLE ARTHUR!
PLEASE DON'T TOUCH THAT!
IT'S THOUSANDS OF YEARS OLD.
GOSH! I'M SORRY, I HAD NO IDEA. WHAT IS IT?
THE CENTERPIECE OF MY COLLECTION. *THE FIRST CHESS SET EVER MADE.*
IT'S ONLY GOT TWO SQUARES!
YES, WELL... THIS WAS THE FIRST RELEASE. IT IMPROVED OVER TIME WITH THE PROPER GAME TESTING.
YOU CAN'T EVEN MAKE A MOVE.
THE WINNER WAS THE FIRST PERSON TO YELL OUT *CHECKMATE!*

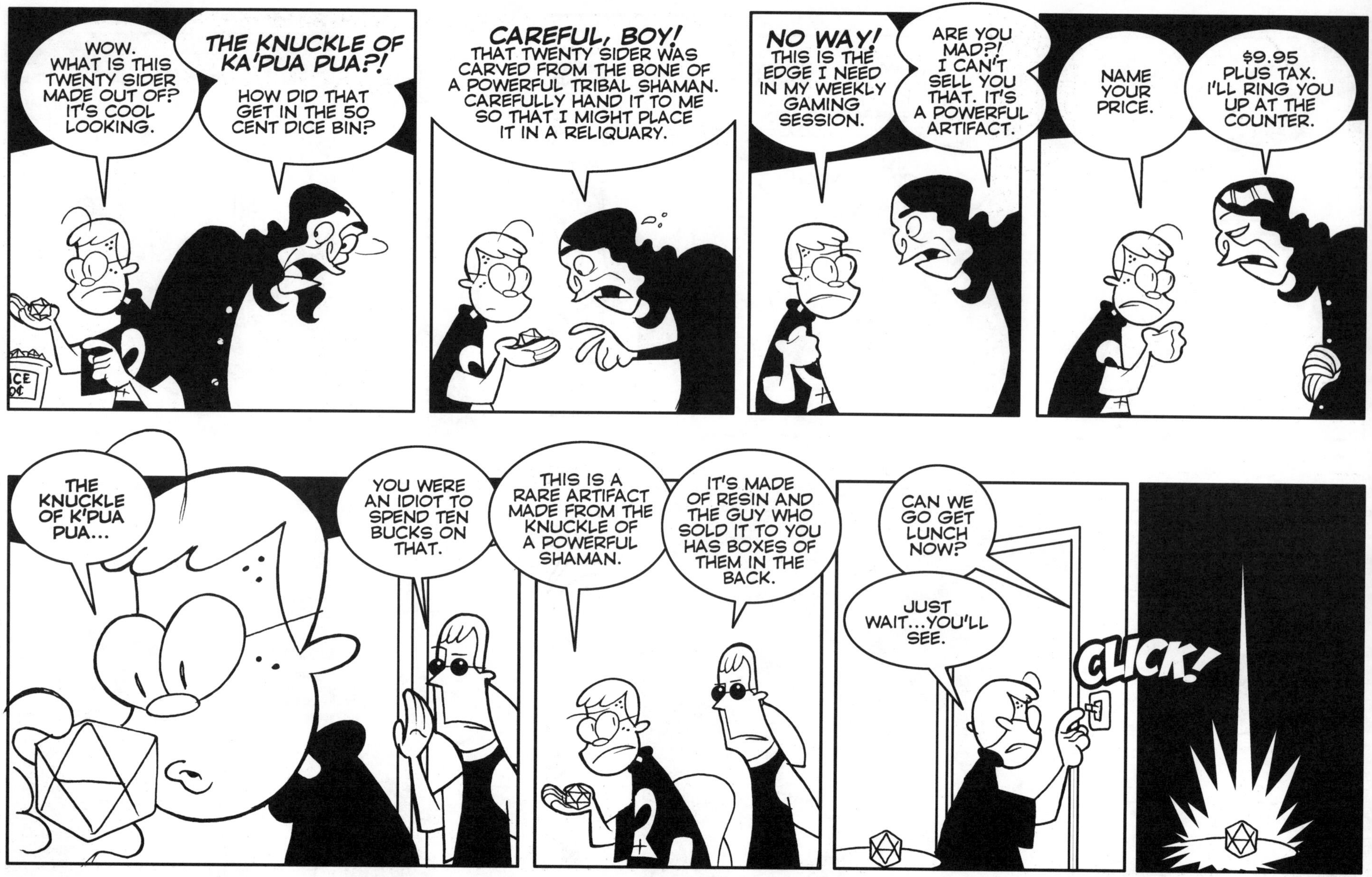
WOW. WHAT IS THIS TWENTY SIDER MADE OUT OF? IT'S COOL LOOKING.
THE KNUCKLE OF KA'PUA PUA?!
HOW DID THAT GET IN THE 50 CENT DICE BIN?
CAREFUL, BOY!
THAT TWENTY SIDER WAS CARVED FROM THE BONE OF A POWERFUL TRIBAL SHAMAN. CAREFULLY HAND IT TO ME SO THAT I MIGHT PLACE IT IN A RELIQUARY.
NO WAY!
THIS IS THE EDGE I NEED IN MY WEEKLY GAMING SESSION.
ARE YOU MAD?! I CAN'T SELL YOU THAT. IT'S A POWERFUL ARTIFACT.
NAME YOUR PRICE.
$9.95 PLUS TAX. I'LL RING YOU UP AT THE COUNTER.
THE KNUCKLE OF K'PUA PUA...
YOU WERE AN IDIOT TO SPEND TEN BUCKS ON THAT.
THIS IS A RARE ARTIFACT MADE FROM THE KNUCKLE OF A POWERFUL SHAMAN.
IT'S MADE OF RESIN AND THE GUY WHO SOLD IT TO YOU HAS BOXES OF THEM IN THE BACK.
CAN WE GO GET LUNCH NOW?
JUST WAIT...YOU'LL SEE.
CLICK!

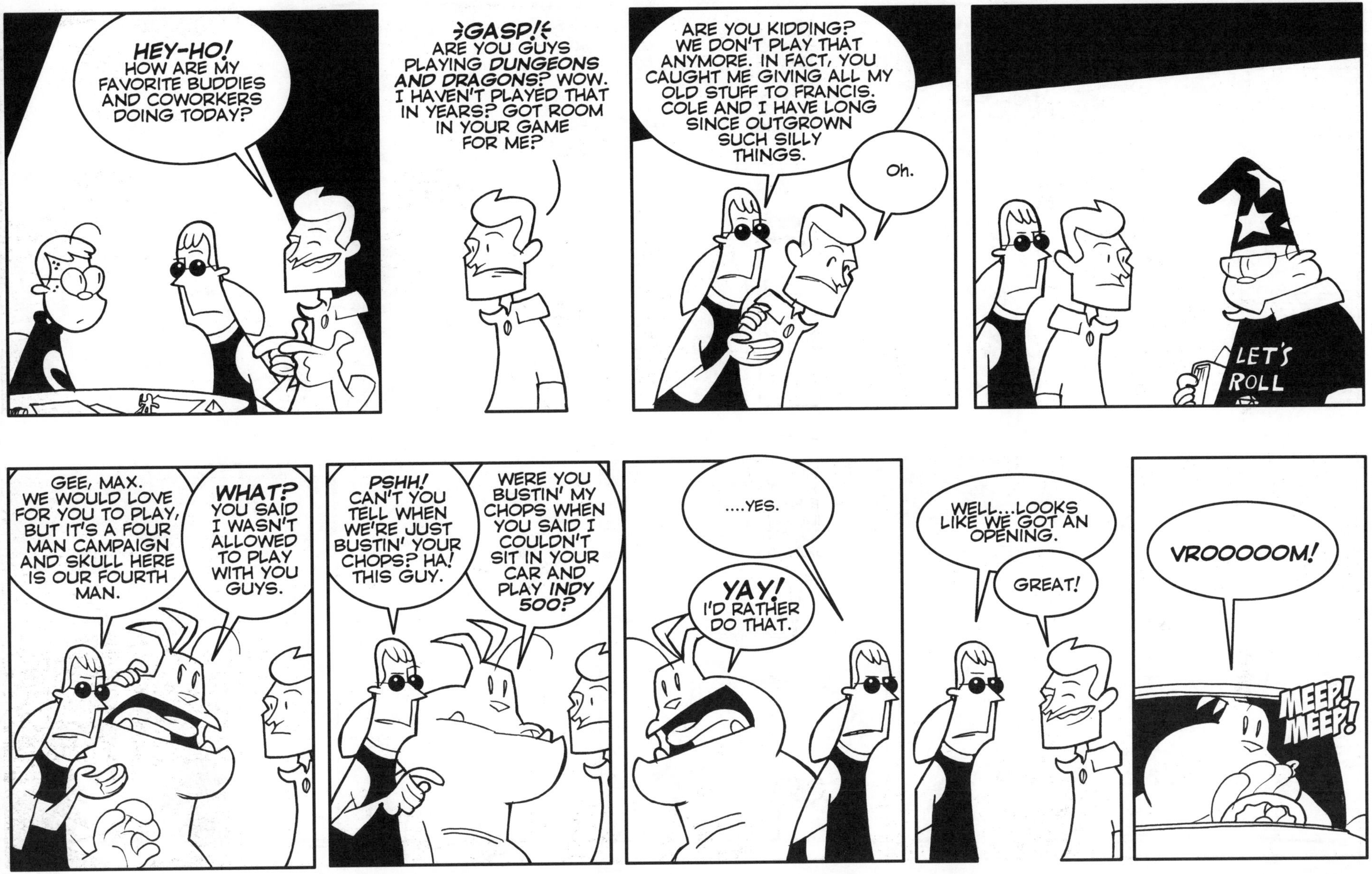
HEY-HO! HOW ARE MY FAVORITE BUDDIES AND COWORKERS DOING TODAY?
GASP! ARE YOU GUYS PLAYING DUNGEONS AND DRAGONS? WOW. I HAVEN'T PLAYED THAT IN YEARS? GOT ROOM IN YOUR GAME FOR ME?
ARE YOU KIDDING? WE DON'T PLAY THAT ANYMORE. IN FACT, YOU CAUGHT ME GIVING ALL MY OLD STUFF TO FRANCIS. COLE AND I HAVE LONG SINCE OUTGROWN SUCH SILLY THINGS.
Oh.
LET'S ROLL
GEE, MAX. WE WOULD LOVE FOR YOU TO PLAY, BUT IT'S A FOUR MAN CAMPAIGN AND SKULL HERE IS OUR FOURTH MAN.
WHAT? YOU SAID I WASN'T ALLOWED TO PLAY WITH YOU GUYS.
PSHH! CAN'T YOU TELL WHEN WE'RE JUST BUSTIN' YOUR CHOPS? HA! THIS GUY.
WERE YOU BUSTIN' MY CHOPS WHEN YOU SAID I COULDN'T SIT IN YOUR CAR AND PLAY INDY 500?
....YES.
YAY! I'D RATHER DO THAT.
WELL...LOOKS LIKE WE GOT AN OPENING.
GREAT!
VROOOOOM!
MEEP! MEEP!

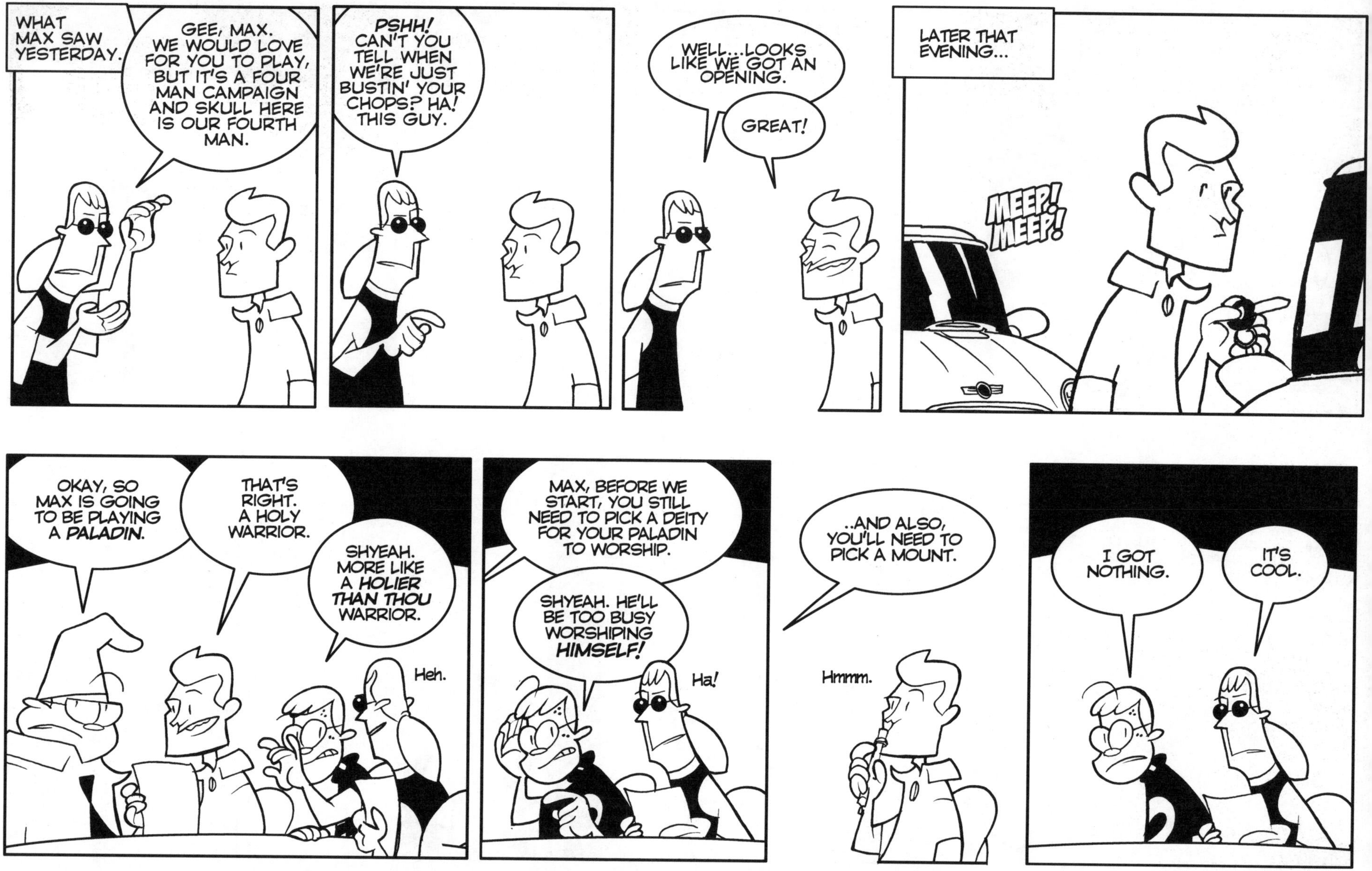
WHAT MAX SAW YESTERDAY.
GEE, MAX. WE WOULD LOVE FOR YOU TO PLAY, BUT IT'S A FOUR MAN CAMPAIGN AND SKULL HERE IS OUR FOURTH MAN.
PSHH! CAN'T YOU TELL WHEN WE'RE JUST BUSTIN' YOUR CHOPS? HA! THIS GUY.
WELL...LOOKS LIKE WE GOT AN OPENING.
GREAT!
LATER THAT EVENING...
MEEP! MEEP!
OKAY, SO MAX IS GOING TO BE PLAYING A PALADIN.
THAT'S RIGHT. A HOLY WARRIOR.
SHYEAH. MORE LIKE A HOLIER THAN THOU WARRIOR.
Heh.
MAX, BEFORE WE START, YOU STILL NEED TO PICK A DEITY FOR YOUR PALADIN TO WORSHIP.
SHYEAH. HE'LL BE TOO BUSY WORSHIPING HIMSELF!
Ha!
..AND ALSO, YOU'LL NEED TO PICK A MOUNT.
Hmmm.
I GOT NOTHING.
IT'S COOL.

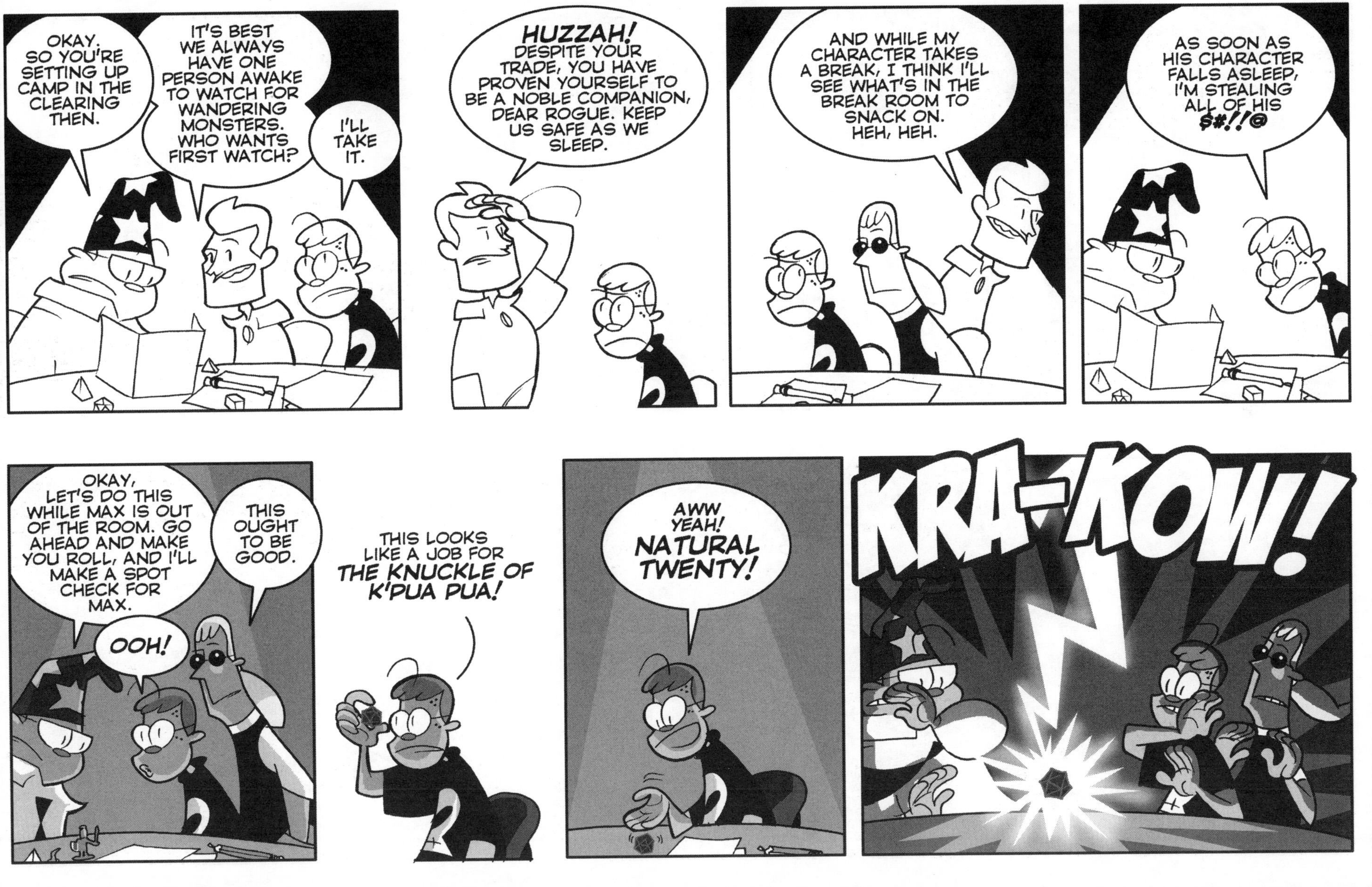
OKAY. SO YOU'RE SETTING UP CAMP IN THE CLEARING THEN.
IT'S BEST WE ALWAYS HAVE ONE PERSON AWAKE TO WATCH FOR WANDERING MONSTERS. WHO WANTS FIRST WATCH?
I'LL TAKE IT.
HUZZAH! DESPITE YOUR TRADE, YOU HAVE PROVEN YOURSELF TO BE A NOBLE COMPANION, DEAR ROGUE. KEEP US SAFE AS WE SLEEP.
AND WHILE MY CHARACTER TAKES A BREAK, I THINK I'LL SEE WHAT'S IN THE BREAK ROOM TO SNACK ON. HEH, HEH.
AS SOON AS HIS CHARACTER FALLS ASLEEP, I'M STEALING ALL OF HIS $#!!@
OKAY, LET'S DO THIS WHILE MAX IS OUT OF THE ROOM. GO AHEAD AND MAKE YOU ROLL, AND I'LL MAKE A SPOT CHECK FOR MAX.
THIS OUGHT TO BE GOOD.
OOH!
THIS LOOKS LIKE A JOB FOR THE KNUCKLE OF K'PUA PUA!
AWW YEAH! NATURAL TWENTY!
KRA-KOW!

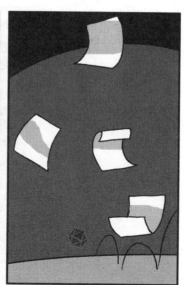

WHAT?
DID YOU GUYS
SAY SOMETHING?
I COULDN'T MAKE
IT OUT.

GUYS?

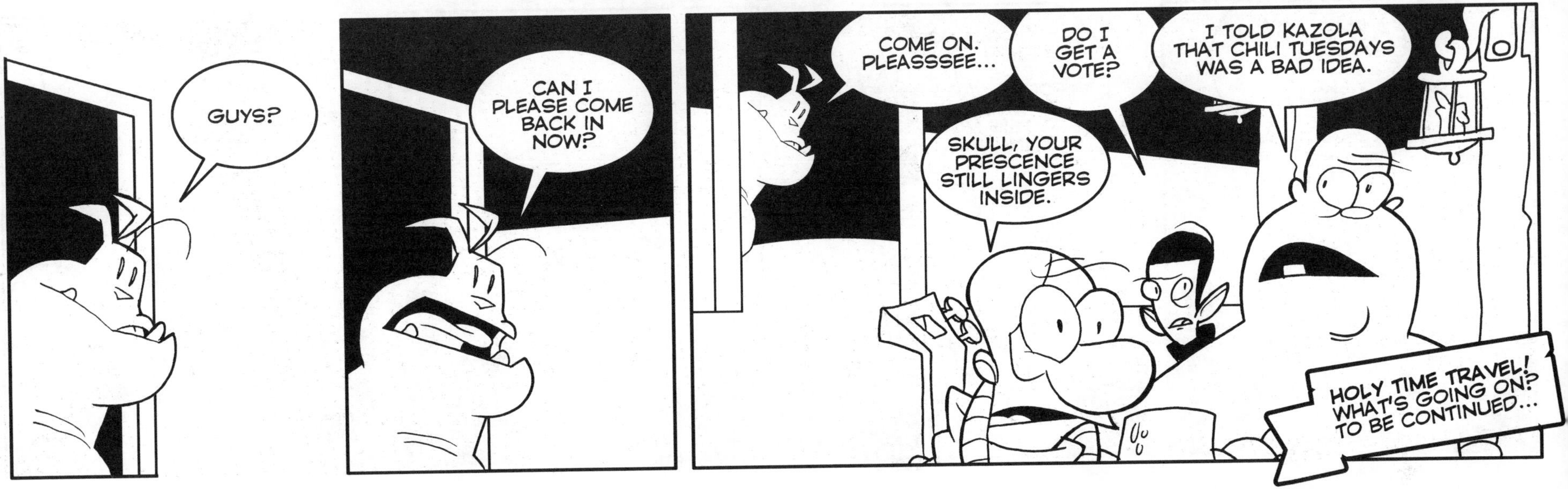
GUYS?
CAN I PLEASE COME BACK IN NOW?
COME ON. PLEASSSEE...
SKULL, YOUR PRESCENCE STILL LINGERS INSIDE.
DO I GET A VOTE?
I TOLD KAZOLA THAT CHILI TUESDAYS WAS A BAD IDEA.
HOLY TIME TRAVEL! WHAT'S GOING ON? TO BE CONTINUED...

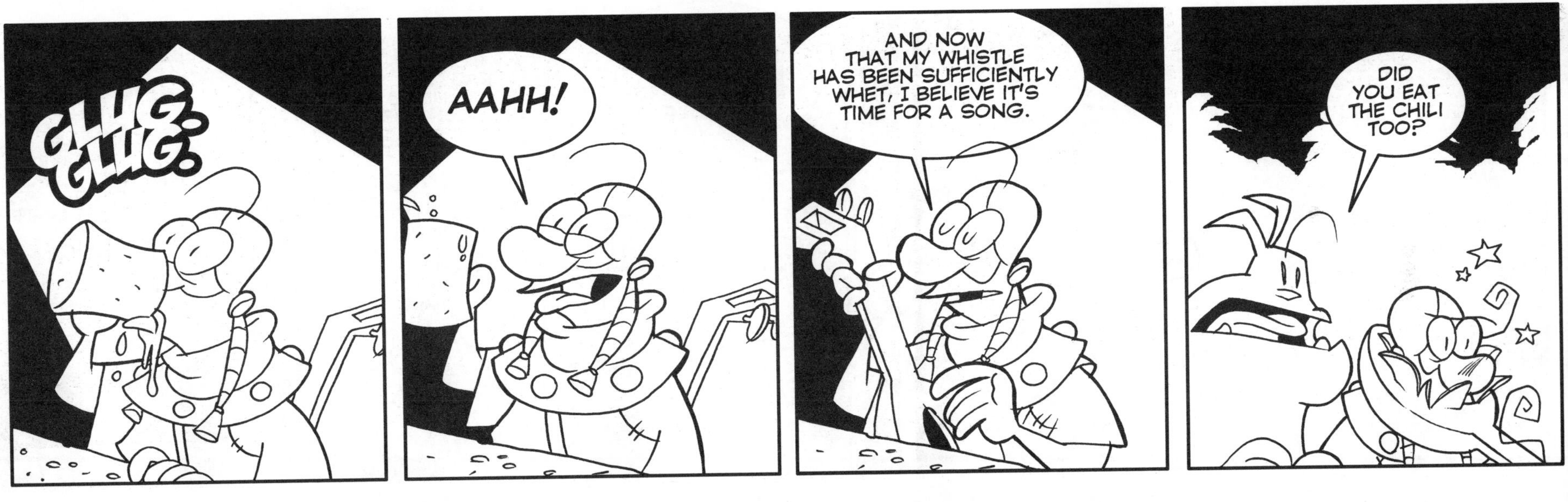
GLUG GLUG
AAHH!
AND NOW THAT MY WHISTLE HAS BEEN SUFFICIENTLY WHET, I BELIEVE IT'S TIME FOR A SONG.
DID YOU EAT THE CHILI TOO?

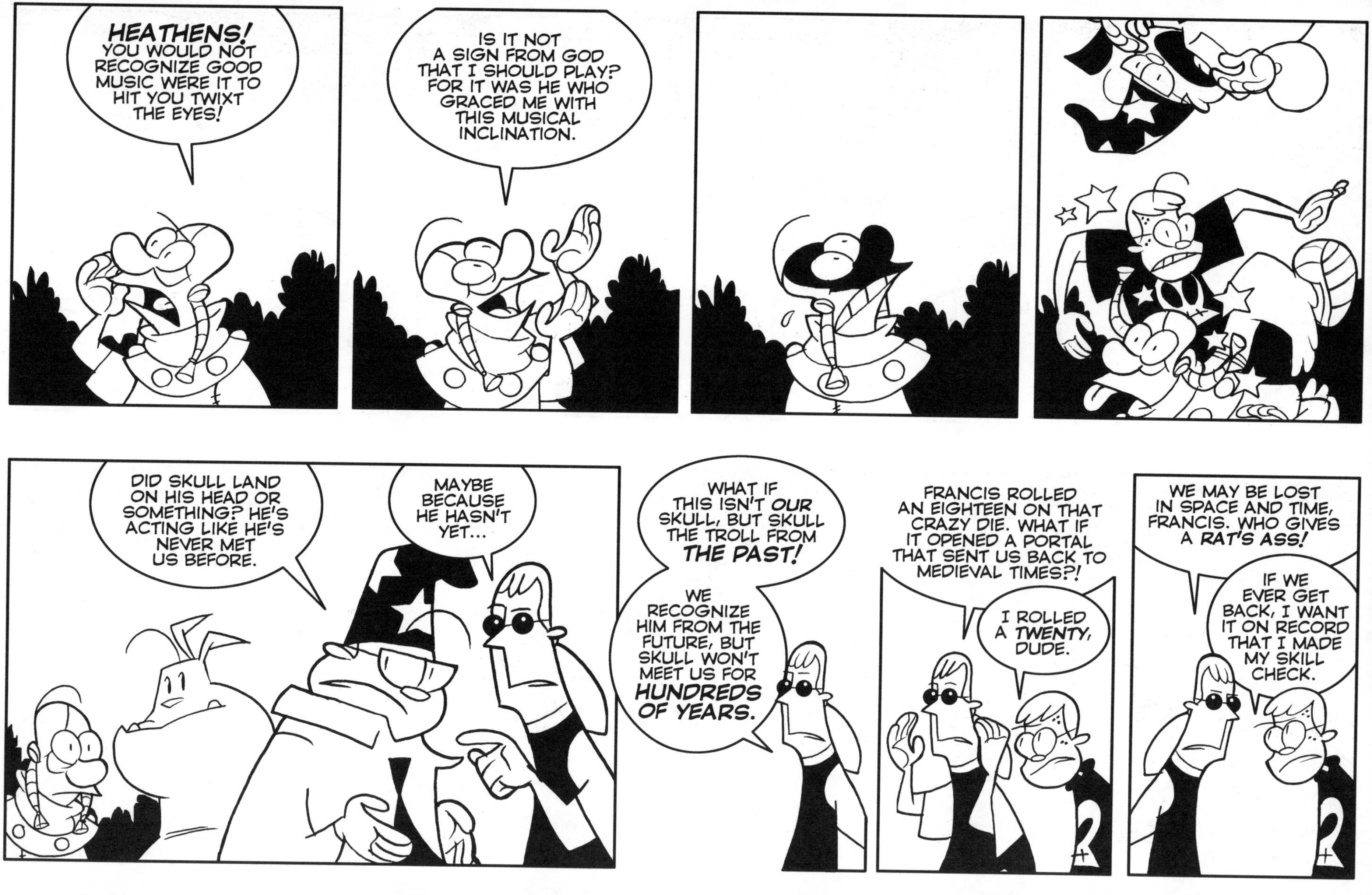

HEATHENS! YOU WOULD NOT RECOGNIZE GOOD MUSIC WERE IT TO HIT YOU TWIXT THE EYES!
IS IT NOT A SIGN FROM GOD THAT I SHOULD PLAY? FOR IT WAS HE WHO GRACED ME WITH THIS MUSICAL INCLINATION.
DID SKULL LAND ON HIS HEAD OR SOMETHING? HE'S ACTING LIKE HE'S NEVER MET US BEFORE.
MAYBE BECAUSE HE HASN'T YET...
WHAT IF THIS ISN'T OUR SKULL, BUT SKULL THE TROLL FROM THE PAST!
WE RECOGNIZE HIM FROM THE FUTURE, BUT SKULL WON'T MEET US FOR HUNDREDS OF YEARS.
FRANCIS ROLLED AN EIGHTEEN ON THAT CRAZY DIE. WHAT IF IT OPENED A PORTAL THAT SENT US BACK TO MEDIEVAL TIMES?!
I ROLLED A TWENTY, DUDE.
WE MAY BE LOST IN SPACE AND TIME, FRANCIS. WHO GIVES A RAT'S ASS!
IF WE EVER GET BACK, I WANT IT ON RECORD THAT I MADE MY SKILL CHECK.

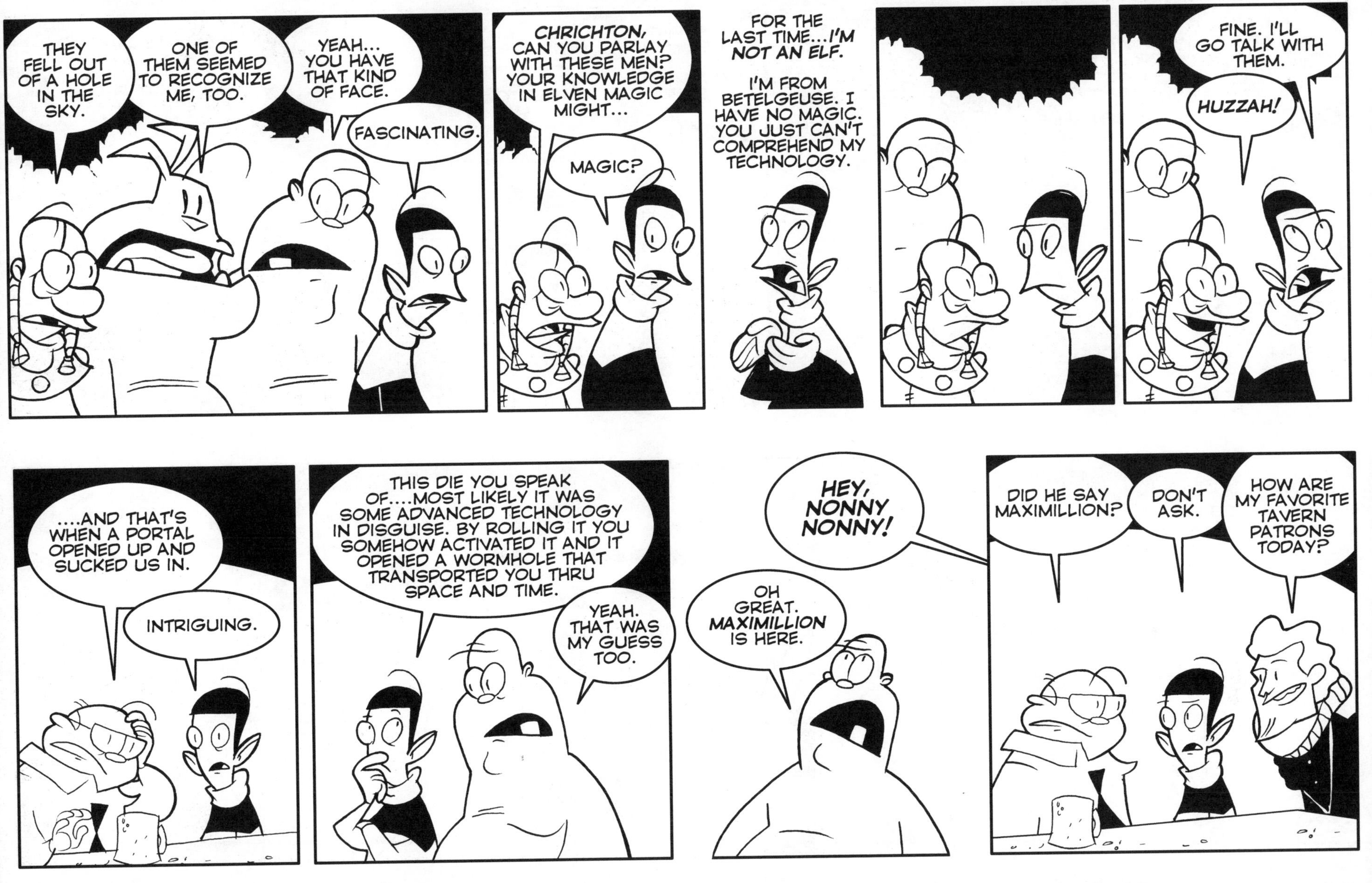
THEY FELL OUT OF A HOLE IN THE SKY.
ONE OF THEM SEEMED TO RECOGNIZE ME, TOO.
YEAH... YOU HAVE THAT KIND OF FACE.
FASCINATING.
CHRICHTON, CAN YOU PARLAY WITH THESE MEN? YOUR KNOWLEDGE IN ELVEN MAGIC MIGHT...
MAGIC?
FOR THE LAST TIME...I'M NOT AN ELF.
I'M FROM BETELGEUSE. I HAVE NO MAGIC. YOU JUST CAN'T COMPREHEND MY TECHNOLOGY.
FINE. I'LL GO TALK WITH THEM.
HUZZAH!
....AND THAT'S WHEN A PORTAL OPENED UP AND SUCKED US IN.
INTRIGUING.
THIS DIE YOU SPEAK OF....MOST LIKELY IT WAS SOME ADVANCED TECHNOLOGY IN DISGUISE. BY ROLLING IT YOU SOMEHOW ACTIVATED IT AND IT OPENED A WORMHOLE THAT TRANSPORTED YOU THRU SPACE AND TIME.
YEAH. THAT WAS MY GUESS TOO.
HEY, NONNY NONNY!
OH GREAT. MAXIMILLION IS HERE.
DID HE SAY MAXIMILLION?
DON'T ASK.
HOW ARE MY FAVORITE TAVERN PATRONS TODAY?

Panel 1:
WOW. LOOK AT THE RESEMBLANCE. IT'S REALLY HIM ISN'T IT?

OH YEAH. *DEFINITELY* ONE OF MAX'S ANCESTORS.

GENTLEMEN, HAVE WE MET BEFORE?

Panel 2:
NO, BUT YOUR GREAT, GREAT, GREAT, GREAT, GREAT, GREAT GREAT, GREAT, GREAT GREAT, GREAT, GREAT GREAT, GREAT, GREAT GREAT, GREAT, GREAT GREAT, GREAT, GREAT GREAT, GREAT, *GREAT* GRANDSON IS A TOTAL *DICKWEED*.

Panel 3:
WHO ARE THESE MEN? THEY SEEM CRAZED WITH FEVER.

THEY'RE FROM THE FUTURE, MAX, AND THEY APPEAR TO BE FAMILIAR WITH ONE OF YOUR DESCENDANTS.

Panel 4:
YOU *RASCALS* AND YOUR TAVERN PRANKS. YOU'VE VEXXED ME ONCE AGAIN. HA! HA! *TWANG!*

UNCANNY.

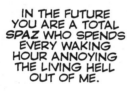

Panel 5:
SO...I WAS WONDERING. ARE WE FRIENDS IN THE FUTURE OR SOMETHING?

NO WE ARE MOST CERTAINLY *NOT.*

Panel 6:
IN THE FUTURE YOU ARE A TOTAL *SPAZ* WHO SPENDS EVERY WAKING HOUR ANNOYING THE LIVING HELL OUT OF ME.

Panel 7:
OKAY, THANKS.

NO PROBLEM.

Panel 8:
WELL?

NOPE. WE'RE NOT FRIENDS.

Panel 9:
I SAY WE EAT HIM.

SOUNDS GOOD.

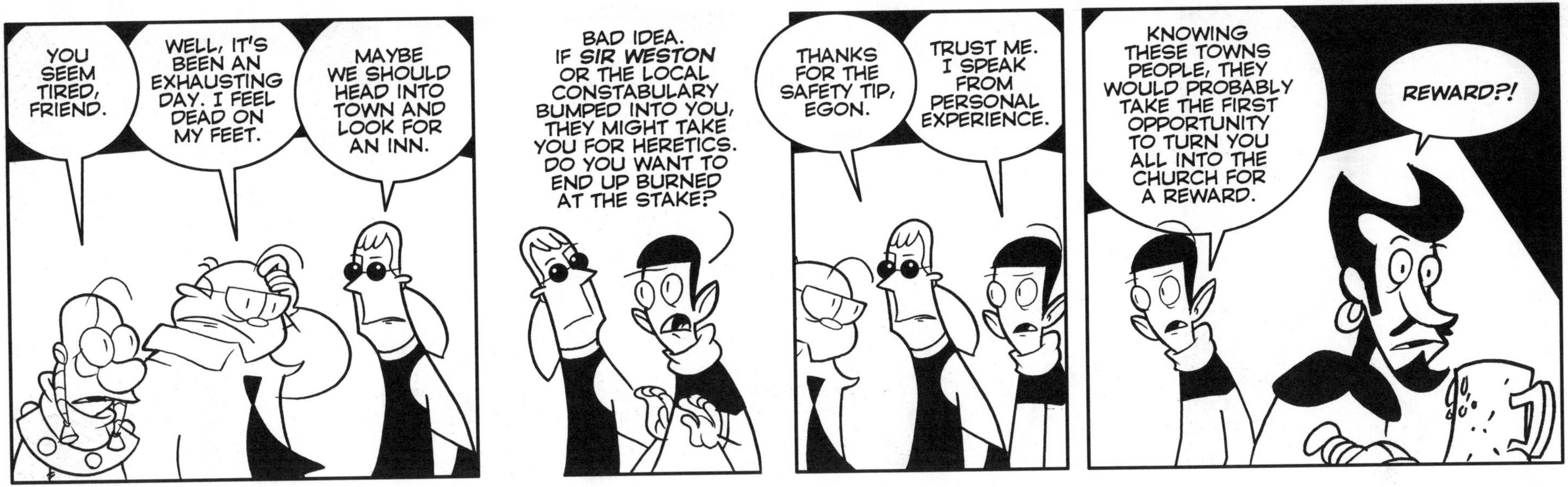
YOU SEEM TIRED, FRIEND.
WELL, IT'S BEEN AN EXHAUSTING DAY. I FEEL DEAD ON MY FEET.
MAYBE WE SHOULD HEAD INTO TOWN AND LOOK FOR AN INN.
BAD IDEA. IF SIR WESTON OR THE LOCAL CONSTABULARY BUMPED INTO YOU, THEY MIGHT TAKE YOU FOR HERETICS. DO YOU WANT TO END UP BURNED AT THE STAKE?
THANKS FOR THE SAFETY TIP, EGON.
TRUST ME. I SPEAK FROM PERSONAL EXPERIENCE.
KNOWING THESE TOWNS PEOPLE, THEY WOULD PROBABLY TAKE THE FIRST OPPORTUNITY TO TURN YOU ALL INTO THE CHURCH FOR A REWARD.
REWARD?!

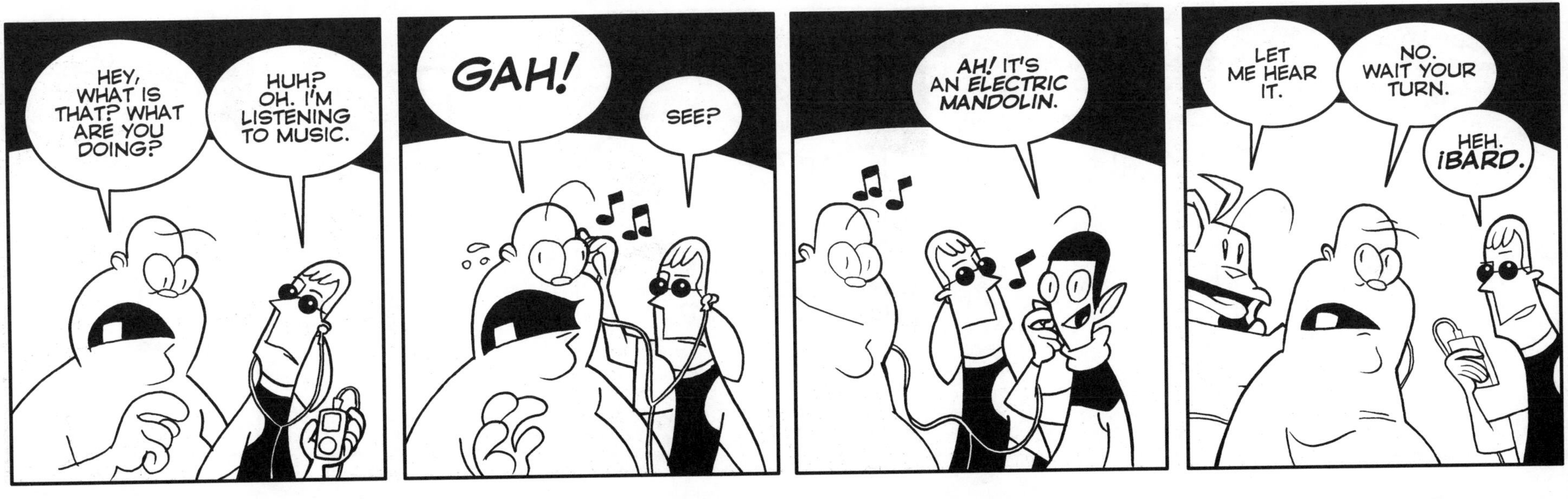
HEY, WHAT IS THAT? WHAT ARE YOU DOING?
HUH? OH. I'M LISTENING TO MUSIC.
GAH!
SEE?
AH! IT'S AN ELECTRIC MANDOLIN.
LET ME HEAR IT.
NO. WAIT YOUR TURN.
HEH. iBARD.

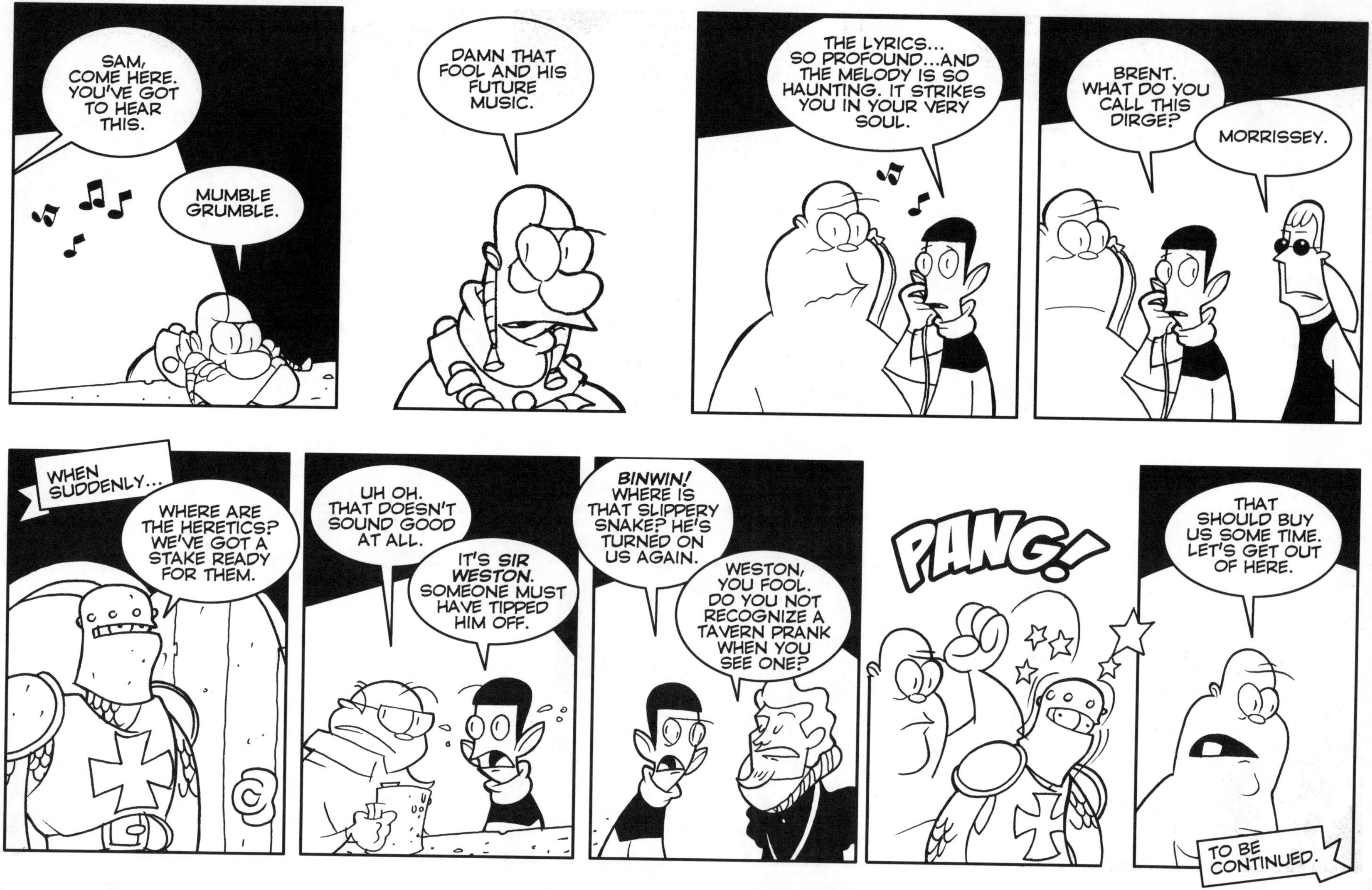
SAM, COME HERE. YOU'VE GOT TO HEAR THIS.
MUMBLE GRUMBLE.
DAMN THAT FOOL AND HIS FUTURE MUSIC.
THE LYRICS... SO PROFOUND...AND THE MELODY IS SO HAUNTING. IT STRIKES YOU IN YOUR VERY SOUL.
BRENT. WHAT DO YOU CALL THIS DIRGE?
MORRISSEY.
WHEN SUDDENLY...
WHERE ARE THE HERETICS? WE'VE GOT A STAKE READY FOR THEM.
UH OH. THAT DOESN'T SOUND GOOD AT ALL.
IT'S *SIR WESTON*. SOMEONE MUST HAVE TIPPED HIM OFF.
BINWIN! WHERE IS THAT SLIPPERY SNAKE? HE'S TURNED ON US AGAIN.
WESTON, YOU FOOL. DO YOU NOT RECOGNIZE A TAVERN PRANK WHEN YOU SEE ONE?
PANG!
THAT SHOULD BUY US SOME TIME. LET'S GET OUT OF HERE.
TO BE CONTINUED.

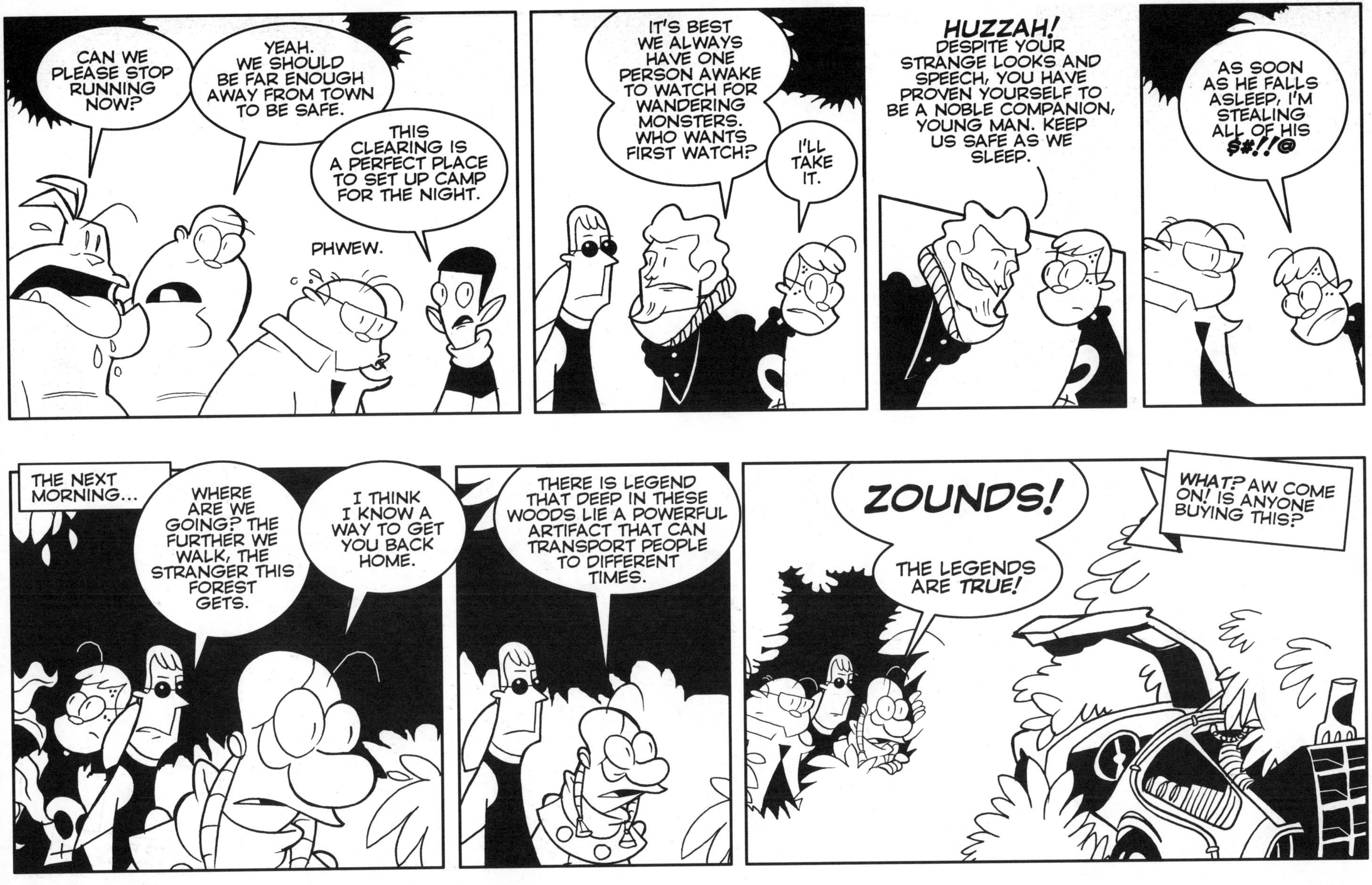
CAN WE PLEASE STOP RUNNING NOW?
YEAH. WE SHOULD BE FAR ENOUGH AWAY FROM TOWN TO BE SAFE.
PHWEW.
THIS CLEARING IS A PERFECT PLACE TO SET UP CAMP FOR THE NIGHT.
IT'S BEST WE ALWAYS HAVE ONE PERSON AWAKE TO WATCH FOR WANDERING MONSTERS. WHO WANTS FIRST WATCH?
I'LL TAKE IT.
HUZZAH! DESPITE YOUR STRANGE LOOKS AND SPEECH, YOU HAVE PROVEN YOURSELF TO BE A NOBLE COMPANION, YOUNG MAN. KEEP US SAFE AS WE SLEEP.
AS SOON AS HE FALLS ASLEEP, I'M STEALING ALL OF HIS $#!!@
THE NEXT MORNING...
WHERE ARE WE GOING? THE FURTHER WE WALK, THE STRANGER THIS FOREST GETS.
I THINK I KNOW A WAY TO GET YOU BACK HOME.
THERE IS LEGEND THAT DEEP IN THESE WOODS LIE A POWERFUL ARTIFACT THAT CAN TRANSPORT PEOPLE TO DIFFERENT TIMES.
ZOUNDS!
THE LEGENDS ARE TRUE!
WHAT? AW COME ON! IS ANYONE BUYING THIS?

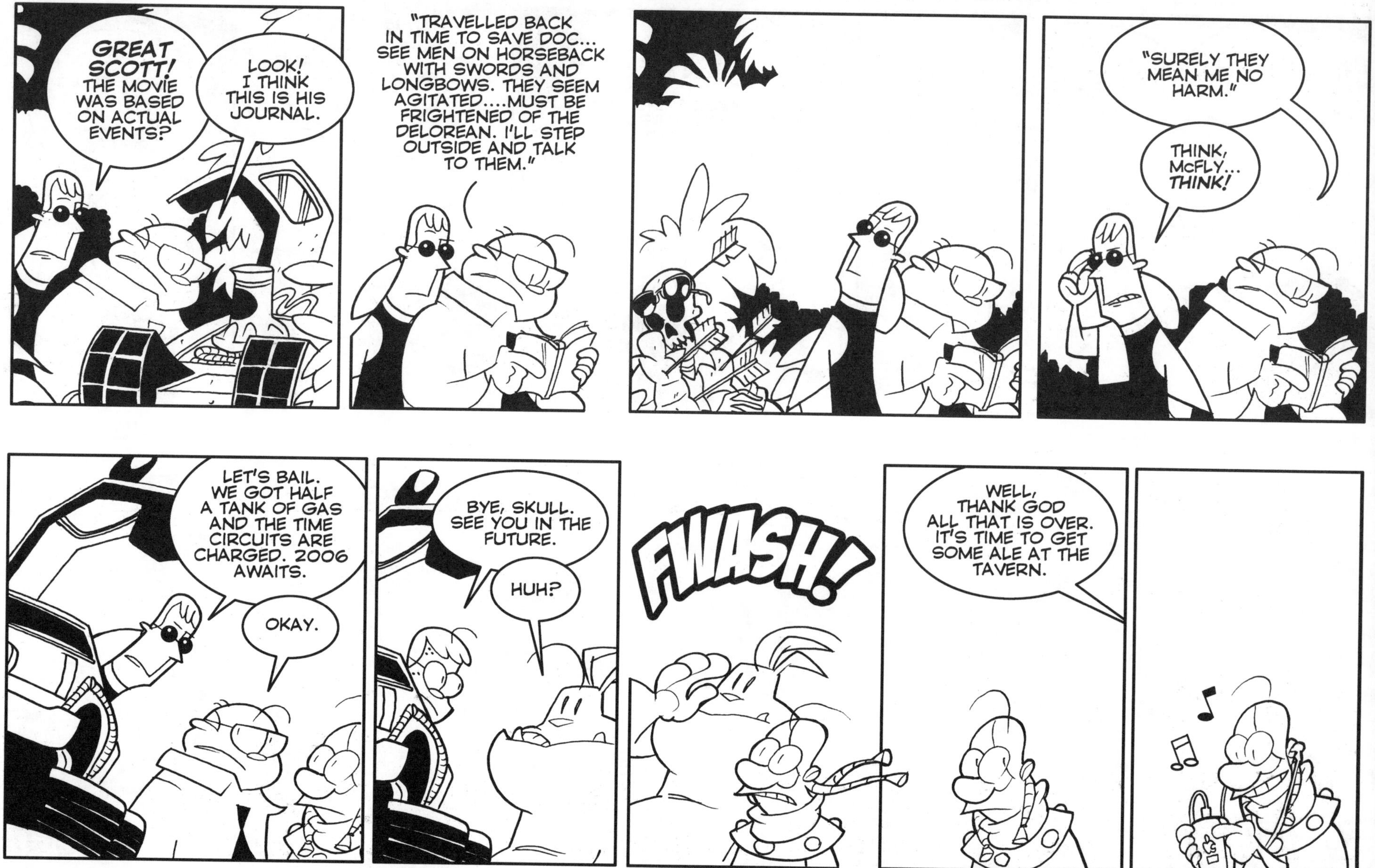
GREAT SCOTT! THE MOVIE WAS BASED ON ACTUAL EVENTS?
LOOK! I THINK THIS IS HIS JOURNAL.
"TRAVELLED BACK IN TIME TO SAVE DOC... SEE MEN ON HORSEBACK WITH SWORDS AND LONGBOWS. THEY SEEM AGITATED....MUST BE FRIGHTENED OF THE DELOREAN. I'LL STEP OUTSIDE AND TALK TO THEM."
"SURELY THEY MEAN ME NO HARM."
THINK, McFLY... THINK!
LET'S BAIL. WE GOT HALF A TANK OF GAS AND THE TIME CIRCUITS ARE CHARGED. 2006 AWAITS.
OKAY.
BYE, SKULL. SEE YOU IN THE FUTURE.
HUH?
FWASH!
WELL, THANK GOD ALL THAT IS OVER. IT'S TIME TO GET SOME ALE AT THE TAVERN.

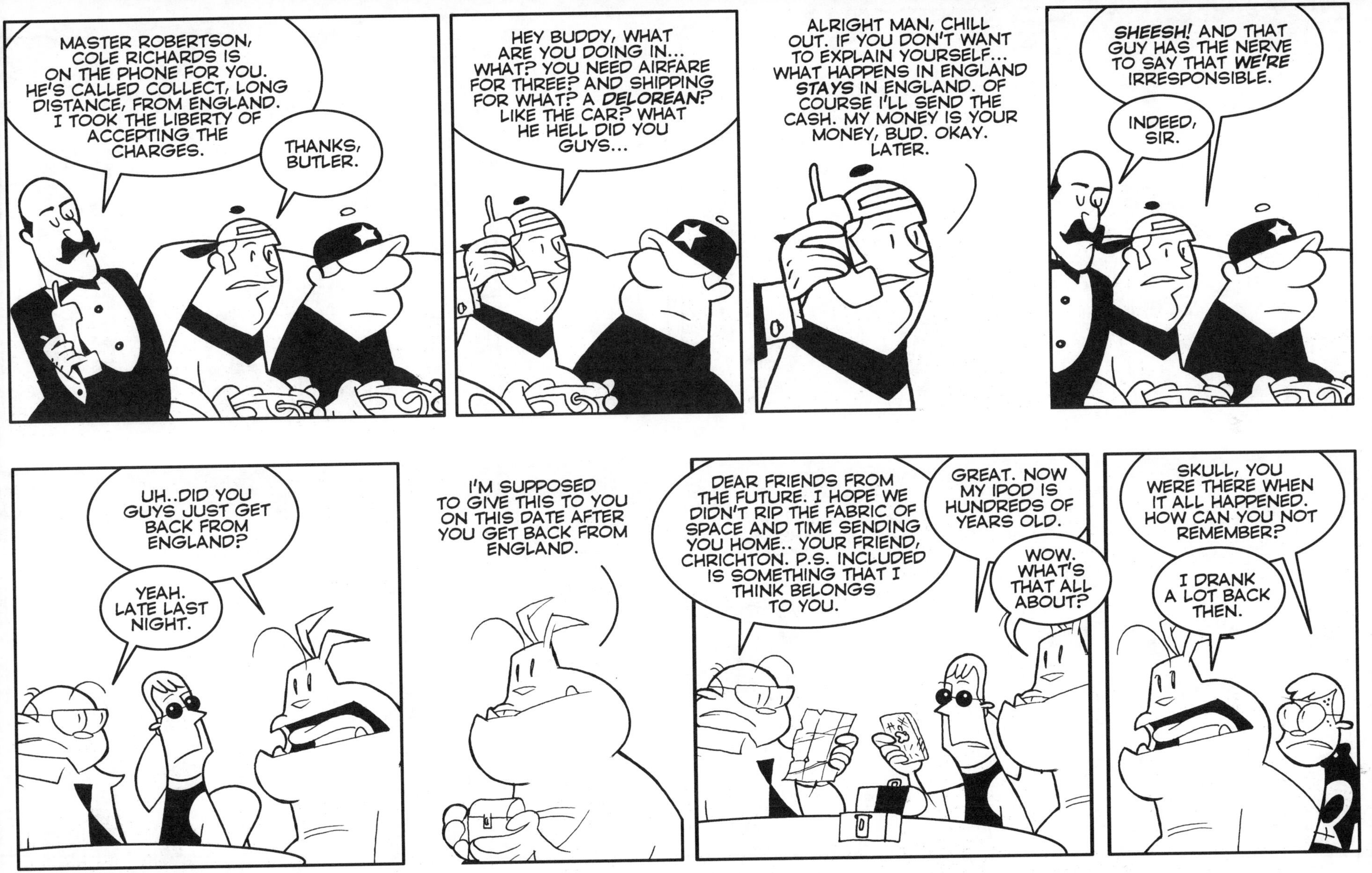
MASTER ROBERTSON, COLE RICHARDS IS ON THE PHONE FOR YOU. HE'S CALLED COLLECT, LONG DISTANCE, FROM ENGLAND. I TOOK THE LIBERTY OF ACCEPTING THE CHARGES.
THANKS, BUTLER.
HEY BUDDY, WHAT ARE YOU DOING IN... WHAT? YOU NEED AIRFARE FOR THREE? AND SHIPPING FOR WHAT? A *DELOREAN*? LIKE THE CAR? WHAT HE HELL DID YOU GUYS...
ALRIGHT MAN, CHILL OUT. IF YOU DON'T WANT TO EXPLAIN YOURSELF... WHAT HAPPENS IN ENGLAND **STAYS** IN ENGLAND. OF COURSE I'LL SEND THE CASH. MY MONEY IS YOUR MONEY, BUD. OKAY. LATER.
SHEESH! AND THAT GUY HAS THE NERVE TO SAY THAT ***WE'RE*** IRRESPONSIBLE.
INDEED, SIR.
UH..DID YOU GUYS JUST GET BACK FROM ENGLAND?
YEAH. LATE LAST NIGHT.
I'M SUPPOSED TO GIVE THIS TO YOU ON THIS DATE AFTER YOU GET BACK FROM ENGLAND.
DEAR FRIENDS FROM THE FUTURE. I HOPE WE DIDN'T RIP THE FABRIC OF SPACE AND TIME SENDING YOU HOME.. YOUR FRIEND, CHRICHTON. P.S. INCLUDED IS SOMETHING THAT I THINK BELONGS TO YOU.
GREAT. NOW MY IPOD IS HUNDREDS OF YEARS OLD.
WOW. WHAT'S THAT ALL ABOUT?
SKULL, YOU WERE THERE WHEN IT ALL HAPPENED. HOW CAN YOU NOT REMEMBER?
I DRANK A LOT BACK THEN.

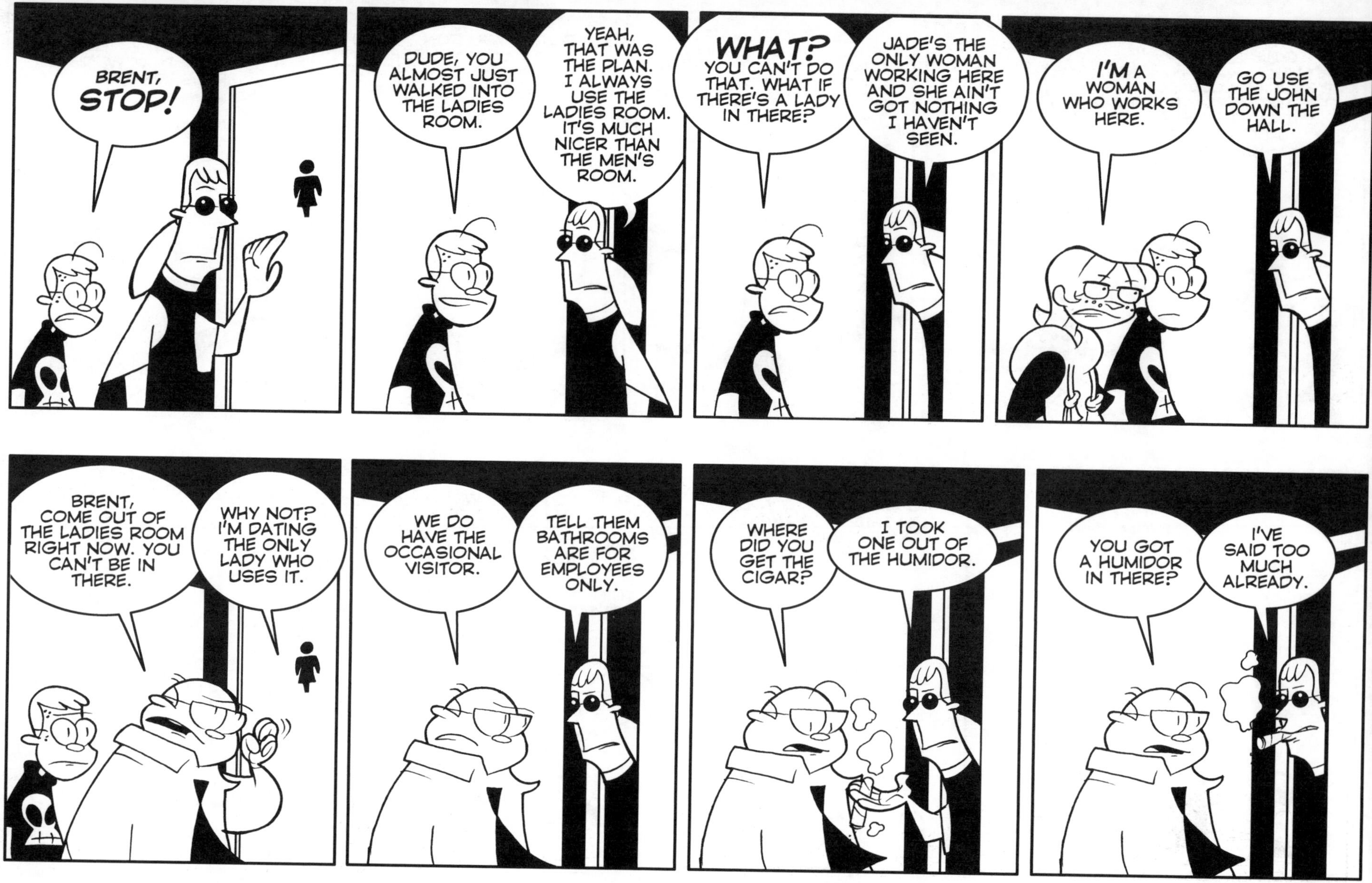
BRENT, STOP!
DUDE, YOU ALMOST JUST WALKED INTO THE LADIES ROOM.
YEAH, THAT WAS THE PLAN. I ALWAYS USE THE LADIES ROOM. IT'S MUCH NICER THAN THE MEN'S ROOM.
WHAT? YOU CAN'T DO THAT. WHAT IF THERE'S A LADY IN THERE?
JADE'S THE ONLY WOMAN WORKING HERE AND SHE AIN'T GOT NOTHING I HAVEN'T SEEN.
I'M A WOMAN WHO WORKS HERE.
GO USE THE JOHN DOWN THE HALL.
BRENT, COME OUT OF THE LADIES ROOM RIGHT NOW. YOU CAN'T BE IN THERE.
WHY NOT? I'M DATING THE ONLY LADY WHO USES IT.
WE DO HAVE THE OCCASIONAL VISITOR.
TELL THEM BATHROOMS ARE FOR EMPLOYEES ONLY.
WHERE DID YOU GET THE CIGAR?
I TOOK ONE OUT OF THE HUMIDOR.
YOU GOT A HUMIDOR IN THERE?
I'VE SAID TOO MUCH ALREADY.

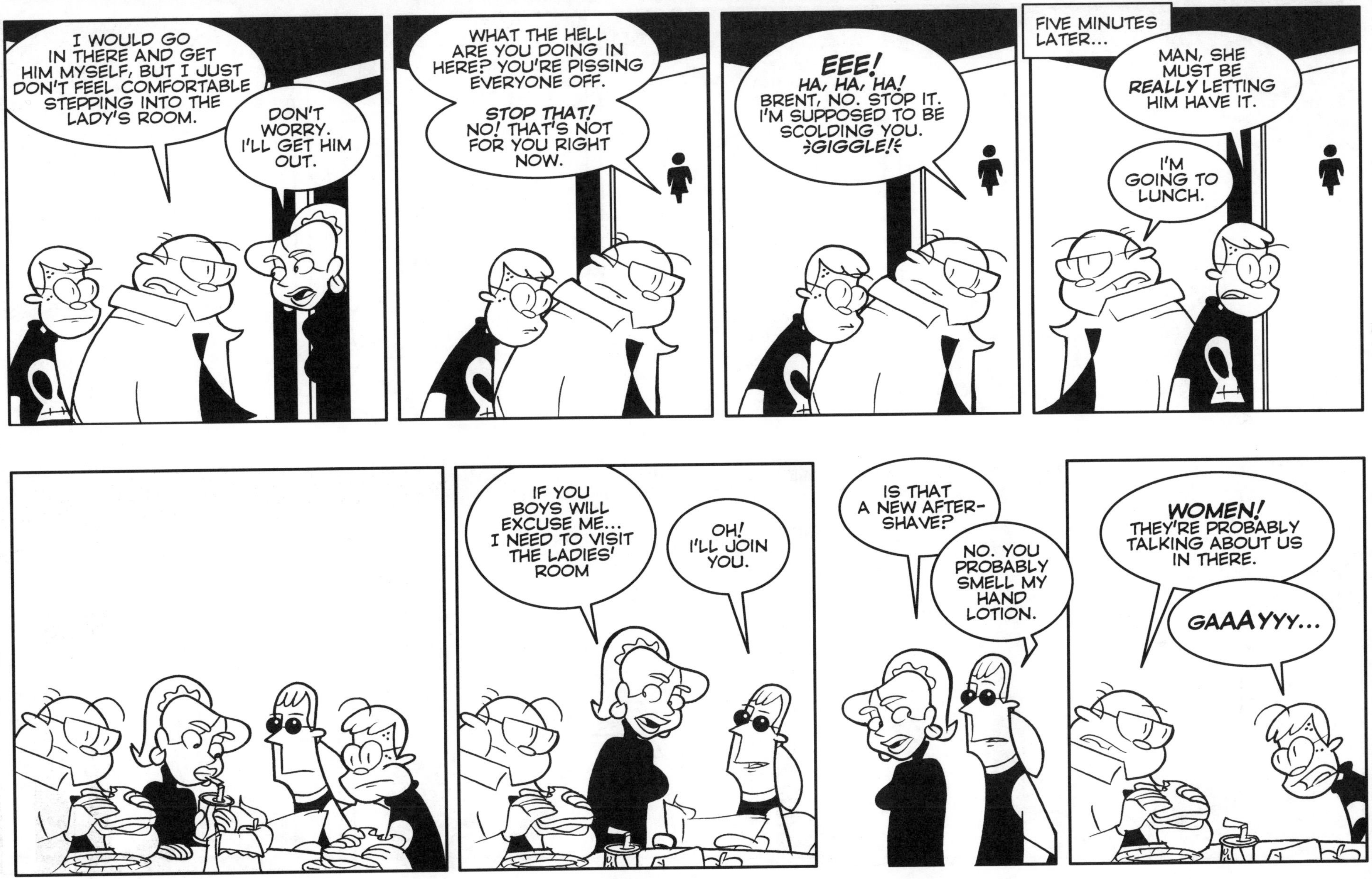
I WOULD GO IN THERE AND GET HIM MYSELF, BUT I JUST DON'T FEEL COMFORTABLE STEPPING INTO THE LADY'S ROOM.
DON'T WORRY. I'LL GET HIM OUT.
WHAT THE HELL ARE YOU DOING IN HERE? YOU'RE PISSING EVERYONE OFF.
STOP THAT! NO! THAT'S NOT FOR YOU RIGHT NOW.
EEE! HA, HA, HA! BRENT, NO. STOP IT. I'M SUPPOSED TO BE SCOLDING YOU. GIGGLE!
FIVE MINUTES LATER...
MAN, SHE MUST BE REALLY LETTING HIM HAVE IT.
I'M GOING TO LUNCH.
IF YOU BOYS WILL EXCUSE ME... I NEED TO VISIT THE LADIES' ROOM
OH! I'LL JOIN YOU.
IS THAT A NEW AFTER-SHAVE?
NO. YOU PROBABLY SMELL MY HAND LOTION.
WOMEN! THEY'RE PROBABLY TALKING ABOUT US IN THERE.
GAAAYYY...

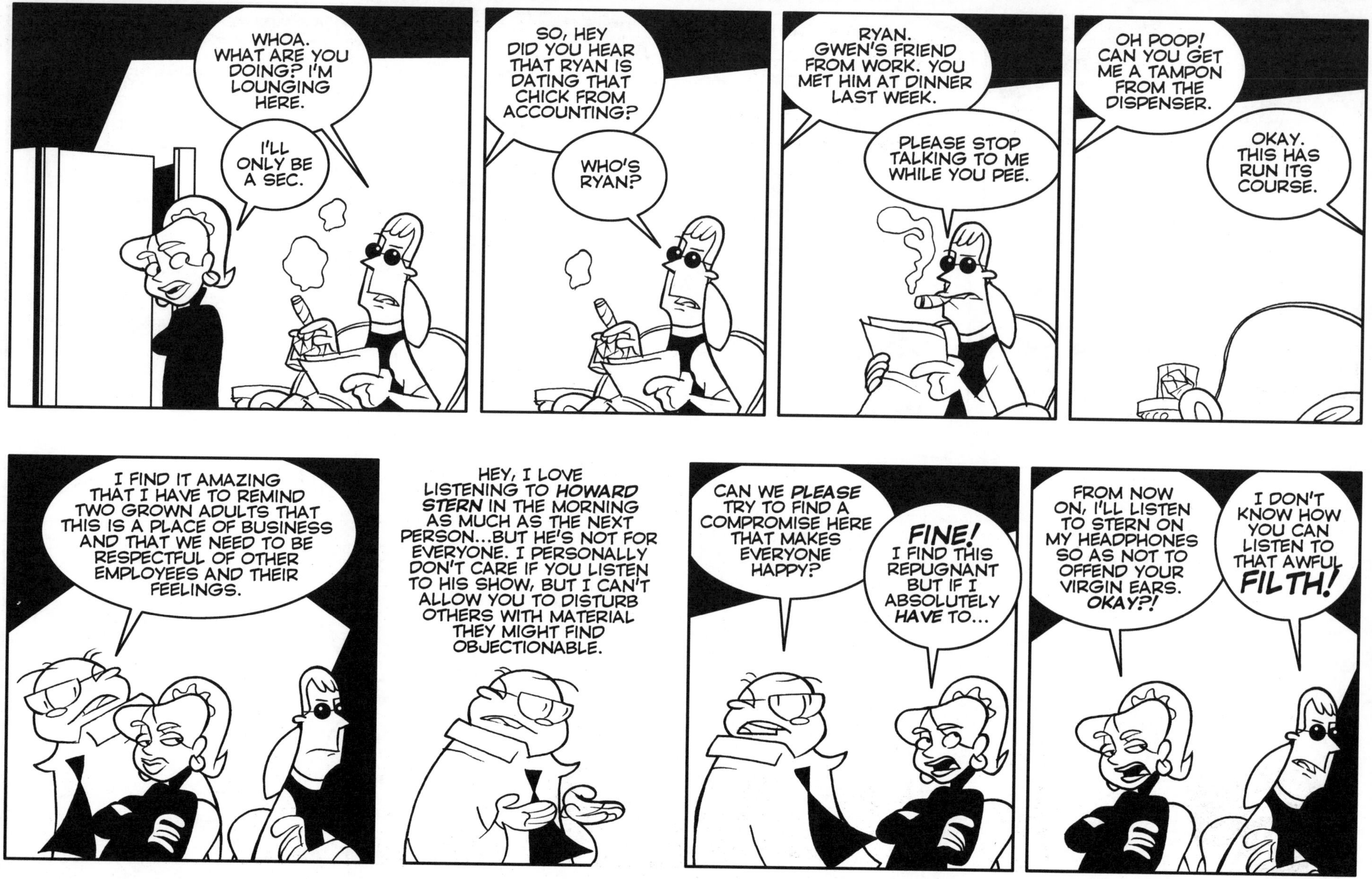
WHOA. WHAT ARE YOU DOING? I'M LOUNGING HERE.
I'LL ONLY BE A SEC.
SO, HEY DID YOU HEAR THAT RYAN IS DATING THAT CHICK FROM ACCOUNTING?
WHO'S RYAN?
RYAN. GWEN'S FRIEND FROM WORK. YOU MET HIM AT DINNER LAST WEEK.
PLEASE STOP TALKING TO ME WHILE YOU PEE.
OH POOP! CAN YOU GET ME A TAMPON FROM THE DISPENSER.
OKAY. THIS HAS RUN ITS COURSE.
I FIND IT AMAZING THAT I HAVE TO REMIND TWO GROWN ADULTS THAT THIS IS A PLACE OF BUSINESS AND THAT WE NEED TO BE RESPECTFUL OF OTHER EMPLOYEES AND THEIR FEELINGS.
HEY, I LOVE LISTENING TO *HOWARD STERN* IN THE MORNING AS MUCH AS THE NEXT PERSON...BUT HE'S NOT FOR EVERYONE. I PERSONALLY DON'T CARE IF YOU LISTEN TO HIS SHOW, BUT I CAN'T ALLOW YOU TO DISTURB OTHERS WITH MATERIAL THEY MIGHT FIND OBJECTIONABLE.
CAN WE *PLEASE* TRY TO FIND A COMPROMISE HERE THAT MAKES EVERYONE HAPPY?
FINE! I FIND THIS REPUGNANT BUT IF I ABSOLUTELY *HAVE* TO...
FROM NOW ON, I'LL LISTEN TO STERN ON MY HEADPHONES SO AS NOT TO OFFEND YOUR VIRGIN EARS. *OKAY?!*
I DON'T KNOW HOW YOU CAN LISTEN TO THAT AWFUL *FILTH!*

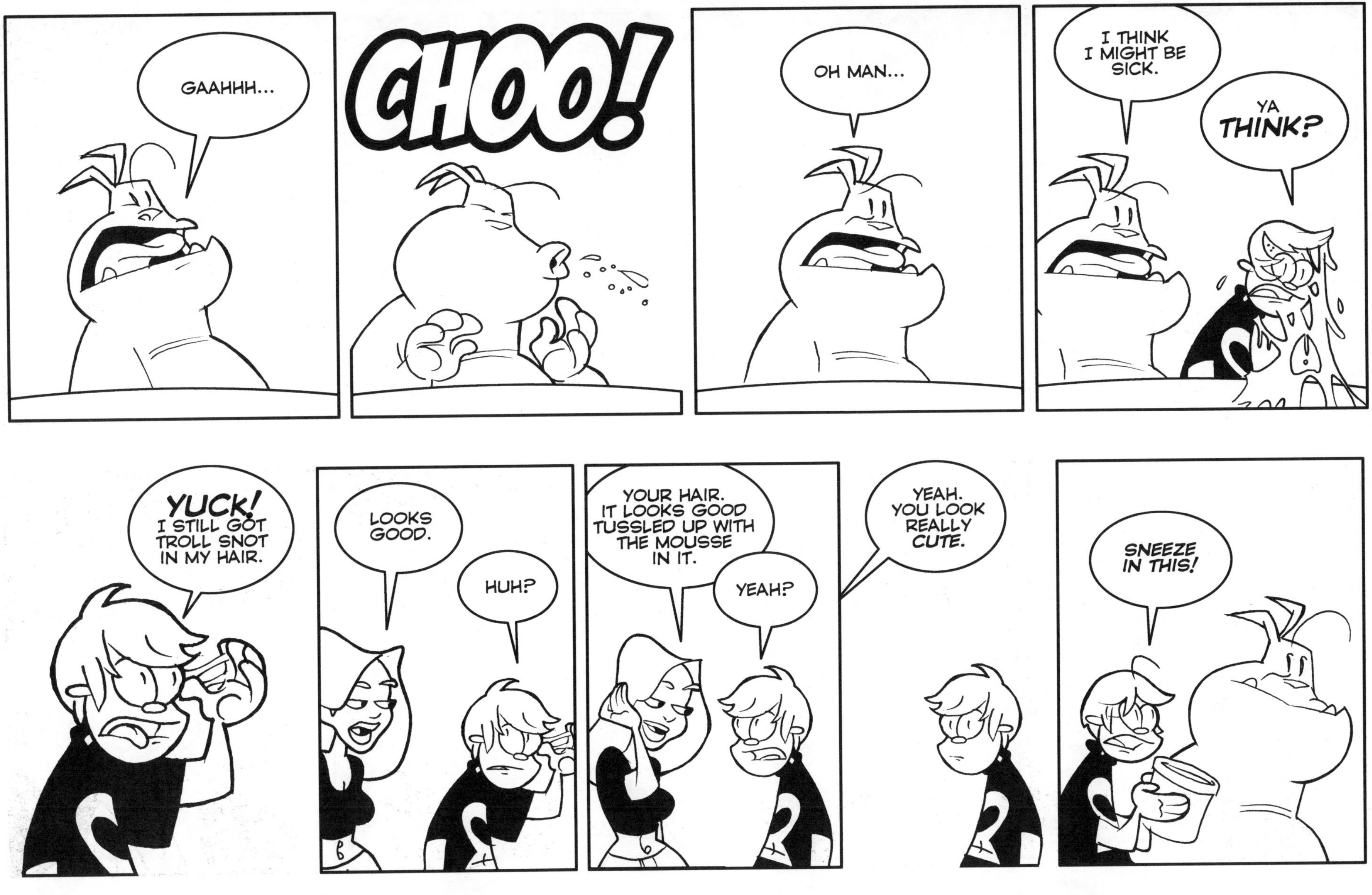
GAAHHH...
CHOO!
OH MAN...
I THINK I MIGHT BE SICK.
YA THINK?
YUCK! I STILL GOT TROLL SNOT IN MY HAIR.
LOOKS GOOD.
HUH?
YOUR HAIR. IT LOOKS GOOD TUSSLED UP WITH THE MOUSSE IN IT.
YEAH?
YEAH. YOU LOOK REALLY CUTE.
SNEEZE IN THIS!

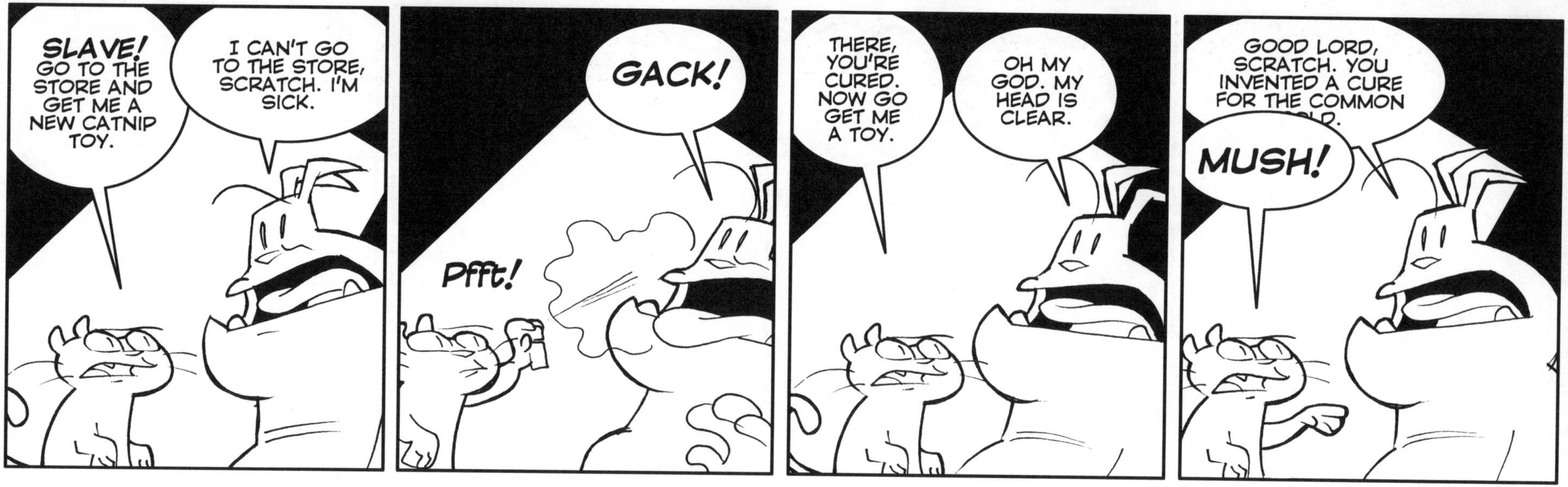
SLAVE! GO TO THE STORE AND GET ME A NEW CATNIP TOY.
I CAN'T GO TO THE STORE, SCRATCH. I'M SICK.
Pfft!
GACK!
THERE, YOU'RE CURED. NOW GO GET ME A TOY.
OH MY GOD. MY HEAD IS CLEAR.
GOOD LORD, SCRATCH. YOU INVENTED A CURE FOR THE COMMON
MUSH!

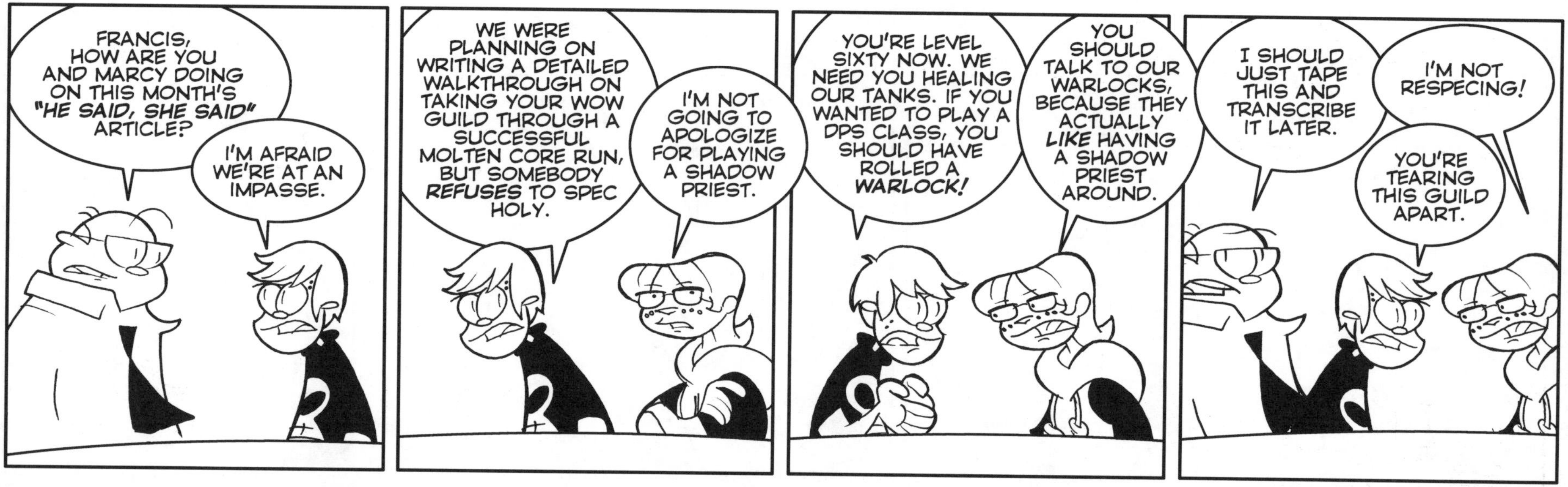
FRANCIS, HOW ARE YOU AND MARCY DOING ON THIS MONTH'S *"HE SAID, SHE SAID"* ARTICLE?
I'M AFRAID WE'RE AT AN IMPASSE.
WE WERE PLANNING ON WRITING A DETAILED WALKTHROUGH ON TAKING YOUR WOW GUILD THROUGH A SUCCESSFUL MOLTEN CORE RUN, BUT SOMEBODY *REFUSES* TO SPEC HOLY.
I'M NOT GOING TO APOLOGIZE FOR PLAYING A SHADOW PRIEST.
YOU'RE LEVEL SIXTY NOW. WE NEED YOU HEALING OUR TANKS. IF YOU WANTED TO PLAY A DPS CLASS, YOU SHOULD HAVE ROLLED A *WARLOCK!*
YOU SHOULD TALK TO OUR WARLOCKS, BECAUSE THEY ACTUALLY *LIKE* HAVING A SHADOW PRIEST AROUND.
I SHOULD JUST TAPE THIS AND TRANSCRIBE IT LATER.
I'M NOT RESPECING!
YOU'RE TEARING THIS GUILD APART.

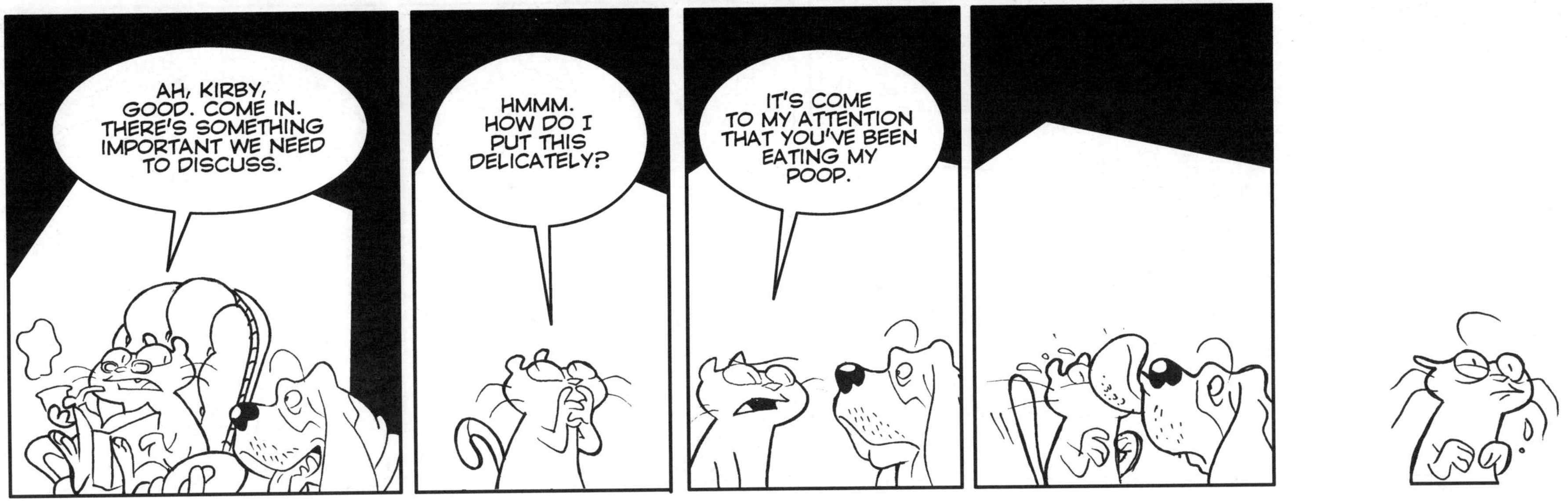
AH, KIRBY, GOOD. COME IN. THERE'S SOMETHING IMPORTANT WE NEED TO DISCUSS.
HMMM. HOW DO I PUT THIS DELICATELY?
IT'S COME TO MY ATTENTION THAT YOU'VE BEEN EATING MY POOP.

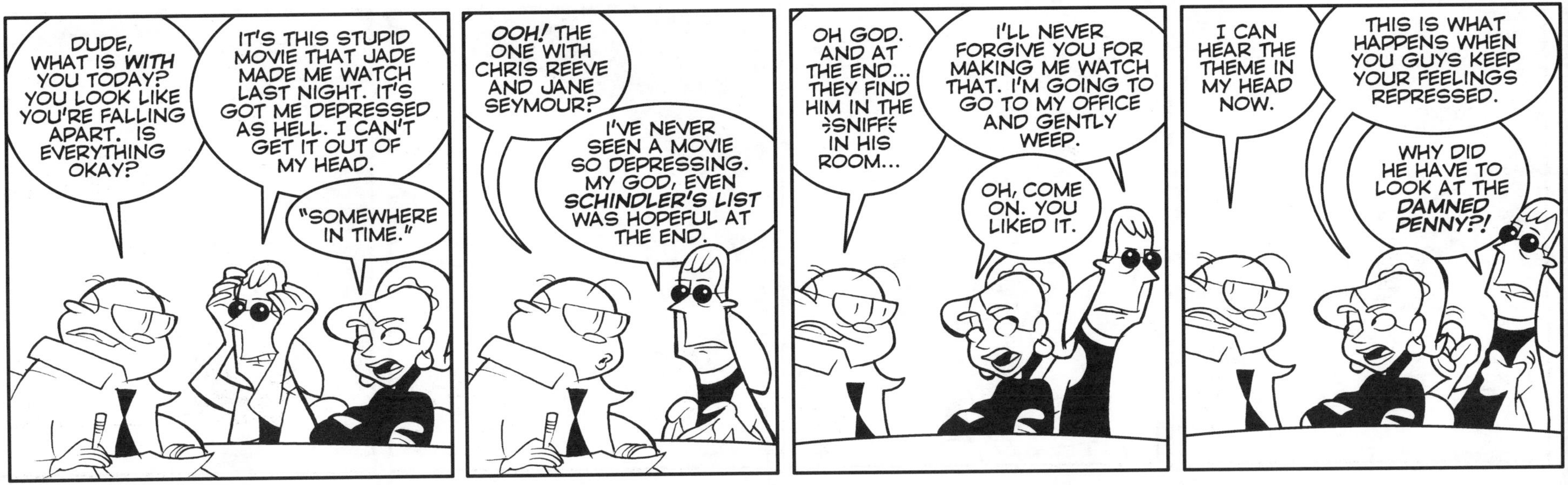
DUDE, WHAT IS *WITH* YOU TODAY? YOU LOOK LIKE YOU'RE FALLING APART. IS EVERYTHING OKAY?
IT'S THIS STUPID MOVIE THAT JADE MADE ME WATCH LAST NIGHT. IT'S GOT ME DEPRESSED AS HELL. I CAN'T GET IT OUT OF MY HEAD.
"SOMEWHERE IN TIME."
OOH! THE ONE WITH CHRIS REEVE AND JANE SEYMOUR?
I'VE NEVER SEEN A MOVIE SO DEPRESSING. MY GOD, EVEN ***SCHINDLER'S LIST*** WAS HOPEFUL AT THE END.
OH GOD. AND AT THE END... THEY FIND HIM IN THE SNIFF IN HIS ROOM...
I'LL NEVER FORGIVE YOU FOR MAKING ME WATCH THAT. I'M GOING TO GO TO MY OFFICE AND GENTLY WEEP.
OH, COME ON. YOU LIKED IT.
I CAN HEAR THE THEME IN MY HEAD NOW.
THIS IS WHAT HAPPENS WHEN YOU GUYS KEEP YOUR FEELINGS REPRESSED.
WHY DID HE HAVE TO LOOK AT THE ***DAMNED PENNY?!***

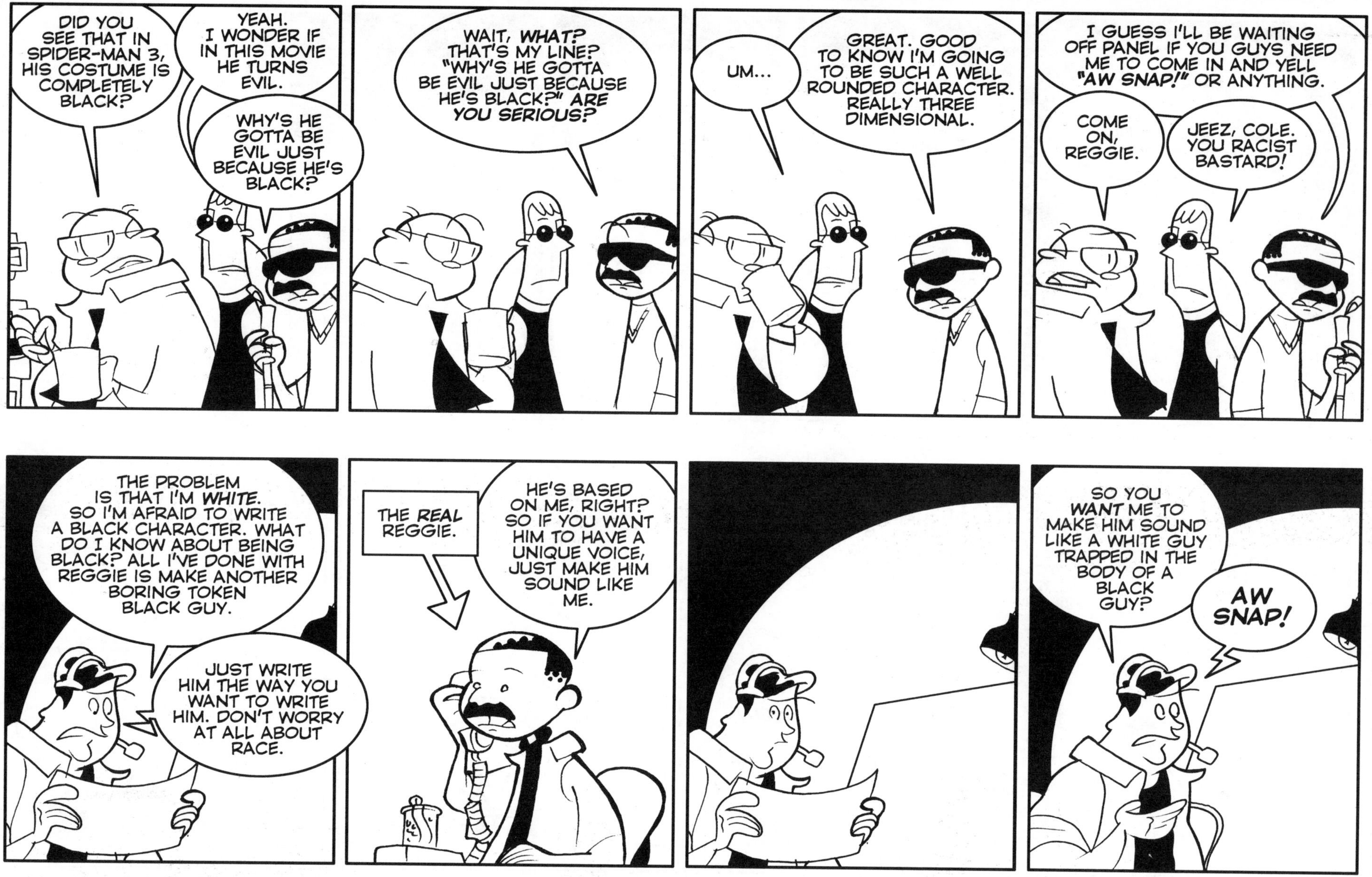
DID YOU SEE THAT IN SPIDER-MAN 3, HIS COSTUME IS COMPLETELY BLACK?
YEAH. I WONDER IF IN THIS MOVIE HE TURNS EVIL.
WHY'S HE GOTTA BE EVIL JUST BECAUSE HE'S BLACK?
WAIT, WHAT? THAT'S MY LINE? "WHY'S HE GOTTA BE EVIL JUST BECAUSE HE'S BLACK?" ARE YOU SERIOUS?
UM...
GREAT. GOOD TO KNOW I'M GOING TO BE SUCH A WELL ROUNDED CHARACTER. REALLY THREE DIMENSIONAL.
I GUESS I'LL BE WAITING OFF PANEL IF YOU GUYS NEED ME TO COME IN AND YELL "AW SNAP!" OR ANYTHING.
COME ON, REGGIE.
JEEZ, COLE. YOU RACIST BASTARD!
THE PROBLEM IS THAT I'M WHITE. SO I'M AFRAID TO WRITE A BLACK CHARACTER. WHAT DO I KNOW ABOUT BEING BLACK? ALL I'VE DONE WITH REGGIE IS MAKE ANOTHER BORING TOKEN BLACK GUY.
JUST WRITE HIM THE WAY YOU WANT TO WRITE HIM. DON'T WORRY AT ALL ABOUT RACE.
THE REAL REGGIE.
HE'S BASED ON ME, RIGHT? SO IF YOU WANT HIM TO HAVE A UNIQUE VOICE, JUST MAKE HIM SOUND LIKE ME.
SO YOU WANT ME TO MAKE HIM SOUND LIKE A WHITE GUY TRAPPED IN THE BODY OF A BLACK GUY?
AW SNAP!

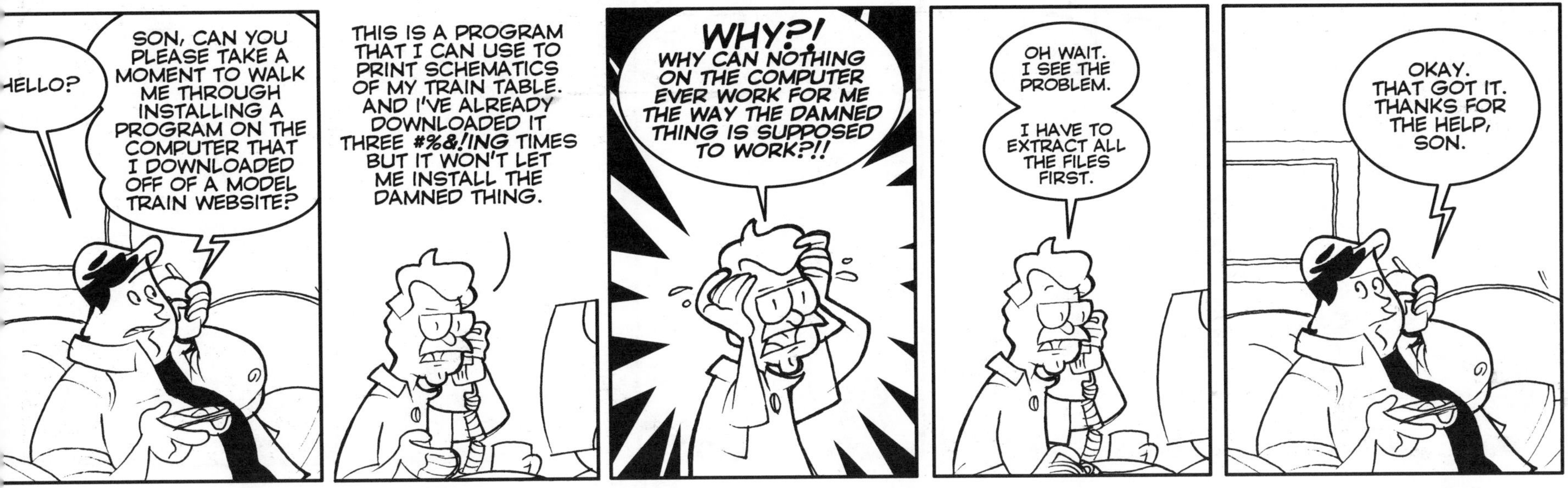
HELLO?
SON, CAN YOU PLEASE TAKE A MOMENT TO WALK ME THROUGH INSTALLING A PROGRAM ON THE COMPUTER THAT I DOWNLOADED OFF OF A MODEL TRAIN WEBSITE?
THIS IS A PROGRAM THAT I CAN USE TO PRINT SCHEMATICS OF MY TRAIN TABLE. AND I'VE ALREADY DOWNLOADED IT THREE #%&!ING TIMES BUT IT WON'T LET ME INSTALL THE DAMNED THING.
WHY?!
WHY CAN NOTHING ON THE COMPUTER EVER WORK FOR ME THE WAY THE DAMNED THING IS SUPPOSED TO WORK?!!
OH WAIT. I SEE THE PROBLEM.
I HAVE TO EXTRACT ALL THE FILES FIRST.
OKAY. THAT GOT IT. THANKS FOR THE HELP, SON.

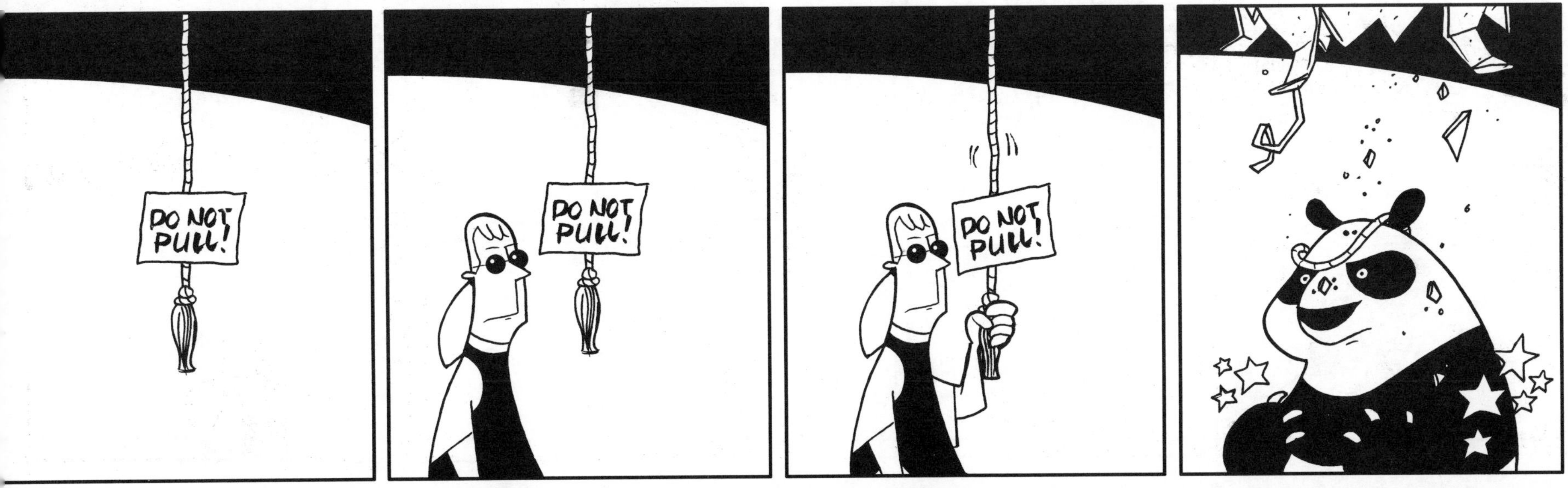
DO NOT PULL!
DO NOT PULL!
DO NOT PULL!

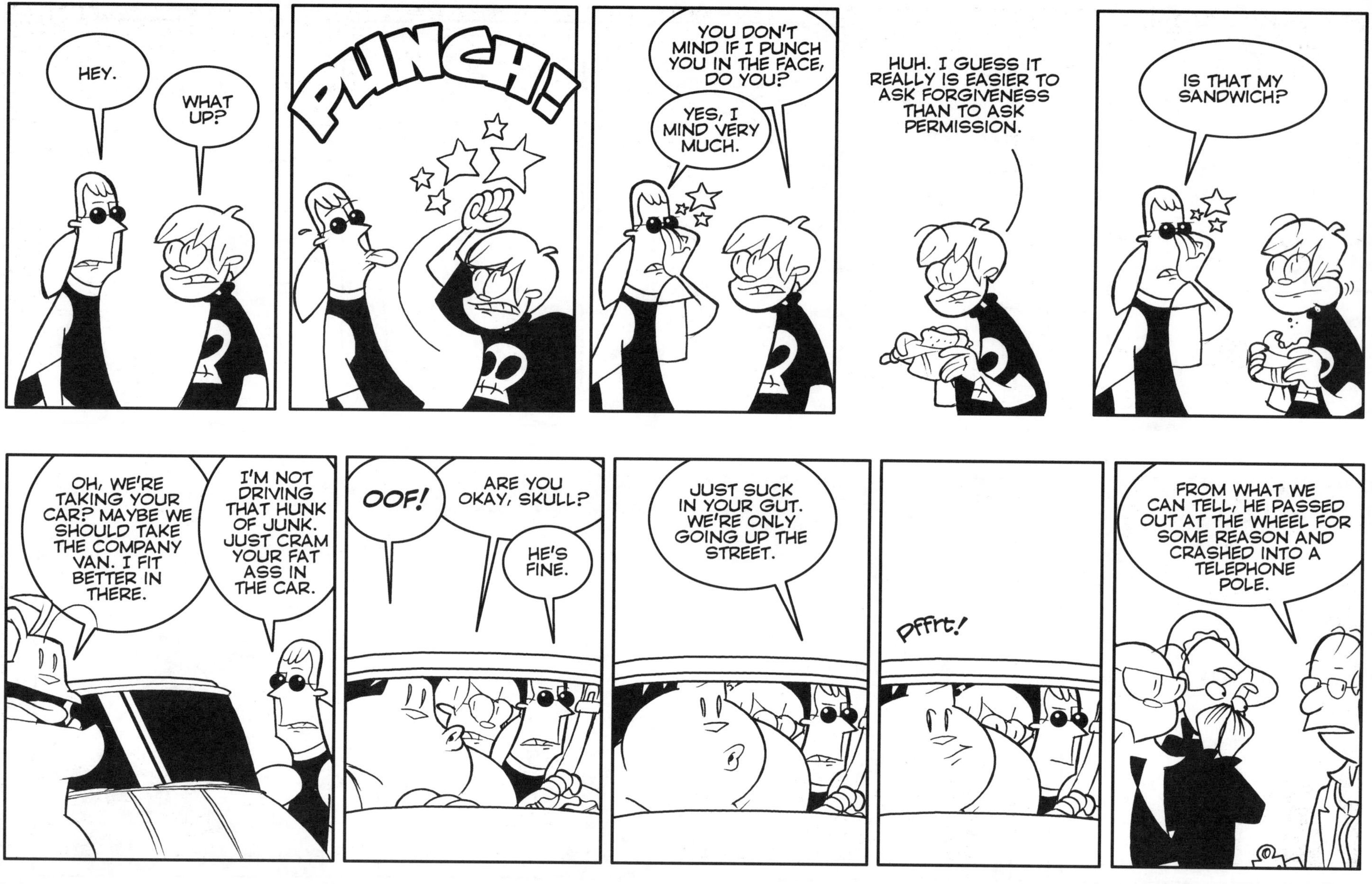
HEY.
WHAT UP?
PUNCH!
YOU DON'T MIND IF I PUNCH YOU IN THE FACE, DO YOU?
YES, I MIND VERY MUCH.
HUH. I GUESS IT REALLY IS EASIER TO ASK FORGIVENESS THAN TO ASK PERMISSION.
IS THAT MY SANDWICH?
OH, WE'RE TAKING YOUR CAR? MAYBE WE SHOULD TAKE THE COMPANY VAN. I FIT BETTER IN THERE.
I'M NOT DRIVING THAT HUNK OF JUNK. JUST CRAM YOUR FAT ASS IN THE CAR.
OOF!
ARE YOU OKAY, SKULL?
HE'S FINE.
JUST SUCK IN YOUR GUT. WE'RE ONLY GOING UP THE STREET.
PFFRT!
FROM WHAT WE CAN TELL, HE PASSED OUT AT THE WHEEL FOR SOME REASON AND CRASHED INTO A TELEPHONE POLE.

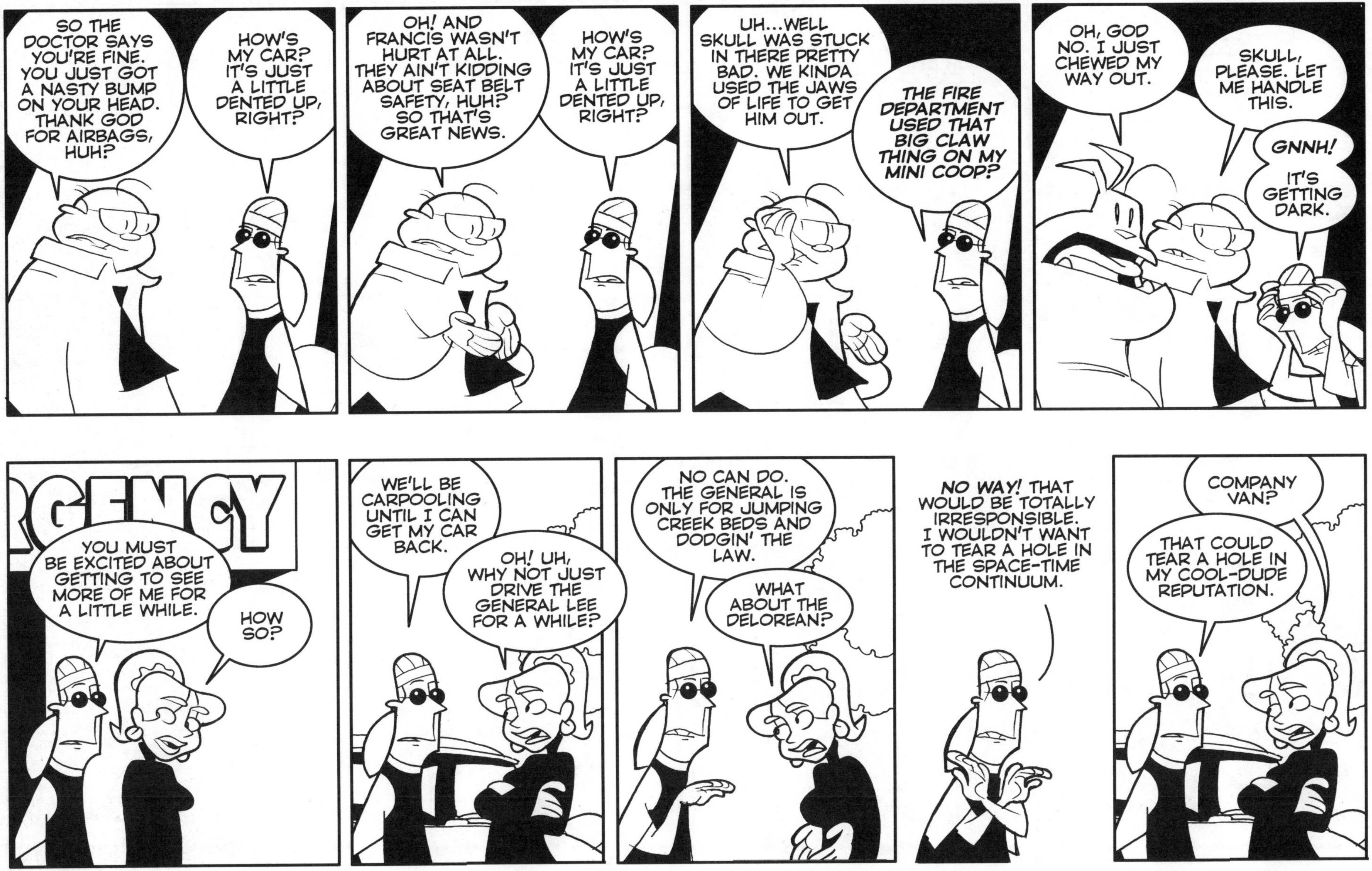
SO THE DOCTOR SAYS YOU'RE FINE. YOU JUST GOT A NASTY BUMP ON YOUR HEAD. THANK GOD FOR AIRBAGS, HUH?
HOW'S MY CAR? IT'S JUST A LITTLE DENTED UP, RIGHT?
OH! AND FRANCIS WASN'T HURT AT ALL. THEY AIN'T KIDDING ABOUT SEAT BELT SAFETY, HUH? SO THAT'S GREAT NEWS.
HOW'S MY CAR? IT'S JUST A LITTLE DENTED UP, RIGHT?
UH...WELL SKULL WAS STUCK IN THERE PRETTY BAD. WE KINDA USED THE JAWS OF LIFE TO GET HIM OUT.
THE FIRE DEPARTMENT USED THAT BIG CLAW THING ON MY MINI COOP?
OH, GOD NO. I JUST CHEWED MY WAY OUT.
SKULL, PLEASE. LET ME HANDLE THIS.
GNNH!
IT'S GETTING DARK.
RGENCY
YOU MUST BE EXCITED ABOUT GETTING TO SEE MORE OF ME FOR A LITTLE WHILE.
HOW SO?
WE'LL BE CARPOOLING UNTIL I CAN GET MY CAR BACK.
OH! UH, WHY NOT JUST DRIVE THE GENERAL LEE FOR A WHILE?
NO CAN DO. THE GENERAL IS ONLY FOR JUMPING CREEK BEDS AND DODGIN' THE LAW.
WHAT ABOUT THE DELOREAN?
NO WAY! THAT WOULD BE TOTALLY IRRESPONSIBLE. I WOULDN'T WANT TO TEAR A HOLE IN THE SPACE-TIME CONTINUUM.
COMPANY VAN?
THAT COULD TEAR A HOLE IN MY COOL-DUDE REPUTATION.

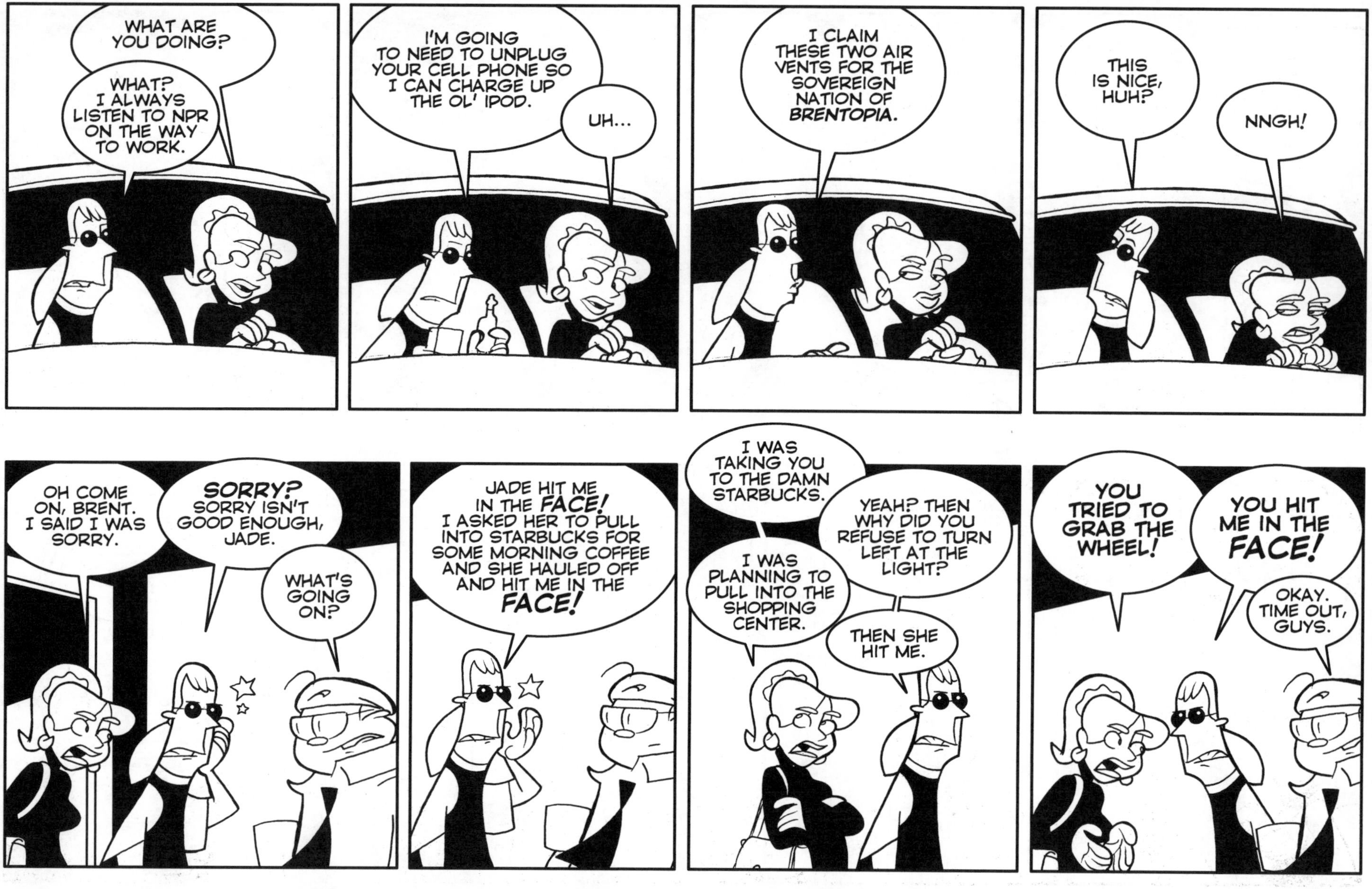
WHAT ARE YOU DOING?
WHAT? I ALWAYS LISTEN TO NPR ON THE WAY TO WORK.
I'M GOING TO NEED TO UNPLUG YOUR CELL PHONE SO I CAN CHARGE UP THE OL' IPOD.
UH...
I CLAIM THESE TWO AIR VENTS FOR THE SOVEREIGN NATION OF *BRENTOPIA*.
THIS IS NICE, HUH?
NNGH!
OH COME ON, BRENT. I SAID I WAS SORRY.
SORRY? SORRY ISN'T GOOD ENOUGH, JADE.
WHAT'S GOING ON?
JADE HIT ME IN THE *FACE!* I ASKED HER TO PULL INTO STARBUCKS FOR SOME MORNING COFFEE AND SHE HAULED OFF AND HIT ME IN THE *FACE!*
I WAS TAKING YOU TO THE DAMN STARBUCKS.
I WAS PLANNING TO PULL INTO THE SHOPPING CENTER.
YEAH? THEN WHY DID YOU REFUSE TO TURN LEFT AT THE LIGHT?
THEN SHE HIT ME.
YOU TRIED TO GRAB THE WHEEL!
YOU HIT ME IN THE *FACE!*
OKAY. TIME OUT, GUYS.

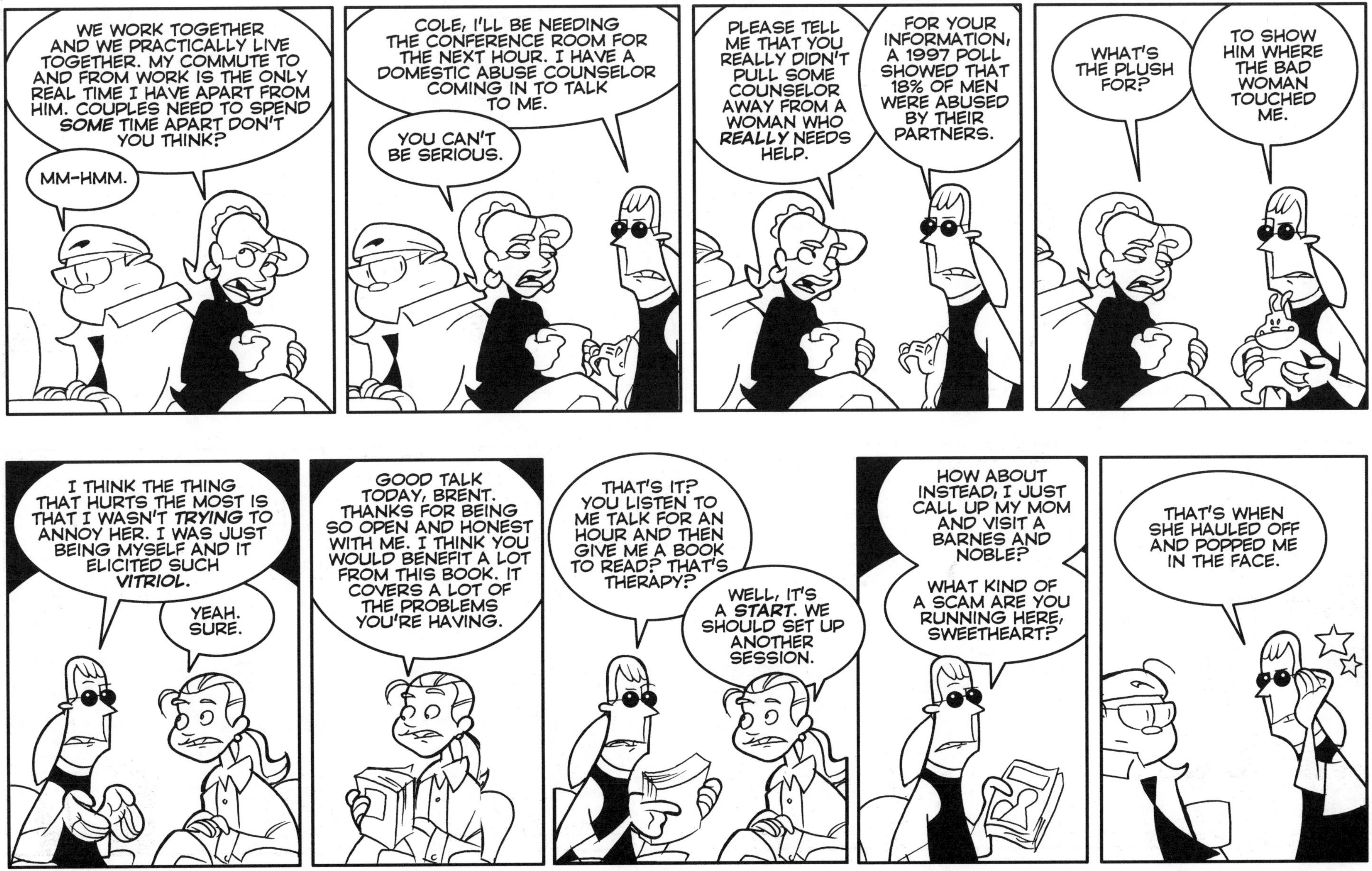
WE WORK TOGETHER AND WE PRACTICALLY LIVE TOGETHER. MY COMMUTE TO AND FROM WORK IS THE ONLY REAL TIME I HAVE APART FROM HIM. COUPLES NEED TO SPEND *SOME* TIME APART DON'T YOU THINK?
MM-HMM.
COLE, I'LL BE NEEDING THE CONFERENCE ROOM FOR THE NEXT HOUR. I HAVE A DOMESTIC ABUSE COUNSELOR COMING IN TO TALK TO ME.
YOU CAN'T BE SERIOUS.
PLEASE TELL ME THAT YOU REALLY DIDN'T PULL SOME COUNSELOR AWAY FROM A WOMAN WHO *REALLY* NEEDS HELP.
FOR YOUR INFORMATION, A 1997 POLL SHOWED THAT 18% OF MEN WERE ABUSED BY THEIR PARTNERS.
WHAT'S THE PLUSH FOR?
TO SHOW HIM WHERE THE BAD WOMAN TOUCHED ME.
I THINK THE THING THAT HURTS THE MOST IS THAT I WASN'T *TRYING* TO ANNOY HER. I WAS JUST BEING MYSELF AND IT ELICITED SUCH *VITRIOL*.
YEAH. SURE.
GOOD TALK TODAY, BRENT. THANKS FOR BEING SO OPEN AND HONEST WITH ME. I THINK YOU WOULD BENEFIT A LOT FROM THIS BOOK. IT COVERS A LOT OF THE PROBLEMS YOU'RE HAVING.
THAT'S IT? YOU LISTEN TO ME TALK FOR AN HOUR AND THEN GIVE ME A BOOK TO READ? THAT'S THERAPY?
WELL, IT'S A *START*. WE SHOULD SET UP ANOTHER SESSION.
HOW ABOUT INSTEAD, I JUST CALL UP MY MOM AND VISIT A BARNES AND NOBLE?
WHAT KIND OF A SCAM ARE YOU RUNNING HERE, SWEETHEART?
THAT'S WHEN SHE HAULED OFF AND POPPED ME IN THE FACE.

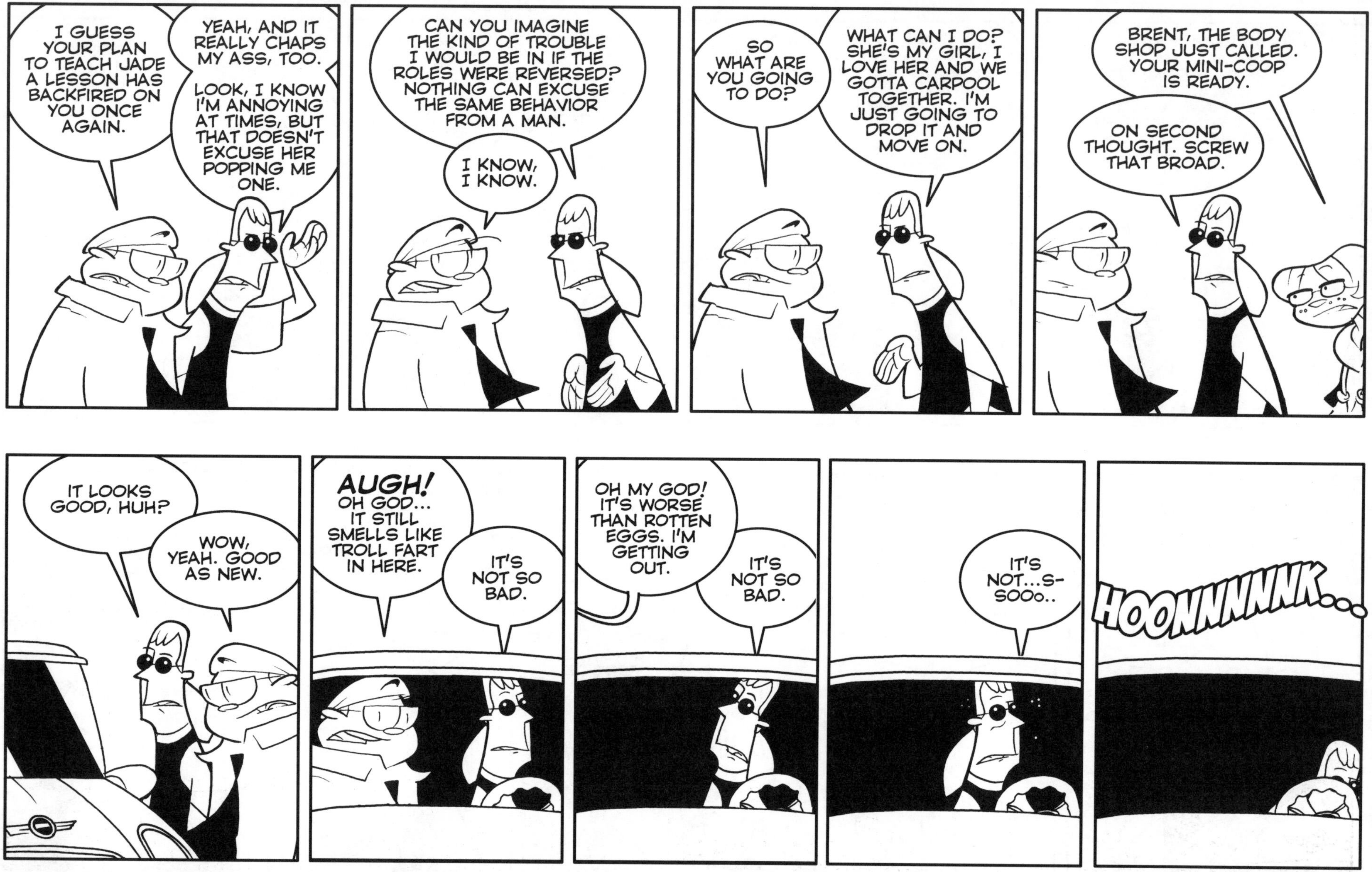

I GUESS YOUR PLAN TO TEACH JADE A LESSON HAS BACKFIRED ON YOU ONCE AGAIN.
YEAH, AND IT REALLY CHAPS MY ASS, TOO.
LOOK, I KNOW I'M ANNOYING AT TIMES, BUT THAT DOESN'T EXCUSE HER POPPING ME ONE.
CAN YOU IMAGINE THE KIND OF TROUBLE I WOULD BE IN IF THE ROLES WERE REVERSED? NOTHING CAN EXCUSE THE SAME BEHAVIOR FROM A MAN.
I KNOW, I KNOW.
SO WHAT ARE YOU GOING TO DO?
WHAT CAN I DO? SHE'S MY GIRL, I LOVE HER AND WE GOTTA CARPOOL TOGETHER. I'M JUST GOING TO DROP IT AND MOVE ON.
BRENT, THE BODY SHOP JUST CALLED. YOUR MINI-COOP IS READY.
ON SECOND THOUGHT. SCREW THAT BROAD.
IT LOOKS GOOD, HUH?
WOW, YEAH. GOOD AS NEW.
AUGH! OH GOD... IT STILL SMELLS LIKE TROLL FART IN HERE.
IT'S NOT SO BAD.
OH MY GOD! IT'S WORSE THAN ROTTEN EGGS. I'M GETTING OUT.
IT'S NOT SO BAD.
IT'S NOT...S-SOOo..
HOONNNNNK...

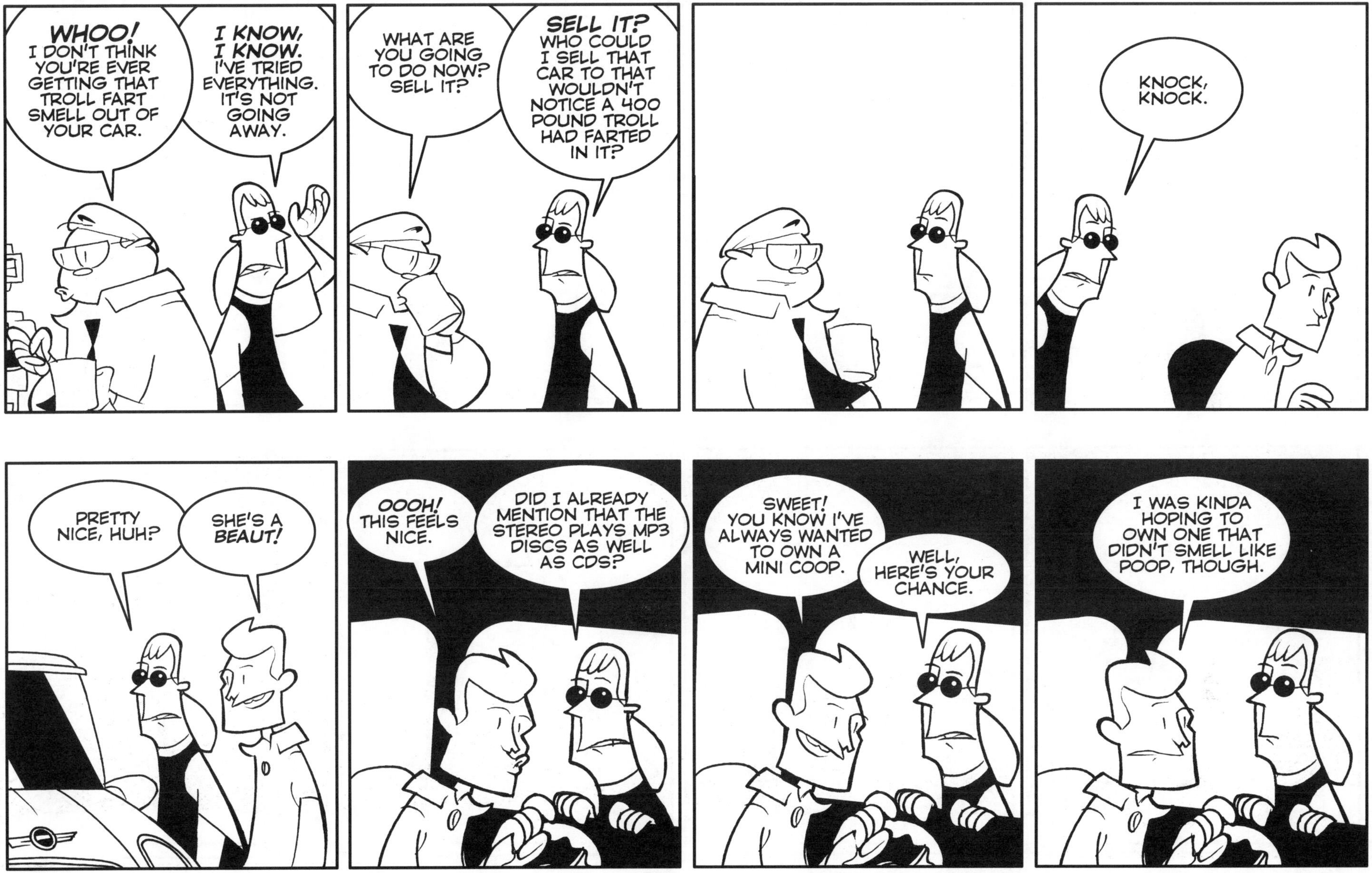
WHOO! I DON'T THINK YOU'RE EVER GETTING THAT TROLL FART SMELL OUT OF YOUR CAR.
I KNOW, I KNOW. I'VE TRIED EVERYTHING. IT'S NOT GOING AWAY.
WHAT ARE YOU GOING TO DO NOW? SELL IT?
SELL IT? WHO COULD I SELL THAT CAR TO THAT WOULDN'T NOTICE A 400 POUND TROLL HAD FARTED IN IT?
KNOCK, KNOCK.
PRETTY NICE, HUH?
SHE'S A BEAUT!
OOOH! THIS FEELS NICE.
DID I ALREADY MENTION THAT THE STEREO PLAYS MP3 DISCS AS WELL AS CDS?
SWEET! YOU KNOW I'VE ALWAYS WANTED TO OWN A MINI COOP.
WELL, HERE'S YOUR CHANCE.
I WAS KINDA HOPING TO OWN ONE THAT DIDN'T SMELL LIKE POOP, THOUGH.

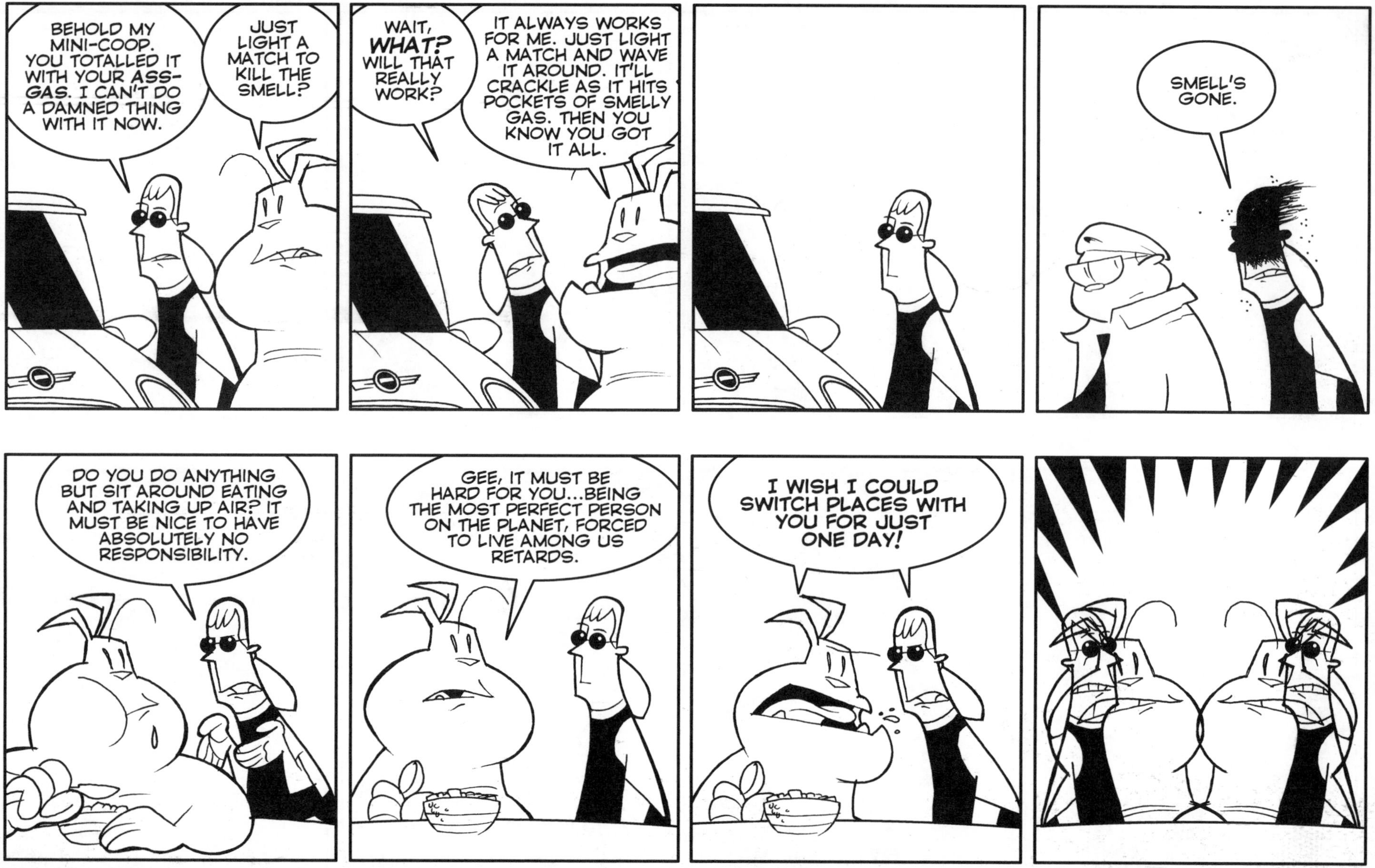
BEHOLD MY MINI-COOP. YOU TOTALLED IT WITH YOUR ASS-GAS. I CAN'T DO A DAMNED THING WITH IT NOW.
JUST LIGHT A MATCH TO KILL THE SMELL?
WAIT, WHAT? WILL THAT REALLY WORK?
IT ALWAYS WORKS FOR ME. JUST LIGHT A MATCH AND WAVE IT AROUND. IT'LL CRACKLE AS IT HITS POCKETS OF SMELLY GAS. THEN YOU KNOW YOU GOT IT ALL.
SMELL'S GONE.
DO YOU DO ANYTHING BUT SIT AROUND EATING AND TAKING UP AIR? IT MUST BE NICE TO HAVE ABSOLUTELY NO RESPONSIBILITY.
GEE, IT MUST BE HARD FOR YOU...BEING THE MOST PERFECT PERSON ON THE PLANET, FORCED TO LIVE AMONG US RETARDS.
I WISH I COULD SWITCH PLACES WITH YOU FOR JUST ONE DAY!

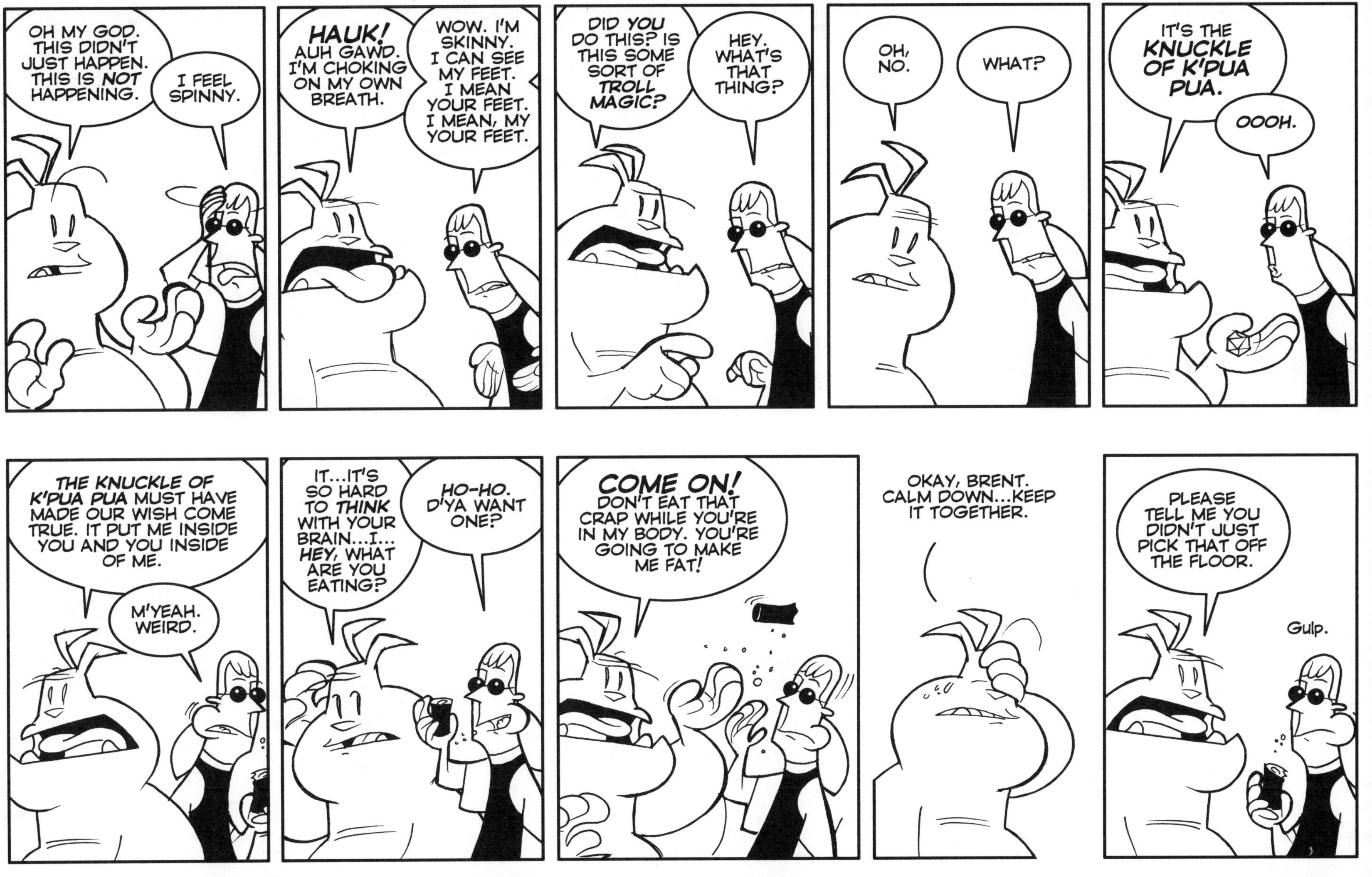
OH MY GOD. THIS DIDN'T JUST HAPPEN. THIS IS NOT HAPPENING.
I FEEL SPINNY.
HAUK! AUH GAWD. I'M CHOKING ON MY OWN BREATH.
WOW. I'M SKINNY. I CAN SEE MY FEET. I MEAN YOUR FEET. I MEAN, MY YOUR FEET.
DID YOU DO THIS? IS THIS SOME SORT OF TROLL MAGIC?
HEY. WHAT'S THAT THING?
OH, NO.
WHAT?
IT'S THE KNUCKLE OF K'PUA PUA.
OOOH.
THE KNUCKLE OF K'PUA PUA MUST HAVE MADE OUR WISH COME TRUE. IT PUT ME INSIDE YOU AND YOU INSIDE OF ME.
M'YEAH. WEIRD.
IT...IT'S SO HARD TO THINK WITH YOUR BRAIN...I... HEY, WHAT ARE YOU EATING?
HO-HO. D'YA WANT ONE?
COME ON! DON'T EAT THAT CRAP WHILE YOU'RE IN MY BODY. YOU'RE GOING TO MAKE ME FAT!
OKAY, BRENT. CALM DOWN...KEEP IT TOGETHER.
PLEASE TELL ME YOU DIDN'T JUST PICK THAT OFF THE FLOOR.
Gulp.

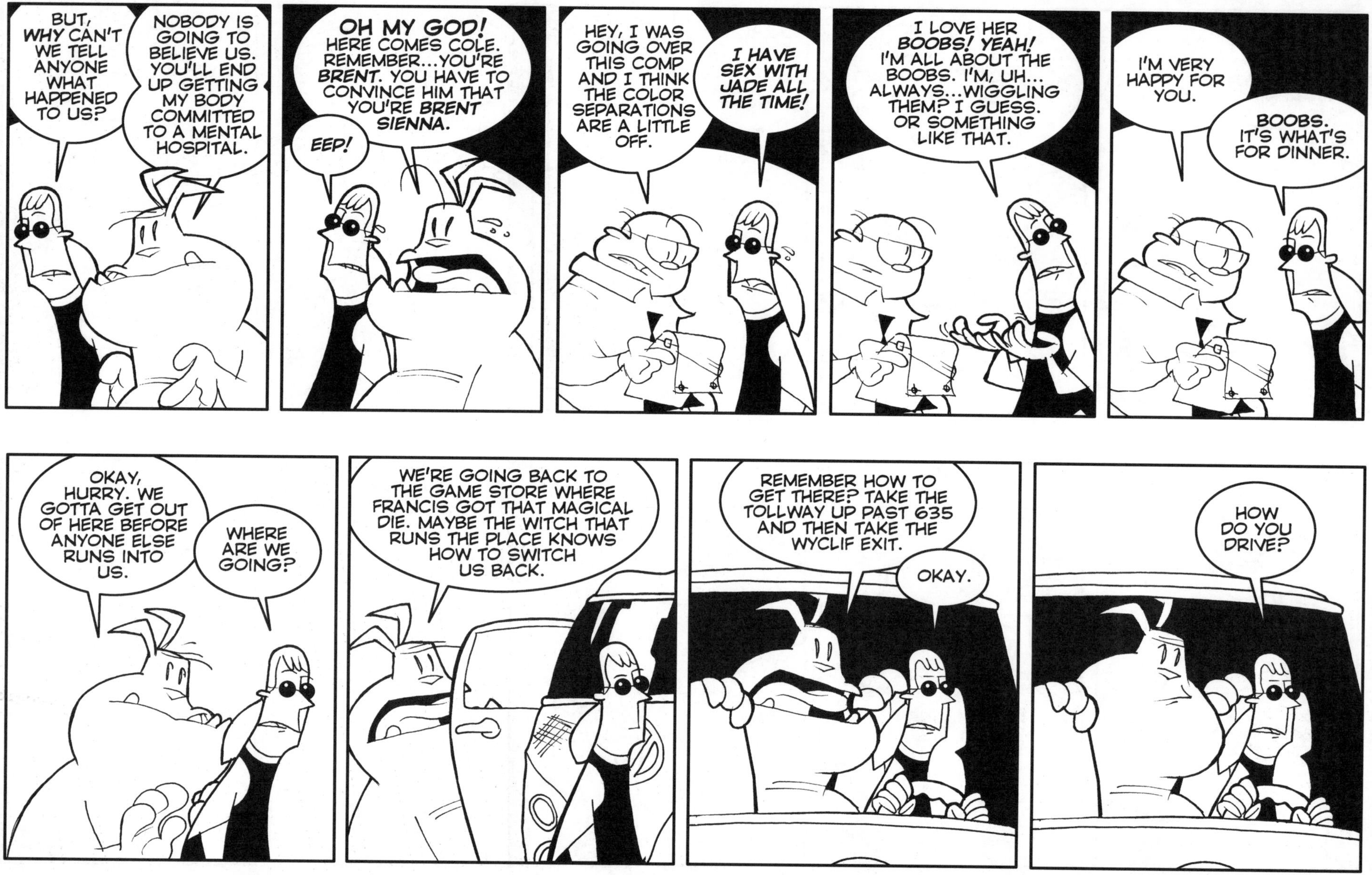
BUT, WHY CAN'T WE TELL ANYONE WHAT HAPPENED TO US?
NOBODY IS GOING TO BELIEVE US. YOU'LL END UP GETTING MY BODY COMMITTED TO A MENTAL HOSPITAL.
OH MY GOD! HERE COMES COLE. REMEMBER...YOU'RE BRENT. YOU HAVE TO CONVINCE HIM THAT YOU'RE BRENT SIENNA.
EEP!
HEY, I WAS GOING OVER THIS COMP AND I THINK THE COLOR SEPARATIONS ARE A LITTLE OFF.
I HAVE SEX WITH JADE ALL THE TIME!
I LOVE HER BOOBS! YEAH! I'M ALL ABOUT THE BOOBS. I'M, UH... ALWAYS...WIGGLING THEM? I GUESS. OR SOMETHING LIKE THAT.
I'M VERY HAPPY FOR YOU.
BOOBS. IT'S WHAT'S FOR DINNER.
OKAY, HURRY. WE GOTTA GET OUT OF HERE BEFORE ANYONE ELSE RUNS INTO US.
WHERE ARE WE GOING?
WE'RE GOING BACK TO THE GAME STORE WHERE FRANCIS GOT THAT MAGICAL DIE. MAYBE THE WITCH THAT RUNS THE PLACE KNOWS HOW TO SWITCH US BACK.
REMEMBER HOW TO GET THERE? TAKE THE TOLLWAY UP PAST 635 AND THEN TAKE THE WYCLIF EXIT.
OKAY.
HOW DO YOU DRIVE?

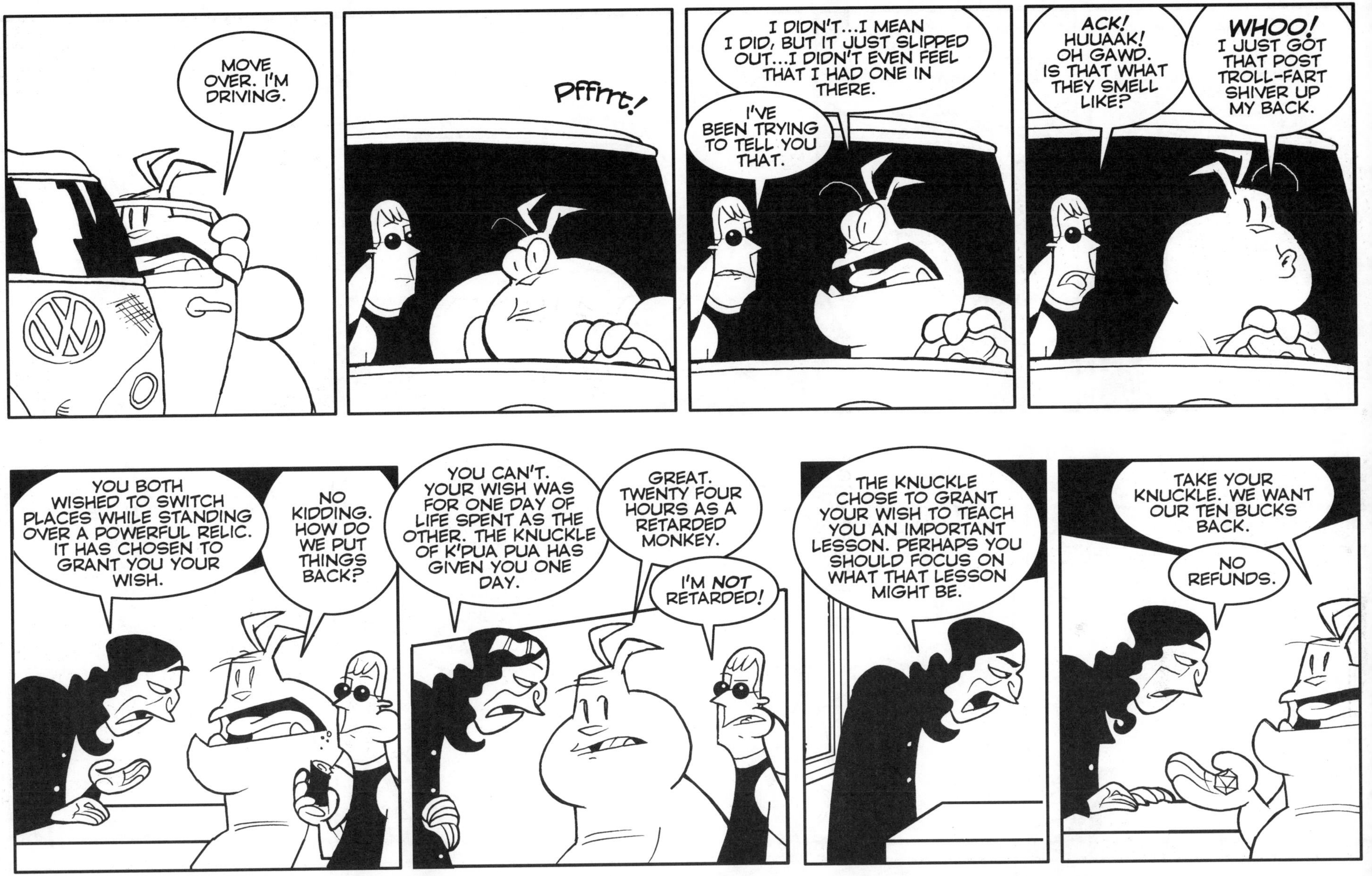
MOVE OVER. I'M DRIVING.
Pffrrt!
I DIDN'T...I MEAN I DID, BUT IT JUST SLIPPED OUT...I DIDN'T EVEN FEEL THAT I HAD ONE IN THERE.
I'VE BEEN TRYING TO TELL YOU THAT.
ACK! HUUAAK! OH GAWD. IS THAT WHAT THEY SMELL LIKE?
WHOO! I JUST GOT THAT POST TROLL-FART SHIVER UP MY BACK.
YOU BOTH WISHED TO SWITCH PLACES WHILE STANDING OVER A POWERFUL RELIC. IT HAS CHOSEN TO GRANT YOU YOUR WISH.
NO KIDDING. HOW DO WE PUT THINGS BACK?
YOU CAN'T. YOUR WISH WAS FOR ONE DAY OF LIFE SPENT AS THE OTHER. THE KNUCKLE OF K'PUA PUA HAS GIVEN YOU ONE DAY.
GREAT. TWENTY FOUR HOURS AS A RETARDED MONKEY.
I'M NOT RETARDED!
THE KNUCKLE CHOSE TO GRANT YOUR WISH TO TEACH YOU AN IMPORTANT LESSON. PERHAPS YOU SHOULD FOCUS ON WHAT THAT LESSON MIGHT BE.
TAKE YOUR KNUCKLE. WE WANT OUR TEN BUCKS BACK.
NO REFUNDS.

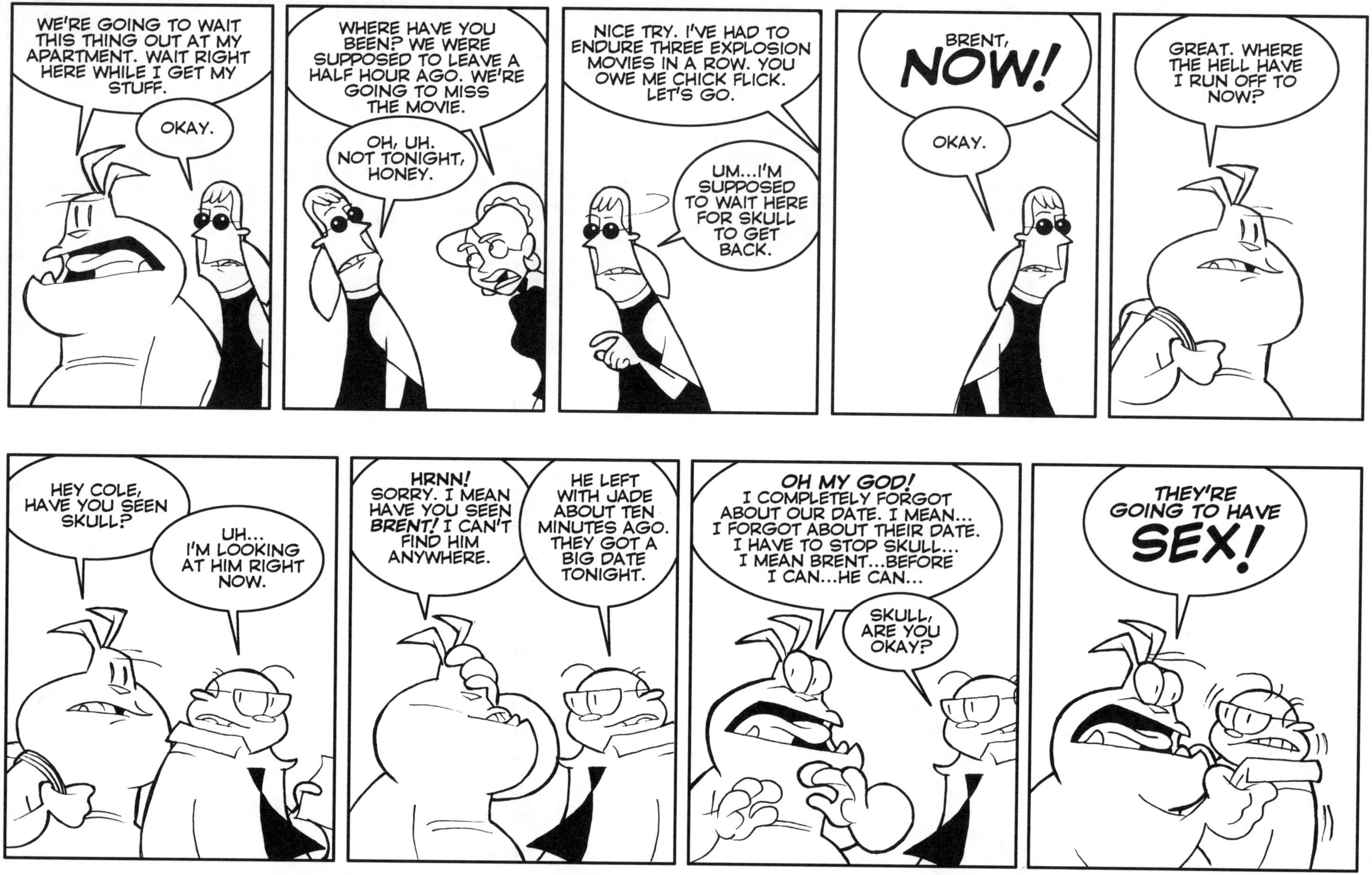
WE'RE GOING TO WAIT THIS THING OUT AT MY APARTMENT. WAIT RIGHT HERE WHILE I GET MY STUFF.
OKAY.
WHERE HAVE YOU BEEN? WE WERE SUPPOSED TO LEAVE A HALF HOUR AGO. WE'RE GOING TO MISS THE MOVIE.
OH, UH. NOT TONIGHT, HONEY.
NICE TRY. I'VE HAD TO ENDURE THREE EXPLOSION MOVIES IN A ROW. YOU OWE ME CHICK FLICK. LET'S GO.
UM...I'M SUPPOSED TO WAIT HERE FOR SKULL TO GET BACK.
BRENT, NOW!
OKAY.
GREAT. WHERE THE HELL HAVE I RUN OFF TO NOW?
HEY COLE, HAVE YOU SEEN SKULL?
UH... I'M LOOKING AT HIM RIGHT NOW.
HRNN! SORRY. I MEAN HAVE YOU SEEN BRENT! I CAN'T FIND HIM ANYWHERE.
HE LEFT WITH JADE ABOUT TEN MINUTES AGO. THEY GOT A BIG DATE TONIGHT.
OH MY GOD! I COMPLETELY FORGOT ABOUT OUR DATE. I MEAN... I FORGOT ABOUT THEIR DATE. I HAVE TO STOP SKULL... I MEAN BRENT...BEFORE I CAN...HE CAN...
SKULL, ARE YOU OKAY?
THEY'RE GOING TO HAVE SEX!

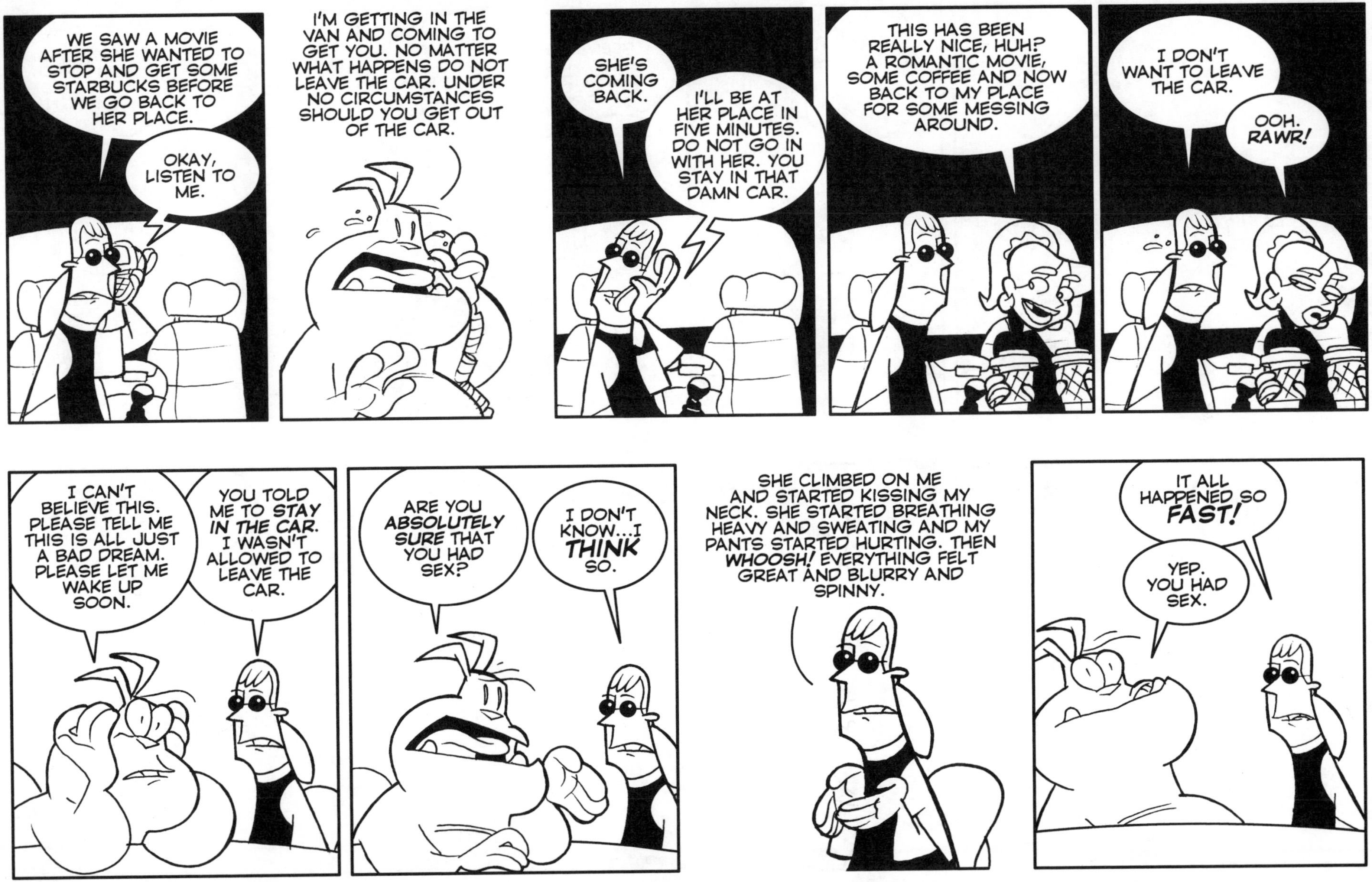
WE SAW A MOVIE AFTER SHE WANTED TO STOP AND GET SOME STARBUCKS BEFORE WE GO BACK TO HER PLACE.
OKAY, LISTEN TO ME.
I'M GETTING IN THE VAN AND COMING TO GET YOU. NO MATTER WHAT HAPPENS DO NOT LEAVE THE CAR. UNDER NO CIRCUMSTANCES SHOULD YOU GET OUT OF THE CAR.
SHE'S COMING BACK.
I'LL BE AT HER PLACE IN FIVE MINUTES. DO NOT GO IN WITH HER. YOU STAY IN THAT DAMN CAR.
THIS HAS BEEN REALLY NICE, HUH? A ROMANTIC MOVIE, SOME COFFEE AND NOW BACK TO MY PLACE FOR SOME MESSING AROUND.
I DON'T WANT TO LEAVE THE CAR.
OOH. *RAWR!*
I CAN'T BELIEVE THIS. PLEASE TELL ME THIS IS ALL JUST A BAD DREAM. PLEASE LET ME WAKE UP SOON.
YOU TOLD ME TO *STAY IN THE CAR*. I WASN'T ALLOWED TO LEAVE THE CAR.
ARE YOU ***ABSOLUTELY SURE*** THAT YOU HAD SEX?
I DON'T KNOW...I ***THINK*** SO.
SHE CLIMBED ON ME AND STARTED KISSING MY NECK. SHE STARTED BREATHING HEAVY AND SWEATING AND MY PANTS STARTED HURTING. THEN ***WHOOSH!*** EVERYTHING FELT GREAT AND BLURRY AND SPINNY.
IT ALL HAPPENED SO ***FAST!***
YEP. YOU HAD SEX.

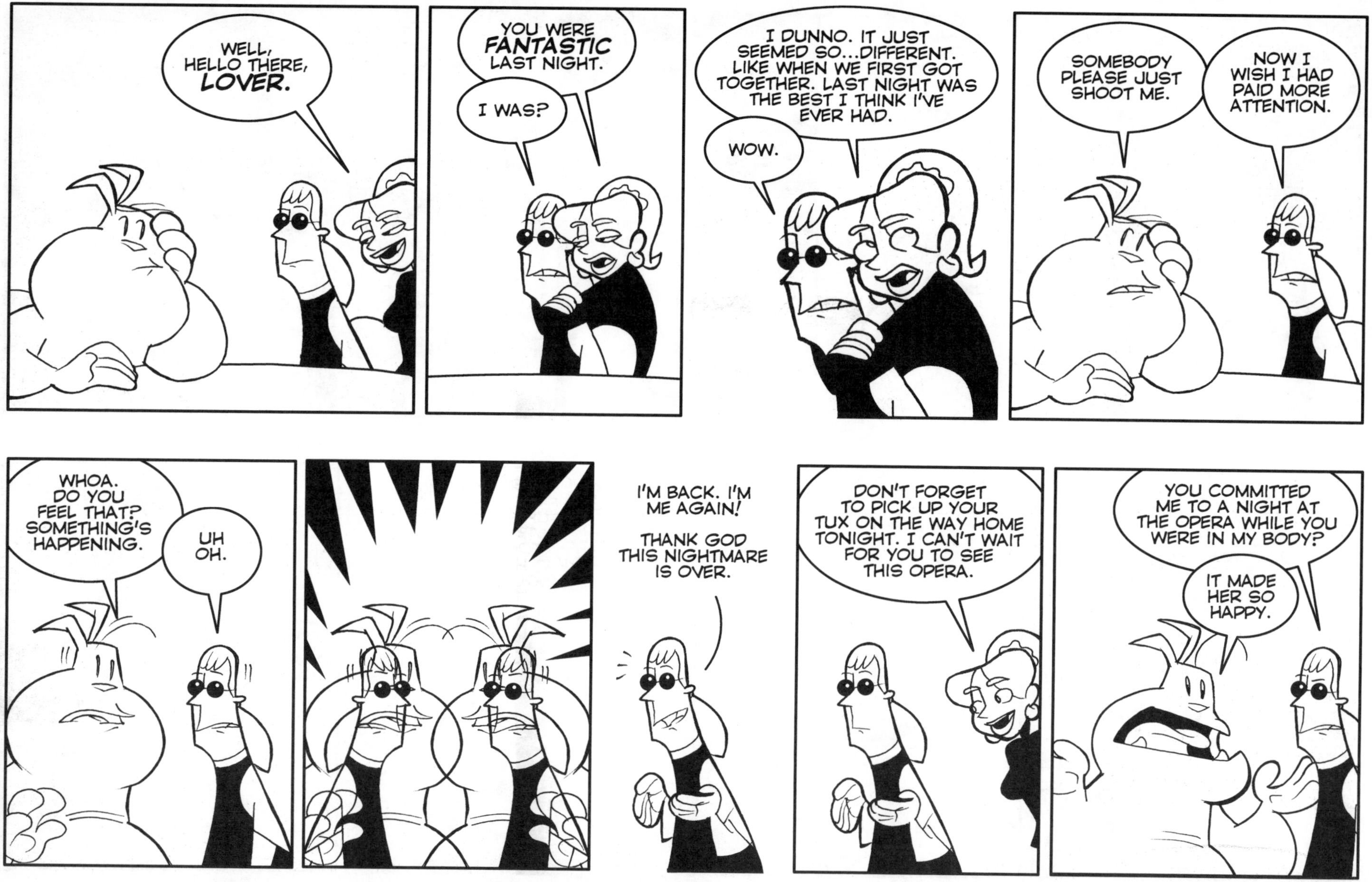

WELL, HELLO THERE, **LOVER.**
YOU WERE **FANTASTIC** LAST NIGHT.
I WAS?
I DUNNO. IT JUST SEEMED SO...DIFFERENT. LIKE WHEN WE FIRST GOT TOGETHER. LAST NIGHT WAS THE BEST I THINK I'VE EVER HAD.
WOW.
SOMEBODY PLEASE JUST SHOOT ME.
NOW I WISH I HAD PAID MORE ATTENTION.
WHOA. DO YOU FEEL THAT? SOMETHING'S HAPPENING.
UH OH.
I'M BACK. I'M ME AGAIN!
THANK GOD THIS NIGHTMARE IS OVER.
DON'T FORGET TO PICK UP YOUR TUX ON THE WAY HOME TONIGHT. I CAN'T WAIT FOR YOU TO SEE THIS OPERA.
YOU COMMITTED ME TO A NIGHT AT THE OPERA WHILE YOU WERE IN MY BODY?
IT MADE HER SO HAPPY.

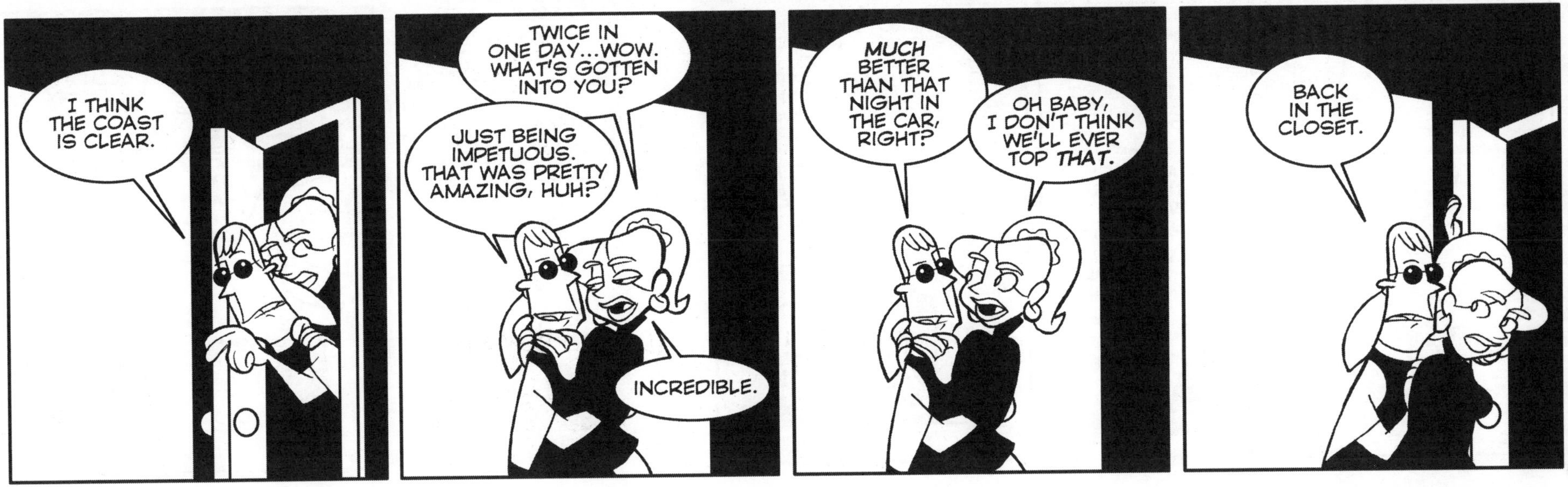
I THINK THE COAST IS CLEAR.
TWICE IN ONE DAY...WOW. WHAT'S GOTTEN INTO YOU?
JUST BEING IMPETUOUS. THAT WAS PRETTY AMAZING, HUH?
INCREDIBLE.
MUCH BETTER THAN THAT NIGHT IN THE CAR, RIGHT?
OH BABY, I DON'T THINK WE'LL EVER TOP *THAT*.
BACK IN THE CLOSET.

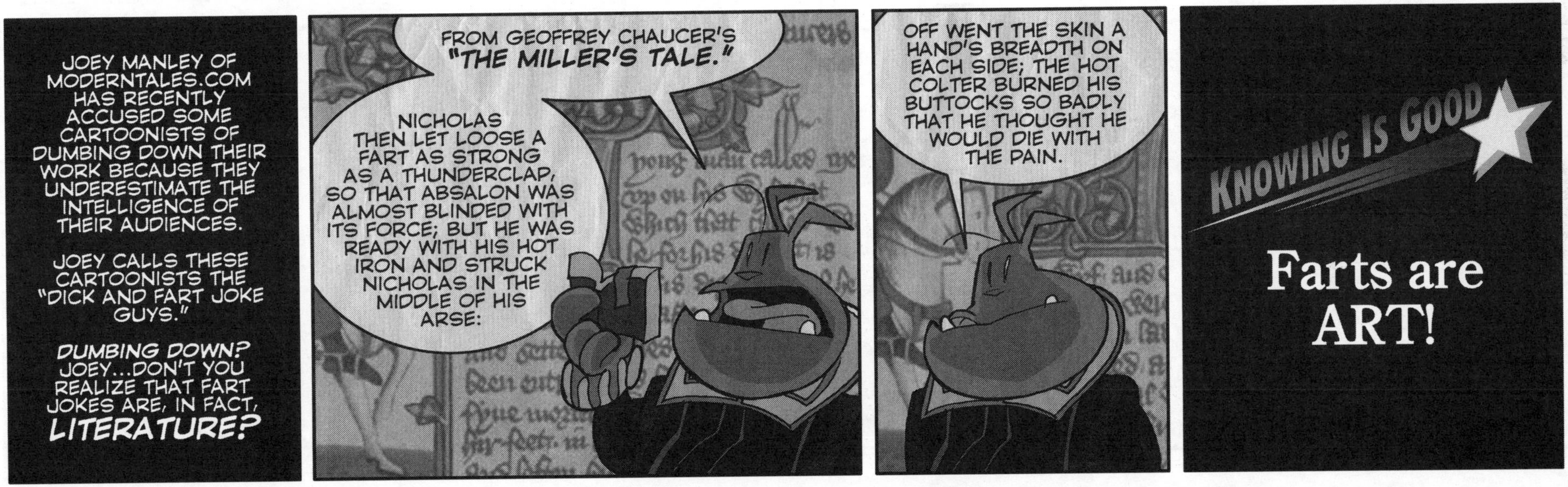
JOEY MANLEY OF MODERNTALES.COM HAS RECENTLY ACCUSED SOME CARTOONISTS OF DUMBING DOWN THEIR WORK BECAUSE THEY UNDERESTIMATE THE INTELLIGENCE OF THEIR AUDIENCES.
JOEY CALLS THESE CARTOONISTS THE "DICK AND FART JOKE GUYS."
DUMBING DOWN? JOEY...DON'T YOU REALIZE THAT FART JOKES ARE, IN FACT, ***LITERATURE?***
FROM GEOFFREY CHAUCER'S ***"THE MILLER'S TALE."***
NICHOLAS THEN LET LOOSE A FART AS STRONG AS A THUNDERCLAP, SO THAT ABSALON WAS ALMOST BLINDED WITH ITS FORCE; BUT HE WAS READY WITH HIS HOT IRON AND STRUCK NICHOLAS IN THE MIDDLE OF HIS ARSE:
OFF WENT THE SKIN A HAND'S BREADTH ON EACH SIDE; THE HOT COLTER BURNED HIS BUTTOCKS SO BADLY THAT HE THOUGHT HE WOULD DIE WITH THE PAIN.
KNOWING IS GOOD
Farts are ART!

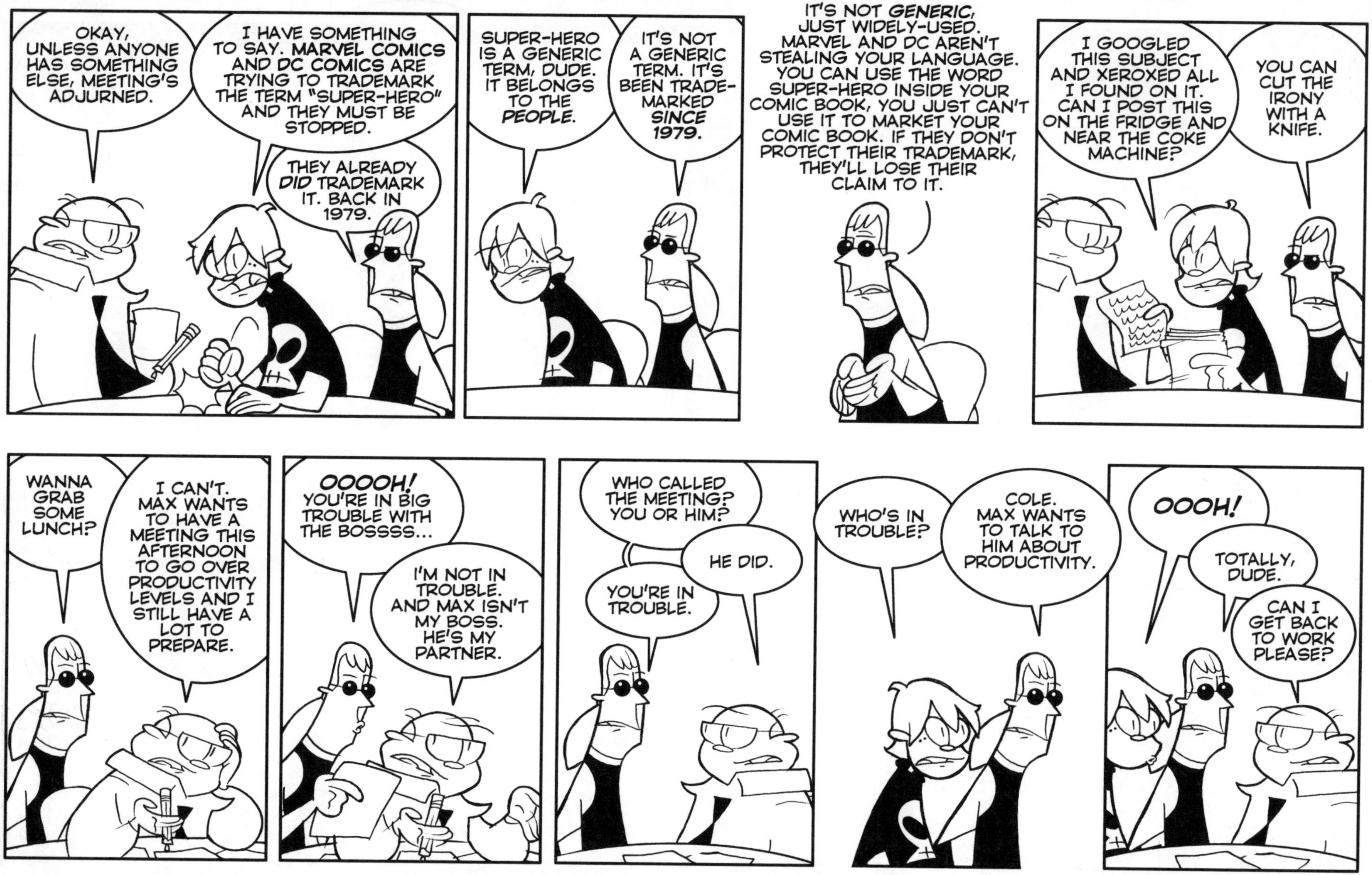
OKAY, UNLESS ANYONE HAS SOMETHING ELSE, MEETING'S ADJURNED.
I HAVE SOMETHING TO SAY. MARVEL COMICS AND DC COMICS ARE TRYING TO TRADEMARK THE TERM "SUPER-HERO" AND THEY MUST BE STOPPED.
THEY ALREADY DID TRADEMARK IT. BACK IN 1979.
SUPER-HERO IS A GENERIC TERM, DUDE. IT BELONGS TO THE PEOPLE.
IT'S NOT A GENERIC TERM. IT'S BEEN TRADE-MARKED SINCE 1979.
IT'S NOT GENERIC, JUST WIDELY-USED. MARVEL AND DC AREN'T STEALING YOUR LANGUAGE. YOU CAN USE THE WORD SUPER-HERO INSIDE YOUR COMIC BOOK, YOU JUST CAN'T USE IT TO MARKET YOUR COMIC BOOK. IF THEY DON'T PROTECT THEIR TRADEMARK, THEY'LL LOSE THEIR CLAIM TO IT.
I GOOGLED THIS SUBJECT AND XEROXED ALL I FOUND ON IT. CAN I POST THIS ON THE FRIDGE AND NEAR THE COKE MACHINE?
YOU CAN CUT THE IRONY WITH A KNIFE.
WANNA GRAB SOME LUNCH?
I CAN'T. MAX WANTS TO HAVE A MEETING THIS AFTERNOON TO GO OVER PRODUCTIVITY LEVELS AND I STILL HAVE A LOT TO PREPARE.
OOOOH! YOU'RE IN BIG TROUBLE WITH THE BOSSSS...
I'M NOT IN TROUBLE. AND MAX ISN'T MY BOSS. HE'S MY PARTNER.
WHO CALLED THE MEETING? YOU OR HIM?
YOU'RE IN TROUBLE.
HE DID.
WHO'S IN TROUBLE?
COLE. MAX WANTS TO TALK TO HIM ABOUT PRODUCTIVITY.
OOOH!
TOTALLY, DUDE.
CAN I GET BACK TO WORK PLEASE?

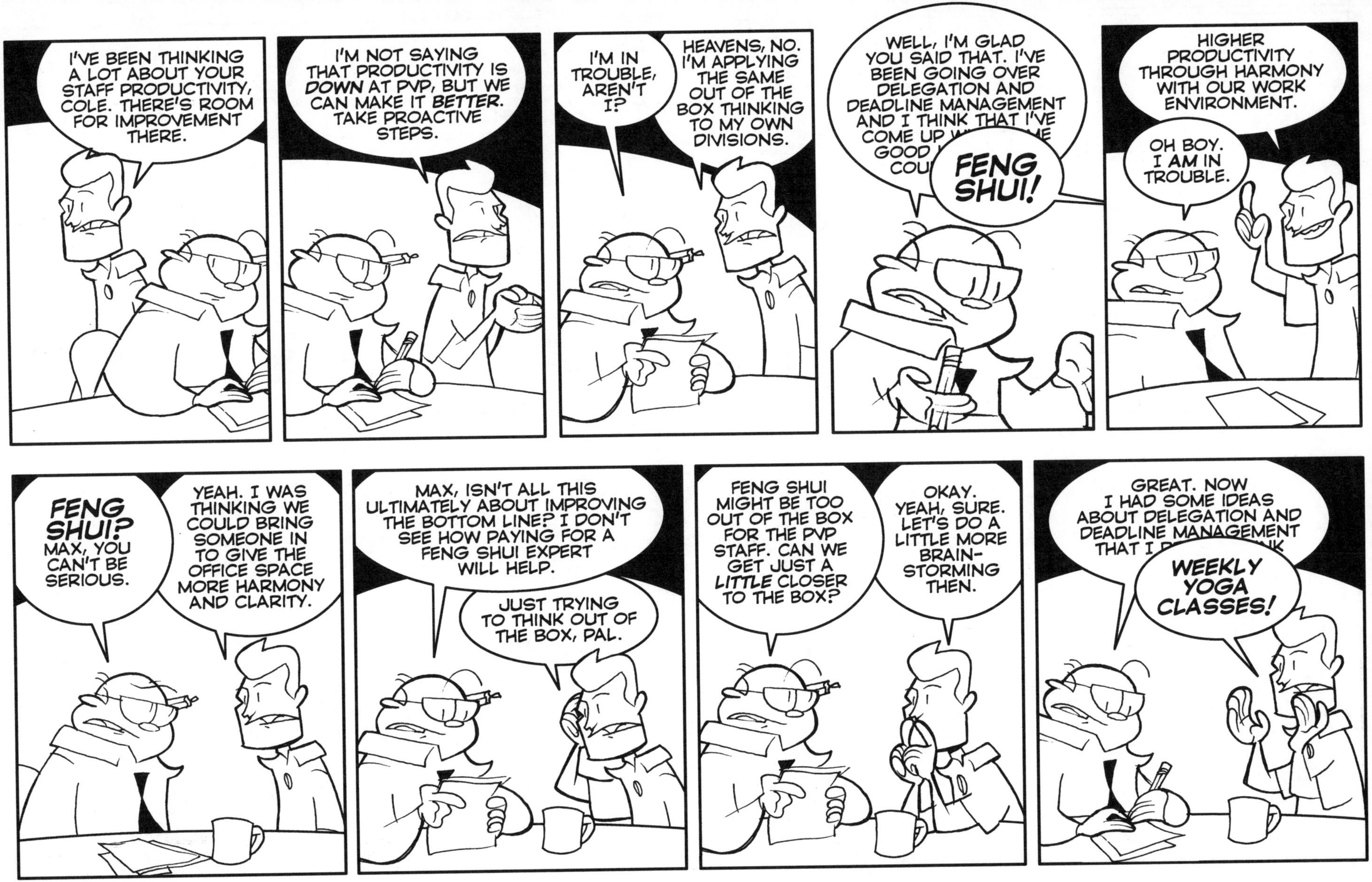

I'VE BEEN THINKING A LOT ABOUT YOUR STAFF PRODUCTIVITY, COLE. THERE'S ROOM FOR IMPROVEMENT THERE.
I'M NOT SAYING THAT PRODUCTIVITY IS *DOWN* AT PVP, BUT WE CAN MAKE IT *BETTER*. TAKE PROACTIVE STEPS.
I'M IN TROUBLE, AREN'T I?
HEAVENS, NO. I'M APPLYING THE SAME OUT OF THE BOX THINKING TO MY OWN DIVISIONS.
WELL, I'M GLAD YOU SAID THAT. I'VE BEEN GOING OVER DELEGATION AND DEADLINE MANAGEMENT AND I THINK THAT I'VE COME UP
FENG SHUI!
HIGHER PRODUCTIVITY THROUGH HARMONY WITH OUR WORK ENVIRONMENT.
OH BOY. I *AM* IN TROUBLE.
FENG SHUI? MAX, YOU CAN'T BE SERIOUS.
YEAH. I WAS THINKING WE COULD BRING SOMEONE IN TO GIVE THE OFFICE SPACE MORE HARMONY AND CLARITY.
MAX, ISN'T ALL THIS ULTIMATELY ABOUT IMPROVING THE BOTTOM LINE? I DON'T SEE HOW PAYING FOR A FENG SHUI EXPERT WILL HELP.
JUST TRYING TO THINK OUT OF THE BOX, PAL.
FENG SHUI MIGHT BE TOO OUT OF THE BOX FOR THE PVP STAFF. CAN WE GET JUST A *LITTLE* CLOSER TO THE BOX?
OKAY. YEAH, SURE. LET'S DO A LITTLE MORE BRAIN-STORMING THEN.
GREAT. NOW I HAD SOME IDEAS ABOUT DELEGATION AND DEADLINE MANAGEMENT THAT I
WEEKLY YOGA CLASSES!

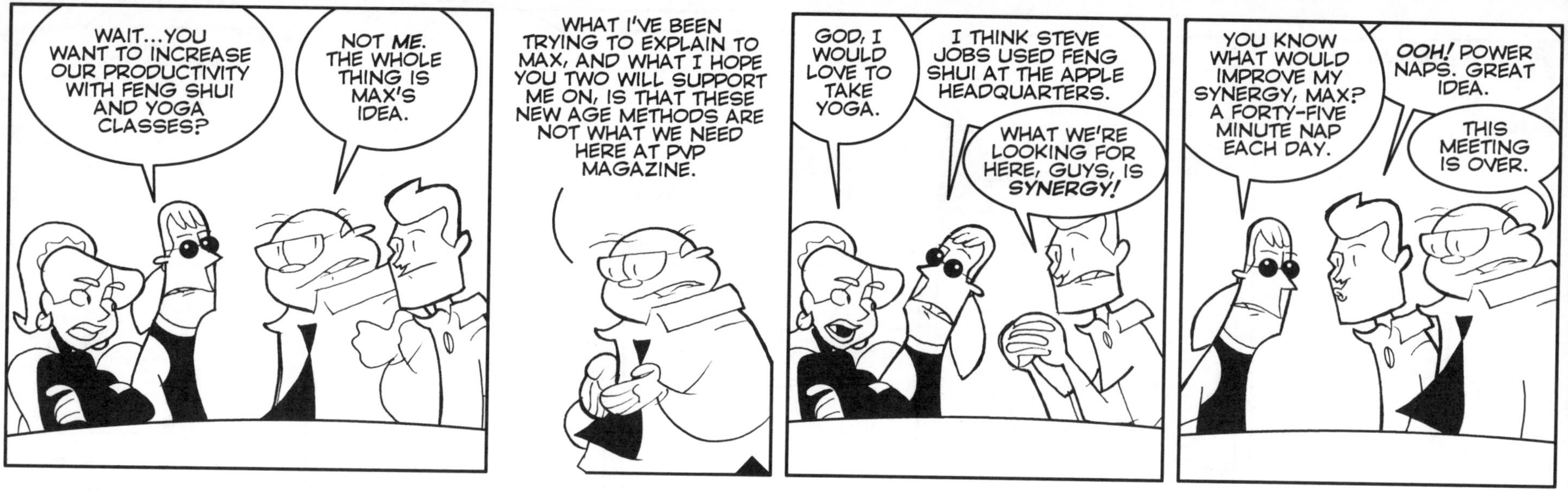
WAIT...YOU WANT TO INCREASE OUR PRODUCTIVITY WITH FENG SHUI AND YOGA CLASSES?
NOT ME. THE WHOLE THING IS MAX'S IDEA.
WHAT I'VE BEEN TRYING TO EXPLAIN TO MAX, AND WHAT I HOPE YOU TWO WILL SUPPORT ME ON, IS THAT THESE NEW AGE METHODS ARE NOT WHAT WE NEED HERE AT PVP MAGAZINE.
GOD, I WOULD LOVE TO TAKE YOGA.
I THINK STEVE JOBS USED FENG SHUI AT THE APPLE HEADQUARTERS.
WHAT WE'RE LOOKING FOR HERE, GUYS, IS SYNERGY!
YOU KNOW WHAT WOULD IMPROVE MY SYNERGY, MAX? A FORTY-FIVE MINUTE NAP EACH DAY.
OOH! POWER NAPS. GREAT IDEA.
THIS MEETING IS OVER.

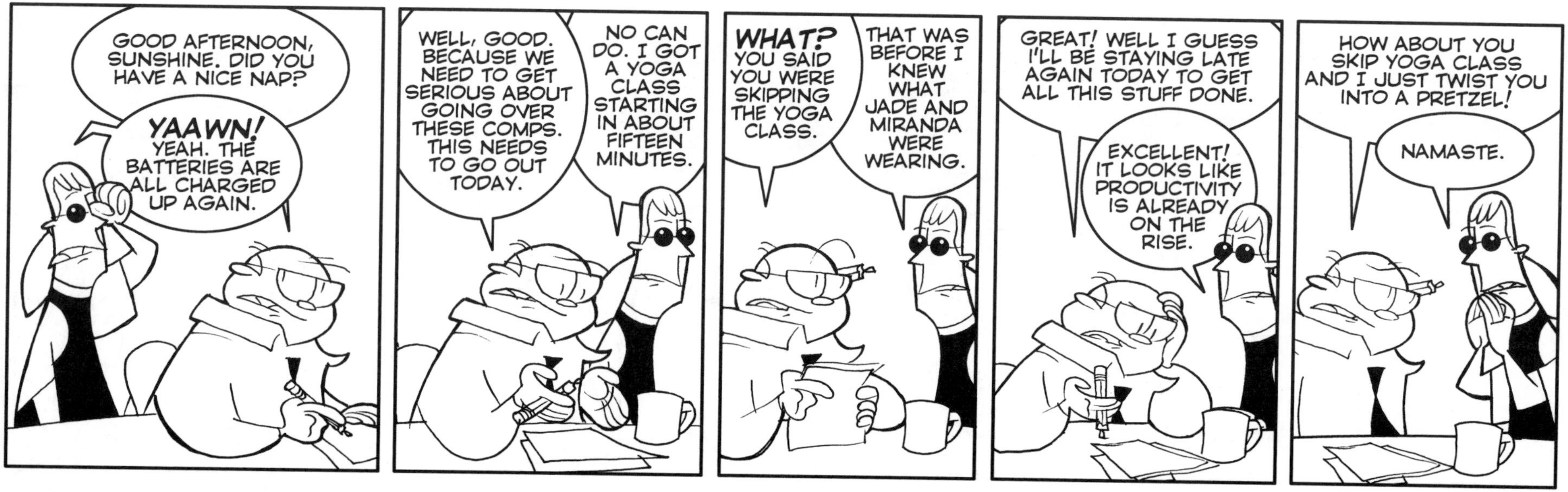
GOOD AFTERNOON, SUNSHINE. DID YOU HAVE A NICE NAP?
YAAWN! YEAH. THE BATTERIES ARE ALL CHARGED UP AGAIN.
WELL, GOOD. BECAUSE WE NEED TO GET SERIOUS ABOUT GOING OVER THESE COMPS. THIS NEEDS TO GO OUT TODAY.
NO CAN DO. I GOT A YOGA CLASS STARTING IN ABOUT FIFTEEN MINUTES.
WHAT? YOU SAID YOU WERE SKIPPING THE YOGA CLASS.
THAT WAS BEFORE I KNEW WHAT JADE AND MIRANDA WERE WEARING.
GREAT! WELL I GUESS I'LL BE STAYING LATE AGAIN TODAY TO GET ALL THIS STUFF DONE.
EXCELLENT! IT LOOKS LIKE PRODUCTIVITY IS ALREADY ON THE RISE.
HOW ABOUT YOU SKIP YOGA CLASS AND I JUST TWIST YOU INTO A PRETZEL!
NAMASTE.

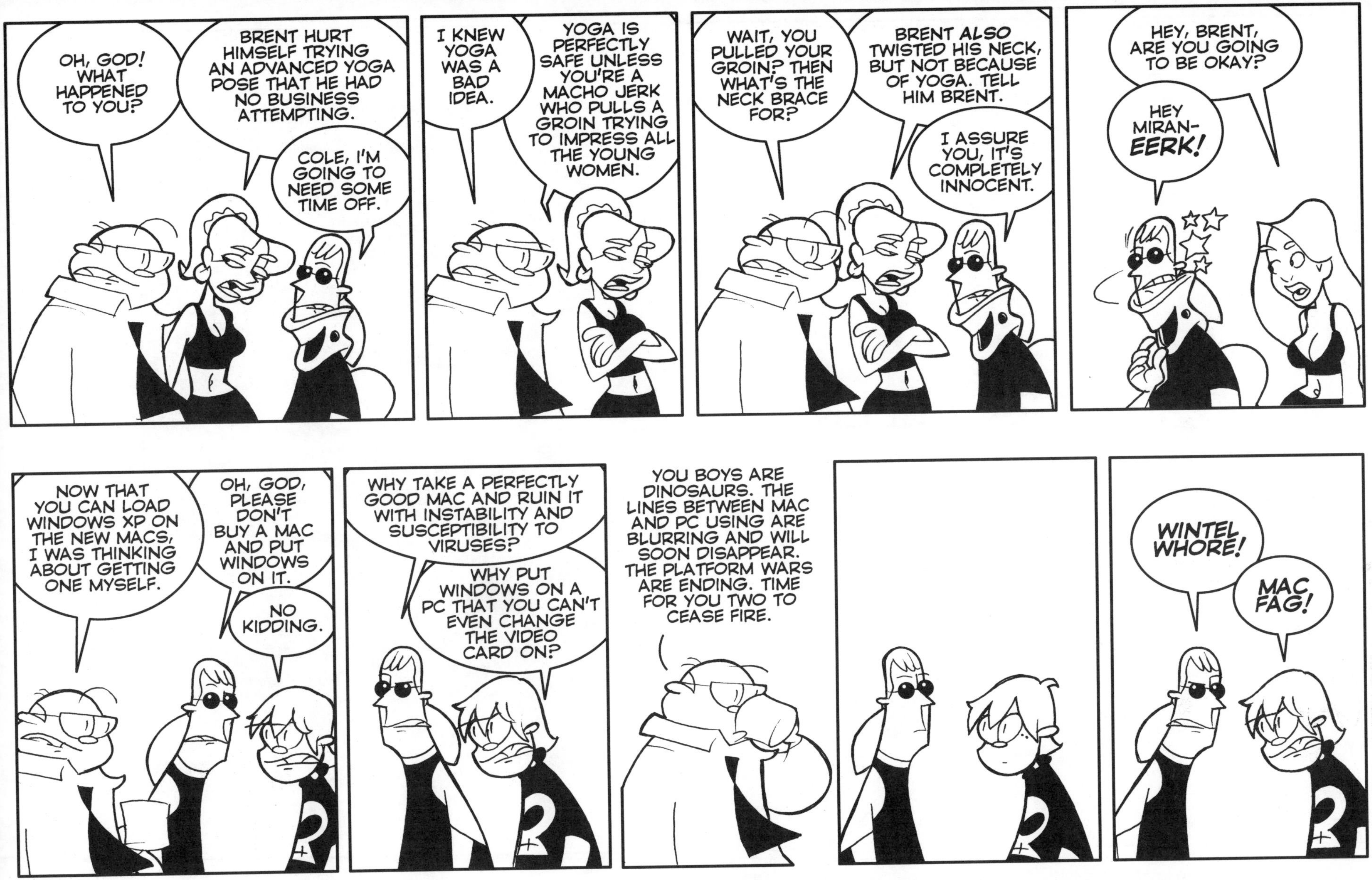

OH, GOD! WHAT HAPPENED TO YOU?
BRENT HURT HIMSELF TRYING AN ADVANCED YOGA POSE THAT HE HAD NO BUSINESS ATTEMPTING.
COLE, I'M GOING TO NEED SOME TIME OFF.
I KNEW YOGA WAS A BAD IDEA.
YOGA IS PERFECTLY SAFE UNLESS YOU'RE A MACHO JERK WHO PULLS A GROIN TRYING TO IMPRESS ALL THE YOUNG WOMEN.
WAIT, YOU PULLED YOUR GROIN? THEN WHAT'S THE NECK BRACE FOR?
BRENT *ALSO* TWISTED HIS NECK, BUT NOT BECAUSE OF YOGA. TELL HIM BRENT.
I ASSURE YOU, IT'S COMPLETELY INNOCENT.
HEY, BRENT, ARE YOU GOING TO BE OKAY?
HEY MIRAN- **EERK!**
NOW THAT YOU CAN LOAD WINDOWS XP ON THE NEW MACS, I WAS THINKING ABOUT GETTING ONE MYSELF.
OH, GOD, PLEASE DON'T BUY A MAC AND PUT WINDOWS ON IT.
NO KIDDING.
WHY TAKE A PERFECTLY GOOD MAC AND RUIN IT WITH INSTABILITY AND SUSCEPTIBILITY TO VIRUSES?
WHY PUT WINDOWS ON A PC THAT YOU CAN'T EVEN CHANGE THE VIDEO CARD ON?
YOU BOYS ARE DINOSAURS. THE LINES BETWEEN MAC AND PC USING ARE BLURRING AND WILL SOON DISAPPEAR. THE PLATFORM WARS ARE ENDING. TIME FOR YOU TWO TO CEASE FIRE.
WINTEL WHORE!
MAC FAG!

COVER GALLERY

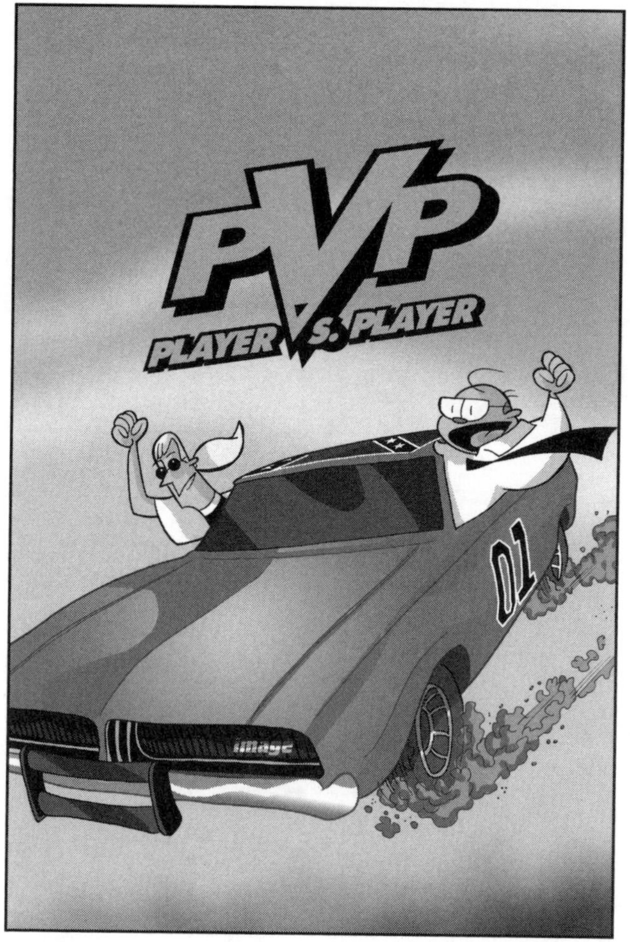
PvP
PLAYER VS. PLAYER
01

PvP 25 cover

COVER GALLERY

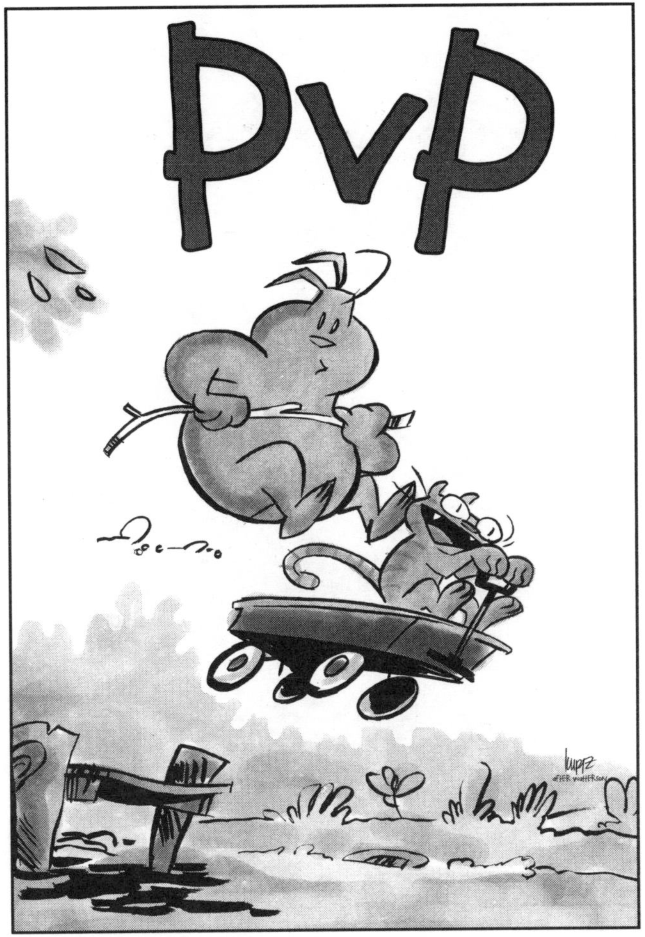
PvP

PvP 26 cover

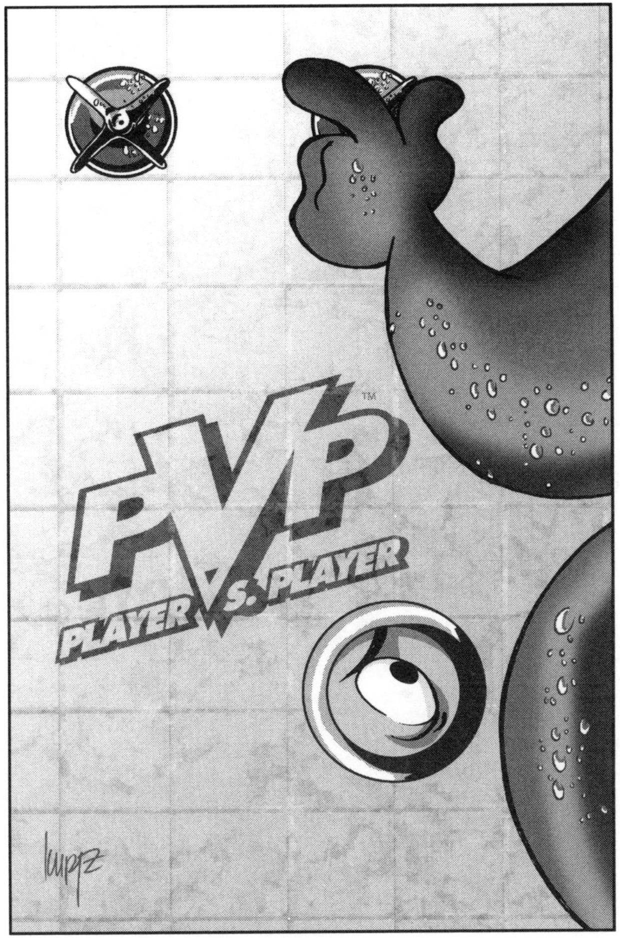
PvP™
PLAYER vs. PLAYER

PvP 27 cover

COVER GALLERY

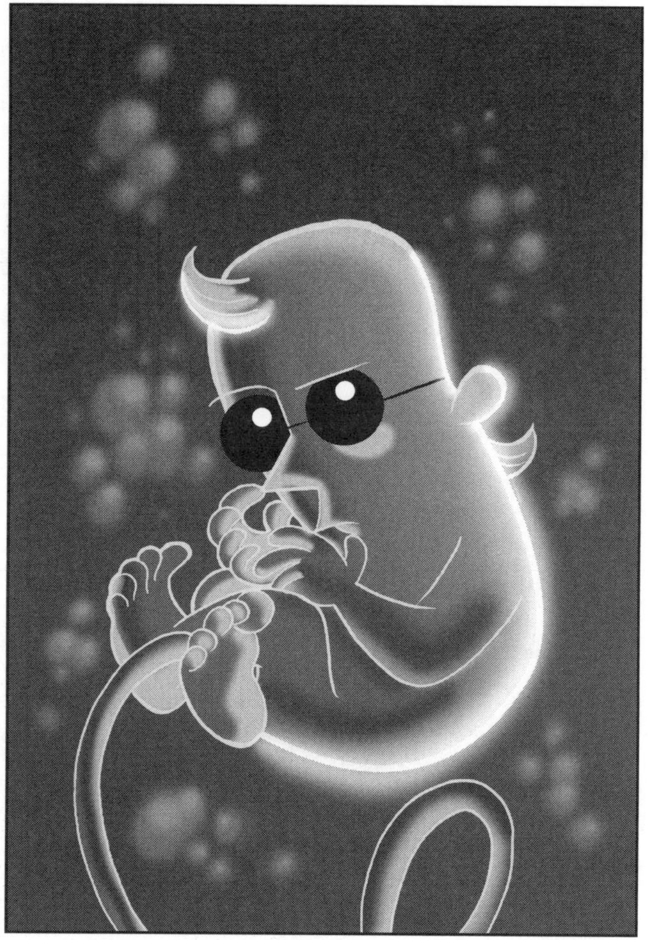

PvP 28 cover

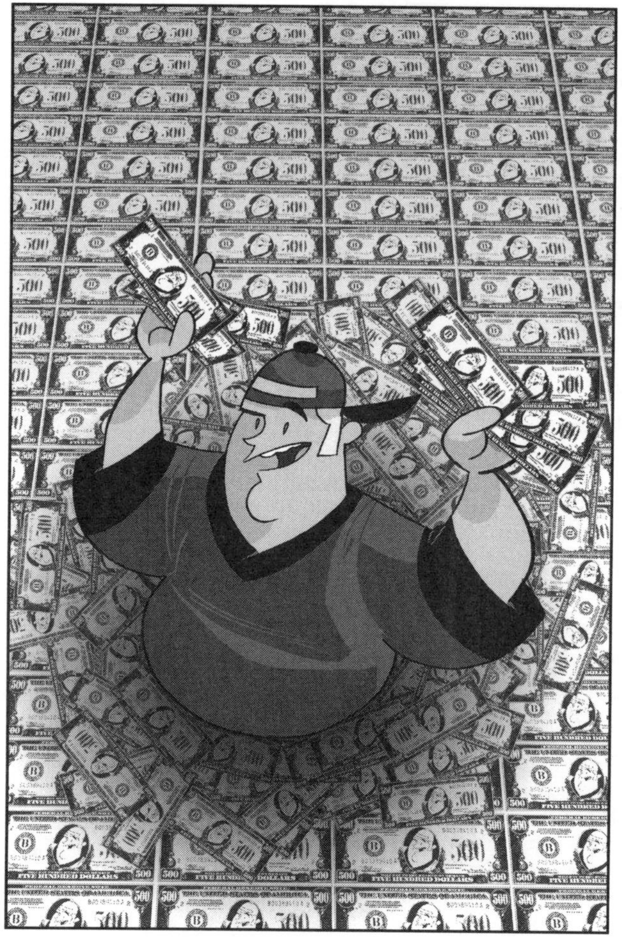

PvP 29 cover

COVER GALLERY

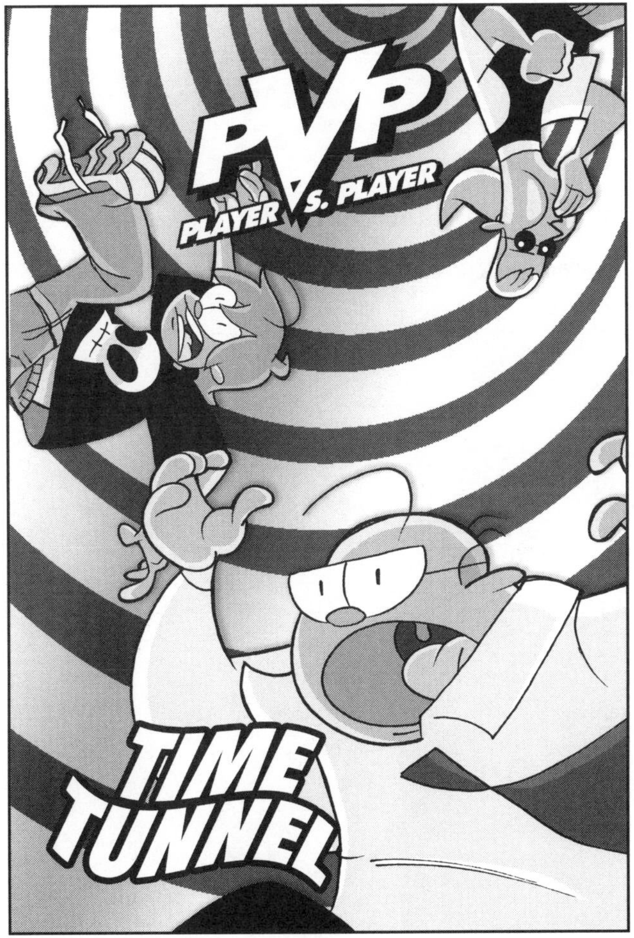
PVP
PLAYER VS. PLAYER
TIME TUNNEL

PvP 30 cover

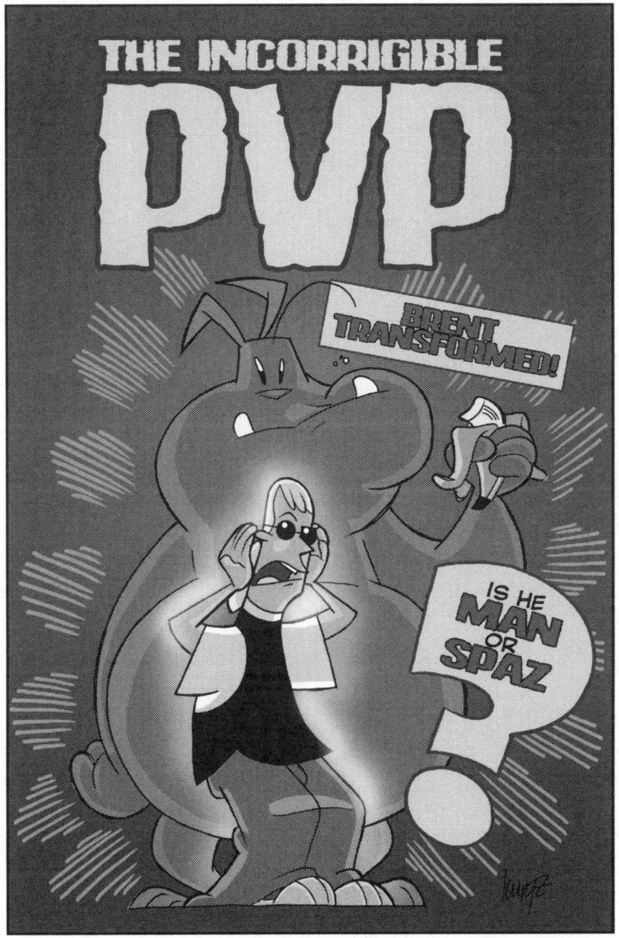
THE INCORRIGIBLE
PVP
BRENT TRANSFORMED!
IS HE MAN OR SPAZ ?

PvP 31 cover

· ABOUT THE AUTHOR ·

Scott Kurtz has been creating comic strips since he was
in the fourth grade. In 1998, his comic strip PvP appeared on the
web for the first time with a couple hundred readers. Today
the strip is read by over 200,000 people daily and
collected each month by Image Comics.

Scott currently resides in suburban North Texas with his
wife Angela, his basset hound Kirby, and Tiffany, the cat
he refuses to admit he likes.

Other books by Scott Kurtz
PvP: The Dork Ages
PvP: At Large
PvP: Reloaded
PvP: Rides Again
Truth, Justin and the American Way
Captain Amazing